WE WERE THE PEOPLE

WE WERE THE PEOPLE

Voices From East Germany's

Revolutionary Autumn of 1989

Dirk Philipsen

943./0878
PSSS

DUKE UNIVERSITY PRESS   Durham and London 1993

© 1993 Duke University Press
All rights reserved
Printed in the United States of America
on acid-free paper ∞
Library of Congress Cataloging-in-Publication Data
appear on the last printed page of this book.

*With admiration and respect, this
book is dedicated to the activists of the
East German civic movement and to my little son
Niklas and his generation in the hope that they, too,
will have the opportunity and strength
to fight for a better future*

CONTENTS

ACKNOWLEDGMENTS

■ Like so many other people I vividly remember where I was the day the Berlin Wall came down: at home in Durham, North Carolina, sitting with incredulous awe in front of my television set. I had gathered all the information I could get my hands on during the previous weeks about mass demonstrations, escalating popular demands, and a faltering Party top-leadership. But this sudden turn of events I had certainly not expected—nor, it is now clear, had anyone else.

As I continued from afar my attempts to keep up with the incredible pace of events in the GDR between November 1989 and April 1990, I soon realized to what extent the East German revolution—hailed *ad nauseam* in the Western world as symbolizing "the end of the Cold War" and the "final death of communism"—offered a unique opportunity for me to study self-generated popular politics. All I had to find were ways and means to go to the GDR in order to conduct "on the ground" research among those who had made this revolution.

As I was taking the first steps to find support and make arrangements for this research trip, it also began to dawn on me that the East German events would have a lasting effect on the country in which I had grown up (West Germany), and that the collapse of the East German one-party state and the GDR's eventual annexation by West Germany would forever alter the quality of life in the city I still considered my home: Berlin.

For all these reasons I was determined early on to travel to the society "on the other side of the Wall." During my university years in Berlin I had crossed the Wall many times, but I had always found life in East Germany strangely impenetrable. Now that the Wall and the many stultifying constraints it had produced for East Germans were gone, I wanted to find out for myself what was lying beneath the fleeting Western media portrayals of the East German revolution.

Two persons in particular deserve my warmest thanks for having contributed to this work in more ways than they probably know: Lawrence Goodwyn, who first introduced me to the subtleties of oral history, and a companion who never stopped having great tolerance for my personal idiosyncrasies. Over the years, we spent countless hours of discussions about the meaning of history and about the tensions (or contradictions?) between democratic social forms and modern industrial societies; and Peter Wood, who has been a close and supportive friend throughout all my years at Duke. He has always been a source of inspiration to me. Without his ceaseless efforts to keep me financially afloat, furthermore, this project would have never passed beyond the stage of mental conceptualization.

In the spring of 1990, I received a travel and research allowance from Duke University for my trip to East Germany, for which I particularly want to thank Dean Malcolm Gillis.

It is most difficult to find appropriate ways to thank the many friends and colleagues who have spent a great deal of time and care in reading all or parts of my manuscript. To say the very least, their comments and suggestions were invaluable. I hope I can pay them back in kind some day. They are William Chafe, Arif Dirlik, Larry and Nell Goodwyn, Justin Hill, Fredric Jameson, Rebecca Karl, Carolyn Lesjak, Andrew Neather, Maike Philipsen, Tom Robisheaux, Michael Speaks, John Srygley, Tim Tyson, and Peter Wood. In most cases I have gladly accepted their criticism and their suggested improvements, but sometimes I also stubbornly resisted. None of these people, therefore, bear responsibility for the final content of this book.

Also, I want to thank the wonderful people at Duke University Press, not only for their interest in and support of this project, but also for their remarkable responsiveness to the various requests that came from this author throughout the months in which this book took shape. It gives me particular pleasure to express my deep appreciation to Bob Mirandon, the editor who labored through my manuscript with great sympathy and care.

Finally, only the cooperation of my East German interviewees made this project possible. It is to them that I would like to express my deepest gratitude. To work with them has been an outstandingly rich experience. I hope they will see this book as a contribution to a better understanding of their efforts.

Dirk Philipsen
Durham, North Carolina
May 1, 1992

LIST OF ABBREVIATIONS

AGL   *Abteilungs-Gewerkschafts-Leitung* (Departmental Union Leadership)

BGL   *Betriebs-Gewerkschafts-Leitung* (Factory Union Leadership)

DA   *Demokratischer Aufbruch* (Democratic Awakening)

DGB   *Deutscher Gewerkschaftsbund* (Confederation of German Trade Unions, FRG)

DJ   *Demokratie Jetzt* (Democracy Now)

EKD   *Evangelische Kirche Deutschlands* (Protestant Church of Germany)

ESG   *Evangelische Studenten Gemeinde* (Protestant Student Community)

FDGB   *Freier Deutscher Gewerkschaftsbund* (Confederation of Free German Trade Unions, GDR)

FDJ   *Freie Deutsche Jugend* (Free German Youth)

FRG   Federal Republic of Germany (West Germany)

GDR   German Democratic Republic (East Germany)

IFM   *Initiative für Frieden und Menschenrechte* (Initiative for Peace and Human Rights)

NVA   *Nationale Volksarmee* (National People's Army)

PDS   *Partei des Demokratischen Sozialismus* (Party of Democratic Socialism)

SDP   *Sozial-Demokratische Partei* (Social-Democratic Party)

SED   *Sozialistische Einheitspartei Deutschlands* (Socialist Unity Party of Germany)

SPD   *Sozial-Demokratische Partei Deutschlands* (Social Democratic Party of Germany)

Stasi   *Staatssicherheitsdienst* (State Security Service)

■ *A precondition for popular democracy means assuming responsibility for one's self, instead of calling for competent people who are supposed to lead out of the crisis, people to whom one will eventually acquiesce again.* ■ *No one shall deny us the responsibility for this country any longer. We also do not want it to be administered by some party or committee again.*
—*Ingrid Köppe, November 1989, Berlin (East)*

East and West Germany at the Time of Unification

INTRODUCTION

The stifling pall of hollow words that has smothered us for so long has cultivated in us such a deep mistrust of the world of deceptive words that we are now better equipped than ever before to see the human world as it really is: a complex community of thousands of millions of unique, individual human beings in whom hundreds of beautiful characteristics are matched by hundreds of faults and negative tendencies. They must never be lumped together into homogeneous masses beneath a welter of hollow clichés and sterile words and then en bloc—as "classes," "nations," or "political forces"—extolled or denounced, loved or hated, maligned or glorified.—Václav Havel, "Words on Words"

■ This book is about the men and women who made possible the revolution of 1989 in the German Democratic Republic. Through extended interviews with East German activists, I have tried to bring back to life the ideas and actions that originally informed the dramatic and peaceful transformation of the GDR. Based on the voices of a wide range of East German protagonists, this study attempts to re-create a rare historical moment of immensely expanded democratic possibility, one, as it were, with social and political significance far beyond the borders of the now extinct German Democratic Republic.

Rarely has a revolution generated a more distinct symbol of victory than the popular upheaval in East Germany: on the night of 9 November 1989, the Berlin Wall came down. Neither the storming of the Bastille in Paris two hundred years earlier, nor the dramatic execution of Romania's dictator, Nicolae Ceaușescu, less than two months later quite matched the almost mythic drama that surrounded the toppling of the Wall. One of the most hideous monuments to political power ever devised was pounded into souvenirs before a global TV audience. People throughout the world celebrated. Perhaps most amazingly, the actions of East German citizens themselves had forced the party to cave in and to allow free travel to the West.

The Wall represented decades of antagonism between East and West, a constant reminder of an apparently insoluble conflict between what people everywhere had learned to call "communism" and "capitalism." It suggested untempered hostility that could conceivably explode into the apocalypse of a worldwide atomic war and result in the extinction of the human race. Simultaneously, this "death strip" with its stark 14-foot barriers cutting through the heart of Berlin provided a gruesome reminder of organized repression and state murder.

And yet—a curious proof of human acquiescence and adaptability—the people on both sides of the concrete divide had learned to live with it. As the historian Robert Darnton perceptively described this phenomenon, "soon after 1961 . . . the million or so inhabitants on the Eastern side and the 2 million or so on the Western began to lose contact. By 1989 a whole generation had come of age within the shadow of the Wall. Most of them never crossed it, even from West to East when that was allowed. They accepted the Wall as a fact of life, as something inexorable, built into the landscape—there when they were born and there when they died. They left it to tourists, took it for granted, forgot about it, or simply stopped seeing it."[1] Indeed, for the two postwar generations of Germans in the East and the West, the Wall over time became a landmark as immutable as the Alps. It literally defined the boundaries of possibility. After a while, it became difficult to imagine a political order without it.

So, when the Wall suddenly and unexpectedly fell on that November evening in 1989, it opened an outpouring of popular emotion that is not easily described. In one sense it was as if the largest prison gate in all history had suddenly swung open. But more than a sense of release underlay the jubilation. Time itself took on a new meaning. A single moment appeared to signal the end of an epoch and the beginning of something new. The startling footage of tens of thousands of East Germans crowding through the newly opened borders for the first time in their lives, celebrating and dancing on top of the Wall with Germans from the other side, coalesced into an indelible image for onlookers throughout the world. Long-accepted political verities now vanished more rapidly than the souvenirs of the crumbling Wall. Out of this maze, one thing

1. Robert Darnton, *Berlin Journal* (New York/London, 1991), 83.

seemed clear: communism was dead, and something everyone called "freedom" was on the rise.

In the weeks that followed, worldwide political commentary was awash with descriptive superlatives: the "massive and nonviolent revolution" had generated "astounding results" that "no one could have foreseen." It was said that a "revolution from below" had "radically altered the political environment of Central Europe," dramatically signaling "the end of the cold war." After the reforming Hungarian CP considered it necessary to tear down its western border fences to Austria in May, and Poland elected its first noncommunist prime minister, the Solidarność advisor Tadeusz Mazowiecki, in August, the fall of the Wall in November was seen as the final death knell to East-Central European communism. East Germans, it was argued, could now pick up the "lost" thread of their history and return to "normal" conditions. In virtually all available reports in the West, the revolution in the GDR was portrayed as an unmitigated success story, a victory of Western values over an Eastern tyranny.

Upon somewhat closer inspection, however, I quickly realized that few voices from East Germany itself seemed to view the transformation in quite this way. Indeed, only days after the opening of the Berlin Wall, East German dissidents and diverse oppositionists who had been active in what they had called the "civic movement"[2] began to express their deep concern that any future political course might be "dictated" by the West rather than being formulated democratically by the East German populace itself.

What distinguished East Germany from all other Eastern European countries in transition was the existence of a much bigger and wealthier Western neighbor, a nation which had never given up on the claim to be the representative of all Germans—West and East.[3] Thus, the very people in the GDR who had risked arrests, beatings, job loss, and (as a frequently employed last resort of the communist regime) oftentimes faced loss of

---

2. The terms "opposition," "opposition activist," and "civic movement" are used in the broadest possible sense here, encompassing the entire range of dissident or oppositional activity in East Germany, including newly founded oppositional parties or large-scale oppositional alliances such as New Forum, but also intellectual circles, shop floor activities, and hundreds of grass-roots groups concerned with issues such as human rights, environmental destruction, discrimination against women, or nuclear disarmament and peace.

3. The preamble to the West German Basic Law (the West German constitution) stated that the document was also formulated "on behalf of those Germans to whom participation was denied" and called for "the entire German people . . . to achieve in free self-determination the unity and freedom of Germany."

citizenship and expulsion for their efforts to change the system were now the ones who most worried about the long-awaited future "beyond the party." The interviews contained herein reveal as much a sense of loss as a sense of success, for many experienced a "drowning of hopes" and a "disappearing of independence and political enthusiasm."

As soon as the debris of celebration had been swept up, the initial joy and sense of collective accomplishment among East Germans gave way to a mood of increasingly sober questioning and reevaluation. What proved difficult for Westerners to understand was the deep sense of loss that most East Germans felt when their hard work was summarily discarded by West Germans as "pitiful" and their high hopes were dismissed as "romantic," while their previous efforts to reform the system—dangerous as these efforts had been—were airily passed over by Westerners. East Germans were in effect told—after the Wall had come down and "freedom" had arrived—that they should now become passive junior partners who dutifully did what West Germans told them to do. Few outsiders understood how inherently condescending and demeaning such a stance was to every East German citizen.

Unlike Poles, Hungarians, or Czechs, the people of East Germany had not only managed to overcome the stultifying constraints of one-party rule;[4] they were also in imminent danger of losing part of their identity, the very part that derived from a 40-year shared history under "actually existing socialism."[5] Most East Germans had never experienced anything

4. Predictably, there has been much debate as to how many East Germans belonged to what has been called "the opposition" and "the civic movement," or, put the other way around, as to how many citizens felt represented by the oppositional movement in the GDR. Any answer to such questions, it seems to me, depends on how one defines "opposition" and what particular period during the revolutionary transformation one takes into consideration. As in all recorded revolutions, for instance, the percentage of citizens who became actively engaged in the process of political change was relatively small. Yet if one were to define "opposition" as "increasing disassociation" from one-party rule, or, similarly, as "sympathetic to the emerging civic movement" during the Fall of 1989, probably well over 80 percent of the East German populace would have considered themselves to be part of the opposition. How complex—and thus how difficult to categorize—the responses of East German citizens were to life under one-party rule has been incisively addressed by the only oral research project conducted in the GDR prior to the system's collapse. See Lutz Niethammer, *Die volkseigene Erfahrung* [The People's Own Experience] (Berlin, 1991). A second volume will deal with East German responses to the radical transformation that took place in their country, a work that should prove of equal significance.
5. The term "actually existing socialism" came into widespread use after the East German dissident and former party member Rudolf Bahro published his book *The Alternative. A Critique of Actually-Existing Socialism* in 1973. Above all, the term came to denote the

else, and it was precisely this younger generation which had constituted the forefront of the revolutionary transformation.[6] As one 28-year-old East German writer told me, the new conditions of overwhelming West German predominance resulted "in a total loss of one's own biography."[7] *We Were the People* thus grew out of my concern that the diverse experiences, aspirations, and, above all, the democratic achievements of all those who had brought about the East German revolution would quickly disappear under the avalanche of Western jubilation.[8]

During the Fall of 1989, the descriptive phrase most often used in East Germany to characterize events had been a ringing superlative—"a peaceful revolution from below." But beginning in the early months of 1990, a new term appeared that sounded much more sober and cautious: "Wende." It means simply "turn" or "turnabout"[9]—a change of termi-

---

assertion by critical left-wing intellectuals that the East German system did not, in fact, represent socialism, but rather a thorough corruption of socialist ideas.

6. It should also be noted that even the majority of the older generation of East Germans, those born between 1933 and 1945, had never experienced life in anything other than an authoritarian state. While life in the GDR can certainly not be compared to life in Nazi Germany, it should nevertheless be kept in mind that those East Germans—unlike their Western counterparts—had never in their lives enjoyed basic human rights such as free speech. The extraordinarily democratic and nonviolent quality of the East German revolution thus also needs to be seen as a deep longing for a self-generated democratic creation of one's own social and political environment that had grown out of a lifetime of tutelage and repression.

7. Andreas Lehmann, see Part III, p. 333.

8. Working within the context of severe time constraints and trying to cope with rapidly changing headlines, political commentators routinely summarized East German events as some kind of "victory for freedom" (the Berlin tabloid *BZ*, 10 November 1989). Similarly, the *Time* cover story on 20 November 1989 was, simply enough, entitled "Freedom!" In the same vein, *Newsweek* wrote in a special report issue on 20 November 1989, "The virtual destruction of the wall that divided Berlin represents the clearest sort of victory for the democratic ideas that the United States and its allies fought for and cherish." So constructed, the message had little to do with the achievements of East German citizens, but was rather meant to imply the superiority of one global system over another. It was this very conclusion, of course, that so deeply troubled East German dissidents. The essential questions for East Germans were avoided or ignored by virtually all media accounts: for whom, exactly, was this a victory? What did the demise of one-party rule in the GDR mean for the future of all East Germans? Exactly who among the East German population would actually profit from the downfall of the nation's peculiar kind of socialism, and who might conceivably suffer? Who, for that matter, would eventually determine the outcome of such questions?

9. Because the East German revolution was an indigenous insurgency within one of the world's competing social systems, but was quickly *not* seen as "indigenous" because its

nology suggesting that the vast openness, the perceived 1989 world of immense opportunity, had become something much narrower in 1990, something far less invested with hope.[10]

So now East Germans and sympathetic outsiders alike began to ask themselves first, how and why did the entrenched communist power crash so completely that its departure seemed to offer almost unlimited prospects for social transformation, and, second, with the absence of the slightest hint of any kind of communist resurgence to dampen hope, what had happened to transform the exhilarating search for a new democratic beginning into a muted "turn" directed largely by others? In the space of a few months, the revolutionary declaration "we are the people" was superseded by the postrevolutionary slogan championed in West Germany: "we are *one* people." How did this enormous change in sensibility and political aspiration, this dramatic shrinkage, come about? And, by the time the Western-controlled merger of the two Germanies appeared all but inevitable, what happened so that the motto among the erstwhile revolutionaries changed yet one more time to the nostalgic "we were the people"?[11]

---

conclusion is taken as proof of the triumph of the "other" system, the linguistic and, thus, the analytical nonsequitors that have emerged are not only frequent, but almost always inherently ironic. For example, the term "Wende" was originally borrowed from a 1983 conservative West German election campaign slogan. After 11 years of governments led by Social Democrats, the Christian Democrats had promised a Wende away from "economic mismanagement" and "welfare-statism." Thus, for progressive citizens in both East and West, the term Wende clearly implied a turn backward.

10. The reason for this was quite obvious. What had seemed a broad-based movement with a rich variety of active participants from all walks of life was quickly transformed into a new game with a strikingly reduced number of players. Most of the key participants in the initial public debate over the future of East Germany did not even appear on the teams that would struggle over the spoils. And, ironically, of those players deemed eligible for the follow-up contests, most who were subsequently sent back to the bench were East Germans. The finalists, it became equally evident, were to consist almost entirely of West Germans.

11. The most common answer among those who had been sympathetic to the aspirations of East German dissidents but nevertheless quickly came to consider it a foregone conclusion that the revolution would fail has been touched upon by the West Berlin writer Klaus Hartung, according to whom the articulation of any political alternative to a Western-dominated unification was fatally missing "a sense of the pressure of time on people who thought that they had lost 40 years of their lives—even if they were only 21. . . . How could a new society emerge out of the debates over a civil society if, at the same time, real estate agents, former property owners, professional gurus, headhunters, and wholesale agents of yogurt, tropical fruits, and inexpensive electronics suddenly dominated the day-to-day life of the GDR?" Klaus Hartung, *Neunzehnhundertneunundachtzig* (Frankfurt, 1990), 124.

Thus, even before the looming prospect of a Western takeover had grown into a settled fact, the most important political questions raised by the East German revolution had already been lost from view. East German oppositionists who had initially been hailed in the West for their "courageous resolve" in rapid succession began to be described as "political idealists" and then, very soon thereafter, to be dismissed as "hopeless dreamers." Once so characterized, they could safely be ignored. In the course of this rapid metamorphosis, the democratic and egalitarian aspirations that had been at the heart of the East German revolution were overwhelmed by the new realpolitik surrounding the annexation of the GDR by West Germany.

Within this paradox reposed a central irony: the politicians and commentators in both East and West who had been quite slow to detect these popular aspirations now proved swift to ignore them. In short, what was truly transforming about the revolution was swept aside in favor of a peculiar kind of political amnesia. This forgetfulness, in turn, effectively isolated the democratically self-organized opposition before it ever had the time to develop and organize a serious political alternative to East Germany's surrender to political arrangements that had their origins elsewhere. In this manner, the core beliefs and independent activism that had energized the revolutionary transformation had vanished from view. It is the purpose of this book to restore them both to visibility before they will have disappeared not only from the current political landscape of the new united Germany, but also from the historical record.[12]

12. Such a disappearance would not be a novum in German historiography. I had my first encounter with a widespread historical amnesia concerning popularly-generated political achievements when I studied the German Revolution of 1918–19. Of the more than 2,000 titles that soon filled my bibliography, no more than a handful had actually dealt with those who had made the revolution—in this case, workers—or the hundreds of workers' and soldiers' councils they had created locally and nationally in their struggle to overcome German militarism and in their attempts to build a democratic society in its stead. A similar disappearance was described by the prominent German oral historian Lutz Niethammer, who was, in the early seventies, among a group of historians who discovered that post-World War II German history had actually begun "with working-class liberation committees in almost every German city. The Antifa [for antifascism], as they were named, were quickly repressed by the occupying powers, whether capitalist or not; and most of the source material about them had been seized and lost in America. So had any trace of the existence of the Antifa in German historiography." Lutz Niethammer, "Oral History as a Channel of Communication between Workers and Historians," in Paul Thompson (ed.), *Our Common History* (Atlantic Highlands, N.J., 1982), 25. The problem focused upon here is not, in the first instance, a product of ideological disagreement among authors, but is, rather, methodological—relating to the kinds of evidence that conclusions are built upon.

Behind the Wall: One Objective, Many Voices

"We do not want to reproduce the twentieth century, neither do we want to copy the Federal Republic of Germany. What we want is to develop the political culture of the twenty-first century. The distinction between left and right . . . is not the only possible way of distinguishing oneself from others—in fact, it is a distinction that does not apply to us. We want to debate politics free of ideology after all of our terrible experiences with all-encompassing ideologies. We don't need those endless empty phrases like democratic, social, market-economic, free, stable, ecological, efficient, and all the rest. A counter position to those is not possible: undemocratic? asocial? against freedom? unstable? hostile to the environment? inefficient? Positions which do not allow for counter positions—those are things we take for granted, but they do not constitute political programs."—Jens Reich[13]

So where in society should one begin to look in order to understand the dynamics of the East German "revolution from below"? How far back in time does one have to go in order to locate the origins of popular politics and trace the emergence of an organized opposition to one-party authoritarianism? And how to conceptualize a period in which everything was in a constant state of flux, so that the goals and analyses of experts and participants alike regularly proved hopelessly out of date within days of having been formulated? If one thing seemed certain to me in the spring of 1990, it was that the quest for answers had to begin with systematic conversations with East Germans themselves.

To be sure, I was not certain what to expect at first. I had crossed the Wall on numerous occasions during my university years in West Berlin. Along with friends from the university or from the Alternative List, I had made intermittent attempts to get to know East Berliner students, artists, and peace activists. Over the years, I had also met numerous East German party members in factories and schools through a fellow student from the Free University who was a member of the West Berlin sister party of the East German CP, called SEW (Socialist Unity Party West Berlin). I had also occasionally visited relatives in a town near Dresden called Sebnitz, not far from the Czech border, the only region in the GDR where West German television could not readily be received. The peculiar combination of complacency about their cozy and secure life on the one hand, and the constant complaints about "the system" on the other, dramatized by

---

13. Jens Reich, prominent opposition activist and founding member of New Forum, at a delegates' conference of New Forum, 27 January 1990 in Berlin, some three months after the Wall had collapsed. Quoted in *Die Tageszeitung*, 29 January 1990. My translation.

the stereotypical model of the man being the one who actively participated in the party, but also by their openly displayed awe toward Western commodities, had left a deep impression. I never learned to feel comfortable within the tension of simultaneously experiencing the degrading treatment by the "official" GDR, as happened each time when we had to register at the local police station, and the role of "well-to-do Western uncle" our relatives and their friends inescapably forced me into.

Each time I went to the closed off society on the other side of the Wall, I had to undergo, like any other visitor, the eerie and humiliating process of applying for a visa, paying the obligatory "visitor's fee," waiting for hours at the check-points, submitting to interrogation as to "what I wanted" in the GDR, and, finally, having my car strip-searched for prohibited Western "propaganda material." If not an entry to a different planet, it was at the very least a police-state exuding a distinctly hostile attitude toward Western visitors. Yet each time I consciously tried to avoid getting so offended by the entry procedure of "our socialist neighbor" as to give up on trying again. If nothing else, it was always an unusual experience, and at least I could use some of the money I had been obliged to exchange in order to purchase very cheaply a good book or two in one of the heavily subsidized, state-run bookstores. In this way, I endeavored to maintain my skepticism toward Western cold war rhetoric which portrayed every single aspect of life in the GDR as a dismal failure. I did this also to keep alive the curiosity necessary to the discovery of anything that conceivably made sense "over there."

Whenever I finally found myself on the other side of the concrete divide, however, my eyes and sensibilities—unaccustomed to the subtleties of life in the GDR—initially detected a depressing greyness of the physical environment and a peculiarly joyless appearance of people populating streets or stores. Again, I rarely knew what to make of this impression, for I was aware how much my perceptions were shaped by the flashy neon-glitter so typical of Western cities that are increasingly organized around the apparent need for ever more consumption. On the other hand, I could not find any reasonable justification for the obvious pragmatic shoddiness of new, box-like concrete structures, and the rampant deterioration of once magnificent Wilhelmine and Weimar buildings. Nor could there be any rational justification for the terrible toll both people and environment had to pay for hopelessly outmoded heating systems operated on cheap coal, industrial facilities without filters, or smoke belching two-stroke cars that provided such a distinct "GDR-smell." Despite all this, I was still never able to settle for the simplistic distinction of "our good" and "their bad" life. If nothing else, I still felt I needed to know much more.

On each trip I tried to learn as much as I could about the day-to-day lives of people I met, about their experiences at work, or their relationship to party and state. Their responses usually struck me as somewhat guarded and apologetic. A typical statement came from a school teacher in Dresden, who responded to my inquiries during a visit in 1986, "of course we don't like it much, but somehow one can get by rather well. You just have to get used to it."

Most East Germans I had encountered prior to 1989 seemed to have internalized a deep inferiority complex toward everything "Western." This attitude ranged from the presumed "freedom" of Westerners "to do whatever you please" to the quality and variety of Western consumer goods. Rarely had I found an East German who was ready to defend the system in which he or she lived. Even those who made attempts in this direction more often than not quickly shifted the conversation to complaints about typical grievances such as the waste and inefficiency seemingly endemic to life in the GDR, lack of travel opportunities, or the general unfriendliness and immobilizing unresponsiveness of party and state employees everywhere from grocery stores to restaurants and municipal administrations. While things clearly did not go well in the German "worker and peasant state," the great majority of citizens nevertheless seemed to have come to various arrangements with party and state, whether due to political conviction, pressure, fear, or opportunism. Perhaps the most revealing indication of this condition were the 3 million citizens who had either joined the East German CP or one of its satellite parties. In addition, as we now know, the party's secret police apparatus employed some 120,000 full time agents and relied on the services of roughly another 100,000 informants—staggering figures for a country with a total population of 16 million. Yet the numbers also provided clear indication of precisely how insecure party and state leaders felt in the presence of their own population. The result was a society in which no one knew whom to trust, and in which few ever made attempts to share their private thoughts with anyone but close friends or colleagues. A popular saying had it that whenever three people engaged in a conversation, one was bound to be a Stasi informant.

As I had come to discover over the years, in short, East Germany constituted a strange and largely impenetrable world for a Westerner such as myself. Life in the GDR clearly followed different rhythms, different rules, and different modes of social interaction from anything familiar to citizens of Western bourgeois democracies. Despite sharing a common language, both the people of East Germany and the world they inhabited remained much less accessible to me than any Western society such as France, Great Britain, or the United States. With the partial exception of some West Germans who maintained contacts with relatives in the East, most Westerners had, in fact, long stopped paying any attention to life in the GDR. The extent to which living in two different political systems had, in just a few decades, resulted in a deep estrangement between Germans West and East remains one of the more puzzling and deeply unsettling realities of the post-World War II order in Europe.

By the time I returned to the GDR in the summer of 1990, of course, so much had changed that it was simply hard to fathom. The party and its ever-present security police apparatus had largely disintegrated, restrictions were gone, and the Wall had collapsed. Since I had only been privy to Western media reporting between September 1989 and April 1990, however, I knew little about the actual dynamics that had brought about this amazingly rapid transformation. Perhaps there was some truth to accounts claiming that people had merely "suffered through" 40 years of actually existing socialism. Perhaps it was also true that they suddenly all longed for what they had come to associate with "the West." On the other hand, such accounts would certainly fail to explain what had happened in 1989, who had generated these events, and how they had done so.[14]

I brought certain expectations to my research on the East German revolution—grounded in earlier studies of social movements and periods of revolutionary change in European history, but also based on prior knowledge of oppositional activities in East Germany. For one, I knew that what social scientists like to describe as "necessary preconditions" for social movements could never, in themselves, generate a movement or a revolution—human beings do. And for people to challenge existing structures of governance—particularly in a severely regulated police state such as the GDR—they need not only to organize, but they need to reach out and communicate to larger sectors of society, rather than remain restricted to small circles of dissidents. In short, given some time and perseverance, I thought that I would be able to locate oppositional ac-

14. For example, Horst Lange (Berlin) and Uwe Matthes (Leipzig), in their analysis of the East German revolutionary transformation, correctly warned against "any monocausal explanations" for the "complex web of contradictory developments" leading up to the revolution; "Ein Jahr danach," *Deutschland Archiv* 11, no. 22 (November 1990), 1747. My translation.

tivities outside and beyond the well-known groups of the civic movement such as New Forum, Democracy Now, or Democratic Awakening, all groups whose founders primarily consisted of college educated dissident intellectuals. What, for example, had taken place in the factories, in the churches and universities, or, perhaps, even inside the party? These were my main questions.

The largest challenge to one-party rule in East-Central Europe to date had been a worker-based movement that materialized out of the Lenin Shipyard in Gdansk, Poland, in August of 1980. In fifteen months of legal existence, Solidarność had recruited more than half of the Polish adult population—workers, teachers, students, professionals, intellectuals, and clergymen. Since Solidarność predated both the reforms in the Soviet Union which have come to be associated with Gorbachev, and the oppositional movements in East-Central Europe, I also expected to find some more or less direct linkages between the opposition movements in Poland and the GDR—if not in form of personal contacts, then at least in terms of a motivating example East Germans may have tried to emulate. On the other hand I was aware that most East German dissidents still couched their opposition to one-party authoritarianism in Marxist (or socialist) terminology, whereas oppositionists virtually everywhere else in East-Central Europe had long given up on socialism. In fact, at least since the brutal crack-down of the Prague Spring in 1968, socialism as an emancipatory goal for the future had been considered, among dissidents within the Soviet sphere of influence, as irretrievably discredited by the reality of Stalinist and neo-Stalinist regimes—that is, with the exception of the GDR.

But then one could never be sure to what extent East German oppositionists continued to use a socialist frame of reference because, in addition to being a relatively safe way to challenge party control on its own terms, it also represented an effective means to show how far removed "actually existing" socialism had become from its own ideological premises. It was, after all, a demonstrable fact that most East German dissidents acknowledged that some form of socialism probably constituted the ultimate raison d'etre for a separate German state. Those who wanted to hold on to an independent GDR seemed naturally drawn to political ideas perceived to be as far removed as possible from those dominant in the bigger, wealthier, and capitalist West Germany. In short, the dynamics that had informed the East German revolution were complex. Nothing at all resembled an open and shut case.

It was with these prior experiences, questions, and expectations that I proceeded to East Germany in May of 1990 to conduct in-depth interviews. I particularly wanted to talk to those people who had, in one way or another, played an important role in the revolutionary transformation of their country—whomever "they" might turn out to be. If one thing seemed clear to me at the time, it was that observers around the world had read enough generalized claims about East Germans and their "peaceful revolution." Now the task was to find those who could concretely reveal and specifically explain the processes that had brought about the revolution, and to let them speak for themselves.

As it turned out, the interviews I conducted with all my East German sources contained elements that were both unexpected and extremely informative. Western readers might share some of this surprise, particularly as it applied to the remarkable willingness of East German citizens suddenly to engage in any topic of discussion, however difficult or painful. Virtually every citizen I talked to seemed eager to convey her or his perspective on the past, on the revolution, and, perhaps most importantly, on the overwhelming problems surrounding the question of "where to go from here." None of these responses are easily captured in a short paragraph, for I encountered a wide range of views which effectively resist easy categorization.

Very few of the people I interviewed, for instance, were strictly and straightforwardly "pro-Western" or "antisocialist," or, for that matter, "anti-Western" or "prosocialist" (even assuming that more than a handful of people could actually agree on what these terms might entail in reality, in the GDR or anywhere else). In fact, most of them made every conceivable effort to steer me away from categories and patterns of thinking that, in the words of a prominent oppositionist, "simply do not apply to our situation." The main difference, it seems to me, was this: to varying degrees the people I talked to had become, through their own actions, what we may call "politicized."[15] This meant different things for different people, but it had one element in common among everyone I encountered: an expanded sense of political possibility, and an engaged, ongoing process of rethinking how their society should be organized. This included such basic questions (mostly forgotten or repressed in the West) as

---

15. This circumstance was confirmed not only by almost all the individuals I interviewed, but by opposition activists in general. For example, the prominent oppositionist pastor Friedrich Schorlemmer, co-founder of Democratic Awakening and currently a member of the Social Democratic Party, repeatedly expressed his disappointment "that the experiences of the Fall [of 1989]—a truly broad politicization of the people—will be lost in our new democracy." *Deutschland Archiv 12*, no. 23 (December 1990), 1935.

to what ideas like "freedom," "democracy," or even a "higher standard of living" actually could mean in daily life. Did these words necessarily signify more automobiles at the cost of a polluted environment, or more efficiency in production at the expense of full employment and a degree of equality among all working citizens?[16] Did one really have to settle for more slogans—as has so often happened in Western societies—at the expense of democratic openness and candor in all the areas of discourse that constitute the public realm? Should one accept, in essence, the capitalist alternative of reviving, in the words of a well-informed chronicler of the East German transformation, "the old abuses of untrammeled competition, labor exploitation, and the destruction of the environment" as the only path toward a future free of Stalinist abuses that had just been collectively overcome?[17] Above all, had the imperative of economic growth, unquestioned by capitalists and communists alike, not proven to be a disastrous formula both for what East Germans described as "the vast majority of human beings" and "for the world they inhabit"?[18] In East Germany, a broad-scale public debate on these questions surfaced the moment the one-party state began to totter. Of course, no one had any

16. As the prominent GDR dissidents Reinhard Weisshuhn and Wolfgang Templin have pointed out, "the relative social equality in the GDR and the moral values which resulted from this daily experience" have generally been underestimated by commentators, and even by party propagandists. In their words, it is "quite remarkable," for instance, "that the ordinary citizen already takes offense at the Volvo of the Politburo member, while he takes for granted the private jet of the Western banker." Reinhard Weisshuhn and Wolfgang Templin, "Hat die DDR eine eigene Identität? oder Vom SED-Staat zur Demokratischen Deutschen Republik," in Axel Lochner (ed.), *Linke Politik in Deutschland* (Hamburg, 1990), 85.

17. Konrad Jarausch, "Toward a Postsocialist Politics?," in Christiane Lemke and Gary Marks, *The Crisis of Socialism in Europe* (Durham, N.C., 1992), 229.

18. Quotation by opposition theorist Ludwig Mehlhorn, personal interview. It should be noted that virtually all opposition activists emphasized the debilitating social and ecological consequences of what they perceived to be the main structural flaw of communist and capitalist economies alike. It can hardly be overemphasized, furthermore, that this debate was in no way restricted to prominent dissidents. What came through in interview after interview was the expanded sense of democratic possibility among the East German populace during the revolutionary months of October to December of 1989, and the concomitant refusal to acquiesce all too quickly in new limitations and inequities. Commenting on this process, Weisshuhn and Templin argued—with the sweep and hope characteristic of those days—that "the attempt to find a new political identity probably contains the unique chance to secure our own existence and, furthermore, for the first time in history to be at the apex of a development which would be significant for all of humanity." "Hat die DDR eine eigene Identität?," 86.

ready-made answers, particularly since the political playing field on which these debates took place changed fundamentally on a day to day basis. Whether the topics concerned domestic issues such as the dissolution of the secret police, the security of jobs, possible participation of the opposition in the government, or external factors such as the role of the Soviet Union or the increasing influence of West Germany, the range of factors that needed to be taken into consideration often became both decisively relevant and rather awesome in scope.

Ironically, my decision to undertake this journey came at a point when the East German chapter in history seemed to most observers to have come to a close. By the late spring of 1990, when I began to conduct interviews, all the East German developments—disappointing as they seemed to many—had generally come to be viewed as more or less "inevitable."[19] A number of explanations of this inevitability were making the rounds—"larger structural necessities," the "will" or the "narrow-mindedness" of "the people," or, more simply, the necessary "costs of freedom."[20]

19. Another traditional assumption comes into view here: the widespread contemporary preoccupation only with things that "work" or "succeed." During the months I spent in the GDR I quite frequently encountered responses along the lines of "why study this movement? Look what happened to it." Shortly before my appointment with the most prominent activist of the East German opposition, Bärbel Bohley, a reporter I had met in East Berlin said to me, "well, she certainly does not play much of a role any longer. She was important once, but now she is pretty much history." In ways quite unintended by the reporter, this is, of course, precisely the point—that is, if we were to conceptualize, as I think we should, "history" as an inquiry into the causes of relevance or irrelevance and the dynamics that shape such outcomes. To be sure, such an exercise would produce very different results from viewing the outcome of the East German revolutionary transformation as "inevitable." See also introduction to Part III, pp. 336–37.

20. For example, in an otherwise nicely framed and vividly phrased short account of the revolutionary days in Berlin, the journalistic chronicler of East European affairs, Timothy Garton Ash, arrives at the astonishing conclusion that East Germans wanted to adopt the Western system simply because "they all knew that a market economy works" (*The Magic Lantern* [New York, 1990], 71). A typical example of the routinely remote and condescending tone that (presumably disappointed) left-wing West German intellectuals employed in order to "make sense" of the West German takeover was offered by the prominent West German political theorist Claus Offe. In specifying historical causation behind the ease with which West Germany achieved total dominance, Offe announced: "At bottom was *a lack of moral and political involvement* on the part of the GDR population: it did not emerge as the winner of a revolution but as a bankrupt estate under new management." Claus Offe, "Prosperity, Nation, Republic: Aspects of the Unique German Journey from Socialism to Capitalism." *German Politics and Society*, no. 22 (Spring 1991), 27. Emphasis added.

These exercises in rationalization, I thought, pointed in a puzzling direction: people had generated high and highly differentiated hopes, their hopes had been dashed, and the process was being characterized as "inevitable." How could this be? The answer, surprisingly enough, was that very few outside observers concretely knew the answer because very few had conducted sustained conversations with those who had been instrumental in bringing about this "stunning" transformation. Prevailing wisdom unquestioningly assumed the basic desire of East Germans to participate in the Western consumer culture. Most commentators argued that there had simply been no choice other than to opt for what amounted to a West German takeover (the economy in shambles, no capital, an insufficiently qualified work force, etc.), but very few considered it necessary to explore the deeper aspirations underlying the East German revolution—or the alternative political routes to which such aspirations pointed.[21]

One particularly common misreading that quickly emerged out of this void was that the events of 1989 were somehow a product of a "spontaneous" rising. In ways that will become clear as these interviews unfold, the years of oppositional activity by the citizens of the GDR provide rich evidence that permanently undermines this notion. It should be noted that the implications of this uncovered evidence extend quite beyond the GDR, because the intuition that political insurgencies are often (or routinely) a result of "spontaneity" is a deep-seated, but I believe quite erroneous, assumption within Western culture.[22]

21. Arguing very much along the lines of the East German civic movement, the British historian of Germany, Geoff Eley, has cogently remarked in this context that there is "no reason to accept the political invitation of the 'death of socialism' rhetoric." "To do so," Eley soberly concludes, "would be profoundly unhistorical," for "such a verdict persuades only if we accept the sufficiency of the crude Cold War opposition between East European state socialism and West European Keynesian-welfare statist social democracy." "In fact," his argument continues, "the most exciting aspect of current events is," on the contrary, "the final destruction of that straightjacket of understanding." Eley's summary appraisal is one to which every East German opposition activist would probably subscribe: "The point is to broaden the space for experiment, diversity, and a genuine pluralism of understanding. In 1956, and then more hopefully in 1968, such opportunities were briefly opened before the fronts were brutally clamped shut. As we enter the 1990s, the space is back." In this reading, however, Eley is a rare exception among the growing number of commentators of either the East German events in particular or the collapse of communism in general. Geoff Eley, "Reviewing the Socialist Tradition," in Lemke and Marks, *The Crisis of Socialism in Europe*, 26.

22. It will be necessary to return to this subject at appropriate junctures in the narrative.

Prior to my arrival in East Germany I had researched the literature on the dynamics of state power and civic opposition in the GDR. On that basis I had created an outline of which people I wanted to interview and what questions I wanted to ask. More often than not, however, the interviews took on a life of their own, proceeding in unanticipated and often surprising directions. This will become readily apparent.

All of this said, there is a final element, I believe, that needs to be addressed in this introduction. Before the reader becomes acquainted with the voices I recorded across the GDR, it seems only fair that I, too, pass through customs inspection—if I may construct a metaphor—laying out as well as I can a few of my own premises and preconceptions. For besides my tape recorder and notepad, I carried with me, as every intellectual traveler inevitably does, a good deal of conceptual baggage.

The research project out of which this book developed was at the same time sparked and informed by the understanding that history is not a "scientific" process that proceeds along one or another theoretically defined trajectory, whether resting upon some presumed "laws" of production relations or some ostensibly "invisible hand" of the market. I do not believe that there are pre-given facts such as "objective laws," "natural developments," or "inevitable results."[23] Despite the contradictions and limitations that are an inherent part of the historical process, what we call "history" is, in the end, a contingent outcome of human effort.[24]

On the other hand, if human affairs rarely proceed along scientific or "inevitable" faultlines, there manifestly are a vast number of customs and traditions that, with varying degrees of rigidity, facilitate what we like to consider as "order." The price of order is, of course, often quite high. It is important to acknowledge that people in all modern industrial societies conform to existing social and political customs most of the time, even if

23. As the Italian historian Luisa Passerini has correctly pointed out, "the interpretative schemes of history and social science . . . almost invariably assume that 'society' is to be conceived of as a series of pre-given facts which only have to be discovered and described. It is one of the great merits of oral sources that they can clearly reveal the poverty and inadequacy of such a crudely positivistic interpretative framework." Luisa Passerini, "Work, Ideology, and Working Class Attitudes to Fascism," in Thompson, *Our Common History,* 54. See also Passerini's excellent oral history, *Fascism in Popular Memory* (Cambridge/New York, 1987).

24. In this context it is worth recalling an insight which I believe continues to have relevance despite the narrowly dogmatic applications that Marx's work received within the Leninist world: "Human beings make their own history," despite the fact that "they do not make it under conditions chosen by themselves." Karl Marx, "The Eighteenth Brumaire of Louis Bonaparte," in Robert C. Tucker, *The Marx-Engels Reader* (New York, 1978), 595.

they don't really wish to. I would submit that this condition prevails as ubiquitously as it does for the simple reason that an alternative way to be, or act, is difficult to imagine, and even more difficult to accomplish—regardless of how strongly people hold their grievances at any given place and time. The routes toward altered modes of behavior are cluttered with social constraints—extending oftentimes to marginalization and ostracism—and enforced when necessary by political repression, ranging from deportation to torture and even extermination. These are social realities for which there is excessively abundant evidence embedded in the history of virtually every modern society. For all of these reasons, most people in most places submit at most times to received practices because, quite simply, they think that nothing can be done about "*it.*"

This systemic "it" encompasses, of course, all of those activities which are perceived as "politics," and, indeed, all of social life itself. In this way, "it" comes to stand for "natural" characteristics of either human beings in the aggregate or entire received political systems. Depending on one's respective ideological background, for instance, either "liberal capitalism" or "communism" can be seen to define "the end of history"—one designed to capitalize on the "greed" presumed inherent to human nature, the other designed to curb the "greed" produced by "all hitherto existing societies."

In terms of the people I interviewed for this book, "it" predominantly encompassed a range of attractions to and grievances about the East German communist party and the social and political system the party constructed and operated. But whether under capitalism or communism, the dynamics inherent in such received practices produce a familiar result: daily life in modern industrial societies is routinely marked by popular conformity and a verifiable thinness of democratic debate. This circumstance, in effect, describes what is regarded as "normal" life—a kind of well-mannered, sometimes weary resignation about the immutability of things as they are. Once alternative social and political options are no longer even thought about in a society, and the potential residing in such options is thereby successfully relegated to a realm "beyond reach," there are no limits to the number of stultifying justifications one can effortlessly generate for "going along" with existing modes of governance, with existing constraints, dangers, and inequities. I would argue that this dynamic can be observed functioning, with greater or lesser intensity, in nominally capitalist, socialist, or theocratic societies around the globe.

What happened in East Germany in 1989 was thus a very rare historical phenomenon indeed. It is rare because it is so difficult to question that which is universally accepted as both "normal" and "inevitable." For this reason, the vast majority of citizens in highly stratified modern societies never find themselves remotely near center stage of political decision-making. This circumstance prevails much more totally all over the world, it seems to me, than people are prepared to acknowledge, or even normally to complain about, much less actively resist.

East Germany's revolutionary autumn revealed not only the transformative potential of large-scale democratic activity, however, but also the limitations and barriers that commonly come to confine the range of such activities. I believe that if these limitations and their causes are intently focused upon and seriously studied, their power to decisively narrow the potential of democratic social relations appears far less imposing, historically, than it otherwise seems to be. Political analysis beyond the current preoccupation with structures of governance can, in turn, expand correspondingly to include the social relations of people who inhabit these structures. This is so, I would suggest, because the potential for enriched social relations, when actually grounded in experiences of collectively self-generated political change, and when thought about with persistence, appears far less unattainable than during times of political normalcy when people routinely are so resigned that they do think about the subject at all. This book has such a purpose—to uncover the elements of social experience that convey this expanded democratic potential that is inherent but largely dormant in all modern societies.

The following interviews, then, are not about theories concerning alternative systems of governance, or about competing ideologies, but rather about a significant chapter in the continuing and troubled search for a more democratic way to live within ever more complex social systems. Of course the term "democratic," misused and abused as much as it is, should be evoked with much caution here. What I encountered in East Germany, however, could summarily be called the "human dimension" of democracy, the social rather than structural elements of democratic forms. While East German oppositionists were obviously greatly concerned about issues such as securing basic human rights or achieving fair electoral representation for each and every citizen in the GDR, their initial and most fundamental concern had to do with the basic problematic that precedes the creation of formal democratic structures. This problematic turns on questions that are truly elemented: how to bring about forms of social interaction that are open and not limiting or repressive, that are inclusive rather than exclusive, that invite people to participate rather than intimidate, drive them away, or otherwise alienate them. Whatever a "functioning democracy" may look like, it was clear to the East German opposition that it would have to consist of more than a separation of powers, parliamentary elections and Western-type parties. By the same token, any ideology proclaiming to give "all power to the working class" in a "free association of producers" had little value if the power of both interpretation and of execution lay in the hands of a single party rather than in the hands of a democratically assembled citizenry. It was in this very sense that oppositionists spoke of a "third way," of learning from the experiences of both Western bourgeois democracies and actually existing socialism, while, at the same time, emulating neither. They called this process of searching for new and vital political forms "democratic" primarily in order to call attention to their belief that it should be based on society rather than on the state or an economic system, that it should include people from all walks of society, and that it should try to redress blatant imbalances of power and influence so endemic to both political systems. It was in this sense, also, that the largest opposition group New Forum refused to turn into a party, and instead wanted to continue functioning as an umbrella organization for a broad-scale civic movement.

In short, what I am here endeavoring to call to the reader's attention in my use of the term "democratic" is not a debate over definitions—inherently static definitions—of what this term of description really means, or, for that matter, what it should mean. Rather, I am attempting to direct attention to the intricate *process necessary* to experiment with (to define and re-define, and eventually to discover) what may be called the human or social elements of democratic forms.

There is no better opportunity, in my opinion, for studying social relations in any given society than during times of collectively self-generated change—that is, when people actually appear on the political scene as actors, and not merely as bystanders. It is only when people's thoughts, aspirations, and actions become effectively "public" that they can produce tangible results—and only then that these results can, in turn, be analyzed with some historical specificity.[25]

25. This understanding is reflected in much of the existing literature on social movements and revolutions. See, for example, Michael Kimmel's recent book on revolution, in which he states that "revolutions are of central importance . . . not only because they are extreme cases of collective action, but also because revolutions provide a lens through which to view the everyday organization of any society." Kimmel, *Revolution* (Philadelphia, 1990), 1. Most students of revolutions/social movements share this understanding. Authors I found most helpful in this respect are E. P. Thompson (*The Making of the English Working Class*), Christopher Hill (*The World Turned Upside Down*), Barrington Moore, Jr. (*Authority and Inequality Under Capitalism and Socialism*), Alain Touraine (*The Voice and the Eye*), Charles

It was for this reason that I have long been interested in organizing efforts directed toward the formation of democratic movements. I researched the German revolution of 1918/19, workers' struggles for collective bargaining rights in the United States during the post-World War I era, and the pivotal breakthrough in U.S. mass-production industries in the 1930s. Later, I studied the student movements of the sixties in Europe and the United States and read broadly about the Spanish Revolution of the late thirties, the Hungarian Revolution of 1956, the Prague Spring of 1968, and the emergence of Solidarność in Poland. My own political seasoning came out of experiences as a shop steward in the late 1970s, participation in the peace movement in West Germany in the early 1980s, and other political activities during my university years in West Berlin.

A final point remains to be clarified. There is, predictably, much debate about whether the East German events should in fact be categorized as a "revolution" at all. Obviously, the term carries very different connotations for different people. In an age in which the introduction of a new hair-coloring method or a diet cola is described as "revolutionary," little common semantic ground exists to describe fundamental social and political changes in any given society.

One possible way to provide an answer to the question of revolution would be to take traditional definitions—political, sociological, philosophical—of what constitutes a revolution and see whether they apply to East Germany's popular upheaval. According to the Oxford English Dictionary, for instance, a revolution is "a complete overthrow of the established government in any country or state by those who were previously subject to it: a forcible substitution of a new ruler or form of government." While East German events would undoubtedly meet these standards, the definition itself is neither very precise nor clearly distinguishable from, for example, a coup. One of the more comprehensive recent definitions, incorporating issues of causation, modes of contention, and ranges of goals, was given by Perez Zagorin in his book *Rebels and Rulers:* "A revolution is any attempt by subordinate groups through the use of violence to bring about (1) a change of government or its policy, (2) a change of regime, or (3) a change of society, whether this attempt is justified by reference to past conditions or to an as yet unattained future ideal."[26]

Tilly (*From Mobilization to Revolution*), Lawrence Goodwyn (*Breaking the Barrier*), and Craig Calhoun (*The Question of Class Struggle*), all of whom have creatively wrestled with interpreting the dynamics of popularly generated social change.

26. Perez Zagorin, *Rebels and Rulers* (Cambridge, 1982; vol. 1), 17.

Again, East German events would meet these criteria, except that the transformation was brought about by nonviolent means.

The larger point, however, is that all definitions—in fact, all of received political description—would be entirely insufficient to capture the complex reality of what happens in a revolution—in East Germany or anywhere else. Depending on one's political perspective, East German events could be characterized as a "revolt," a "popular upheaval," an "insurrection," or simply the collapse of a decrepit totalitarian regime. And yet none of this descriptively vivid but wholly inexact terminology can do justice to the underlying meaning of the East German transformation. The controlling historical fact, it seems to me, is this: through their own actions, East Germans created a popularly generated political space for themselves. Within it, vastly expanded democratic possibilities emerged. Between October and December of 1989, these possibilities clearly constituted a "revolutionary moment," fully commensurate with that which existed in the revolutions of 1848 in France and Germany, 1956 in Hungary, or 1968 in Czechoslovakia. One deals, therefore, with a "revolution."

These, then, were the interests and presumptions I carried with me when I decided that I had to go to East Germany in 1990. When I first stepped out of the subway in the newly reopened station on Friedrichsstrasse, East Berlin, on 28 May of that year, I was nevertheless concerned that those whom I had preselected as "important" members of the opposition movement might prove to be too busy, or generally not interested in talking to a Western scholar. Neither my West German nor my American background, I feared, would be very helpful, for I was aware that Western reporters, politicians, and scholars were often viewed with suspicion by East German political activists.

Almost everywhere I went, however, people were overwhelmingly cooperative. East Germans I met generally responded very positively to the idea of an in-depth inquiry into events that, they believed, had too frequently been telescoped into sensational and misleading headlines. Whether I talked to people well-known in the GDR and beyond, or those known only within a small community, whether these people were pastors, workers, teachers, scientists, or party functionaries, East Germans, after a few minutes spent "checking out the scholar from the other side," quickly expressed interest in helping push forward my project. They demonstrated a remarkable willingness to confront the most complex dilemmas that were an inevitable consequence of their own actions and—often— their own nonactions. In the few instances in which I did not manage to get an interview, the reasons had to do with lack of time on my own part, inability to establish contact because of nonexistent or malfunctioning telephone lines, gas stations that did not have the gasoline I needed for my Western car, or unanticipated obligations that carried people away from a scheduled appointment.

Between May and August of 1990, I conducted 106 interviews in the GDR. Of these, 48 were taped. They lasted between 45 minutes and four hours. Since I had never intended for the list of people I interviewed to be "representative" of the East German population at large, I tried to focus on those who had played, in widely varying ways, active roles in these unfolding events. This book consequently does not focus on the "silent majority," but rather on those East Germans who actually "made history" through their own actions.[27] I did attempt, however, to find a rough cross section of East Germans in terms of occupation, political convictions, gender, age, and place of residence. Roughly one-third of my interviewees had been, or still were, communist party members,[28] while over half of them had been active in the oppositional civic movement. My youngest interviewee was 18, my oldest 79, while the age bracket with the highest number of interviewees ranged from 30 to 40 years. Though a few of them were religious, most would have described themselves as atheists. Occupationally, they ranged from former prime minister to bricklayer.[29] Finally, I tried to visit as many cities across the GDR as my schedule allowed in the search for political networks that might prove relevant to an understanding of the revolution.[30]

27. As in any recorded revolution, those who became politically active at one point or another most likely make up a relatively small minority among the East German population. Yet it is important to point out that the some 300,000 demonstrators in Leipzig on 23 October 1989, or the estimated 1 million demonstrators in East Berlin on 4 November 1989—both, that is, before the opening of the Wall and the subsequent disintegration of one-party rule—constitute a significant portion of a total population of 16 million (based on the total U.S. population, the American equivalent would be a demonstration of about 4.5 million U.S. citizens in Chicago or about 15 million in New York).

28. Of the 35 people who belong in this category, 29 had left the party at the time of the interview. All of the 12 workers who had been party members had handed in their membership cards within weeks after the opening of the Wall. The 6 persons who stayed in the renamed party belong to the group of 23 who had either an academic or a professional degree.

29. The exact breakdown according to occupation is as follows: 43 people with academic or professional degree, 34 workers, 9 pastors, 9 students, 8 full-time politicians, 3 artists.

30. Beyond the activity of a few prominent intellectuals, few observers paid any sustained attention to the views and actions of "normal" East German citizens. Usually lumped together as one big mass of faceless "people," it seemed sufficient to most observers to

When I returned home to Durham, North Carolina, I was, of course, confronted with the necessity of reducing literally thousands of pages of narrative to a manageable body that could be shaped into a coherent account of the origins, course, and outcome of these complex events. It

analyze East Germans on the basis of highly elusive election results or by the fact that many of them seemed eager to go on frequent shopping sprees in the West.

In the meantime, a few books have begun to appear that in different ways have helped to undermine the two previously prevailing views which have simplistically portrayed the East German revolution either as an unmitigated failure or, alternately, as a full-blown success in its quest for Western freedom and prosperity. Not surprisingly, all are based on some form of oral investigation among East German citizens. See particularly John Borneman's critical and perceptive evaluation of the revolution's effects on Berliners East and West in *After the Wall* (New York, 1991), in which he calls the unification process a "corporate take-over" by West Germany and argues that what "sapped the revolution's strength . . . was the terrifying feeling of inferiority, the sense that everything they had stood and lived for, their sacrifices and self-satisfactions alike, were worthless in the face of Western prosperity. . . . East Germans were taking a beating not as individuals, but as a society." Surprisingly, Borneman nevertheless goes along with the predominant Western conclusion that "in response, collectively, they demanded West Germany's rich way of living for themselves" (p. 33). See also Robert Darnton's *Berlin Journal* (New York, 1991), an imaginatively conceptualized report on revolutionary East Germany in which he laments that the opposition movement has been "relegated to the sidelines, and East German political life is conforming to a West German pattern." Darnton adds: "In fact, the West Germans seem to be taking it over. The [election] campaign [of 1990] has been dominated by the media, personality cults, and a foreign variety of political professionalism imported from the Federal Republic" (p. 259). Like many others who conducted interviews in East Germany, Darnton argues that "there was little left of the excitement and idealism that pulsated through the body politic last autumn." Darnton concludes: "The citizen's groups identified with the revolution nearly disappeared in the wave of votes for the conservative Alliance for Germany sponsored by Chancellor Helmut Kohl" (p. 262). Also relevant in this context is Helga Königsdorf, who, in her *Adieu DDR* (Reinbek bei Hamburg, 1990), successfully managed in a short amount of time to put together a fairly wide range of complex East German responses to the revolutionary transformation. Also of interest is Christina Wilkening's fascinating accounts of former Stasi agents in *Staat im Staate* (Berlin, 1990). None of the available studies, however, have actually attempted to trace the emergence of the East German civic movement (and thus have not dealt with what specific experiences informed the revolutionary effort), nor did they particularly focus on those who, in one way or another, played an active role in the transformation of their society. Unlike the above-mentioned authors, I have also attempted to give a full account, with as little editing as possible, of the interviews chosen for publication. Other valuable books on the East German revolution, among them a variety of document collections, so-called "instant histories," and essay collections, including analyses of the revolution by participants, political commentators, and journalists, can be found in the bibliography. All of them, however, greatly differ from the present study in both focus and conceptualization.

was with some relief that after months of review and re-review of this dense body of material, I found myself able to shape these passionate, thoughtful, doubt-ridden, sometimes modest, sometimes arrogant responses into the structure that constitutes this book.[31] Its essence consists of fifteen prolonged conversations which I feel best represent both the variety of protagonists and the range of answers I received.

The study is divided into three parts, a pre-revolutionary, a revolutionary, and a postrevolutionary period. This order is essential, I believe, for uncovering the long sequential building process of an organized opposition in the GDR, and it helps to elucidate the diverging, and sometimes contradictory, responses among members of different sectors of society to life in East Germany during the evolving stages of this transformation. In terms of text, I have tried throughout to retain the direction, style, and idiosyncrasies of the interviews. Minor alterations have been made only where they seemed absolutely essential for clarity.[32] One of the larger problems, undoubtedly, lay in having to translate everything from German, and sometimes from marvelously vivid German idioms at that.

In each case, I have introduced the interviewee and provided necessary background on the interview itself. My questions were retained only where they appeared essential for the answers to be understood. Whenever I cut a sentence or a longer section, I marked these places with ellipses (. . .). In a few cases, names have been changed to preserve

31. Despite their unique potential to reveal complex historical dynamics, oral history accounts, it perhaps needs to be emphasized, should never be used as one's only source, nor should they be taken at face value. People intentionally or unintentionally forget or misconstrue, they are selective, and, in a most personal way, they are very subjective. Additionally, answers are highly contingent upon the interviewer, the particular context at the time of the interview, and the questions asked (or not asked). Since the researcher usually walks away—interview in hand—from both the source and the situation which produced the interview in the first place, interviews inherently contain a number of difficult moral and political issues for the interviewer. Feminist oral historians in particular have begun to stress the social, psychological, and literary problems surrounding the interview process. See, for example, the excellent collection of essays by Sherna Berger Gluck and Daphne Patai, *Women's Words: The Feminist Practice of Oral History* (New York/London, 1991). For a good general discussion of oral history, see also Lutz Niethammer, *"Lebenserfahrung und kollektives Gedächtnis"—Die Praxis der Oral History* (Frankfurt, 1980), and Paul Thompson, *The Voice of the Past: Oral History* (Oxford/New York, 1988).

32. Such alterations were strictly confined to the following: completing sentences in which a word or two were missing; occasionally putting together sections of the interview that belonged to the same topic; adding statements that were made after I had turned off my tape recorder (but which I was given permission to use); and, finally, clarifying otherwise incomprehensible references.

promised anonymity. Such instances are identified in the text each time they occur.

At the end of the book's main text, the reader will find a chronology from 1945 to 1990, which I believe will prove useful as a guide to the names, dates, and events alluded to by the interviewees. The chronology also offers an extremely condensed overview of 41 years of East German history.

PART I
A LONG TIME COMING
Roots of Dissent and Opposition in the
German Democratic Republic

There is really not a soul who has a conception of what's to become of this divided,
mixed-up country.—Soviet party functionary one day before the workers' upris-
ing in June 1953, in Stefan Heym's novel 5 DAYS IN JUNE

One task of human thought is to try to perceive what the range of possibilities may
be in a future that always carries on its back the burden of the present and the
past.—Barrington Moore, REFLECTIONS ON THE CAUSES OF HUMAN MISERY

■ Shortly before the tumultuous events of 1989, the British journalist
Michael Simmons observed that "the German Democratic Republic . . .
has been in its time the most maligned, most disparaged, and most
misunderstood state in Europe."[1] Founded in 1949 on territory that had
been "liberated from fascism" by Soviet forces during the defeat of
Hitler's Germany in World War II, the GDR indeed proved difficult to
understand. Was it a legitimate, popularly supported attempt "to build
socialism on German soil," or merely a state whose continuance depended entirely on the Soviet occupying power? To what extent was the
existence of an independent East German state determined by its role as a
socialist cold war frontier in the heart of Europe? And above all, how did
East German citizens see themselves, or perceive their own society? Over
time, considerable evidence has accrued which indicates that they saw the
world—whether party members or not—in a distinct way. The American
historian Robert Darnton, for example, has vividly summarized his own
realization of how different East Germans were from Westerners, despite
their common historical roots: "I soon discovered, East Germans did not

1. Michael Simmons, *The Unloved Country* (London, 1989), 1.

think like Westerners. They began from different assumptions, and lived in a different world. . . . They spoke the same language and shared the same culture [with West Germans], but they had lived apart for 40 years. I had not realized how effectively they had been divided and how deeply the division had cut into the two societies. It extended to the everyday lives of ordinary people, their ways of handling social contacts, time and money, friendship and family, and even words, despite their common language." In the same vein, the historian of Germany, V. R. Berghahn, concluded that "East Germans certainly appear to identify more strongly than ever before with the State in which they live."[2]

Insightful as these qualifications are, however, they are not meant to imply that East Germans were content with life in a one-party state. The forty-year history of the GDR also contains some readily available evidence which suggests that things had not always been as calm, complacent, and orderly as they appeared at first sight. Two events in particular have come to symbolize early popular disaffection with state socialism. The first was the large-scale uprising of workers against new wage and work regulations in June 1953. The rebellion ended in a massive wave of repression in the GDR.[3] The second development that verified the existence of popular disaffection was the building of the Berlin Wall in August 1961. This government action was designed, quite simply, to prevent any further permanent exodus of hundreds of thousands of citizens from the GDR.[4] Both events left deep psychological and political rents in the fab-

2. Darnton, *Berlin Journal*, 16; V. R. Berghahn, *Modern Germany* (New York, 1990), 237–38.
3. In response to a 10 percent increase in work norms without a corresponding raise in pay, the worker strikes began on 16 June in Berlin and subsequently spread throughout the GDR, involving some 370,000 workers. The demands of the workers ranged from the reduction of work norms to the holding of free elections. What had generally come to be seen as the first large-scale uprising in the Eastern Bloc ended, like numerous later uprisings, with the Soviet occupying forces imposing martial law. According to various estimates, 21 demonstrators and four policemen were killed, more than 1,000 demonstrators were sent to prison, and seven were sentenced to death. See particularly Arnulf Baring, *Uprising in East Germany: June 17, 1953* (Ithaca, N.Y., 1972).
4. About 200,000 citizens fled the country in 1960, and another 155,000 between January and 13 August 1961 alone. Young people, skilled industrial workers, and professionals composed a majority of those who decided to leave everything behind for good. See Bundesministerium für innerdeutsche Beziehungen, *DDR Handbuch* (Cologne, 1979), 400–401. Mike Dennis, a historian of East Germany, quotes Erich Honecker, in charge of building the Wall and later general secretary of the Socialist Unity Party, as describing the crisis in 1961 as follows: "Could we afford to look on passively while the open border was exploited to bleed our republic to death by means of an unprecedented economic war?

ric of East German society. Among a growing number of citizens, both the underlying causes and the outcome of these events also strengthened the appeal of the "other" German state. The very continuance of the German Democratic Republic thus basically came to depend on two extremely tenuous factors: its frail legitimacy among its own population, and the willingness of the Soviet leadership to guarantee its permanent existence.

"Leadership" in East Germany thus constituted an occupation beset by chronic nervousness. In the aggregate, the East German party elite faced dismal preconditions in its attempts to build "actually existing socialism" under one-party control. To be sure, the party elite tried hard to leave the impression of success. Over the postwar decades, everywhere one looked, billboards, slogans, and flags attested to the distinct quality of the "socialist worker and peasant state." For the most part, child care programs, schoolbooks, university seminars, radio and television shows all were dedicated to portraying the "outstanding successes of socialism." The whole society was flooded with the politics of symbolism—of heroes, great deeds, and unprecedented accomplishments. Yet the more the party engaged in such desperate efforts to create an autonomous identity among its citizens, the less the people of East Germany displayed any indication of possessing a genuine East German sense of self.

The Wall, nevertheless, did serve the party's basic purpose. After the practical option of leaving the country had been effectively foreclosed by a heavily guarded 12-foot barrier along the entire 965-mile border with West Germany, most East Germans appeared resigned to life in a society organized around "the leading role of the communist party." Until the early eighties, organized public opposition, and thus open democratic debate, disappeared from sight.

As the economy grew throughout the sixties and into the early seventies, and such basic necessities as jobs, housing, social services, and limited

---

Could we afford to remain inactive when a situation had arisen in the heart of Europe, with its hardly hidden mobilisations and intensified war hysteria on the Western side resembling that of the eve of the Second War? Could we afford to twiddle our thumbs while Berlin-West was built up into a 'bridgehead' of the Cold War and exercised its 'nuisance function' more and more uninhibitedly?" Erich Honecker, *From My Life* (Oxford/New York, 1981), 209; also in Mike Dennis, *German Democratic Republic* (London/New York, 1988), 31. Commenting on this line of reasoning, David Childs correctly points out that "by destroying the centre of a great city, by risking super-power confrontation and internal revolt, the ruler of the GDR built the Wall and took the explosive pressures off their state and society. At the same time they built a permanent, massive, anti-Communist propaganda exhibition." In *The GDR: Moscow's German Ally* (London, 1988), 65.

travel opportunities became more available to everyone,[5] this resigned acceptance of the system deepened. Whether East Germans liked it or not, it seemed, they all made compromises on a daily basis.

Even though the GDR—unlike its Western counterpart, the Federal Republic of Germany—had been widely understood as an artificial creation, its independent existence within the political order of postwar Europe was soon generally recognized, despite the fact that its leaders and policies were not trusted by its neighbors. West European elites continued to be offended by East Germany's communist ideology, while party functionaries in Poland, Czechoslovakia, and elsewhere in East-Central Europe feared its Germanic heritage. Michael Simmons quotes a Polish associate who gave voice to a sentiment widely shared by both Eastern and Western neighbors of East Germany: "The GDR? It is nothing. It is warmed and fed by its brothers to the West and it is kept in order by its brothers to the East."[6]

Nevertheless, experts in both camps agreed with one another in crediting the GDR with having the most successful and most stable regime in the Eastern Bloc.[7] Accordingly the one-party state, behind its vast security

5. See particularly Christiane Lemke, *The Quality of Life in the GDR* (Armonk, N.Y., 1989), and G. E. Edwards, *GDR Society and Social Institutions* (New York, 1985).

6. Simmons, *The Unloved Country*, 1. This perspective is, understandably enough, also visible in scholarly literature. In one of the last publications about the GDR prior to the Fall of 1989, a prominent historian of East Germany, David Childs, writes: "In the final analysis, what the SED can and cannot do is circumscribed by the Soviet Union and the Federal Republic. It is dependent on their political and economic good will." In David Childs, Thomas A. Baylis, Marilyn Rueschemeyer (eds.), *East Germany in Comparative Perspective* (London/New York, 1989), 18. It should be noted that this was a thoroughly reasonable assessment in the nonrevolutionary context prevailing at the time Childs wrote. It became less descriptively accurate only because the East German Revolution fundamentally changed all contexts.

7. Four recent examples of such conclusions can be found in V. R. Berghahn, *Modern Germany* (Cambridge, 1990); William E. Griffith, "The German Democratic Republic," in William E. Griffith (ed.), *Central and Eastern Europe: The Opening Curtain?* (San Francisco/London, 1989); Childs, *The GDR;* and Dennis, *German Democratic Republic.* Berghahn comes to the clear conclusion that East Germany "has an important political voice and can currently boast greater prosperity and stability than all other socialist regimes" (p. 238). Griffith writes: "Although [East Germany's] cities were mostly bombed into destruction during World War II, and what was left of its factories was largely dragged away to the Soviet Union as reparations, [the GDR] is today the most prosperous Communist country in the world and one of the top twenty world industrial powers" (p. 314). Similarly, Childs states in his introduction that "[the GDR] has continued to make economic progress . . . and retains a respectable place among the industrial states of the world: and it is apparently one of the

apparatus, seemed virtually impregnable to change. Few if any political analysts were surprised when the East German party leadership openly rejected Gorbachev-type reforms in the late 1980s. For a long time to come, it was assumed, East Germany would withstand the turmoil of reform occurring all around it in the Eastern Bloc. Even members of the marginalized opposition within the GDR had taken for granted that the Berlin Wall—the most glaring reminder and ultimate safeguard of communist party domination—would remain in place for the foreseeable future.

East Germans, it seemed, had come to terms with a reality that appeared more or less unalterable. During the entire postwar period the party and state apparatus had expanded tremendously, reaching into every sphere of social life. With an increasingly elaborate network of functionaries and secret police forces, the party state planned, informed, disinformed, organized, decided, supervised, and controlled virtually all aspects of life.[8]

In so doing, however, the communist regime could point to undeniable

---

world's most stable regimes." In the same vein, finally, Dennis expresses his impression that "the GDR of today appears to be a politically stable, relatively prosperous and increasingly self-assured state. It is often upheld as a model for its particular brand of socialism" (p. 197). Again, these judgments were quite reasonable in the context prevailing as late as 1988. The persisting point: the collective activities of East German citizens which brought down the Wall (and with it its builders) fundamentally altered the political conditions in which the East German state had previously been understood to have existed.

8. By and large, this condition was true within all Eastern European nations that had come under the Soviet Union's domination after 1945. Following the effective political consolidation by Stalinist parties in the late 1940s and early 1950s across Eastern Europe, any public opposition in these societies carried the immediate risk of arrest, often torture, and, among prominent dissidents, even execution. The British socialist Chris Harman has pointedly summarized conditions in Eastern Europe since those days: "The end product was a group of societies, rigidly and hierarchically organized, in which a monolithic bureaucracy and police apparatus continually fragmented other social forces; where political debate amounted to the dull, uniform reiteration of platitudes that were patently untrue; and where cultural life became a deadening apology for those same platitudes. Life within the bureaucracy was characterized by cringing fear, and at the same time cynical enjoyment of enhanced privileges. In the factories the joyless toil to accumulate was intensified without even the marginal protection obtainable in the advanced west from trade-union organization. In every sphere, spies and informers . . . could be relied upon to betray those who tried to resist the system by collective organization from below." Chris Harman, *Bureaucracy and Revolution in Eastern Europe* (London, 1974), 64–65. The only institutional exception to involvement in this closure was the church. It was a most provocative exception, indeed, as the interviews in this book repeatedly demonstrate.

achievements during the 1960s and early '70s—full employment, a nationwide system of day care for children, and comprehensive health coverage. Nevertheless, in terms of modern industrial production, the economy was in shambles. Supplies were disorganized, much of the infrastructure oversized and badly outmoded, the environment increasingly threatened by industrial pollution, and inefficiency so institutionalized that work itself proceeded at a desultory pace. As the growth of the East German economy came to a grinding halt in the mid-seventies, the inefficiency, waste, corruption, and lies that were an organic part of this peculiar Leninist mode of production tangibly began to undermine the system's legitimacy. Although this condition was never visible as part of a public debate, people increasingly complained to each other, and, above all, lost hope "that there is anything we can do to make things work."

As a result—imperceptibly at first to outsiders and high-ranking party functionaries alike—a culture of noncooperation began to spread through the interstices of East German society. Early on, however, this fact did not yet translate into any kind of open, or even publicly organized, opposition, for the meticulous organization of every aspect of day-to-day life by the state apparatus left a crippling mark on any efforts of self-generated activity within the official realm. Nevertheless, East Germans found complex ways of minimizing personal initiative and, in turn, developed elaborate individual escapes to conditions that increasingly appeared to be beyond their personal influence. In fact, common wisdom began to consider any attempt to offer open criticism for the sake of improvement as downright dangerous, and thus not intelligent. East Germans came to call this reality "a society of private niches" in which "individual emigration" took place on a massive scale. From all walks of life, East German citizens fled to the world of weekend dachas, alcohol, and West German television.

Yet small-scale attempts to articulate and organize dissent materialized. On issues such as human rights, the militarization of society, or environmental destruction, disparate voices can be detected as far back as the mid- to late seventies.[9] Despite numerous setbacks, such efforts grew in number and diversity throughout the eighties.[10] By the time the society

9. For a valuable overview in English of dissent in the GDR, see Roger Woods, *Opposition in the GDR Under Honecker, 1971–1985* (New York, 1986), and, in German, Ferdinand Kroh, *"Freiheit ist immer Freiheit . . .": Die Andersdenkenden in der DDR* (Frankfurt am Main, 1988).
10. By the summer of 1989, more than 600 such grass-roots groups had come into existence. It would be difficult to ascertain the number of committed and experienced activists at the time, but the estimates range from a very conservative 2,000 to more than 10,000.

"opened" in 1989, this entire past history of social and psychological oppression, on the one hand, and various attempts to carve out a bit of free space, on the other, had left an enormously complex residue.

This residue is one that poses subtle problems for the Western scholar. While, in all interviews the initial questions I asked concerned how life proceeded within such conditions, and the answers can be swiftly summarized as "not so well," it is important to specify that the common tone of these answers concealed a wide range of very different—and very revealing—responses. I quickly realized that it was precisely in this embattled social realm where one ran headlong into an entire substructure of perceptions and aspirations that were central and yet at the same time hard to pin down. Different people responded to the existing conditions in many different ways. Nowhere did I find simple and clear-cut forms of what is variously and routinely called insurgency, disaffection, apathy, acquiescence, support, or protest. On the contrary, everyone had, at some point and to varying degrees, "gone along." People acquiesced and cooperated, and yet they also disassociated themselves from the ruling power. At the same time, it can be said that, in subtle ways, many resisted.

As the following interviews indicate, just below the routine of daily life smoldered a growing sense of discontent—about lies and corruption, blatant inefficiencies and hazards in the workplace, arbitrary rule, and social restrictions in general. For a long time such discontent seemed an essentially individual expression, existing principally in the privacy of one's mind or surfacing solely in the safe environment provided by one's close friends.

But it was there nonetheless. Even though such discontent rarely translated into public acts of protest or opposition, it still manifested itself—even prior to 1989—in the endless variety of subtle ways people in East Germany disassociated themselves from party and state. Over time, I gradually began to understand the importance of this "suppressed" longing, this "hidden" resistance. In fact, fully considered, these emerging social forms constituted the beginning of the East German revolution.

1 THE TROUBLED
EMERGENCE OF AN IDEA

■ FRANK EIGENFELD, biologist and founding member of New Forum, and HARALD WAGNER, mathematician, pastor, and founding member of Democratic Awakening. ■ *"I had felt imprisoned ever since 1961."—Eigenfeld* ■ *"I learned from my sports experiences that there is nothing I cannot do just because someone tells me that I can't."—Wagner*

About two months into my research on the East German revolution, in July of 1990, I was invited to an oppositional Summer Academy in Erfurt, created two years earlier as an informal annual gathering ground for oppositionists from all parts of the GDR. This event had initially been set up by members of a dissident circle within the church, called the "Solidaristic Church." The overriding purpose behind the Summer Academy was to provide a relatively secure space for communication among disparate sectors of the East German opposition under the aegis of the Protestant church. As some of the founders told me, the strong but distant hope was that something collective, something "bigger," might come out of such a meeting. This hope was not entirely misplaced, as later events proved. In fact, the list of participants in the meetings during the previous summer of 1989 reads like a "Who's Who" of the East German opposition leadership. At the time of my 1990 visit, most of these people held some kind of elected position, in stark contrast to the year before.

The Summer Academy took place in the rooms of the Protestant church in Erfurt, a city of medieval origin and great beauty, despite the fact that large portions of its centuries-old architecture have been badly neglected over the last 40 years. The historic center of Erfurt is surrounded by the kind of shoddy, pragmatic, and cold architecture one can find in most "socialist" cities: six- to eight-story concrete blocks, as cheaply built as they appear overwhelmingly inhumane. Erfurt was a city of tensions and contradictions, a city in which Luther spent five years studying theology (1501–5), and where, a little less than 400 years later, in 1891, the German Social Democrats voted to adopt a "Marxist" program which they hoped would help lead Germany to a free and egalitarian future. Narrow cobblestone roads, little marketplaces, solid stone houses, some built as far back as the sixteenth century, and more than 60 churches and cathedrals exude an atmosphere of "lived history" like few other places in Europe.

Oppositionists from every Eastern European country, including the Baltic republics and the Soviet Union, participated in the 1990 Summer Academy. For seven intense days, 46 people from 11 countries (I was the only "Westerner") talked, debated, ate, drank, laughed, sang, and argued with each other. We read prepared papers to each other and had discussions about the past, present, and possible future of each and every East-Central European nation; it was an experience, in short, that was as unusual as it was exhausting, energizing, and enhancing.

On the very first day of the conference, I had a long conversation with two East German oppositionists, Frank Eigenfeld from Halle and Harald Wagner from a small town near Leipzig. Neither of these men had been mere spare-time oppositionists; they had quite literally lived for "a free and democratic but also egalitarian" East Germany all their adult lives. Both turned out to be invaluable sources on the internal dynamics of the growing civic opposition movement during the 1980s. But above all, they in many ways represented—as close as one can get to "typical" examples—the organized East German opposition at large. Not nationally known, yet widely respected in their communities, not fighting for personal fame but rather for a better society to live in, articulate but not condescending, they had consistently pursued their objectives despite great personal hardships and many severe setbacks. Both were quite unpretentious, which I initially misread as a possible sign of insecurity, or even weakness. At first, I thus viewed them as people who could not really be "serious candidates" according to my notion of "genuine and dedicated oppositionists in a police state." The quiet but very determined way in which they explained the intricacies of political dissent in the GDR quickly revealed that this impression was quite wrong. Much of the Western cultural baggage I had brought with me concerning how people think, or how they "usually" interact with each other, it turned out, simply did not apply in the opposition milieu of the GDR.

In the following section, Frank Eigenfeld and Harald Wagner incisively address some of the problems and presumptions shaping democratic political organizing. For instance, one of the most basic issues of political activism—in East Germany as in any other modern society—revolves around the question of what to do in order to translate a "good idea" into a "tangible result"—a frustrating problem routinely simplified into the elementary decision of whether to work "within the system" or "outside of it." As the following interview makes clear, the real political issues were, and are, much more complex. In many cases the very distinction between "inside" and "outside" seemed impossible to make. In the movement's initial stages—and this interview focuses on these early stages—the tasks of simple survival far outweighed such lofty strategic questions. Eigenfeld and Wagner here illuminate the many arduous steps that needed to be taken in order to get from articulating political grievances to organizing local grass-roots groups and, ultimately, to some kind of larger network of oppositional groups nationwide.

The two activists agreed to participate in a joint interview late one evening, after a full day of discussions and events. As the three of us sat around a small table, Eigenfeld unpacked a bag full of home-grown fresh vegetables and some Czechoslovak beer ("you never know whether you can find good stuff when you go on a trip in the GDR, so I always take along as much as I can") and began to tell me about his childhood and youth, his experiences with the East German state, and about the twists and turns of how his initial grudging acquiescence to communist party control developed over the years from private dissent to increasingly outspoken resistance. He was born in 1943.

■ *Frank Eigenfeld:* I had realized very early, even before the Wall was built, what it meant to live in the "East" as opposed to the "West." The exchange rate, for example, was 1 Mark West for 5 Mark East at the time, and in addition our wages were much lower than in the West. So even though there were plenty of things in the stores in West Berlin, there was very little I could buy with my money. . . .

The Wall was erected one week before my eighteenth birthday. This was the first genuine shock in my life. All of a sudden it became strikingly clear to me that there are certain people out there who have the power fundamentally to curtail your wishes and your plans. This was something I wasn't used to from home, and something I was never able to accept. To this very day I am deeply moved by resentment when I am in Berlin and I see the Wall.

Back in 1961, just like today, I simply perceived such constraints, whether on a political level or on a personal level, as very unjust. Wherever I can, I try to defend myself against it. I don't think the implementation of such restrictions can ever be justified, whatever the cause may be. A political structure like that simply has no right to exist. . . . But still I, as most everyone else, did not know how to respond to all this. I felt unable to respond; I felt completely powerless. . . .

Of course, these things were part of our discussions at home or at work, but there was nothing we could do. We all felt a sort of helpless rage. We talked about it, we felt angry and shocked, but we never did much about it.

Political discussions picked up in earnest during the Prague Spring of 1968. I can remember—we listened a lot to Radio Prague—that we invested a lot of hope in a possible new development. Most of all we hoped that this new development would also begin to take place in the GDR. . . .

So you can imagine the horror we felt when Czechoslovakia was occupied in '68. During that period we spent most of our days listening to the radio, hearing the calls for help from Prague. Again we experienced this feeling of powerlessness, the feeling that there was nothing we could possibly do. . . .

There were very few signs of solidarity in East Germany. A small number of people wrote slogans on streets or on walls, but we could not find anything meaningful to do in terms of putting up some resistance [to the violent crackdown of the Prague Spring].

So this was my second experience with a system that cold-bloodedly killed certain important developments, a system that I thus came to perceive as simply inhumane. . . .

During the seventies, hope blossomed again because of the Warsaw Pact treaties with the Federal Republic, and when those did not end up changing much, we began to hope again during the so-called Helsinki process. . . .

In 1977–78, the debates surrounding the arms buildup began. Again, it became very clear to me that a danger was developing here that could be potentially disastrous. The saying at the time was that "the Germans can see each other from now on only through a fence of missiles." . . .

In light of all these developments, it increasingly dawned on me that one cannot always continue to sit still as a victim and say "it's terrible what's happening around us, but basically we are helpless."

Once I had fully realized that, I consciously moved away from this position of powerlessness and began to think about what one can do, at least as an individual. You see, this was, for me, very similar to the dynamics of the Third Reich. We had asked our parents about their position during that time, knowing, or at least being able to know, what had happened around them. But what had their role been? To what extent had they been responsible? In short, there was a growing desire in me to become active in order not to have to accuse myself of not having "done anything."

My wife and I thus joined a so-called "open group" [in 1978] that had been founded by a open-minded pastor in Halle. We quickly developed good contacts with the members of this group since they pretty much shared our objectives. Soon thereafter we began to organize a number of initiatives. . . .[11]

There were only a few older people like us. Most of them were young activists. . . . The group called itself "Open Work." We dealt with a variety of problems, concerning the school, the workplace, or the parents of some members. We were open toward all these problems and tried to deal with them in any way possible, always trying to point out the larger political relevance. . . .

In addition, we began to develop ideas as to how we could try to get involved with the whole debate surrounding the arms race. For example, we began to stage small demonstrations. To our utter surprise, we actually managed to conduct these demonstrations in the beginning. Obviously, nobody within the state apparatus had expected any such activities. I can remember when we organized the first one in Halle, on the occasion of a so-called official "peace meeting"—it must have been around '81—all the "blueshirts" [members of the party-controlled Free German Youth, an organization not dissimilar to the Girl Scouts or Boy Scouts in the United States, except that it had a more blatantly ideological, party-oriented emphasis] were ordered to go there, and we, a colorful and mixed bunch as we were, started off in order to participate as well. The official slogan back then was "Make Peace Against NATO Weapons" [Frieden Schaffen und gegen NATO-Waffen]. Sure, we were opposed to NATO missiles as well, but we were also against the Soviet missiles that were supposed to be deployed throughout the country.

In any case, we successfully "participated" and got all the way to the grandstand where all the district party bosses were standing. At first, they simply did not seem able to grasp at all what was happening down there.

11. Frank Eigenfeld is here describing the genesis of the grass-roots groups in Halle, which, as reproduced in other East German cities, became the energizing fulcrum of the opposition movement.

But immediately after they had realized what we were doing, they attempted to cover us up by surrounding us with blueshirts who carried flags, banners, and so on.

Those blueshirts, of course, also did not understand what was happening at all. When we began singing a few harmless songs (we numbered about 80) they began to yell "long live the party." Nobody else was yelling that, so everyone else began to look at what was going on, and we suddenly got a lot of attention. Anyway, we caused a great stir, and they could not prevent it anymore. But this was the only time we were that successful and did not have to deal with any forms of repression, summonses, and such. . . . They only took pictures of us that time. . . .

Since you were talking about these stages between resignation and hope, how would you characterize your relationship toward the existing state in East Germany, to socialism—however one may interpret that word—and what specifically did you mean when you said that you had hope that something might open up or change? Was it hope for . . .

Eigenfeld: . . . Well, hope for liberalization, for more freedom. Something free and democratic, but still egalitarian.

I had felt imprisoned ever since 1961. I never got rid of this feeling. For me, the people who were responsible for that fact were the state's leaders; it was the party, it was the society in which I lived. Therefore, I also always argued against the excuse invoked by many of being merely "normal fellow travelers," because we all had to realize what the actual situation in our country was like, and that most of us were not doing anything about it. I simply could not fathom that, particularly in light of what had happened in the Third Reich. I thus never, in any way, identified with this state, or with what it represented.

My only hope was to get out of this prison, to get out legally, through normal channels, as a result of a normal development, without having to leave it. My hope was that this could be achieved through the so-called "East Treaties" and with the Helsinki process.

And beyond this opening, did you have any ideas as to what should become of the GDR?

Eigenfeld: I cannot remember that I had any concrete ideas about that. My hopes did not encompass the idea that the existing state had to be toppled, if that's what you mean. . . . I would always have accepted the existing state if it had only lived up to its promise of granting basic human rights.

In fact, I believe to this very day that citizens all over the world care very little about who exercises political power, that is, as long as it is exercised in such a manner that everybody can move around freely. Whether it is a monarchy, Mr. Kohl, Mr. Ulbricht, or the New Forum, that, to me, is not significant. And I don't believe it is significant to most other people either.

Well, that is in fact a fascinating question which we should come back to when we talk about New Forum and what it did and could have done during the Fall of 1989. But let's first turn to you, Harald. Could you also provide us with some relevant biographical information?

Harald Wagner: Perhaps in contrast to Frank, I am a person with close ties to home. I was born in 1950 and grew up in a tiny village with a population of 70. I am still living there. I was raised with a deep appreciation for the environment and for some sort of inner freedom. My parents were completely apolitical. With the exception of one person, there was no one in my environment who could have been considered "political." Yet when it was time to go through Jugendweihe [the party substitute for church confirmation], I simply refused to go along. If someone asks you to do something you don't want to . . . well, from very early on I valued my right of self-determination, even against my parents' will . . .

. . . It sounds as if you were not socialized "properly." Were you some sort of genetic rebel?

Wagner: [laughing] . . . Well, maybe. Since I really wanted to finish school and get my Abitur [highest German school diploma, required for university entrance], I probably should have . . . well, but I didn't.

In the fifth grade I got to know someone who would turn out to be a very important person not only for me, but in fact for this country, a man who later became state representative of the Saxon state church for environmental questions. He was the son of my parish's pastor. He became a very significant person in my life.

In a small circle which he organized, we began to read things like the first report of the Club of Rome as early as 1970–71, and subsequently wrote a petition to the Council of Ministers. One could say that I was thus politicized early on concerning environmental questions.

The other experience that was very important to me was that I did a lot of sports—decathlon, to be specific. I continuously moved up, first participating in competitions in the biggest district town, then in the state's capital, and then on the national level, and I realized that I was just as good as all the others. That experience would later turn out to be extremely important in political terms as well. . . .

I learned from my sports experiences that there is nothing I *cannot* do just because someone tells me I can't. . . . I think the barrier which one has to overcome in order to realize something like that, however, is very high.

There are too many pseudo-needs. In any case, in 1970 I began to study math in Leipzig, and ever since that time we tried to do environmental information work within the church. . . . The church was the only place that was relatively safe from the encroachments of the security police.

Anyway, early on in our church group in Leipzig, we began to learn about Marxism because we thought that the party did not at all live up to its own ideology. We also thought that a critique that stayed within the dominant field of thought would be the most promising. Around 1975–76, we began to read Rosa Luxemburg, for example. . . . We read texts, debated them, and tried to figure out what our relationship was to all of this. We also tried to connect with other groups and tried to work together with them—in activities such as putting provocative graffiti on walls, or writing and distributing pamphlets. Even such minor activities were extremely dangerous at the time.

One interesting thing we did was to write up lists of all the books that were in our possession, and to exchange these lists among ourselves. This turned out to have disastrous consequences for me. I had given my list to one of my friends, a politically very active person who was specifically working on trying to establish contacts to people who would later form Solidarność in Poland. Shortly thereafter, they arrested him. . . .

Of course, they found my list of books when they searched his apartment. Ever since that day I was arrested on numerous occasions, questioned by the Stasi [the East German secret police], and constantly followed and observed by them. At one point, I drove to Berlin and I was followed by three Stasi cars. . . .

First they tried to catch me by surprise, searching my apartment, but they discovered that the books on the list were not even in my possession at the time. Of course, I did not tell them why I did not have them or where they could find them. Instead, I told them that I had merely compiled a list of books I might be interested in taking a look at when the International Book Fair came to Leipzig. Probably they did not believe a word, but they could not prove the opposite either.

The next thing that happened had to do with my job as a teacher at the Karl Marx University. They told me "we can see that you are very engaged and extremely talented, and it would be nice if you could advance in terms of your career, perhaps you want to become a professor," and so on. In short, they tried to buy me through possible job-advancement offers and such. I brusquely turned them down, however.

After that we continued our work, smuggling hundreds of copies of Rudolf Bahro's book [*The Alternative: A Critique of Real Existing Socialism*] into the GDR, copying his articles and putting them into people's mailboxes. The friends of mine who had organized these particular actions were later indicted and given jail sentences of between five and seven years. . . .

Since they did not seem to have enough on me, they just constantly summoned me. It was stunning to discover later on, after they arrested me, that they had detailed day-to-day knowledge of what I had done over the previous years. For example, they would ask me questions such as "what were you doing on 15 August 1977 in the early afternoon"? Since I did not know, of course, they would then proceed to tell me.

Incredible. What was the specific reason why they arrested you in 1980?

Wagner: Obviously they successfully tricked one of those imprisoned into some kind of statement implicating me with the possession of some of this literature. They worked with vicious tricks. . . .

They subsequently arrested me, and I spent seven months in jail just awaiting trial, and 11 months later I was sentenced for "collaboration in derogating the state" by possessing and disseminating subversive literature. Wolfgang Schnur was my lawyer. [Ed. note: Schnur defended most political dissidents during the eighties. Later, he was active in the opposition movement himself and became the first chairman of Democratic Awakening in October of 1989. In the spring of 1990, however, it was revealed that he had been a secret police informant whose task it had been to infiltrate the opposition.]

A question I would like to ask both of you. Did you know about comparable activities by other people, and if so, did you try to establish contacts with them?

Eigenfeld: Not in the beginning. At first, our activities completely centered on our own group. The first contact we had with the outside was to [the Protestant pastor] Rainer Eppelmann [see pp. 55–67]. In 1980, we went to see him in Berlin simply in order to find out what was happening there and to establish first contacts.

Why Eppelmann and not someone else?

Eigenfeld: Even then, Eppelmann was already a kind of leading figure for us. He was generally well known. We knew about his contacts with Robert Havemann [a former cellmate of later General Secretary Erich Honecker in a Nazi prison camp, who became a leading communist dissident after the 1960s], for example. . . .

But we did not know anything about other, similar groups. Perhaps this was partly due to our initial assumption that we might, in fact, be the only ones engaging in oppositional activities. We simply did not know that other groups existed as well. That did not change, in fact, until we established contact with Eppelmann in 1982. Even afterward, a long period of time ensued in which nothing happened. . . .

Wagner: I always had good contacts with other groups—artists, human rights activists, and so on—and that turned out to be, I think, very important later on. We even worked together with Marxist groups. . . . We had a lot of conspiratorial meetings with scholars from the university, debating Marxist theories of revolution, or the works of Rudi Dutschke [spokesperson of the late '60s student movement in West Germany, author of the widely read tract, "The Attempt to Turn Lenin Upside Down"], or of Rudolf Bahro [former party member until deported for publishing his book *The Alternative*].

In other words, you also had good contacts with party people, like those in the university?

Wagner: Oh, yes. If I may jump ahead a little, just to give you an example. Of the seven people who wrote the new party program for the PDS [Party for Democratic Socialism, the successor party of the Socialist Unity Party, the East German communist party] in November of 1989, I know four people personally, and one is a close personal friend. It all goes back to the early eighties, when they all began to talk to one another more or less clandestinely . . .

. . . So you also trusted people in the party?

Wagner: . . . Sure, I trusted these people; in fact, I still do. . . . You see, on the one hand, I would be in favor of the total disintegration of the party. On the other hand, I also believe that people who want to do that kind of politics should be able to do it; after all, it's completely legitimate. . . . There are some good people among them, I have really no doubt about that.

Of course, out of the seven I know, four have subsequently left the party for Democratic Socialism, because they also came to realize that it doesn't work, that the party *is*, in fact, the corruption. My close friend ended up with Democracy Now in Leipzig. . . .

But, politically speaking, you had no problems with people who remained in the party, or had most of them left at some point?

Wagner: Either they left, or they were people like Michael Brie [brother of André Brie, see pp. 171–81], people for whom I had great respect because they tried to do everything that was possible within the limits imposed by the party. They spoke up to the extent they could. They had problems with the secret police themselves. Therefore, they also represented the people with whom we started the local round tables, such as in Leipzig. The people around the brothers Brie also played a key role in convincing the local party leadership in Leipzig to rescind their order to suppress the demonstrations on 9 October "with all means necessary." They were the ones who wrote a petition to the Politburo on 6 October that tried to explain the situation in the country, and they did so after they had first consulted us.

To what extent is what Harald described different from your situation, Frank?

Eigenfeld: I have to say that *our* goal was not primarily to engage the system in a theoretical debate, but rather to confront it with realities.

Our early experiences had been that the party pretty much determined people's lives, that nobody had the opportunity to participate freely in this society, that "they" always decided everything. Above all else, we wanted to defend ourselves against such repressive domination.

The theoretical debate as to why conditions were the way they were picked up much later. In fact, it always happened after we had tried something practical and failed, after we had realized that we had little or no chance of achieving much with what we were doing, after we had realized that we were dealing with a structural problem within the system, and not just a few flaws here or there. . .

Wagner: . . . Your goals were probably very similar [to ours], we just approached the problems from two different directions. But we *also* massively fought against the system, against what was being done in this country. . . .

Eigenfeld: Later on, we organized various demonstrations that, each and every time, resulted in our short-term arrest, such as an environmental demonstration in which we wanted to bike to Buna [an extremely polluted industrial center near Halle], with banners, signs, petitions, and so on.

At about the same time, four of us had also founded a little group that wanted to draft a particular petition about the current situation in the GDR. This was, by the way, the first time that we tried to approach the problems in theoretical terms, even though it was still very much based on our own specific experiences. The attempt failed, however, because we got arrested. Two of the group were subsequently indicted. . . . Another guy and I were detained only temporarily, and no legal proceedings were initiated against us.

How did they know about your group and your plans?

Eigenfeld: Apparently all of our meetings had been bugged. They had very detailed knowledge about our plans, details that only the four of us could have possibly known about. And I am certain that none of the four of us were informants. . . . [The group was defended by Schnur, who was an informant.]

The next big event was the arrest of my wife on 31 August 1983. We had planned a peace demonstration for the "peace day" on September 1st. We wanted to march from one church across the city to another church. Again, because many activists were arrested, the event never took place. They wanted to send a message to all circles of opposition activists that they could stop us anytime they wanted to by simply arresting the initiators of such demonstrations.

To some extent, of course, they were successful in these attempts. Again Schnur came, and his main line of argument was "no publicity." He said he could only do something for us without any publicity. Publicity would only hurt us.

Fourteen days later Sebastian Pflugbeil [grass-roots activists from Berlin, see p. 160] was arrested on the street in Berlin. Richard von Weizsäcker was mayor of West Berlin at the time [later elected president of West Germany and, since October of 1990, president of the new united Germany]. He had a meeting with Honecker and asked for Pflugbeil's release, which in turn was immediately granted.

What was important about this event was that it became clear to us that the strategy of quietly waiting in the dark and letting other people handle the affair was wrong. What we needed was publicity.

How did you hear about this whole affair?

Eigenfeld: Well, that's precisely the point. We heard through the Western media. So then I drove to Berlin and told people our entire story, about my wife's arrest, and so on. Very few people had heard anything about that. . . . Our group knew about the women involved in the Berliner group "Women for Peace" [Bärbel Bohley, Ulrike Poppe, et al., see pp. 131–39 and 292–303], and I knew their addresses. In Halle we also had a group, Women for Peace, which my wife had helped to organize. Yet we had no previous contact with the Berliners. You see, everyone had vague notions about other groups, but until then we had not attempted to establish any contacts.

So in this emergency situation, after we had realized that only publicity could help, I drove to Berlin and asked for help . . .

If I understand you correctly, Harald, you had a slightly different relationship to the state, the party, and to the question of what could be done. You said you had good contacts with "reasonable" people within the party. Did that mean that you also had hopes that something could be done through the party as well?

Wagner: This very question was always an issue of dispute in our groups. Personally, I never thought anything positive could be achieved through the party. But those who were members of the party carried around this idea about "the march through the institutions," an idea that had been developed by West German left-wing intellectuals during the late sixties and early seventies.

Our friends in the party had taken Bahro's idea seriously that the party could, in fact, be reformed. Their argument against our strategy was "you will not achieve anything anyway, you are too much on the margins, you are too far below, things will only change through the Politburo. If, one day, we manage to gain access to the Politburo, then fundamental change can finally take place." Our reply usually was to point out that this was exactly the path that would not work, that would not result in anything.

In short, we worked together with them because we shared many of the same ideas, but we did not agree with their strategic vision as to how to achieve anything. . . .

Let me ask you how much you knew at the time about two other issues that seem to have been important.

First, the peace movement that called itself "Swords to Ploughshares" [after a monument that was donated by the Soviet Union to the UN and erected in Geneva in 1963]. What exactly did you know about this group of people, and did you have any contact with them?

And related to that, could you tell me something about the whole affair surrounding Roland Jahn of Jena, who was arrested for nothing more than riding his bicycle with a Polish flag across the marketplace in Jena on the second anniversary of the formal recognition of Solidarność in Poland?

Eigenfeld: It had been my impression early on that there was a very active circle of people in Jena. It seemed to me that they focused primarily on the question of emigration . . .

Wagner: . . . That's not true. At least the inner circle did not. Only those who increasingly began to hang on to such grass-roots groups were mainly would-be émigrés [people who had applied for exit visas in order to move to the West]. The core people like Jahn, however, did very similar work to what you and others did in Halle. They did not work so much on a theoretical level as they tried to organize an opposition against people in high places, who completely determined their lives. It is true, though, that the Jenaer circles were quickly taken over and instrumentalized by would-be émigrés . . .

Eigenfeld: . . . This is precisely what our impression was . . .

Wagner: . . . I knew Jahn pretty well. I don't think one can accuse him or his group of focusing on emigration issues.

Basically, we are talking about very small groups, political grass-roots groups, six to seven people who tried to organize something until, all of a sudden, a large number of new people tried to attach themselves to the already existing groups. What happened after that was usually beyond the control of the initial groups. . . .

When exactly did this would-be emigration movement pick up—in '83 or so?

Eigenfeld: Well, in single cases as early as the late seventies, but those people did not then get any publicity. In Halle it did not develop into a larger movement until 1983, when they began to bombard West German politicians with letters asking for support in their emigration efforts. But at that time, they did not yet try to flood our groups that much—that did not begin to happen until about 1985.

In 1984–85 was the time when big waves of emigration occurred, a time in which it was apparently not yet necessary to engage in political activities in order to get out quickly. Emigration applications were dealt with much more speedily by the authorities back then. In '86, the overall number of people who were let out suddenly dropped sharply. I think in '84 about 44,000 were let out, in '85 again about 35,000, and in '86 the number had all of a sudden dropped to about 15,000, and that despite the fact that the numbers of people who wanted to get out had drastically increased.[12]

That's why people began to think about what they could do to speed up their emigration process, and, as a result, began to invade our groups for that purpose. . . .

What about the "Swords to Ploughshares" movement? When and how did that get started?

Eigenfeld: It started in 1980, as an idea that emanated from the Brandenburg Youth Convention. They had called upon people to organize a Friedensdekade ["Peace Decade"] in the context of the entire arms race debate going on at the time. They were also the ones who first used both the slogan and the symbol "Swords to Ploughshares" in this context . . .

. . . Which is a statue that the Soviet Union donated to the UN, if I am not mistaken . . .

Eigenfeld: . . . Yes, in 1963. It is a symbol that has been around for a very long time, but now it was suddenly made into the symbol for the unofficial GDR peace movement. These Friedensdekaden were always very active and very exciting events. Peace activists came together for some 10 days before the day of prayer and repentance. Such events were organized wherever peace initiatives existed within the church, that is, at least in all the big cities. . . .

12. The actual numbers of GDR emigrants and refugees to the West were 1983: 11,343; 1984: 40,974; 1985: 24,912; 1986: 26,178; 1987: 18,958. See *Fischer Welt Almanach, Sonderband DDR* (1990), 135.

Halle was one of the first to organize relatively big events around these Friedensdekaden with demonstrations of up to 1,000 people, marching from one church to another, always terribly harassed by the Stasi and the People's Police [as the regular police forces were called].

It was quite some job to keep people calm, yet we continued to be successful in keeping everything peaceful, despite the fact that it sometimes got quite dangerous. The police forces did everything they could to provoke the outbreak of violence. . . . For example, they drove their police trucks right into the crowd of demonstrators, sometimes at up to 60 miles per hour.

Wagner: You see, I know of no other city except Halle in which such a movement existed that early. Nothing comparable occurred in Leipzig at the time. The really terrible thing about all of this is that nobody knew that these things were going on in other places. Just knowing about it would have made a big difference. Then you wouldn't have felt so alone. It would have encouraged us a great deal.

Only a small number of people knew about anything going on outside of their own hometown, mostly about things that happened in Berlin. Rainer Eppelmann, Ulrike and Gerd Poppe, and Bärbel Bohley were all rather well-known, mostly through their oppositional activities. But no one knew about what was going on in Halle, for example. There was just not much of a chance that one would hear about that, even though we lived in Leipzig, which is quite close to Halle.

Eigenfeld: Well, that was partly our mistake as well. It was our position at the time that we were doing this for ourselves, and not for anyone else. In fact, we never tried to gain any publicity. At that point the Western media constantly reported about Jena, even though probably more was happening in Halle. . . .

Wagner: You see, this "publicity business" was really a very new thing for us. Friends in the West had told me that "what doesn't appear in our media might as well simply not have occurred at all." That was a new aspect for us. Events apparently had to be publicized, at least by some newspaper. Because otherwise, whatever you do, while it may anger some and please others, on the whole it has no effect, it just hasn't happened.

So no one outside knew anything about events in Leipzig, despite the fact that we did at least as much as the Berliners. In Berlin the route to the Western media was just much shorter and simpler. And the situation in Halle, of course, was even worse than in Leipzig. At least we had the International Trade Fair, so twice a year at least we could try to give the world an insight into the internal affairs of the GDR.

Eigenfeld: You know, it's very curious. For a long time we shied away from making anything public because we thought that this was not the way to go about doing things. When we decided to write this public petition about the current conditions in the country in September 1982, for example, we came together over a weekend and wrote this document. But what did we do with it? We sent it to the local party secretary, that is, we approached party and state officials, quite consciously, and told them what we planned to do. We also sent one copy to the church leadership. In other words, we very consciously did not channel these kinds of statements into the Western media, because we figured that this was something we were doing as East German citizens—it was an internal affair of the GDR that had nothing to do with the West . . .

. . . In other words, you still had hopes that the existing system could be reformed?

Eigenfeld: . . . Yes, precisely. We still nurtured the naive hope that some day we would receive a positive response through official avenues.

Wagner: The other side of the coin is that the people who now act as if they had always been against the party and everything it stood for—back then, when you cited some source concerning the terrors of Stalinism, for example, they always replied "but how do you know this? You could have only read this in a West book," and that was something largely discredited as a reliable source of information. So it really was a very desperate situation.

In that sense, Gorbachev was also very important for us in the GDR. For the first time he made it possible for us to cite "official primary sources" for crimes committed by communist regimes.

But it was still very difficult, because we certainly did not want to end up unwittingly applauding the wrong side . . . I mean, the West.

Eigenfeld: I agree, those were precisely the arguments . . .

Wagner: . . . It is in this sense that our actions, but also our options, were extremely limited. I think you have to understand that it was absolutely necessary first to try everything conceivable without making use of the Western media. People around us would simply not have understood and would not have supported it if we had gone public with the help of the Western media. . . .

Right up to 6 October [1989], Protestant pastors in Leipzig were blamed for talking to the Western media with the argument, "Why do you need to do this? Don't we have our own media? Don't you have any patience?," etc.

In other words, it took us a long time to understand the dynamics behind this question. In '82–'83 we were still completely caught within this trap. . . .

Eigenfeld: . . . The main point is that we initially wanted to reform our own country by ourselves, that is, without any help from outside . . .

Wagner: . . . And fear continued to exist as to what any contact with the West might do to our movement—with plenty of justification, I might add.

I had a lot to do with Western media people over the last couple of years, I gave a lot of interviews, and what not. But often when I read afterward what they had done with what I had said, or with the information I had given them, I frequently thought, "This is absolutely unbelievable; they must have talked to someone else!"

I know many GDR oppositionists who were very angry and frustrated because of their terrible experiences with the Western media, because of reports that were completely distorted and that, in many cases, seriously hurt our cause. . . .

Eigenfeld: . . . Furthermore, the commentary of the Western media often did not at all reflect our intentions, did not represent what it was we wanted to achieve . . .

Wagner: . . . It took us a very long time to realize that the media in the West has to worry mainly about selling a product, and not about substance. Consequently, they have to work under a lot of pressure and strict confinements. . . .

Also, we did not know these newspapers, simply because we had never read them. If someone came to see us from the [West German] *FAZ* or the *Süddeutsche Zeitung* [comparable to the *Wall Street Journal* and the *Boston Globe*, respectively], I did not know what to expect. . . .

But there were groups who directed their political activities very much toward the Western media. The group Initiative for Peace and Human Rights, for example, founded in 1985, focused most of their political attention right from the beginning toward an efficient use of the Western media [primarily Western radio programs, which could be received throughout the GDR]. And it seems to me they did not do that with the strategy of using the means of the enemy, but rather in order to reach fellow East Germans through the only channels available.

Eigenfeld: My first political experience with the possible role and significance of the Western media had to do with the arrest and release of my wife, Kathrin. She got out on 1 November 1983, as a result of the intervention of the West German Greens who had petitioned Honecker to release her. One day after they had petitioned she was out.

So this public petitioning had proved effective twice, once with Sebastian Pflugbeil, and once with Kathrin. When we went to Berlin we had already decided that we should try use the Western media as a source of security, because if we continued to work in isolation and engage in actions without letting the Western media know about it, no one would find out about them. Without them, we were perfectly walled in. . . .

Even though we had previously organized our marches and events right in the middle of the city, hardly anyone ever found out about it. That's really the curious thing about it, the Stasi pretty much functioned in the public sphere, but the public was somehow not aware of it. I guess most people simply repressed it. But if the information came in via the West, then all of a sudden it did exist, and people began to talk about it.

So after we had fully realized this dynamic—after all, what we did was very dangerous, you had to expect arrest without release any day—we said to ourselves that we need the kind of security that the Western media can provide for us.

We subsequently began to make use of them with great purposefulness, informing them of whatever we deemed helpful. So ever since 1983 this strategy represented an important component of our political work. . . .

We drove up to Berlin at least twice a month in order to inform them about what happened in Halle. That way we also gained our first experiences about what was going on in Berlin, and how to deal with media people.

Thus, when we wrote our public petition in '86 to the party congress, we also sent it to the West. I have to say, however, even then we gave the party a little time to respond first. So we first sent the petition to the Central Committee, to the Politburo, and to *Neues Deutschland* [main official party newspaper] about four weeks before the party congress was due to convene. In other words, we gave them 4 weeks to respond, which they did not. After those four weeks had passed, we no longer saw any reason to withhold it, and so we publicized the petition in the West. . . .

But let me return to 1983 for a moment. We already had some good political contacts with Westerners, like the Green Party.

As I said before, after the Greens went to see Honecker,[13] (it was a Monday) my wife was released the very next day. I immediately drove up to Berlin, and we all met each other in Bärbel Bohley's house. For the following Friday we had all planned the first German/German peace initiative [with peace activists from both East and West Germany]. We wanted to hand over a petition to both the Soviet and the American embassies, demanding that they both abandon their plans of deploying

13. Members of the Green Party presidium: Petra Kelly, Gert Bastian, and Antje Vollmer.

further nuclear missiles in their respective halves of Germany. We had even informed Honecker about it.

On Wednesday, there was a press conference in Bonn with a close advisor of Honecker and member of the Politburo. From Wednesday on we were also subjected to heavy surveillance by the Stasi, even though this Honecker crony said in Bonn that same day that the East German government perceived our plan as "helpful activity," something they wanted to support—which he said in front of the international press. But on Wednesday afternoon we discovered carloads of Stasi people following us around. The planned action never took place. Instead, we were all arrested. Even church superintendent Forck was put under house arrest; in fact the Stasi blocked off roads that led to our and Forck's houses. The Berliners were picked up at home, and so were we in Halle.

In other words, it was quite obvious that this action had been initiated single-handedly by the Stasi, without prior arrangement or consultation with Honecker—it just couldn't have been any other way. Otherwise, Honecker's crony couldn't have said in front of the international press that this was a "good thing," while, at the same time, having us all arrested . . .

. . . *You don't think that it could have been an intentionally deceptive move on Honecker's part?*

Eigenfeld: No, I simply refuse to believe to this very day that Honecker was capable of intentionally double-crossing us like this. . . .

After that failed action, we wanted to organize a human rights seminar in Berlin, within the space of the church, because that was the only place where one did not have to apply for official permission, which would have been impossible to get. . . .

One parish had agreed to house the human rights seminar, but then we received a negative reply from the church leadership, because what we wanted to do somehow went beyond the state-imposed restrictions as to what was permissible within the church. In the aftermath, not only the Stasi, but also officers of the criminal division of the police came to see us, and we were subsequently prohibited from making any further trips to Berlin.

That was precisely the point in time when many of us realized that, despite the relative freedom within the church, we had to find some space independent of the constraints of the church. After that, we founded the "Initiative for Peace and Human Rights" [IFM], which was the first, and for many years the only group, that functioned outside the realm of the church.

Wagner: We should first mention, however, that there was a real downward turn between about 1983 and 1985. During this period, very little happened in terms of political activity. It was not until '85 that things began to pick up again due to the founding of various human rights groups.

. . . You mean human rights groups also existed, aside from the IFM, inside the church?

Wagner: Oh yes, quite a few already existed within the church . . .

Eigenfeld: . . . These groups had already established themselves at the time of the first "Frieden Konkret," where they displayed their various activities with info tables. In the course of the peace movement against the arms race in general and the further deployment of nuclear missiles in both East and West, we realized that we were not at all accepted by the powers that be, and that we had little opportunity to articulate ourselves in public. That was essentially the reason for fighting for opportunities and space to make our voices heard publicly. We had simply realized that this was a "must," that without it we couldn't do anything. We had to demand this right of free speech.

So that's when the focus changed from the arms race toward human rights. In the beginning, human rights were not at the forefront of our attention. In other words, only after we had begun to run into enormous organizing difficulties did our focus begin to change.

Listening to both of you, I get the impression that you knew quite a bit about each other and about what was going on in other places in the GDR after all. More and more groups were founded everywhere, so that you had almost 200 different groups by early 1989. I don't know whether the exact number was ever established. How do you explain such variety, such a large number of different groups?

Eigenfeld: The variety of groups, in fact, became more and more color-ful. Two hundred different groups is probably a conservative estimate. All sorts of topics were covered. In addition to various peace, human rights, and environmental groups, gay and lesbian groups were founded, groups for alcoholics, groups for students, and so on. . . .

So these problems and issues were ultimately "picked up" by what you might call "self-help" groups, which finally dealt with all those topics that the "official" society refused to deal with, with the things that were considered "taboo." . . .

And then there were groups like the "Church from Below" which consisted of people who wanted to pressure the church to support grass-roots groups, and, at the same time, provide space for people outside of the church as well. In that endeavor they constantly ran into problems with the church hierarchy.

You see, we had very basic problems, such as finding rooms for people to meet. We had always depended on specific parishes to support such efforts and provide rooms for grass-roots groups. In most cases, it was far from easy to obtain such support from the parishes. In Halle, for example, only three out of fourteen parishes ever 'provided space for us. Even though it is always claimed that the church played such a crucial role in the formation of the East German opposition, most churches wanted to have nothing to do with us.

■ RAINER EPPELMANN, prominent oppositionist, founder of Democratic Awakening, subsequently minister for disarmament and defense.
▌ *"The topics that came up had to do with hopelessness, feeling incarcerated, fear, fear of the police, fear of the Stasi, fear of superiors . . . . He played a few blues songs, then we read a few texts . . . and 200 people showed up, for heaven's sake."*

Minister for disarmament and defense, pacifist, and Protestant pastor, Rainer Eppelmann, early on chose to be one of those church dignitaries who "wanted to have something to do" with dissident sectors in the GDR. Yet Eppelmann represents a very different kind of East German oppositionist from either Frank Eigenfeld or Harald Wagner, for he operated from the relatively safe realm of the church, not being subjected himself for the most part to the vicissitudes and dangers to which most other activists were invariably exposed.

Eppelmann not only started numerous political initiatives, but he was a much sought after contact person for political activists from across the country. A veteran "rebel," he became during the eighties one of the most prominent dissidents within and outside the German Democratic Republic.

Unlike most of his former friends and colleagues in the dissident movement, however, Eppelmann did not seem to have any problems accustoming himself to conventional forms of politics. In common with many Westerners, he deeply resisted communist party authoritarianism without questioning inherently hierarchical modes of political decision-making characteristic of both communist and capitalist systems. In fact, he never concealed his desires to play a significant political role as a "leader" himself.

On my 50-minute subway trip from West Berlin to Alexanderplatz in downtown East Berlin to interview Eppelmann, I reviewed for a final time the notes I had collected on him, and I stumbled upon a telling statement which I found particularly revealing in the political context existing at that moment. At the time when the East German civic opposition movement (the same one that had provided him with national prominence and political fortune) was once again forced into a position of political marginality, Eppelmann told reporters of the largest West German political newsweekly magazine, *Der Spiegel,* from behind his new desk at the ministry: "Yes, the civic movements will always be necessary for the lime tree at the corner and for the clean table in the village. But concerning the big political decisions, they are no more than folklore."[14] This was a startling remark for a former opposition "leader." It certainly shed some light on what forms of politics Eppelmann could imagine for the future.

Rainer Eppelmann was born in 1943 in what later became the Soviet-occupied part of Berlin (East Berlin). He went to school in West Berlin until the Wall was erected by the communist-led East German government in August of 1961. In 1969 he began to study theology at a seminary in East Berlin "because the church was the only place in which one could breathe in this country." Since 1974 he has been a Protestant pastor of the East Berliner Samariter Parish and district youth pastor of the city borough of Friedrichshain.

Together with his associate Robert Havemann, Eppelmann wrote a petition to the government in 1982 calling for "peace without arms," a document that soon thereafter not only caught the attention of the security police, but also of the international media. By this circuitous process, East German censorship was breached, and Eppelmann became known to the many East German citizens who regularly listened to West German news programs.

In the mid- to late eighties, he developed into one of the most vocal and best-known oppositionists in the German Democratic Republic. In September 1989 he played an instrumental role in the founding of the first opposition party, Democratic Awakening, which he cochaired after its inception and subsequently represented at the Central Round Table.

In the transitional "Government of National Responsibility" under Prime Minister Modrow, Eppelmann was chosen as minister without portfolio on 6 February 1990, following Modrow's offer to the opposition to participate in his government.

After the first free elections in the GDR on 18 March 1990, Eppelmann became minister for disarmament and defense in the government of the Christian Democrat Lothar de Maizière, a post he occupied until the day of formal political unification between the two Germanies,

14. Rainer Eppelmann, quoted in *Der Spiegel,* no. 14, 1990.

3 October 1990. Shortly thereafter, his political fortunes seemed to fade. After the annexation of Democratic Awakening by the Christian Democrats and many internal debates surrounding Eppelmann's conduct as minister of disarmament and defense, he did not even succeed initially in obtaining a nomination for his own party's ticket for the upcoming national elections. It was in the midst of these tumultuous events that I interviewed Eppelmann in July 1990, a time during which he still served as minister for disarmament and defense.

The environment in which this interview was conducted struck me as quite eerie, to say the least. Eppelmann's office was located in the former Berlin Soviet military headquarters near Alexanderplatz. The building was heavily guarded by young men of the National People's Army, of which the Protestant pastor and pacifist Rainer Eppelmann was now in charge. More than half of his staff consisted of officers from the same army, adding a chilling formality and strictness to the already existing coldness of this Prussian military edifice. The pictures of Gorbachev and Honecker had been taken down, leaving nothing but the square light spots on the walls which could be found in offices throughout the country at the time. In place of these portraits, many of Eppelmann's staff had put on their desks a little black-and-white picture of their new boss.

Eppelmann turned out to be a small man with a beard and uncombed hair. Soft-spoken in his thick Berliner dialect, he was quite cooperative while, at the same time, exhibiting a profound sense of prerogative. He was, in short, very much a minister of the state. Indeed, after the interview he felt the need to tell me, "I want you to know that this was by far the longest interview I have given since things began to fall apart in the GDR—you should feel honored." I did.

The following interview with Eppelmann, I believe, allows an instructive view into the possibilities and constraints of life in the GDR. Eppelmann's entire biography can be seen as a persistent struggle to carve out a bit of space "in which one could breathe freely." Above all, what becomes evident are the various twists and turns to which Eppelmann had habituated himself in his effort to play a meaningful role in East German life, a series of stances that could perhaps best be described as energetic and courageous, while, at the same time, proceeding from premises which were neither very specific nor very well-directed. From wanting to be a fighter pilot to becoming a pacifist, from being a close friend of the dedicated communist Robert Havemann to being a close associate of outspoken conservatives, from being a "lone fighter" to joining the governing Christian Democratic Party, Eppelmann's personal trajectory is full of telling contradictions that often serve as an accurate reflection of developments in the larger society.

■ *What were your first experiences leading you to question aspects of the East German political system?*

I would have to start with 13 August 1961 [the day the Wall was erected], and I would have to take it from there, 30 years of my life, not always as dramatic and condensed as during the last few months, but perhaps somewhat indicative of this period of postwar German history. In fact, one important foundation for my later development dates back to the one and a half years prior to August of 1961.

I was one of the few thousand students in East Berlin who went to the Gymnasium (secondary school) in West Berlin. The postwar school laws at the time applied to all of Berlin, which made it possible for people from the eastern part of the city [controlled by the Soviets] to go to school in the western part [which was controlled by the three Western Allies, the United States, Great Britain, and France]. Until the eighth grade, however, very few people took advantage of this opportunity because there was not that much difference between the two systems in terms of elementary and lower school education.

During those days, one began with upper school in the ninth grade, and many people, despite the fact that they had the qualifications, were not allowed to go to the upper school in the East due to a lack of so-called "political participation" [in one of the numerous party organizations]. I was one of those. Consequently, I went to the upper school in West Berlin (Neukoelln), that is, until August of 1961. After that, of course, I could not go there any longer. This was a decisive point in my life, since I had planned on getting an Abitur[15]—which was the wish of my parents—and then I probably would have gone on to the university. I was in the eleventh grade, and I either wanted to study architecture (my father was a carpenter, and therefore I was interested in the construction business) or—irony of history—become an officer in the West German army.

So you were not a pacifist at the time?

No, at that time I had dreams of becoming a pilot of fighter planes. I have a clear memory of getting information brochures about this, trying to figure out what else one would need besides the Abitur and good health in order to get in. I sometimes smilingly think about the kinds of changes, the

15. The examination taken by graduates of the most qualifying secondary school in Germany (Gymnasium) after the thirteenth grade, roughly equivalent to the British A-level exam and the French baccalaureate.

kinds of traps and turns that are part of a biography like mine.

So that was 1961. I subsequently was employed as an unskilled worker—it was a sort of revenge by the East German government to punish all those who had profited from crossing the border (Grenzgewinnler), which referred to those thousands who had gone to work in the West, and also included students who had gone to school in the West [prior to August 1961]. All those people now had to prove themselves worthy somehow. That was particularly hard on students because typically it was the parents who had decided to send their kids to the West. I had to work as a roofer's mate for a year, which was a very hard year for me. . . .

There was no chance to continue your schoolwork?

No, that was absolutely impossible. I could not even get an apprenticeship. What I did as a roofer's mate was to carry these big baskets filled with tiles on my back, climbing ladders all day long with this heavy load. In the beginning that was terribly hard for me. After this first year they offered me the opportunity of applying for an apprenticeship—of course, not the opportunity to enter the university or even to finish my degree at the upper school. I have to add that my father was in a West Berlin hospital until 13 August 1961. He had worked in the West. Therefore, it was simply impossible for us kids to even think about a university career, and that despite the fact that "collective guilt" did not exist as an official concept in East German law. My sister was caught in the same situation. . . .

There was no way for us to return to school. My mother usually handled the family's necessary dealings with the party bureaucrats. Probably they told her that there were no more spots available and that they had to reserve the available ones for those people who faithfully supported the "workers' and peasants' state." Of course, they couldn't respond with their "working-class child" line of argument[16] since my sister and I were, in fact, working-class children.

The next important thing happened in 1964 when the Department for National Defense passed a decree concerning the conscription of construction units [brigades of conscientious objectors, so-called "shovel soldiers"] within the Department of National Defense. This decree was a result of the negotiations between the Thuringian state bishop, Moritz Mitzenheim, and the then head of government, Walter Ulbricht. The background for these talks was the period between 1961 and 1964—

16. Eppelmann here refers to the preferential treatment of working-class children in the GDR, and the fact that non-working-class children were often prevented from entering institutions of higher learning.

before that time they had not dared to introduce the draft in the GDR due to the fear that most people simply would have run away. Thus, the introduction of the draft did not occur before the building of the Wall,[17] and fortunately there were numerous young men who said: "I will never pick up a gun." That was something absolutely exotic at the time; people went to prison for that. The Protestant church began to support these people, I suppose because most of them were religiously motivated. So in 1964 they passed this decree, and ever since then—for more than 20 years only in the GDR among the Warsaw Pact countries—the GDR citizens were allowed to refuse armed military service. Conscientious objectors were still soldiers; they had to wear uniforms, and they lived in camps, but they did not have to take part in armed exercises.

It is my understanding, however, that this opportunity was not generally known about . . .

. . . Well, of course it was not advertised. When a young man was called to the military district command they did not tell him that he could decide for or against armed duty within the military. Of course, they only told him about the various possibilities within the national defense forces. So the Protestant church had to make a major effort to inform people about these possibilities. They also had to hope for a change of consciousness among the population, because very few people initially chose to refuse armed service.

I was in the second year of those who joined the construction brigades. . . . I was drafted in 1966. The construction soldiers had to serve exactly as long as common soldiers, and in that way it was not like conscientious objection in West Germany [where conscientious objectors serve substantially longer than common soldiers]. Either orally or by written statement—in my case it was written—you had to give a justification as to why you refused armed duty.

So one difference was that you did not have to touch a weapon; the other was that our oath to the flag did not include the passage "with a weapon in my hand." The vow everybody had to take, however, was the same. So then came the day when I was drafted. As it turned out, however, I was only part of my division for 14 days, because after that we had to take our vow, which I refused to do.

Oh, and something else I wanted to tell you: altogether there were about 120 construction soldiers across the GDR that year—in fact, a relatively small number. The construction soldiers represented pretty rare

17. Conscription was introduced in the GDR on 24 January 1962.

birds in the GDR. There were quite a few officers who made it very clear that they thought we were absolutely insane.

In any case: I was one of two in my company who refused to take this vow. The result was that I was jailed for eight months, and after my release I was allowed to begin my 18 months' duties, so that I came back home after 26 months. At that time I began with my construction apprenticeship, something that would perhaps allow me to go on to study construction engineering later on. I finished the apprenticeship, and subsequently managed to get into construction engineering at a college. I did not last long, because I quickly realized that I could not survive in that environment. I was constantly irritated at this place. You have to imagine that I had experienced a free school in West Berlin. . . .

A woman who previously had had a great impact on me was a history teacher, an old social democratic comrade at my former high school in West Berlin. There I had learned intellectual disputation, how to argue, how to defend yourself, how to be open toward different ideas, to question yourself. And now in this new school everything went according to party line, and nothing else. That just destroyed me. I had simply not expected such a thing at this particular school. After all, I did not want to become a polit-propagandist, but rather a construction engineer. So after three months I left the program again, and the director of the program unequivocally told me that "if you ever change your mind about this, don't even think about applying to this program again." So I went back to working in construction, this time as a bricklayer. . . .

Tell me what your response was to the Prague Spring in particular and to the political developments—as you perceived them—in Czechoslovakia in general.

I can remember this very well. I was one of the few GDR citizens who, after they had learned about events in the CSSR, went to the Czechoslovakian Embassy and put their signature into a book of solidarity declarations, and I did so with a clearly legible name and full address. I went there with my sister and a good friend of mine. It was very important to us during those days to show our solidarity with the Czechoslovakian people. As I said earlier, I was working as a bricklayer at the time, so for me this signature did not create any problems. My sister, on the other hand, worked as a teacher, and they fired her ruthlessly after this. . . .

I worked as a bricklayer for one year, but even at the time when I returned from the army I knew that I could not spend the rest of my life doing this kind of work. And then I began to ask myself, considering the closed border, what can I do here with my basic attitudes, with my expectations, with my notions about my own life? The only thing I could think of in this closed society was to become a Protestant pastor. This involved immense risks for me, however. . . . I could easily have failed completely.

If I may interrupt at this point. If I understand you correctly, you are saying you chose to become a pastor not so much out of conviction, but rather because this was the only way, in your opinion, to fulfill some of the expectations you had toward your own life?

That's exactly right. I do have to say, however, that I was confirmed and that I had gone to the youth services. But if you had asked me two years earlier what I wanted to become, I most certainly would not have thought of becoming a pastor. So it really involved an immense risk. I can only say that I had tremendous luck—perhaps it was even a wise decision. I studied at the theological seminary here in Berlin for six years. . . .

A prerequisite for this seminary was that you had the Mittlere Reife [roughly equivalent to a high school diploma], a finished apprenticeship, and that you had actually worked for some time. So you could not just get out of school, pass through an apprenticeship, and then begin to study theology. You had to prove that you had work experience and that you had not been kicked out of your job, that is, you had to have letters of recommendation. . . . It was important to them that people had made their way in life already, that you were a person whom they could confidently send into the parishes. So for the people who started at the theological seminary in Berlin it was basically clear right from the start that they would do parish work. In other words, we did not have the same options as a university student, that is, either to take the scholarly route or do parish work.

Was your decision to become a pastor more a political choice because you thought the church could provide space for political work, or was it more a personal one in favor of a somewhat freer life?

Well, at the time I was 26. I said to myself: if I am going to start all over again, having to live with very little money—which was not very easy to do, after having earned 800 to 900 Marks[18]—if I am going to put all this effort into it, then at least it has to be something that I can imagine doing for 40 years. And under the existing circumstances in the GDR, I could think of nothing else except becoming a Protestant pastor. It was a vague hope; I did not really know what it would mean.

In addition to this, I had the fantastic luck of being at this school during

18. An amount which was, at the time, roughly equal to the same amount in dollars today. However, both food and housing were heavily subsidized in the GDR.

the *only* three years in which I could have survived there. One year earlier they would not have taken me, and one year after I had finished the new seminary, students started walking around as "new converts" with wooden crosses, so again I would have been in constant conflict with them. . . .

The people that had the most impact on me in theological terms were Dietrich Bonhoeffer and Dorothee Sölle. Without the ideas they expressed, I could have never become a Protestant pastor. If it had ended with Luther or had been limited to certain forms of pietism, I would never even have entertained the thought of becoming a pastor, or I would have eventually quit the school.

How many years did you go to the seminary?

The training took six years. In 1974 I was assigned to my first parish in Friedrichshain. One of the six years of my training had been a practical year in which I focused my attention on working with adolescents, first in a church circle and later under the auspices of the Berliner City Youths' Pastor's Office. After that, I became district pastor at the Samariter Church in Berlin and, simultaneously, district youth pastor for the region. It was during this time that I began to conduct church services that were very unusual for the time, so-called "Blues Masses."

Perhaps it is important to point out that the common thing to do at youth masses until then had been to find a biblical theme as a motto for the month or year, and it was my opinion that this would no longer suffice; it might have been OK for previous years, but at this point in time we should have let ourselves be guided by the themes that were important to those we wanted to show up and join us, themes that had something to do with their lives, with the circumstances of their lives. . . .

The topics that came up had to do with hopelessness, feeling incarcerated, fear, fear of the police, fear of the Stasi, fear of superiors—all these were topics that we tried to pick up on, even during public events. We also tried to provide answers to the best of our knowledge. When we started all this in 1976, it was extremely exotic within the conditions of the GDR.

You see, before the time when certain people began to wear the buttons "Swords to Ploughshares" and such, citizens of the GDR only expressed what they really thought among circles of close friends, the family, or at the neighborhood bar after they got drunk—but never publicly. Everyone was scared that negative repercussions would automatically follow. And for most people, the expression of political opinions was not important enough to risk that. So we were among the first who began to express such things publicly.

The whole thing got started when a young man came to me and said: "I can fill up your church, I am going to organize blues concerts in your church, I don't even want anything for it, I just want to do it for a good cause." I replied, "well, just a blues concert, then you can just as easily go to the concert house; I want the church to get the money—let us find some kind of church service as a format for your concerts."

So we started with biblical texts about love, then he played a few blues songs, then we read a few texts, and so on, and 200 people showed up, for heaven's sake. For a normal church service in downtown Berlin you would never have gotten together 200 people. The next time we chose our own theme, wrote our own texts while still using some biblical texts, and then 400 people showed up. This kept on growing—growing so much, in fact, that people began to come from all over the country, with backpacks on their shoulders, lining up in front of the church because they were worried they wouldn't be able to get in. During peak times—that must have been in the early '80s—10,000 people showed up. We had to repeat some services three to five times.

Of course, at this point we already began to experience some scary things. This ranged from neighbors complaining about participants who, after five hours of standing around, had to take a pee, or something bigger, and sometimes they did so in the hallways of neighboring buildings. Bars in the vicinity, of course, were booming. Later, we had to move out of our church because we were causing traffic jams. We subsequently moved to another church with more surrounding grounds, which, of course, were flattened after we had conducted the service four or five times in a row. We also performed small experimental plays. We had people smoking and drinking in church. You could tell that these folks had never been to a church in their lives; they came because they loved the music, and they were really interested in the topics that were addressed.

Who, concretely, was involved in organizing all of this and how did you do it?

At first a colleague of mine and I did it by ourselves. When we reached 10,000, a group of 10 to 12 people was responsible for the content and a group of about 50 organized it. . . .

Were those people who had previously gone to church as well, or people who had been drawn to this for the same reasons as almost everybody else?

We recruited people from the participants. Of course, we were confronted with immense attacks by the Stasi and the local police. It turned into a real ritual later on: we knew that whenever the date became known, Eppelmann would be called to see the mayor who told us: "No, we cannot allow something like that to take place. What if they march to the Wall? Besides, this has got nothing to do with a religious service anymore." Terrible, terrible. I can't remember all the details anymore, but eventually they stopped talking to me and instead barred me from entering city hall. The last time we met, they threatened me by saying "if you will proceed with your service tomorrow, we will march in!"

March into the church?

Yes. Fortunately, the general superintendent of the Protestant church at the time said in response: "Well, we cannot and will not cancel a church service."

I was just going to ask you about that: did the church hierarchy generally support your efforts?

Well, yes, with trembling and hesitation at that point. They frequently told me, "Eppelmann, you're putting the fate of the entire church at risk with your activities." And this was, of course, a very painful issue for me.

A mother once came to see me, for instance, and told me that her daughter was not admitted to a higher school despite the fact that she was a straight-A student. When she talked to the director of the school she was told that her daughter attended the same church as Eppelmann. These were heavy burdens to bear.

Did you make any attempts to contact people outside of your church who were possibly interested in the same kind of political work as you were?

There were none. I was—and I have to say this in all modesty—the first swallow of spring, together with those co-organizing these events. There was nothing comparable happening anywhere else in the GDR. That's why they came from everywhere, from the Baltic Sea to the Thuringian Forest. . . .

I did not mean so much to ask whether you knew people who were already engaged in similar or the same things, but rather to ask about attempts *to approach people who were* interested *in similar or the same kinds of things.*

Oftentimes sheer coincidences played a role in my life, like my friendship with Robert Havemann. Two houses away from where Robert Havemann lived in Grünheide there was a Lutheran meeting center. Some clerical coworkers and I had gone to a conference there on the topic "Outsiders"—it must have been a year and a half before Havemann died [in April of 1982]. On that occasion I made a proposal by saying: "Let's not just talk about outsiders. Let's go to a so-called outsider and see whether he is willing to talk to us." I had previously only known him by name. So three of us went to see Havemann and he talked to us for an hour. Then he invited the whole group over; we again talked for some time, and I was the only one who stayed after the others had left. I told him that I wanted to see him again and he agreed.

Our subsequent relationship became more and more intense, despite the fact that we lived relatively far away from each other. In most cases, on my way back home I was followed by the Stasi who made a point of showing all of us that we should not assume that they did not know that we had gone to see Havemann. More and more conscious political talk, and later some specific actions, grew out of this relationship.

In the fall of 1981 I wrote an open letter to Honecker. After I did not receive an answer, I gave it—mediated through Robert Havemann—to a Western journalist. This was the first time that my name appeared in public. At that time, this act [using the Western media to publicly criticize the leadership] was, of course, still considered to be a criminal offense.

In February of 1982, I coauthored the "Berliner Appeal" with Robert Havemann [calling for the demilitarization and disarmament of the GDR, and—going beyond most other appeals—calling for the withdrawal of "all occupation troops from Germany," which quite clearly included the 400,000-strong Red Army contingent in the GDR]. It was my hope to disseminate this pamphlet throughout East Germany with the help of the internal church network. Such an appeal, of course, would not have made any sense if it was just sent to somebody, and then 20 years later people found out what was happening. For example, a Protestant pastor from Dresden, Wonneberger, had written a similar appeal [in 1980] concerning the Social Peace Service (SOFD), and even I, who was part of the religious youth work, did not find out about it until a year later. We thought this was ridiculous. Of course, Robert Havemann already had much more experience with the press due to the books he had written and published in the West. So it was very clear to us that we were going to make an attempt to use the inner GDR communication network first, and if that would not work out, we would make use of the Western media.[19]

So it was your understanding that you would be pretty secure engaging in such activities because of your position as a pastor within the international framework of the church, or did you too have reason to be worried about the Stasi, the police, and the party?

Well, in the meantime we had done another thing which I need to tell

19. Robert Havemann's plea attached to the Berlin Appeal represents an instructive example of how important the Western media was considered to be for the formation of any kind of opposition in the GDR. It stated: "We address ourselves to our friends in the peace movement in the West, to writers, scientists, representatives of the Christian Churches. . . . Use every means at your disposal to provide the people of the GDR—via West German radio and TV—with the important facts about our peace movement. Disseminate this article in radio broadcasts, and arrange interviews on television about the Berlin Appeal with writers, scientists, politicians, and theologians." Quoted in Wolfgang Büscher et al., *Friedensbewegung in der DDR: Texte, 1978–1982* (Hattingen, 1982), 228f. My translation.

you about: a video-recorded interview of Robert Havemann and me. My wife was asking the questions, but we did not film her, because, for obvious reasons, we wanted to conceal her identity. When Robert Havemann gave the video to his Western liaison, he ordered them to give the interviewer a different voice in order to protect her, so the only ones that could be seen and heard on the video were Robert Havemann and Rainer Eppelmann. Once the tape was gone—I don't know what Robert thought at that point—I was not at all sure whether I would not be picked up by the Stasi half an hour later. . . .

■ CORNELIA MATZKE, opposition activist, founding member of the Independent Women's Alliance, Leipzig. ■ *"Actually I was trying to find the women's movement."*

The fabric of dissent in East Germany was woven of many threads. Cornelia Matzke grew up in Leipzig, in many ways far removed from all the publicized political decisions taking shape in East Berlin. In common with hundreds of other oppositionists in the GDR, she was neither well-known nor well-connected to the small circles of prominent dissenters working mainly out of the East German capital. Yet—it is now clear—without the courage, creativity, and sustained hard work of men and women like Cornelia Matzke, the revolution would never have taken place. People like her were the ones who organized, set up meetings, distributed pamphlets, and recruited fellow citizens to the varied activities that made up "the civic movement."

I first learned about Matzke when I went to the "House of Democracy" in Leipzig, a building that housed the newly founded opposition groups. These groups ranged from "big" new parties like the East German Social Democrats to small self-help circles such as "parents for an independent school system." As always, when encountering such groups, I asked for names of activists who could tell me about the development of their grass-roots groups, or could enlighten me about the emergence of an organized opposition in their city in general. Matzke's name was mentioned by several people as someone who was not only well-informed, but extremely approachable and open. So I called her, and she promptly invited me to come by her place for breakfast the next morning.

About five minutes from downtown Leipzig, her apartment was on the third floor of a typical 1920s five-story German apartment building, the kind I had learned to like a great deal during my college years in West

Berlin. The difference between the buildings I had seen or inhabited in the West and Matzke's, however, was nothing short of dismaying. The facades of the buildings on her street had not seen any repair work since World War II; there were no trees or shrubs in her neighborhood, and most apartments did not have running warm water or indoor toilets—a situation that described living conditions for more than 30 percent of all dwellings (and in the majority of old buildings) in the GDR. The whole scene reminded me of drawings that try to provide a realistic impression of modern cities after a neutron bomb attack: gray, void of anything alive, and in dismal condition. The streets were covered with so many huge potholes that I still don't know how my aged little car survived.

Cornelia Matzke's apartment turned out to be very pleasant, furnished with care and a love for details; a sort of oasis in a hostile environment. She brewed a fresh pot of coffee, and as we began chatting a bit about current events in the GDR, she remarked in passing that "this whole thing must be very strange and difficult for you to grasp." Before I could respond, she added: "I would very much like to visit the U.S. once, just out of curiosity. But I don't think I could ever live there." I only had slightly more than one hour, so I did not ask her what exactly she had meant. Instead, we started with the interview.

Matzke had just recently finished her training as a general physician. In the Fall of 1989 she had initiated the Women's Initiative in Leipzig. She was, right from the start, active within New Forum. At the time of my visit she was 29.

■ So much has happened lately that I haven't thought about me and my development for a long time. . . .

I am a woman who has been interested in political issues as far back as I can remember. I always had a desire to have influence. Of course, one would have to reflect on the question as to what it means to "have influence," but it represented a basic motivation to become active politically; otherwise, I could have continued to live a normal life, like most others. I already wanted to have this influence as a child. I was very active in the Pioneer organization, but quickly began to feel very exploited by them. I just felt treated unfairly, having to do things and being exploited for things that I did not agree with, that I did not support. . . .

I had a pretty high position within the structure of the Pioneer organization; I was chairperson of the friendship council. And in this position you had quite a few privileges and responsibilities. I remember at one time we participated in the so-called Weltjugendspiele [World Youth Games].

That was in 1973; Walter Ulbricht [first secretary of the Socialist Unity Party until 1971] had just died. We had to stay in one of those camps, guarded and everything, and we were not allowed to move around freely, to go places and meet young people from other countries. I perceived that as an outrageous restriction at the time. And then we were told to go to an official demonstration—not to participate, but to stand on the sidelines and to sort of "fill in." They did not tell us what this was all about, why we could not participate actively, or anything. We were just puppets being moved around according to their plans. I was so angry that I got sick and did not participate, which, of course, was considered to be a disciplinary offense for someone in my position. . . .

During my training at the university I began to seek contact with grass-roots groups here in Leipzig and with the ESG [Evangelical Student Community]. In November of 1985 I organized a presentation on the fortieth anniversary of the victory over fascism within the context of the Protestant Peace Decade that was held in Leipzig at the time. Before that, I had only had sporadic contacts with the church. . . .

My problem had always been to find a way to express myself politically, to find a context or people with whom I could work. . . .

Actually, I was trying to find the women's movement, except that I had not yet quite realized that at the time. . . .

You see, the church was the only possible alternative for any kind of political activism. There was absolutely nothing else. For a while I had considered joining one of the satellite parties, such as the LDPD [Liberal Democratic Party of Germany], but all of them were really the same as the SED; they were completely controlled by the SED and followed in every respect the party line. Just the language these people were using was appalling to me. One cannot express oneself in these abstract party-line categories.

So trying to change something from within the party, perhaps with friends who thought along the same lines as you, was never an option for you?

Well, maybe if I had fallen in love with a party member or something like that, but short of that, no. I don't think this would have been possible at all. You see, I always perceived myself as someone from the left, and I had always been very angry about how this party was ruining and corrupting left-wing ideas. I just felt betrayed by this party which claimed to be the bearer of an ideology which they themselves did not live up to at all. But this never resulted in my giving up on left-wing ideas, on the idea of socialism, on a more democratic and egalitarian alternative to capitalism. And I still think that way. . . .

My experiences with working in environmental groups was, on the other hand, that men were always in charge of everything, and they knew they were. . . .

Were women's issues ever debated in any of those groups?

No, not really. It was simply not an issue, mostly because the women's movement was not an issue in the GDR. Women had no support for their grievances or their issues anywhere in the country. Which is, by the way, the main reason why I think women should organize their own groups: so that they can have a support network, a place where their issues and problems are taken seriously, and a forum through which to form some kind of political lobby. Because if women simply join male-dominated groups and parties—and I am not saying they should not do that as well—they will never get this kind of support; they will not be able to identify themselves as women. Women can only achieve some kind of identity by organizing as women, by having a network which allows them to realize that their problems are not individual problems, but rather that many other women have the same problems. . . .

Had you heard about the group "Women for Peace" that was founded in Berlin in 1983?

Yes, I had heard about it, but I did not know much about them. It was very difficult to find out things like that. We did not have any contacts with them; the linkages were simply missing. It was very difficult to obtain certain pieces of information in the GDR; one always depended on personal contacts. Only afterward did I find out that there was a group "Women for Peace" in Leipzig as well. I don't know how they came into existence, but very few people knew about them. . . .

It was very difficult in the GDR to realize that your problems as a woman might not have personal causes, but instead were indicative of a larger problem, of gender antagonisms permeating all of society. As you know, the official ideology claimed that emancipation and equal rights had already been achieved in the GDR—in short, they claimed that there were no gender-related problems.

What helped me a great deal was when I met a woman from Marburg who was active in the West German feminist movement. Only by talking to her did I realize how much was going on out there in terms of women's issues, how large the women's movement was, and for how long they had been organizing. Of course, discrimination against women was probably also not as clear-cut as it is in the West. I could not claim, for example, that I was discriminated against in terms of my own education or job in the GDR. It had more to do with smaller things, with things that were not as tangible. I had always perceived disadvantages or unfair treatment as my private matter, as a problem that had only to do with me, but not as something that might perhaps be tied into the larger issue of gender relations in the GDR.

Quite a number of very tangible things come to mind, however. There was not a single woman in the Politburo. In general, women were grossly underrepresented in the political hierarchy. Or the fact that women still had to bear the double burden of working and doing the housework at the same time, without much help by men.

Yes, that's true, but you first have to learn to see this as a woman. I remember initially being rather insensitive to these things, not being able to see some of these blatant inequalities. On the other hand, this had also to do with the fact that the kind of politics represented by the party did not fit women at all. It would almost have been more of a contradiction if women had occupied more leadership positions. In terms of the double burden most women have to carry, I simply have to say that I came out of a family in which the father had to do his share as well, and since all my siblings were female I did not encounter many forms of discrimination against women in my family. . . .

How or when did you realize that you wanted to focus your political activities on women's issues?

The discussions with the men in the environmental group were just dreadful to me. In fact, that was true in all the groups I participated in. One of those was a so-called "discussion group." We met about once a month and talked about certain issues that had been decided upon earlier. Of course, we particularly focused on issues that one could not talk about in public anywhere else. What always bothered me a great deal was that if women came with their partners or husbands, they always ended up not saying anything. I was always drawn to these women in an emotional sense. I just wanted to find out how it would be to have such discussions only with women. . . .

There was an incredible atmosphere in the country during most of 1989, a sort of depression, a feeling of being severely oppressed, a sense that all the things we had put up with and we had suffered could not go on much longer. Everyone felt like that in one way or another.

We had organized a street music festival in June 1989, where I was arrested. I was totally depressed afterward. We simply could not believe that they could be that stupid, that they actually dared to arrest people at a street music festival. They simply went beyond their limits, or at least they did not seem to know anymore where those limits were. If they ever had, they certainly no longer understood where they had to allow some space in order then to be able to crack down on people when it *really* got dangerous for them. They were not even clever as holders of power. They certainly did not belong in the category of "intelligent dictators." In retrospect, it is amazing to see how many blatant mistakes they made from their point of view—in fact, it is astonishing how long they managed to hold on to power.

It was my understanding that this street music festival in 1989 was concep-tualized not merely as a cultural event, but rather as a political statement as well. Is that correct?

Well, yes and no. It was not a political rally of any sort. But it was supposed to be a test as to whether the party would in fact react as if it were a political event. We had even tried to get an official permit for this festival, which we did not receive. But we decided to go ahead and invite bands and people anyway. Prior to this, the musicians were put under a lot of pressure from the officials who said that if the musicians participated in the festival, they would lose their licenses. Most of the musicians buckled under this pressure and did not show up. So we mostly had amateur musicians and bands from other cities.

At first, the festival did not really get started, because the Stasi had a lot of agents there who were talking to the musicians, trying to convince them not to play, putting pressure on them and such. A few friends and I walked up to one of those conversations between Stasi officials and musicians and just began to sing—which was difficult, because we didn't really have any songs everyone readily knew.

Well, in the end we found one, and this idea of just beginning to sing and play spread rapidly. So this is how the festival started. Everything was OK until about noon, when the police drove up with trucks and began to arrest people. First, they arrested the musicians, and then others who had played any active role in putting together this festival.

Later on, I got to know quite a few very interesting people in the detention cell, people who had organized the monitoring of the elections in May and who had made public the large-scale election fraud that had been revealed by those members of the grass-roots groups who had organized this. It was a very interesting experience.

Why exactly did they arrest you?

Well, at the end they pretty much picked up people at random in front of the Thomas Church. Of course, they were particularly looking for people who they already knew were engaged in "subversive activities" and those who somehow looked conspicuously "alternative." I did not particularly look "alternative," and I could probably have avoided arrest. But first of all

I thought that it was time for me to go through this experience as well, and second of all I figured it would be important for them also to arrest people once who did not fit into their preconceptions of who was and who was not opposed to the regime they were serving.

How long did they keep you in detention?

Until about 2:30 at night.

How did they treat you?

Not too badly. The guy who interrogated me was talking about "enemies of the state" and things like that, but that was normal. Surprisingly, I was also not scared at all. We knew, for example, that they were eavesdropping on us, but that did not matter to us at all; we talked to one another completely freely. There was a mood among us—the kind of mood that prevailed until October and, I think, that goes a long way in explaining the mass demonstrations of October—that it did not matter anymore. Things were so bad, it really no longer mattered. Something just *had* to happen, and people were increasingly willing to take risks in order to bring about change. That so many people took the tremendous risks they did on 9 October, even though they knew what the state apparatus could potentially do to us, and even though it was absolutely unclear as to what would happen, I think can only be explained by people having reached a tremendous degree of alienation and resignation. In retrospect, after we have found out what some of their plans were . . . it was really quite scary.

Anyway, I did not get treated badly, but I think that mostly had to do with the fact that there were so many of us. But after I had gotten out, I was severely depressed, and my partner Matthias and I concluded that it was time for us to become more active ourselves. We decided to play the role of the naive citizen who had seen innocent people being arrested. So we wrote three official letters inquiring about what had happened and wondering as to why the state was conducting itself in this fashion. We sent one letter to the city councilman for cultural affairs, one we sent to the editor in chief of the *FAZ* [West German daily in Frankfurt], and the third to Kurt Masur [director of the Leipzig orchestra]. We got no answer to the first letter; the second was answered in a very unresponsive fashion, which depressed us even more. But Professor Masur wrote back, telling us that he had taken notice of this and that he was surprised how the police had apparently treated people and so on. And then he wrote that he would plan a session on 28 August in which he would invite all the people who were interested in street music.

You can imagine what a big success this was for us. A high-ranking personality with connections to Honecker was actually paying attention to us and responding to us. In fact, from then on he became active as a sort of mediator in critical events—before that he had not done anything.

So you think that had to do with the letter you wrote him?

Well, yes, at least that's what he said himself. Of course, we went to this event. I had told all the organizers of the earlier street music festival about this, and many, many showed up. During the introduction Masur said that a "concerned citizen of the city" had written this letter to him and that he wanted to do whatever he could, and that he was moved by the fact that the letter writer obviously thought that he could make a difference.

How did you originally come up with the idea of writing to Masur?

Well, it was to be expected that the city officials would not respond, and it was also to be expected that we would not get much help from an editor of a West German newspaper. We just figured that Masur was somebody who had a lot of high-up connections—something that became very clear when they built this outrageously expensive Orchestra House for him right in the center of Leipzig. On the other hand, he was not a party official proper, so we thought that this was worth an attempt. We didn't even expect that much. Even if he had only said a word to the city councilman for cultural affairs, that would already have been a success. Furthermore, in this kind of feudal state it was normal for the underlings to write to the ruler, and he more or less belonged in the category of rulers. There is a long history in this country of people writing letters and petitions to Honecker: again, the underlings trying to receive recognition from the ruler. So our attempt was part of a long tradition, part of the system, in fact.

Did anything change in response to this meeting organized by Masur?

Well, first of all it was nice that somebody who was in a position of relative power had acknowledged the problem, and, second, from then on Masur became very actively involved in things that were going on in Leipzig. His best-known and most important intervention, of course, was this open letter he and five others [among them three party district secretaries] wrote prior to the demonstration on 9 October, calling for peaceful negotiations.[20] It was also wonderful how he tried to encourage

---

20. The letter stated, among other things, "we are troubled by the developments occurring in our city, and we are searching for a peaceful resolution. We need the free exchange of opinions for the continuation of socialism in our country. . . . We herewith promise all citizens to do everything in our power in order to make this dialogue possible." Document in author's possession. My translation.

us, how he tried to give us hope at this meeting. He said, quite explicitly, that we should not let others push us around too much, that we should do more by ourselves, because there was really nobody who could prevent us from doing this, and so on. It really was quite wonderful.

Many things happened after this meeting in August, the wave of emigration through Hungary and such. What also seemed important to me at the time was the fact that Honecker was sick, and that the entire party leadership simply came across as desolate. They seemed no longer capable of any real decisions. All of this, of course, left the impression that this "power"—this party and state leadership that we had come to know simply as "the power"—that this power had disintegrated so much primarily because Honecker was sick. It was somehow encouraging, because if that was true, it could not be all that great a "power" after all. I at least experienced it that way, and I believe many others did as well. It just signified that such power cannot be infinite.

I well remember a meeting we had in September among opposition activists and church members, and one person said "the whole system is so well organized, so stable, that it will certainly defend itself to the last man." Particularly older citizens, due to all their experiences, thought that this entire party apparatus could never be broken.

Many thought that inertia, or a kind of self-perpetuating dynamic would keep the apparatus in place indefinitely. How wrong everybody was.

Did you ever participate in the Monday Prayers at the Nikolai Church or the demonstrations that always followed?

No, because I was always on duty at this time [as a physician]. It was interesting, however, that all my colleagues and friends expected me to go. After I had been arrested at the street music festival, for example, they called my boss who, in turn, put me under quite some pressure to quit these kinds of political activities. He in effect threatened me by making it very clear that I could easily lose my job.

He is an interesting case: he is now a supporter of the CDU [the conservative Christian Democratic Party]; in other words, he is one of those many opportunists who just made a quick 180-degree turn. In any case, I had told him at the time that he should not worry about me because I was quite capable of deciding what to do myself.

■ LUDWIG MEHLHORN, prominent oppositionist, expert on Eastern Europe, founding member of Democracy Now. ■ *"Most of our energy was spent just trying to create a bit of free space. . . . It was an attempt to step out of our isolation."*

Ludwig Mehlhorn, born in 1950, mathematician, translator, and cofounder of the opposition group Democracy Now, was one of the most prominent spokespersons of the opposition in the Fall of 1989. He was my first "insider" contact in East Berlin, a contact that subsequently developed into a close and candid relationship for the duration of my visit. He seemed to enjoy taking off some time from his various tasks in order to reflect calmly on the tremendous and unexpected changes in the GDR, the role of the opposition, the many twists and turns of the revolution, and, above all, his own role in these events. Mehlhorn subsequently set up numerous contacts for me and tried to help out whenever I ran into seemingly insurmountable obstacles, either in contacting people, or in terms of apparent nonsequitors concerning new details I had unearthed about the "revolutionary process."

I had my first appointment with him on 6 June 1990 in East Berlin at the "House of Democracy," the largest one of its kind in the GDR. When I first entered this imposing building which had previously served as an administrative party headquarter, I was struck by the liveliness pulsating through every room and down every hallway. Posters and announcements were plastered all over the walls, and one could constantly hear people debating or laughing, making phone calls, typing letters or using the printers. Virtually all the groups, organizations, and parties that had been founded since the collapse of the regime shared the building. Sometimes members of different groups worked together in the same office. At the time, membership to different groups had not been considered an obstacle to close cooperation, but rather was appreciated as essential to the diversity that society needed after years of suffocating one-party centralism.

It not only felt like, it was, in fact, "democracy at work." People who had never previously thought about "doing politics" joined in. Throughout the day citizens who just happened to be in the neighborhood dropped in "to see what is going on" or "to find out whether I can help out some way." Every age group was represented, children played in the hallways, and in some groups entire families were active. For a time, it seemed, politics had been successfully torn away from the state and brought into an emerging civil society. It may be said that, during the moment of revolutionary transition, the personal had become political, and the political had become personal.

Mehlhorn impressed me as a soft-spoken, thoughtful, and determined man. Answers did not come quickly or easily to him, but they were clear and precise. He seemed to be comfortable with doubt and ambiguity. Clear-cut positions sparked his suspicion. He was not the kind of person who seeks the limelight of public attention, but rather one who likes to act in the background.

Through persistent work of a seemingly selfless character, Mehlhorn had become an important organizer, mediator, and spokesperson for the East Berlin opposition. He had equally good contacts with activists in and outside the realm of the church; he had himself been active in grass-roots groups that were either organized under the roof of the church or set up independently, and he had acquired a name for himself as a well-informed and extremely reliable contact person.

He said to me at one point, "even though things have turned out very differently from what we were striving for, we should nevertheless not forget the real achievements that came out of our struggle." His frustration about the current situation was tangible, yet he considered the worst to be over. "At least now we can say what we want to—it may not have much of an effect anymore, but it helps."

■ *Could you first tell me a little about your personal background, particularly concerning your own political socialization?*

Perhaps I should start with the prehistory of Democracy Now. One could say that it started with the twenty-fifth anniversary of the building of the Wall. A number of personal experiences are connected with this date. On 13 August 1986, the two Protestant bishops from Berlin [West and East], Kruse and Forck, had written open letters to one another concerning the duties of the church considering the separation of the city, the separation of Germany, and the problems that were connected to that for both the people and the church. Their analysis was very superficial in our opinion. They remained confined to pastoral advice of one kind or another, saying that one should accept the separation and that all one could do was take small steps toward trying to "alleviate the problems" people had as a result of this separation. They had no concept that could have indicated how one might change this situation, change it in a fundamental sense.

So we started two initiatives in response to this exchange of letters. The first one was started by me. I wrote a letter to both of them, pointing out and criticizing this deficiency. At the same time, I demanded a clearer stance by the church toward what I considered to be the scandal of Germany's separation. My reasoning behind this was that this separation not only resulted in the demarcation of the GDR, but it also represented the basic reason why this particular dictatorial system could survive in the GDR.

The church had, during the East-West conflict of the early eighties, taken the position concerning the question of military confrontation between East and West that "the church is against the spirit, logic, and practice of deterrence." So I had written in my letter that one could reasonably expect the church also to take a clear stance against the spirit, logic, and practice of demarcation, that is, if the peace policy and the peace pedagogy that the church had subscribed to were to remain credible.

What exactly did "demarcation" mean to you?

Demarcation was synonymous with being walled in in the GDR, with this kind of dome that was erected over the country, which not only systematically prevented travel, but also closed down any kind of access to information and ideas. The entire cultural development in the West passed us by. We were, in effect, condemned to a ghetto existence. This not only included being walled off from the West, but also from the East. Opportunities for travel or establishing contacts with Eastern Bloc countries were extremely restricted as well. There were times when it would probably have been easier to get permission to travel to the West than to Poland, such as during the era of Solidarność, for instance [1980–88]. Our conditions resembled the conditions of a prison camp, one in which people had made themselves relatively comfortable, mostly in their own private niches.

The other action that took place on the same day [13 August 1986]— without our knowing about it—was the one by Reinhart Lampe. He had chained himself to a window crossbar facing the Wall at Bernauer Street. It was a sort of one-person happening, a one-person demonstration with two banners that he had tied to the window. One said "Twenty-five years is enough," and the other stated "One dies due to the wall in one's head." Lampe, of course, was arrested for this. The action lasted for about a half an hour. The group out of which Democracy Now would later emerge actually constituted itself as a group around the struggle for Lampe's release. We tried to intervene in the trial, we gathered support signatures, we established contacts with Western journalists, we hired an attorney for him, we wrote petitions, and things of that sort. . . .

Could you explain that a little more? What specifically did you do?

We tried to stage public actions or to organize public lectures. We wrote petitions to the church synod, because it was very difficult to reach the public, and the church at least had some access to the media. And we tried to talk to and write to various people about this topic. We asked theologians, writers, psychologists, and others to begin to think and write about this problem. In short, we tried to get people to focus on this problem of demarcation and, particularly, on the Wall as the starkest symbol for this imprisonment. Of course, the whole thing was also meant as a metaphor for all the interior conditions in this state, imposed on us by the kind of execution of power that is typical of communist dictatorships. Out of all this came a petition to the synod of the Protestant church in which we again demanded the rejection of the spirit, logic, and practice of the principle of demarcation. We produced a whole journal on this question . . .

. . . which you produced illegally and which you wanted to distribute among as many people as possible?

Right. We called the journal *Aufrisse* [which means "outline/sketch" as well as "breaking open"], which was also meant as a metaphor for breaking apart the structures, for an opening. . . . The target groups were mainly those people who we thought might potentially contribute to the building of an organized opposition in the GDR. Those were the grass-roots peace groups, the human rights groups, all those who were trying to create some independent public space—writers, environmental activists, people who were part of the youth subculture, or of the literary subculture. In other words, people from various different social backgrounds, but people who had one thing in common: a deep dissatisfaction with the existing conditions in the GDR. Actually, the point was to create a mutually shared conceptual basis, to come up with a minimal consensus for a platform from which we could proceed to fight or challenge the structures of oppression that had been established domestically with the help of the Wall.

Is it correct that practically all the groups you just mentioned, with the exception of the Initiative for Peace and Human Rights, were operating within the realm of the church?

Well, yes and no. I was, for example, also talking about a literary subculture. The dividing lines were very fluid. We did not only work within the church either. For example, in the years 1985 to '87, we organized a number of readings by authors who were not allowed to publish officially, and we did this in private homes. Sometimes more than 80 people showed up to events like this. . . .

You were working as a mathematician at the time. Did you work in industry?
No, I worked at the mathematics center of the university, that is, until
1985. That year I left the university. Actually, I was fired. There was a
political reason behind that, even though the actual cause was rather
banal. What I am about to tell you can actually be used as a very indicative
symptom for the whole issue of demarcation. As a subclause to our job
contract, we were asked to sign "that we would give notification of any and
every contact, be it by phone, by letter, or personally with anyone from the
West." Ultimately, this meant that they demanded from you cooperation
with the Stasi. And they also demanded from you that such contacts
should be limited to purely personal ones. I refused to sign this document.
The result was that they told me that my qualifications were no longer
sufficient to hold the position I then occupied.

In such cold-blooded ways they destroyed, among various other things,
many professional careers. It was a rather normal thing around here. My
attitude at the time was simply to try "to make the best of it." You always
had two options: either you decided that you had to leave; in other words,
you applied for an exit visa, which meant three or four years of mere
survival, being unemployed and generally in a very unstable situation. But
at some point you usually managed to get out. Or, the other possibility, the
one I chose for myself, was to say, "I will not seek this kind of personal,
individual solution to these problems, but instead, since this situation
requires an overall political solution, I will try to work for such a general
solution." This meant a general opening of the society and a fundamental
change of the political system.

So, after I was out of my professional job—I subsequently worked as a
night security guard in a home for mentally retarded children—I began to
get more engaged politically. The main goal was to build what one might
call an "oppositional structure." After 1985, that turned into the main
content of my life.

After that we began to engage in oppositional activity more systematically. The main impetus driving us from our initial phase of oppositional
activity to the other was that we realized that it would not suffice any
longer to base oppositional contacts on mere oral communication—we
needed something on paper that could reach beyond the circle of friends
or people we already knew. This was a decisive step, one that happened
simultaneously in other groups as well. I certainly do not want to make it
sound as if we were the only ones engaged in such activities . . .

. . . *The Initiative for Peace and Human Rights (IFM) got started in 1985 as
well . . .*

. . . Right. The IFM was founded mainly because these people were, in effect, pushed out of a church which did not want to provide facilities for a human rights seminar they had planned. So they had to resort to a private home, where the group was born.

But you still wanted to build your own group?

Well, yes. We did not have any differences with the IFM in principle; we were in full agreement with their assessment of the political situation. We simply opted for a different organizational framework, for different forms of work. But we still maintained a continuous line of communication with one another. We also published a number of samizdat journals in cooperation with the IFM.

Could you tell me what happened between September of 1987 and October of 1989, when Democracy Now was founded? What activities did you initiate, how did the group develop?

Through the work on these samizdat journals we were able to establish a permanent discussion forum, mainly of people who lived in Berlin, but also of some others. We worked on two levels at the same time. On the one hand, we tried to push forward the discussion process about these problems within the official committees of the church. We constantly put them under immense pressure with petitions, requests, and initiatives. We were quite successful in that.

And on the other hand, independently of that, we continued the publication of samizdat journals. We never tried to turn these into regular publications, because all such previous attempts had been systematically destroyed. So we did not want to run into their open knife by producing periodic issues. Instead, we came out with a journal whenever something particular was happening, like when there was a synod, or a Church Day. This also made it a bit easier to get it distributed, and it was easier to calculate the problems we would have with the security police.

Did you also try to expand the group during this time by recruiting people?

Well, the group did expand. We managed to reach a wider audience by organizing a large panel discussion with about 200 participants in January of 1988 . . .

. . . *This meeting happened in a church?*

Yes, in a church in Oranienburg, because the Stasi had exerted a lot of pressure on the church not to allow such an event to take place in Berlin.

How did you publicize such an event?

In this case it happened through church channels. People who had read our journals had written so many letters to the church officials that they simply could no longer ignore our initiatives. They would have lost all credibility if they had not reacted to this. Of course, from today's perspective it was an extremely laborious effort just to reach a minimum of a general public for such issues. Most of our energy was spent just trying to create a bit of free space . . .

. . . *Even within the church?*

Yes, even within the church.

Lotte Templin [founding member and spokesperson of the Initiative for Peace and Human Rights] told me in this context that the role of the church had always been mainly reactive; in other words, that church officials had to be put under immense pressure before they would react or go along.

Yes, I think that is a fair assessment. The difference between the IFM and us is that we continued to try to put pressure on the church until the end. That was mainly because a larger percentage of us had originally come out of the context of the church ourselves, while most people in the IFM did not have this personal religious background and therefore gave up trying much quicker. So in general I agree that we had to exert pressure before they reacted. On the other hand, I have to say that even though this assessment is correct as far as it concerns the church as an institution, it is certainly not correct with respect to quite a few church employees and pastors. There were a number of people inside the church who were also not at all satisfied with the positions of the church committees, of the church hierarchy. . . .

Let me ask you once more about the growth of the group. You said that the group was expanding, and you told me about this large-scale public meeting at which, I suppose, you tried to recruit some people. Could you tell me a little about who exactly showed interest, what they did, and how they came to be part of your group?

Well, I think at this meeting we managed to create a consciousness of the fact that we had to do something about the general situation in this society, a situation with which people had up till then tried to come to terms only on a purely personal, individual level.

The reason I am asking about this again simply has to do with the fact that I find it rather difficult as an outsider to understand what exactly the conditions were like in the GDR at the time, what was possible to do, and what was dangerous or impossible to do. I would thus like you to help me understand what the specific obstacles for organizing any political opposition were . . .

I believe it is extremely difficult to explain the entire situation to somebody from the outside—this heavily weighing pressure of silent consent with the regime; this strange peace that everyone had found with the system; this total suppression within oneself of any reflex of rebellion against the deeply ingrained conventions in every sphere of society.

Even within the realm of the church, a certain attitude of resignation had dominated everything since the sixties, a stance that assumed that we could not fundamentally change anything, that we could only try to alleviate some of the worst consequences, and that in this effort we had succeeded in some ways.

Shortly after the Wall had been built in the sixties, the church came up with the thesis of "living with the division." This implied that "our duty now was to make the best of it." We were to accept it as something that was brought upon us, something for which Germans are in some ways responsible due to their history. So therefore we consciously had to accept this division as a fate. "Living with the division" was also the title of a widely read book published in the sixties.[21]

Such a stance was probably justified from the perspective of the sixties, that is, to offer people some perspective for the future, trying to prevent people from simply getting bitter and cynical. But we just thought that the answers of the sixties were no longer applicable 20 years later. We needed different answers in the eighties, answers that would help overcome the division, answers that would help build the preconditions for easing the East-West confrontation and thus help overcome the division of the entire continent.

You have to realize that even international politics in the framework of East-West relations had been pushed toward a dead end through the policies of the GDR leadership, at least since the mid-eighties. The GDR leadership blocked all policies of détente that were associated with Gorbachev, and that were pushed forward when countries such as Poland and Hungary began to open up toward the West. During all this time, the GDR remained the last Stalinist bastion in Central Europe.

So, if you wanted to take yourself seriously as an opposition within the GDR, you had to take this into consideration and come up with specific political strategies that could lead out of this dead end, and not just keep rehearsing the classical rhetoric of détente typical of the seventies; that is, all we can do is take small steps in alleviating the worst human hardships. What we needed was a fundamentally new starting point—this is what we

---

21. It was not until 1969 that the West and East German Protestant Churches began to go separate institutional ways, which, in turn, allowed the newly-founded East German Bund der Evangelischen Kirche to define its role within the political realities of the GDR. The best-known and most succinct statement concerning the role of the Protestant church in the GDR was made in 1971 by the then bishop of Berlin, Albrecht Schönherr: "We do not wish to be a Church alongside Socialism, nor a Church against Socialism: we wish to be a Church within Socialism." Quoted in John Sanford, *The Sword and the Ploughshare* (London, 1983), 15.

tried in our samizdat journals, to find such a starting point, to develop such a strategy. What we did was certainly insufficient—after all, we had very limited possibilities—but it was a start catching up with the developments occurring all around us. It was an attempt to step out of our isolation.

Let me ask you a question that may sound a bit naive or simplistic. If I try to imagine the attempt to build some kind of political opposition in the then existing political system in the GDR—and you say that most people lived in a state of quiet consent to the system, and, furthermore, that there were very limited means of communication and only a few spaces for open debate available for people—what specifically did you do in order to find out which specific people might be interested in becoming active in some sort of opposition? Can you tell me how you did this?

There were various ways of doing that, but ultimately we never reached a very large public. We reached the most people at those Church Days which were attended by some 5,000 to 10,000 people. So we went to those events with about 500 copies of our journal and tried to distribute it among various groups, or we printed pamphlets in larger numbers and tried to get those out to people. But a kind of working network could only be established through personal relations, on the basis of personal trust. We had to be pretty certain that the people with whom we worked were not employed by the Stasi, or would not use our group for any other personal gain.

How confident could you be about that among the participants of the Church Day?

Well, you have to distinguish between those among whom we distributed our journals and pamphlets, and those with whom we started to work on a constant basis. We were, in other words, not afraid of contacting almost anyone, but in order to work with someone we needed to have some kind of guarantee that they could be trusted.

What about people in the factories, people in the satellite parties, or even reformers within the party? Did you ever attempt to establish contacts in those circles? You mentioned Gregor Gysi earlier on, for example, someone who was a party member but also someone who was obviously interested in change?

Well, you see, Gysi [party member, attorney, defender of numerous oppositionists, later chairman of PDS] and his friends tried to change the system from within the party. They wanted to democratize the party and rebuild it so that it could acquire a "leading role in society" that was genuine. We did have some contacts with people like him, and we were also interested in maintaining such contacts. But with Gysi, for example, his role was largely confined to defending oppositionists. Others limited themselves to having private conversations with members of the opposition.

We had tried at one point, for example, to get the members of the Institute for Social Sciences at the Central Committee of the Socialist Unity Party [the East German CP] to write some articles for our next journal. This, however, they refused to do, because they were afraid that this would mean the end of their career and thus the end of their potential ability to change the party from within. Of course, this was a gross miscalculation on their part.

If some of them, like Rolf Reissig, could have presented themselves in the Fall of 1989 as the authors of such articles, they of course would have had much more credibility. And then they could also have simply left the party without any loss of face. But none of them did that, probably because they did not want to lose what they perceived to be their potential influence in the party.

Would you say that this "miscalculation" was absolutely predictable early on, or would you characterize it as "understandable" that some people thought that the only possible change could only come from within the party?

Well, first of all you can only begin to understand or criticize those people if you take notice of the framework in which they thought, a framework that had no relevance for us anymore. They based their political hopes on a renewal of socialism through a transformed party. We were already beyond thinking about the future in socialist terms—not in the sense that we predicted or even wanted the GDR to disappear as a nation in the near future; that was a process that overwhelmed us as well, a process for which we had no concepts or strategic responses either. No one had anticipated the speed of this process, and we certainly did not want it. But the reason we did not want it had nothing to do with the preservation of socialism, whatever that may be.

You have said in one of your earlier interviews that the term socialism was not of much use anymore, because it was utterly corrupted by the party . . .

Yes, in this sense we had learned from the other Eastern European opposition movements. Václav Havel captured this best when he once said that the idea of socialism, for which generations of people went to jails and risked their lives, has turned into nothing more than a police truncheon.[22]

22. The actual citation reads "'socialism' was transformed long ago into just an ordinary truncheon used by certain cynical, parvenu bureaucrats to bludgeon their liberal-minded fellow citizens from morning until night, labeling them 'enemies of socialism' and 'anti-

And in this very sense "socialism" was no longer a term on which we could possibly build a concept or a plan for the future. Of course, this did not mean to us that the values which were historically connected to the international socialist movement were passé. It certainly did not mean that.

What we tried to do, and you can read about this in our journals, was to find a different term in order to capture these values: we called it "solidaristic society" [solidarische Gesellschaft].[23] We tried to restore a certain valuable substance of the socialist tradition, something that was, of course, part of other traditions as well. But we had certainly separated ourselves from any attempts to define our own ideas and goals solely within the parameters of Marxism. Of course, all of us responded to the situation in slightly different ways, but at least in our group we had pretty much dropped the Marxist paradigm. . . .

You are probably the foremost expert on Eastern Europe within the opposition. How would you compare the developments in East Germany to the ones in Poland and Czechoslovakia? I have read in one of your articles that you called the period between 1953 and the late '80s in East Germany the "Ice Age" compared to other Eastern European countries. Could you explain that?

Yes, generally speaking I think very little had happened in the GDR. If you look at Poland, for example, workers had their first big strikes in 1956, which resulted in a number of important structural changes. Among other things, they managed to create a relatively open press, they had certain political clubs that could organize relatively freely, the church obtained more liberties, the collectivization of farms was reversed, and so on. The people who were part of the clubs of the Catholic intelligentsia—Prime Minister Tadeusz Mazowiecki [original advisor to shipyard strikers 1980 in Gdansk; defeated in his bid for the presidency by Solidarność leader Lech Wałęsa in 1990] came out of these clubs—and those who later represented part of the Solidarność movement by forming the intellectual leadership of the movement were already dissidents in 1956. Of course,

---

socialist forces.' " In Václav Havel, "Words on Words," *New York Review of Books*, 18 January 1990, pp. 5–6.

23. The more appropriate translation would actually be "communitarian"—a word, however, which progressive German political activists, in both East and West, try to avoid because of its highly problematic connotations in German history. Ever since 1871 the far right in Germany, including the Nazis, has routinely invoked the "Community," the "Community of German People" [Deutsche Volksgemeinschaft], or, like the fascists in the thirties, the "Aryan People's Community" [Arische Volksgemeinschaft].

they could not do much at the time. But they had, for example, a small symbolic circle of representatives in parliament.

We experienced nothing comparable. And Czechoslovakians generated an event in 1968 which would subsequently shape an entire generation of citizens. There is a very vivid memory in Czechoslovakia of the 1968 revolution. Nothing happened here at the time, so we more or less lost a whole generation.

What about Solidarność in Poland, a movement which, if I understand it correctly, was almost completely organized by workers themselves . . .

. . . Yes, the next big event was in Poland in 1980. This was a very significant movement in which large portions of the intellectual dissident movement that existed throughout the Eastern Bloc joined large portions of the working-class movement. Even though the initial thrust of the movement had mainly to do with social problems, a wide-scale democracy and human rights movement followed immediately in its wake.

So suddenly there was, throughout Polish society, a structure in which certain ideas found a receptive audience. And these ideas, in turn, were defended by large segments of the population during the era of martial law. All of this combined created a strong oppositional tradition in Poland, and it led to the incorporation of all sorts of sectors of society into the oppositional struggle.

There was a long period of oppositional activity, in other words, which one could structurally rely on at the time when the party was finally defeated and when it was time to begin actually to implement the transformation into some kind of democratic society. In our case it was very different; here, everything happened much more quickly. We were forced to act during a period when we were not yet ready to act, because we had no organizational structures that were in any way sufficiently developed. . . .

Could we say that the difference was not so much that intellectuals were better organized or had different ideas in Poland, but rather that Poland saw the emergence and successful building process of a massive working-class movement that was largely self-generated?

Well, there is no question that the working-class movement was much better organized in Poland than in the GDR. But it is not true that the intellectuals in the GDR had similar ideas to their counterparts in Poland. Intellectuals here were thinking much more within a left paradigm, within the concept of a "third way." They wanted to "improve socialism." This did not only have to do with the German-German conflict, but also with the lack of experience that I was talking about earlier. You see, the Czechs buried their hopes for a democratic socialism after 1968. The Poles also talked about "workers' self-management" and similar things in the context of the early Solidarność movement. But after 13 December [1981, the day martial law was declared in Poland], this was also passé. After that, even the intellectuals realized that this was the wrong route to take. "Project Socialism" had simply not passed the historical test. To be sure, we should not betray all of the values that are associated with the socialist movement; quite the opposite. But in order to fulfill the values and visions of socialism, we need radically different structures, we need a democratic state. And this line of argument was much clearer in the other Eastern European nations.

But is that not a little too much of a fixation on the term socialism? It is correct that a Bronisław Geremek [medieval historian, chairman of the 1980 Solidarność action program, prominent Solidarność member of parliament], a Jacek Kuron [founder of the Polish opposition group KOR, *minister of labor in the Solidarność government], or a Václav Havel do not call themselves socialists, but on the other hand they may be representing many of the ideas and values that the opposition in East Germany came to call "democratic socialism."*

Well, yes, but it does make a big difference in our context whether one still declares him/herself to be a socialist or not. Large portions of the opposition in the GDR did exactly that, even within the church. Almost everyone was talking about improving socialism—in other words, the route Gorbachev was perceived to be taking.

I see. What I still don't quite understand, however, is whether you think this represents a substantial difference, a difference in political goals and concepts, or rather more of a tactical/stylistic difference?

No, I really think it is a substantial difference. And that may have to do with the fact that we did not have any national tradition. It was always our dilemma that we wanted to "reform the state." Yet this state had not emerged out of a national tradition, but instead was a political creation. Its basis for legitimacy was the supposed so-called "antifascist consensus of all democratic forces."

This consensus, if it had ever existed like that, certainly no longer supported this kind of state. Yet the opposition was operating on the basis of this consensus as well, for the simple reason that you could not abolish what you wanted to reform. Therefore, we were continuously under pressure to hold on to "socialism" as the only legitimacy of this state, in clear distinction to the Federal Republic of Germany.

We never succeeded in resolving this dilemma. Only now, in retrospect, do we realize that the foundation on which we had based our political concepts was already irreversibly eroded; in fact, it was completely devastated. Look, for example, how many members of the opposition still said during the Fall of last year that they fully supported the foreign peace policies of the GDR. And just shortly thereafter, we found out how high-ranking party officials had traded in arms with anyone who was willing to pay in hard currency, such as both Iran and Iraq, and that with full knowledge of the entire party leadership.

In short, everything one ever heard or feared concerning the corruption of the party was far surpassed by the reality as it came to be revealed. The degree of hypocrisy on the part of party officials was simply overwhelming.

In other words, you are saying that there was still a large degree of illusion about the party among the members of the opposition?

Yes.

In addition to that, I guess, any opposition within the party, to the extent it ever existed, never went public and never tried to establish any contacts with the opposition outside of the party?

That's exactly right. That's precisely what was missing in the GDR. Again we could compare this to Poland. In Poland one finds much more distinct social milieus—the farmers, the workers, the intelligentsia. Those are very distinct, very different social formations. This kind of social differentiation did not exist in the GDR to any comparable degree.

On the other hand, we had much sharper boundaries within a particular social formation, like among the intellectuals, between those who belonged to the party, and those who were in the opposition, and those who were somewhere in between. Those boundaries were clearly marked, much more clearly than in Poland.

Here, there was virtually no communication between those groups. We also had virtually no one who was willing or capable of mediating between those groups. In countries like Poland, people from these different groups or factions, if you like, at least still talked to one another. The command structures of the GDR system—again something very German—simply functioned much more effectively. It would have been unthinkable in the GDR that someone like Adam Michnik [Polish opposition activist, journalist, and political strategist] could be in prison and yet still be able to write manifestoes that actually reached the outside. The repressive apparatus worked much better in the GDR, there is no question about that.

■ HANS MODROW, last communist prime minister in East Germany.
▮ *"It had already become clear by the late '70s that things could not go on like that."*

Before becoming the last communist party prime minister of the GDR on 13 November 1989, Hans Modrow had come to represent the hopes of all those who either wanted to continue a party-led form of socialism in the GDR, albeit in a reformed and democratized fashion, or those who could simply not yet fathom a future for the GDR "beyond the party." A quiet and principled man, Modrow had won sympathy among many citizens for his modest life-style and his reformist political views. For a time, party members and nonparty members alike saw prospects for him becoming a possible Gorbachev-like figure for East Germany.

Hans Modrow was born in 1928. He learned to be a machine fitter and toolmaker. During the last years of World War II he was drafted into the German army and was subsequently captured as a POW by the Soviets in 1945. In 1949 (the year in which the German Democratic Republic was formally founded on the Soviet-occupied territory of Germany), he joined the SED (Socialist Unity Party), which had been founded in 1946 as a product of the Soviet-dominated merger of the former Social Democratic Party and the Communist Party.

From 1953–61 he was chairman of the East Berlin district leadership of the FDJ (Free German Youth, the official SED youth organization); from 1961–67 he was secretary of the SED district leadership of Berlin-Köpenick, and from 1967 on he was a member of the SED Central Committee.

During this time, he acquired a diploma in social sciences from the SED party school, a diploma in economics at the University of Economics in East Berlin, and he received a doctorate in economic sciences from Humboldt University, East Berlin—all through correspondence degree courses.

After Erich Honecker became first secretary general of the SED, Modrow took over the chairmanship of the Department for Agitation at the SED Central Committee. In 1973 he became the first secretary of the SED district leadership in Dresden. Ever since that time he has apparently been a controversial figure in the SED, praised by some for his reform-mindedness and modest life-style, criticized by others for his lackadaisical support of the central party leadership. He was the only first district party secretary in the GDR never to be nominated for the Politburo.

On 7 October 1989 he decided to be the first party district leader to consent to negotiations with the opposition in Dresden. Soon thereafter he was widely considered to be a likely reform-minded candidate for a central party leadership position. On 13 October he was nominated and elected prime minister, assumed leadership of the government, entered negotiations with the Federal Republic of Germany (West Germany), and prepared the ground for unification. In March of 1990 Modrow was the leading candidate for the PDS, which captured slightly more than 16 percent of the overall vote in the GDR.

After a total of 14 telephone conversations with Modrow's advisors and secretaries, all of whom showed little interest in setting up an interview appointment for me, I finally convinced one of his aides to let me speak to him on the phone. Modrow immediately consented to an interview and said he would try to "escape" for half an hour from the then ongoing parliamentary debates concerning a new constitution. I should come to one of the conference rooms of the PDS at the People's Assembly [the East German parliament] on the following afternoon, 20 July 1990.

The energy he devoted to the interview seemed to suggest that he had for many months simply been too busy to "think out loud" about the underlying realities informing the tumultuous events in East Germany, that he knew it was important to do so, and was, in fact, determined to seize the opportunity to do so. Despite frequent interruptions by his aides that "time was up," he continued to talk to me. As he put it when dispatching, once again, one of his aides from the room, "I have not yet answered all this gentleman's questions."

The following interview portrays a man in conflicted transition—from being a leading representative of an extremely authoritarian yet nominally socialist system, to a person striving to be a mediator between the old and the new. My impression was that Modrow had still not quite realized that his and his party's time as a leading force in the country had passed for good. The categories in which he seemed to be thinking, and through which he expressed himself, were obvious derivatives of the old system. Yet he was also clearly struggling not to be left behind by political dynamics that were emerging, for the first time in the history of the GDR, from sources completely divorced from the party. Unlike many of his former comrades, Modrow was enough of a realist, however, to acknowledge that some kind of fundamental rethinking of former party premises was imperative in order not to lose touch with a rapidly changing political environment.

It is almost unavoidable to consider him more of a pragmatist than a creative thinker, for Modrow has continued to focus his attention on tactical adjustments rather than on a fundamental rethinking of long-internalized beliefs about "society." Despite these limitations, the following interview represents, in my opinion, an extremely instructive example of the particular kind of thinking typical of reform-minded Eastern European communist functionaries.

In addition, Modrow here makes a telling effort to help "somebody from the West" comprehend the goals and responsibilities of the last communist prime minister in the GDR. It was striking to discover in this respect that his thoughts seemed to be governed less by a sense of "political opening," than by an immobilizing preoccupation with the presumed constraints on the newly acquired democratic possibilities. He apparently found it very difficult to think outside the boundaries of the party, boundaries to which he had become deeply habituated over the last forty years.

At the time of the interview, July 1990, the situation in the GDR had drastically deteriorated. In many sectors of society, dislocation and bitterness had replaced the joy of newly gained freedom; observers were predicting up to 50 percent unemployment by the end of 1991;[24] and the bargaining power of the East German government vis-à-vis their West German counterpart was rapidly moving toward zero.

Whatever Modrow's vision of a new East Germany might have been, it certainly would not become a reality. Meanwhile, the party of which he was honorary chairman, and which he led in parliament, found itself under severe attack from all quarters. The political left questioned its credibility, the right saw it as a last remnant of Stalinism, while the Social Democratic center, in fear of much-needed percentage points in its electoral race with the Christian Democratic government, wanted to see the party destroyed as quickly as possible. Complicating matters still further, the PDS provided an easy and much-welcomed target for everyone who needed a villain on whom they could blame the "whole mess." By the summer of 1989, East Germany seemed to consist mainly of "victims." Responsibility, one was told, rested with "those in the party." Even some of the busiest former defenders of the system now preferred to portray themselves as people who "had actually been oppositionists all along."

In this situation, Hans Modrow was the last of "the old guard" of party leaders who could still play anything remotely approaching a significant political role, and he gave no indication of wanting to leave the political stage anytime soon.

---

24. The actual figure turned out to be in the vicinity of about 35 percent, even though the official statistics only showed between 12 and 14 percent, effectively concealing those citizens out of work who continued to be listed as "short-time" workers or employees.

■ *First of all, I would like to ask you a question that will probably strike you as somewhat unusual. As a social historian and a student of social dynamics, I am particularly interested in early beginnings of social change. Since you had just reached adulthood in 1945, you have consciously experienced the 40 years of East German existence. Do you remember any forms of organized political dissent in those 40 years—which does not necessarily mean against the party or the state, but just any form of oppositional collective self-assertion before 1988–89?*

To the extent to which there may have been structures in East Germany that one could directly call "forms of organized opposition," I wouldn't be able to characterize them because I never, due to my positions in the party, participated in anything like that.

Wherever I myself tried to think about forms of opposition, like when I attempted to establish contact with like-minded people, I never really succeeded. That was mostly due to the fact, at least ever since the eighties, that I represented for others the kind of person with whom oppositionists certainly did not want to be seen. . . .

Did you have any contact with people outside of the party?

No, I did not have any contact with outside oppositionists.

How do you explain your special role in the party as a person who is widely perceived to be a reformer?

Well, there are different reasons. For one thing I cannot deny that for a long period of time I had reservations about a number of developments in the country, particularly in terms of the interpretation of our particular brand of Marxism. After all, that was our worldview, and it still plays a very important role in our thinking. I was simply convinced that its contemporary implementation did not meet the requirements of its objective scientific character. . . .

Secondly, I did things like protecting the director of the Dresden theater, Gerhard Wolfram, against unfounded charges concerning a political counterplatform that had ostensibly emanated from his theater. . . . It was unprecedented that the district party secretary protected someone like Wolfram so that he would not have to bear the brunt of the accusations. You see, I assumed responsibility for a controversy that went all the way up, instead of blaming everything on the theater. Such things all left impressions that contributed to the image of me as a party reformer.

Did you ever have any contacts with reformers or dissidents within the party? For example, as you may recall, in 1978, after Bahro had been expelled, there appeared a letter criticizing the party in a fundamental way, written by party members, calling themselves "the alliance of democratic communists." Did you have contact with these people or did you at least know who they were?

No, I did not know any of them. I can also understand why they did not attempt to contact me because, after all, I was too much a part of it all. My contact was more with reformers at Humboldt University. . . .

Could you quickly describe your reaction in 1985 to Gorbachev and to the beginnings of perestroika *and* glasnost *and, connected to that, the very obvious attempts by the East German communist party to foil such developments in the GDR?*

Well, first of all, I want to make it very clear that, at that time, reforms [along the lines of perestroika and glasnost] were very close to my own thinking. . . . I have long had contacts with reformers in Leningrad. . . . There, they had already come up with a concept called "Intensification 90," which was based on the premise that the economy had to be restructured and modernized. Through this channel, I got involved in such ideas very early on. . . . Through all these contacts, the party reformers in the Soviet Union, of course, were conscious of my opinions. I know that Solovjov [first secretary of the CPSU in Leningrad] in particular had talked about me with Gorbachev, with whom I did not have any personal contact until I became prime minister in 1989. Only after I had become prime minister did Gorbachev and I have direct consultations with each other. Yet I knew that my ideas had played a role all along.

It was, of course, obvious that Honecker knew about these contacts. . . . He repeatedly accused me of not having analyzed the Soviet Union "thoroughly enough." He thought that my views were perhaps "blurred" by Leningrad.

So that was his stance toward me. Of course, he knew that I had different ideas from his. My attitude also bore consequences because I never wrote any critical reports about what happened in Leningrad, something other district party secretaries frequently did. So therefore Honecker must have noticed that he could not fully rely on me. . . .

I was always in full agreement with my partners in Leningrad that we should make full use of every possible opportunity for cooperation [on perestroika], but that we should keep our hands out of it at points where it would only lead to conflict. . . .

It was crucial that I could speak Russian with them, and furthermore it was common that we debated these questions on a one-to-one basis, that is, without an interpreter, which is of course also not unimportant concerning such important issues. . . .

In light of current developments, what do you think should have been done in the GDR after 1985 in order to maintain the sovereignty of the GDR and to ensure the continuation of "Project Socialism"?

First of all—and that, of course, also concerns the fate of Gorbachev—

we should have taken much more decisive action following the stagnation of the Brezhnev era. That is to say that the real chances for Gorbachev were also in this early period—I personally think that he lost too much time as well. One can clearly see in retrospect that he was still able to have a great effect on the outside after his rise to power, but on the inside he was dealing with a time-frame that created tremendous problems for him. . . .

But for the GDR, it had already become clear by the late seventies that things could not go on like that. If I look back at my own thinking and conduct, including the reports I wrote to Honecker at the time, then it becomes clear that the late seventies or early eighties definitely represented the point in time where we should have started a fundamental restructuring. Our concept concerning the unity of social and economic policy had already been superseded and should, in my opinion, have been corrected. I say this for the following reasons: first, it meant overburdening the "socialist society"—to use this expression—if the economic performance could not keep up with our programs in the social sphere. This leveling down, to give people something in order to satisfy them without a possibility of challenging them, to implant a mediocrity into society to the extent we did—that could not, in my opinion, continue any longer . . .

. . . so you mean performance-oriented payment, or incentives . . .

. . . Yes, exactly, including the question of how to foster talent. This problem went right across society. Even though people talked a lot about competence, there were too many mediocre figures in leading positions. If I look at the Politburo, for example, who of those people was in any way extraordinary? Mittag [member of the Politburo, responsible for economic affairs], for example, was not at all a strategist, but rather simply a pragmatist, somebody who based the economy on a pragmatic footing but also somebody who never had a strategy, otherwise all of these problems would have become obvious much earlier.

Secondly, it always represented a cheap excuse to claim that our national debt was merely due to the rise in oil prices. This was not the main problem. I once had a one-on-one argument with Honecker about this in which I clearly stated that I did not think it was right to import items such as blue jeans, and that we should instead buy the appropriate machinery to produce denim fabric ourselves in Saxony.

My understanding was simply different. I thought that we should organize production so that we would not have to run up a debt; instead, we should have channeled production to meet whatever consumer demands arose. At Christmas, for example, our production was never ready for consumer demands.

And thirdly, we should have begun to realize that the new developments of glasnost and perestroika were not a phenomenon that applied to the Soviet Union alone—which is not to say that we should have made the mistake of simply copying that model in some sort of schematic fashion. But I think [what was going on in the Soviet Union] should have constituted a starting point for us from which we could have proceeded. But this did not happen—not only did it not happen here but, if you look closely, the other [Eastern European nations] did not really go along either.

You see, this was really always a tremendous limitation of perestroika; even in the current situation, it never entered a creative discourse with the other Eastern Bloc countries. On the contrary, it always resulted in a sort of simplistic, primitive application, . . . but a real creative discussion about the meaning of perestroika simply never occurred. And so Gorbachev has been, up to the present, left alone. . . .

At what point in time did you receive the first clear signals, perhaps even from your own party members, that something had to change fundamentally or the whole thing would break apart?

Beyond a doubt I would point to the mid-eighties for that. At that point it became clear that not only my own thinking favoring change might have a chance, but also that we were right in the middle of a process that clearly required fundamental change.

And how did you try to respond to that?

I responded by trying to point out to the people in my own circle in Dresden, as well as to comrades in the Central Committee in Berlin, that things such as the cult of personality surrounding Honecker and so on did not work. You can easily read in the minutes of the Central Committee meetings over all these years that I, aside from the duties one has with respect to the elected first secretary, never excessively praised Honecker.

Do you think that a change of the leading clique of the party would have . . .

. . . I thought change was absolutely necessary by the mid-eighties . . .

. . . And you thought that a change of leadership would have been sufficient in order to begin implementing structural changes as well?

Well, there should have been people committed to implementing such changes, that is, people who would not have simply continued things as they were. You see, the politics of mere continuation that are now associated with Krenz would not have been sufficient, even back then. . . .

[Ed. Note: In the context of this chapter, "The Troubled Emergence of an Idea," it is clear that serious social initiatives emanated not from the ranks of "party reformers," but rather from oppositionists like Eigenfeld, Wagner, Eppelmann, Bohley, Köppe, and Matzke. The troubled life and thought of Hans Modrow is further pursued in Part II, chapter 5, "The Constraints of a Party-Centered Perspective."]

2 THE PARTY, THE WORKERS, AND OPPOSITION INTELLECTUALS

■ WERNER BRAMKE, long-time party member, chairman of the history department of the Karl Marx University, Leipzig. ■ *"I still had hopes that there might be a chance to save socialism . . ."*

Werner Bramke, though himself a middle-ranking party official, never seems to have aspired to the kind of leading political positions party functionaries like Hans Modrow had been accustomed to for many years. More of a theoretician than a political practitioner, Bramke represented one of the numerous critical yet often rather timid intellectual "believers in the socialist cause" within the party. Like many other GDR citizens from all walks of life, Bramke had continued to hold on to the notion that "while things may not be good, at least in the GDR the first steps toward socialism have been made." This fateful belief, combined with the desire to "play a meaningful role" in the workings of one's society, prevented a host of serious egalitarian-minded people like Bramke from taking a clear stance against the party—year after year, even decade after decade.

Not until the party had effectively collapsed under pressure from both the opposition and from internal corruption did many of its intellectual members finally give up any hope of a party-dominated "socialist renewal." Herein lies the much deeper and more complex tragedy of the twentieth-century history of communism. It is a tragedy which goes back at least as far as the October Revolution in Russia, but one which extended to millions of dedicated and faithful followers of the communist cause in countries all over the world. The root cause of this tragedy lay in strained justifications for the excesses of a strong centralized party—rationalizations turning on the "necessities of survival" in a hostile capitalist environment. Such rationalizations were all the more useful because they were grounded in observable social reality—namely, the stifling social consequences which communists like Bramke could readily detect as the persisting substructure of the capitalist alternative. Whatever problems party members perceived within the communist camp, defecting from it necessarily seemed to involve the abandonment of the struggle for "socialist ideals," for a "free and just society." Worst of all, however, fundamental criticism of "actually existing socialism" seemed to imply acceptance of "capitalist hegemony." The ultimate question posed by these global dynamics thus always generated a numbing dilemma: how far did one "go along" with something that at least promised eventually to build a better alternative to capitalism, to a system that socialists throughout the world agreed could not possibly provide for a humane and peaceful future?

It is clear that professor Bramke in the following interview wanted to convey some sense of the agonizing political dilemmas he had lived with for so many years. It is also clear, however, that he initially harbored many suspicions as to how I would use the information he was trying to convey, or whether I would really be able to understand the complicated intricacies of life under one-party rule in the GDR. Yet doubts and all, it became equally evident that the interview offered him some moments of relief, and that he actually welcomed the opportunity to discuss East German matters with a colleague from the United States.

Bramke's own field of study covers the history of working-class movements in general, and the history of the communist party of Germany in particular.[25] More recently, he also did research on German resistance to National Socialism/fascism. Indeed, it was the latter fact that provided the principal reason as to why I asked him for an interview just months after East German had collectively brought down communist one-party rule.

Despite his willingness to discuss difficult political—and sometimes personal—issues with me, Bramke's responses can clearly be seen as guarded or, at the very least, extremely cautious. Perhaps this was typical for a good German professor. On the other hand recent events, although

---

25. I should note, at the outset, that as this kind of scholarly work took shape in the academic environment of East Germany, he did not, in fact, study "workers" within "the working-class movement." Rather, he studied the emergence of party socialism as the energizing fulcrum of what some elected to describe as an "organized socialist movement." So conceptualized, this research design yields a history of "the working class" that is largely devoid of workers.

not entirely unwelcomed, had left him at a fundamental loss, for not only the party, but with it most of Bramke's deeply-held convictions had collapsed. From one day to the next, an inhabitable environment simply seemed to have disappeared for East German socialists previously associated with the party. Whatever the party's terrible shortcomings, it had at least helped to uphold the legitimacy of the socialist tradition for people like Bramke. After the withering away of both party and state, it was as if his deepest thoughts, whatever had become of them at this point, no longer possessed any usable context in which they could be expressed.

Various non-party students as well as academic colleagues of Bramke told me that "he was one of the few within the party apparatus one could actually talk to, and get along with." Despite his long-time party membership, he seemed to have enjoyed an unusual degree of credibility among dissenting sectors of the university student body and faculty.

Bramke had joined the party in 1956, the year he had turned 18, but also the year of popular unrest in Hungary and Poland.

■ *Could you explain why you joined the party?*

In some ways this goes directly back to the way I grew up. My parents were what you would call Christian conservatives, but, at the same time, very socially minded, which is not a very rare occurrence among German conservatives. From this vantage point it was very easy to end up either with the fascists, or somewhere the opposite of them.

The position of my parents was quite nationalistic, and they thought something had gone fundamentally wrong with German history, but they believed that this could only be corrected if people participated in society on a day-to-day basis. We inherited a Germany which was somehow alien and occupied, yet it nevertheless afforded certain opportunities. And if you want to participate, you have to do that at the very place where you are officially able to. My parents represented an example of that to me, and they passed this understanding on to me. Influenced by school and by reading a lot of literature, I subsequently turned toward socialism—not simply under Marxist auspices, but rather through a turn toward the question of social fairness.

I was always simultaneously an alien as well as an active participant in the party. Alien in the sense that I was never, due to my background, a believer in the party. I was never lured into some kind of Stalin cult. My attitude to this man, as well as to other leading figures, was distant and cold—not hostile, but detached.

Right from the start I had first a mild and then a profound distrust toward the apparatus of the party, but I always believed that even though this was not the best socialism, it was the only one possible for the foreseeable future due to the constellation of external political factors. Therefore, I thought that I had to make the very best of it at the place I worked.

I frequently had collisions with the party, but I also got to know many people in it full of integrity, people who time and again stood by my side and with whom, time and again, I achieved full agreement.

Before we pursue this theme in some specific historical contexts, one preliminary question about what you call "socialism." You just mentioned that as it existed in the GDR it was not the best kind of socialism. Do I understand you correctly, however, that you did or do think it was some kind of socialism nevertheless?

No, this is just the way I saw it back then. My reasoning was simply that another kind of socialism has never existed anywhere else. It is a kind of socialism that is, of course, very much shaped by the occupying power [the Soviet Union]. Therefore, one had to try, within those conditions, to make use of the foundations of this society—which did have a little to do with socialism—and to wait until a comprehensive reform movement would become possible.

It was quite obvious to me relatively early on, from the early to mid-sixties on, that this kind of socialism—in practice and in theory—was rather far removed from Marx's intentions. So it is not as if I could claim I was being lied to. My attitude was very pragmatic: I said to myself, "a few elements of socialism are in place," for instance the socialization of the means of production—even though it was a very formal kind, which in reality was state ownership. Nevertheless, it was a beginning.

Another example: there was something like an equalization of previous class differences; the differences in social status between people were actually narrowing. And, again, the fact that there was not only decreed solidarity, but also real solidarity among people. Therefore, I said to myself, "I will make use of these conditions."

In terms of different kinds of socialism, what was your reaction to Hungary in 1956 or Czechoslovakia in 1968?

In regard to Hungary I did not yet detect a different model of socialism, but rather simply a political rebellion against oppression. At the time I simply did not know enough about Hungarian theoreticians.

But all of this was very different in 1968. I and many of my friends watched the events in Czechoslovakia with great sympathy, and the outcome of 1968 represented a great shock to me. In retrospect, ever since the mid-eighties, I see 1968 as the most decisive year, a year after which a reform of socialism, I think, no longer was possible. At the time, of course, I did not quite understand that. Not until 1985, when I realized that the other countries of the socialist camp did not go along with the reform process that Gorbachev had initiated, did I understand that the results of 1968 now made it impossible to make use of the unique chance offered to us by the rise of Gorbachev in 1985. But, of course, I unfortunately realized that about 17 years too late.

If you characterized 1968 as the last and missed opportunity, how would you characterize 1980/81 with Solidarność in Poland?

No, Solidarność could not generate the necessary impulses for a reform process that could go beyond Poland, because under Brezhnev's leadership the "socialist camp" was under such a firm grip that a transformation of the entire system was not possible if it only emanated from one country. The only thing one could have hoped for was that a cautious development in Poland would have sent some impulses to others as well. But right from the start, this was a balancing act that could hardly be sustained. So, here again, we had great sympathy for what was going on with Solidarność, we discussed it a lot, but we never had any hope that it could possibly result in a kind of movement we had envisioned in 1968.

But many would see a huge difference between 1968 and 1980–81—that the former was a movement from above, whereas the latter was a movement from below? Solidarność was a movement almost entirely generated by the Polish working class, while the Prague Spring came from intellectual circles inside and outside the Czechoslovakian CP. Therefore, of course, the potential effects of these two different movements on other Eastern Bloc countries were, or perhaps would have been, very different.

Yes. [long pause, continuing until the next question]

Did you see the Polish movement as representing the attempt not only by intellectuals, but actually by large segments of the population, to become engaged in a struggle to overcome the power monopoly of the one-party state? My impression, so far, has been that this understanding did not materialize in East Germany, but rather that anti-Polish resentments, such as "Poles want to strike because they are just lazy," were quite widespread among East Germans. How do you explain that?

Well, this did happen in a few cases, but it was certainly not a mass phenomenon. It caused me a great deal of concern when I heard comments like that. I talked frequently to my brother, who is a coal miner. He worked together with a lot of Polish guest workers. He *did* talk about phenomena like that, but he said that such sentiments were not representative of the majority of workers; instead, most of his coworkers were acutely interested in the kinds of effects Solidarność was having in Poland. I think there were a lot of hopes.

Please do not forget that the resentments, that the clear anti-Polish tendencies until the late eighties, were fed by particular examples that came from experiences with Poles at the workplace, where single negative examples were generalized.

And then, of course, you have to look at the way Poles behaved as consumers. My mother lived close to the border in Cottbus, where I visited her every once in a while. It was indeed very problematic to remain calm at the sight of droves of Poles falling upon the stores. Of course, their conduct was very understandable—if you come from a place where it is hard to get anything, you go to a place where there is more. The reason that the workers from the GDR and from Czechoslovakia—from places, in other words, where one would have expected to see attempts to emulate the Solidarność experience because of old mutual traditions—did not comprehend this, was, first, because they had never been forced to live as poorly as the Poles and, secondly, because we never had any real unions in the socialist countries of the Eastern Bloc. We only had organizations that resembled unions, which means that workers had been disempowered to such an extent, for more than 30 years by that time, that their turning to another union movement would almost have resembled a miracle.

Furthermore, the Poles had one other motive, aside from their extremely low standard of living, which was nationalism; that was not the case in the other countries. In Poland, you find a virulent nationalist consciousness of a kind which you will not find in any other socialist country. Therefore, Poland could not generate the kinds of sparks that the Prague Spring had in 1968. This is not something I merely say in hindsight, just because it happened that way, but because this is the way we talked about it at the time. It was our understanding all along that Solidarność would not—unfortunately not—result in any fundamental changes.

You just said that one of the reasons why East German and Czechoslovakian workers did not feel inspired by the Polish example was because of the 30-year history of disempowerment, having had no voice or representation by real unions. But isn't the same true for Polish workers? They did not seem to be bothered by that, and instead set out to organize their own, independent union. How do you explain that?

Yes. But what you have to take into consideration at this point is the fact that their social conditions were much worse. There was an immediate pressure to change something. . . .

. . . But don't we know as social historians that this "theory of deprivation"

does not always work at all; in fact, in most cases it is not true? Economic and/or social deprivation may be a necessary prerequisite for a social movement, but it certainly is not sufficient. . . .

. . . You are absolutely right. . . .

. . . In fact, in Poland we had two groups of workers who were particularly active: first the unskilled workers who were extremely badly off, and, second, the group of highly skilled workers who seemed to be doing relatively well.

Yes, you are right. But on the other hand, it is also true that need makes one inventive [Not macht erfinderisch], even in the organizational sense.

And there is yet another factor, aside from the nationalist factor, which is that Solidarność, from the very beginning, was not only a social organization, but also one in which very strong tendencies toward a nationalist democratization could be found. And, as one last factor, we have to take into consideration the role of the church. Wałęsa was not only a faithful son of the church, but the church generally played a very important role in the growth of Solidarność. Again, these are factors that did not have that kind of importance in other socialist countries.

Well, this would be a long discussion. I think that the role of the church, the role of the national question, and, not least of all, the importance of intellectuals in the organization of Solidarność are all vastly exaggerated at the expense of a sustained analysis of the decisive role of workers' own efforts in making this movement possible.

I do not want to doubt that, but still, the reason that the movement could reach the kind of depth and size it did had decisively to do with these other factors. Solidarność would otherwise possibly have remained an ephemeral phenomenon.

Of course, what also played a decisive role in the case of the GDR and of Czechoslovakia were the negative prior experiences with 1953 and 1968. Poland also had something like that, in 1956, but that did not have such far-reaching effects. And after 1956, Poland opened up, which is extremely important for the later development.

And, one more comment about the nationalist component: the Poles knew, despite their rampant anti-Semitic and anti-Russian sentiments, that the Soviets were forced to grant the Poles special conditions as the link between the USSR and the western outpost of East Germany.

But in what ways did that concretely manifest itself in the day-to-day life of the vast majority of Poles?

Well, the Polish man in the underground or in the union could easily figure out that his room for maneuver was somewhat bigger than that of his German or Czechoslovakian counterpart.

Perhaps we could move on at this point. Would it be correct to say that 1980/81 with Solidarność was also very important in terms of understanding how Gorbachev became possible in the Soviet Union? In many conversations I recently had with East Germans, the rise to power of Gorbachev in 1985 seemed to have been a tremendous source of hope. People seemed to think "if the same things that Gorbachev is initiating in the Soviet Union begin to happen in the GDR, then we will be content with this kind of socialism." What was your opinion about and attitude toward all this?

Well, of course, I also had a lot of hopes that if the same kinds of changes were to occur in the GDR, we might actually have the chance to build a kind of socialism that actually deserved the name. Why? Quite simply because I thought the GDR is a much smaller country, it has an infinitely more favorable social and economic infrastructure, we have a much older democratic and socialist tradition, and in the GDR the example of the West plays a much more decisive role in pushing us forward—we were always forced by the West German example to push forward if we wanted to have any chance of survival; it had always represented a challenge of the first degree.

On the other hand, I did not think that it could be a reform movement that would only expand the room to maneuver a little, but instead it was clear to me that it would have to be a reform movement that would have to push toward a "third way," a movement that would break open the existing structures and move toward a pluralist society. This one-party model without any real opposition had to be the death of *every* democracy.

Furthermore, we definitely would have needed the formation of real industrial unions, because a modern society cannot exist without the interplay of different [social and economic] forces. All of that I clearly saw. But what I did not take into consideration was this: in 1985, when Gorbachev rose to power, I still thought the party could be reformed. I knew that the top tier could not be reformed; neither could the second highest tier; but I counted on a third and fourth tier that could quickly reproduce itself, and I did *not* expect that the first and second layer would be strong enough to prevent this from happening.

But by 1987 it became strikingly obvious that this kind of reform inside the party would not take place. And at this point in time I began to lose hope. The only hope I still had was that a change of leadership could still bring about a sudden enough push from below that an explosion could still be prevented. Not until December of 1989 did I entirely give up this hope. Since then it has been clear to me that the path toward a fundamental reform of socialism did not exist anymore—socialism was dead for the foreseeable future. . . .

You stated earlier that while you did not agree with the existing kind of socialism, you still thought that there were people in the party who not only shared most of your views, but with whom a reform would have been possible from within the party.

Yes.

Do you still see it that way, and, if so, could you give me specific examples as to how and with whom such reforms were attempted within the apparatus of the party?

We have, I think, quite successfully attempted to establish some kind of democracy within the ivory tower, which is to say that we were quite successful in creating a relationship between colleagues, and between students and scientists, that could very well be described as democratic.

For example, we never had any witch hunts of dissidents around here. We never dealt with applications for exit visas restrictively, but instead very reasonably. And, of course, when students approached us with complaints about particular scholars, we always successfully attempted to reestablish contacts between the students and those scholars, and that without giving orders. Instead, again through the party, we said "please, dialogue is essential," and usually dialogue is what followed.

Or, let's just take the critical year before the "Wende," a year that was very much shaped by the ban of *Sputnik* [a journalistic voice of critical Soviet reformers] in the fall of 1988, which led to a dramatic eruption. We did not suppress this eruption of outrage by the students, but rather encouraged it. We also tried to help find ways of allowing this eruption of anger and outrage to reach the outside, so that it could be debated freely on the inside. We had a student newspaper here, for example, and we had to fight hard in order to get permission for its publication, and it got published. Of course, we tried to steer the students toward thinking within the parameters that were available, but without ever telling them what to do. So those are a number of factors that allowed us to say to ourselves that we had, under the existing circumstances, made an effort to create democratic relations around here.

When you say "we," you are referring to party comrades within the department of history?

Yes, party members in the department. Similar things happened, however, during the monthly meetings of the department directors with the president of the university. The president allowed all these efforts and discussions to take place. In fact, he supported them. I remember very well the meeting of the department directors right after the *Sputnik* ban. I was the first to bring up this issue, and I said "I am ashamed of this measure. I cannot understand the substance of this ban nor do I agree with the reasoning behind it." Not one word of criticism was uttered in response to what I had said. And when a number of department directors asked for a decision that supported the students, instead of suppressing them, the leadership of the university agreed and supported this policy against the explicit will of the district party leadership.

But I have to say that many did not make use of the relative openness that existed at this university—in fact, we could have done a lot more. The following months, of course, were very difficult, because we were subjected to a barrage of attacks from the party district leadership and from the Central Committee. The kind of unrest that could be found here existed at other universities as well. In Leipzig, however, we had the largest social science potential; we conducted the training program for Marxism-Leninism teachers. Thus the comrades in Berlin got so nervous because the most severe protests emanated from the very department in which Marxism-Leninism was taught. Which is, somehow, very understandable, because those were the people they thought they could really rely on, and now it turned out they could not. Many of us tried hard during this time to move together and to provide mutual support for each other in order to prevent an atmosphere of denunciation and hopelessness at the university. We did not always succeed, but we earned respect for our attempts, even among students.

Let me ask you in this context: as an outsider it is, of course, sometimes very difficult to evaluate such a situation correctly. Does what you just told me pretty much describe the possibilities and limits of what could be done inside the party? And, was that in any way sufficient for somebody like you, somebody who is politically active and who perceives himself as a critical democratic socialist?

Well, of course not. I reached these limits and asked myself this question repeatedly. Ever since 1961 (which represented an outstandingly negative experience for me) I got into situations like this at least five or six times. Each time I asked myself whether I should not leave the party. Every time I wondered what I would do if I resigned—I would automatically become a dissident, and as a dissident I would automatically be pushed into a fundamentally antisocialist position. Anything else would be an illusion. I had always admired those who still defined themselves as socialists but who were, in effect, expatriated. Their situation was just hopeless. They might still have been able to help the opposition in some ways, but they could not do it in terms of socialist impulses. That is precisely what my problem was time and again.

There was only one time that I acquired a genuine dropout mentality, which was in 1984. I had not been a so-called "travel cadre" ["reliable" exponents of the party who were allowed to travel on certain occasions]. I also knew that I had been considered to be a "risk factor" for quite some time and that I had been systematically spied on, but I did not know exactly why. I was not so much concerned about my travel privileges. But since I was called upon—in fact, was instructed—to work as professor for the "socialist cause," and since I, furthermore, had been a party member for 30 years, yet apparently was still looked upon as a risk factor by the party . . . that was something I just could not and would not tolerate anymore. At this point, after so many years of party membership, I was just worn out, and I decided to ask the minister for education to recall me from my position. I had already made plans as to how exactly I would resign, and how I would do a few things afterward as a private scholar.

At the time, I tried to talk myself into believing, particularly when I approached the first party district secretary about this, that it was some kind of resistance. But when I received the notification—completely opposite to my expectations, because they usually did not meet such requests but rather repressed them—that I would be a travel cadre from now on, I was not happy; I was deeply disappointed. That is when I realized that I had developed a deep dropout mentality.

Could you describe the communicational processes inside the party for me? I suppose you continuously tried to find comrades who might have shared your problems and views and who pushed the limits as much as you did. And, in connection with that, I would like to ask you whether you knew anything about the open letter of the so-called "Alliance of Democratic Communists" within the SED, and whether you had read and discussed, in this context, the book The Alternative *by ex-party member Rudolf Bahro?*

In our party organization, and sometimes even beyond that, we had very open discussions. Practically nothing was taboo. So that was one of the ways to discuss things and to find out about others. On the other hand, I had many friends, some of them party members, but most of them not in the party. Most of our conversations were dominated by political discussions, which could not be avoided. So you knew who was in agreement, who opposed you. Of course, we heard about the "Alliance of Democratic Communists," but I did not have any contacts with them. I tried to get in touch with them, but it was not possible. Bahro, of course, we debated intensely. Such things did take place, but there were no contacts with organized groups in or outside the party—informal discussions is all we had.

So would it be correct to say that you had made up your mind right from the start that any contacts with radical democrats, socialists, communists, Marxists, or other dissidents outside the party would automatically cost you your position in the party, and thus your job?

No, that's not quite correct. I would have risked losing all that, but these contacts just never took place. I am not quite clear why they did not. It may have had something to do with Leipzig as well. Here, any contacts with oppositionists did not occur until about late 1988. In Berlin this happened much earlier, but I had very few personal contacts with people in Berlin. I also had problems as an atheist in finding contacts with the circles organizing from within the Nikolai Church in Leipzig. . . .

. . . *But there were a number of atheists in those circles all along. . . .*

. . . Yes, and I knew that, but I still felt a strong resistance. I felt this would be a misuse of the church.

On the other hand, I have talked to Protestant pastors in the GDR for whom one of the main reasons for joining the church and becoming pastors had been the fact that they were socialists, but the kind of socialists who would never be able to find a home in the Socialist Unity Party. . . .

. . . Well, I knew some Protestant pastors, I had some contacts with pastors, mainly through professional channels, and those were very different from what you just described. They were all strongly believing Christians, very critical, but with plenty of reservations toward the opposition movement. So this stood in the way toward further contacts with the church.

How much did you know about oppositional activities by socialists and communists in Berlin, such as Women for Peace with Bärbel Bohley and Ulrike Poppe, or the Initiative for Peace and Human Rights, also an organization founded and organized by people who saw themselves as socialists or communists.

Initially, I found out about these groups from the Western media, mainly through the Deutschlandfunk [a radio news program that was widely listened to, particularly between 5 A.M. and 8 A.M.]. I always tried to make arrangements so that I could listen to their early morning news program. I did this for many years. So I knew about these groups, but I had an ambivalent attitude toward them. Generally speaking, I followed their activities with sympathy, because I perceived them as a possible beginning of a democratic opposition movement with which it might have been possible to build bridges. On the other hand, some of their positions caused me to remain distant from them. Part of the reason for that might have been that we did not have any personal contacts; thus, I only had intermediary experiences of them.

Could you give me an example or two of positions or ideas of theirs with which you disagreed?

Well, I was especially irritated by the January demonstration in 1988. Because I knew that the people who were using the words of Rosa Luxemburg there were either doing so simply as a means toward some ulterior motive, or out of a fundamental misunderstanding of Rosa Luxemburg and her ideas [oppositionists and would-be émigrés joined the official demonstrations commemorating Rosa Luxemburg and Karl Liebknecht in Berlin and carried banners with Luxemburg's famous phrase "Freedom is always the freedom of the one who thinks differently"]. And then I was very bothered by the positions of the then most vocal representatives, Freya Klier and . . . I forget . . .

. . . *Stephan Krawczyk* . . .

. . . Right. I just got a very clear impression that their positions were not socialist positions. In retrospect, I have been asking myself, particularly because I have extensively dealt with the resistance to the Nazi regime, whether it would not have been necessary for me to say "socialism should not play a role in this. Should I not seek contact with virtually everyone who is standing up against this ossified dictatorial system?" But back then I did not see it like that, because I still had hopes that there would be a chance to save the underlying tenets of socialism by turning over the system completely with the help of a reform movement.

I have a little problem with this. Again you are arguing with the term "socialist" despite the fact that you admitted earlier that the very term itself had become highly problematic in the context of the GDR, because nobody knew any longer what it was supposed to mean. To call members of this opposition "non-socialist" strikes me, quite frankly, as somewhat awkward if it comes from somebody who had been a member of the SED for 30 years and thus had, at least to some extent, identified himself with the policies of that party—policies that would also not pass any serious test of being "socialist." Isn't this distinction a very complicated one?

Well, no, let me put it this way: among those forces I did not even perceive a starting point for what is commonly referred to as a "third way."

I don't exactly know whom you are referring to if you speak of "forces," but it is my understanding that the vast majority of people in the Initiative for Peace and Human Rights, for example, would much more easily pass the test of being socialist than most SED members. Perhaps you could give me an example as to what specifically you would include as "socialist" by your yardstick?

The most decisive element concerns the political moment. Precisely when some of these people ran into conflicts with the state, they made use of means and medias which were unequivocally against this state, namely the Western media. This, for me, was the threshold they had passed.

You don't think this was a legitimate means?
For them, yes, but not for me at that time.
How would you evaluate that from today's perspective?
If I were confronted with the same situation again today, I would probably not respond very differently. Today I know that this crippled form of socialism could not have been reformed, but at the time I still thought it might be possible—actually more than just reform it, namely, to turn it upside down. Therefore, my position was that people who call themselves socialists, but on the other hand work together with a state that is clearly antisocialist, that is, a parliamentary democracy, that they had gone beyond the limits of what I could accept . . .

. . . I am having difficulties following you here: why is making use of their media the same as "working together" with them?
Of course, that is what it means. . . .
. . . Didn't they only make use of Western media because media in the GDR was simply not available to them?
Sure, but those who did this should have known that using outside forces that push the state to the edge of survival necessarily preempts any opportunity for an interior reform process. It would have been an illusion to assume that you could be in communication with the Western media and the political public in the Federal Republic of Germany on the one hand, and simultaneously pursue a socialist goal in the GDR.

Could one not reasonably argue that, first, newspapers like the West Berliner "taz" cannot be equated with the capitalist or antisocialist West, and, secondly, that changes or reforms, in the same way as you had hoped for, cannot be achieved without some democratic sphere of debate, without some access to the media? In that sense, was it not much more the attempt to create a debate within the GDR than an attempt to create pressure from without?

The *taz* only played a marginal role in this; I am talking about different media. Everybody should have understood, and the reasonable ones did understand, that anyone who makes use of the entire Western media in order to articulate their opposition will have to forgo any chance of shaping the reform process from within, and particularly from within the opposition itself. Of course, that would never work; there is no doubt about it. The only thing that could be achieved by those means would be the breaking apart of society as it existed, something that we clearly saw later on.

Please take into consideration that anyone who still nurtured hopes that this society could be reformed could only see the use of Western media as a route that could lead to nothing other than the breaking apart of the existing society and its movement toward a bourgeois parliamentary society. And this is exactly what happened. On this issue I was right, whereas on some of the others I was not.

Let me ask you this: would you accept that someone who consciously used this strategy as a means to get a public debate going within the GDR had a fundamentally different understanding of these dynamics from you?

Of course. I *did* understand this. I perceived it as an illusion, however. It was an illusion, just as much as my hopes proved to be an illusion. What comes through clearly here is the fact that all the different camps of the opposition had been sustained mainly by illusions. Some of these illusions were even beneficial for the opposition. I found out through many conversations with oppositionists that many would have backed off had they only seen what would follow after November. Thus, I clearly accept such illusions, because they were productive illusions, perhaps in some ways even more productive than my own illusions. . . .

■ Joint interview with industrial workers at the largest heavy machinery plant in East Berlin. ■ Worker, describing trade union leaders' dazed response to worker's complaints: *"They told me that they did not understand the world anymore"*

In many cases, unbeknown to Protestant pastors such as Eppelmann, academics such as Bramke, or intellectuals such as Mehlhorn, grass-roots groups did not represent the only site of dissent in East Germany. The following joint interview with five workers at a large heavy machinery plant in Berlin explores a different sector of East German life and opposition. The interview took place in August of 1990, one month after the social and currency union with the Federal Republic had been established. It was already becoming obvious that many plants would be closed and hundreds of thousands of workers would lose their jobs.

I arrived at this supposed "pearl of East German industrial achievement" at 9 o'clock in the morning. I told the security guard in a small, shabby booth next to the imposing entry gate who I was and with whom I had an appointment. He wanted to see my ID, nodded, reached for a heavy, black telephone right next to him, and dialed a three-digit number. Then he muttered, "just wait here." So I did. Ten minutes later a man walked across the factory courtyard in our direction, greeted me with a friendly "good morning," and asked me to follow. We soon entered a four-story building, climbed three flights of concrete stairs, and came into a room which apparently was occupied by the factory union representative. Five workers, two women and three men, sat around a table, talking and drinking coffee. Yet the atmosphere seemed formal, as if they had expected some high-ranking official. They had placed flowers on the table and served their coffee using china obviously reserved for special occasions. I began to wonder what, if anything, they had been told about me or about the purpose of my visit.

Through contacts with officials of the new metal workers union IGM, I had asked for a group interview with workers who had been politically active during the revolution, and who could tell me about any possible oppositional activities prior to the Fall of 1989. Who had selected the five workers I now encountered, and on what grounds, I unfortunately had no way of knowing. They, on the other hand, were apparently quite surprised when the man who had brought me in introduced me by saying "here is Mr. Philipsen." It seemed as if I was a bit too young and too casually dressed to meet their expectations of a Western scholar—a circumstance, however, which I think eventually proved helpful during the course of the interview. In any case, after I had shared with them some of my own experiences as a previous metal worker and union activist, we proceeded with the interview in a refreshingly candid and unreserved manner.

The conversation that ensued is in some ways unlike any other reproduced in this book. It has a certain kind of richness that, curiously enough, draws some of its power from its indirectness. It also contains a series of qualifications about things already said that on some occasions deepen the meaning, while on others fundamentally altering it. And there are revealing nonsequitors as well. The discussion of Polish Solidarność, for instance, can only be described as oddly misinformed. Besides revealing a peculiarly German way of condescending to Poles, it also reflects a relatively primitive grasp of the function of workers' strikes in redressing grievances. As one of the workers in this interview said with quiet confidence, Poles "did not want to work anyway, so that is why they started all those strikes and so on." East German workers made similar statements in my presence across the GDR. The significant, and to me unexpected, point here is that the remarkable insurgent Polish institution, Solidarność, apparently had no motivating impact on workers in the GDR. On the contrary, a widespread nationalist pride seems to have prevented many East German workers from acknowledging that anything positive could originate in Poland.

Aside from such qualification, it is necessary to point out that the group of workers in this interview represent what might be called a "distinct range of dissenting opinions." Though some participants in the discussion were loyal party functionaries until quite late in the reform process, others had been more clearly oppositional for many years. The range of responses I received in this interview, I believe, are symptomatic of the crisis which increasingly afflicted the Eastern European communist camp. This interview brings into vivid relief the dearth of information, the lack of open debate, and the pervasiveness of fear throughout East German society. Fundamental problems had been apparent for quite some time, but no one found—or dared to explore—effective ways to bring the ensuing grievances out into the open. As such, the following interview helps explain the dynamics of protest in the Fall of 1989 as much as it illuminates why protest had not become public earlier and why it was so quickly silenced afterward.

Bernd K.: [Born 1935, began his factory apprenticeship in 1950 as a machinist.] Until 1980 I worked as a skilled worker, and, I believe, a darn good skilled worker. In 1975 they "joined me" for the party; they had trampled on my nose for such a long time that I finally said, "Well, hell, why not, they won't leave you alone otherwise." They were interested in me because I was such a good skilled worker, I had received the honorary medal of the GDR for my services as a skilled worker, which was a pretty high reward. I had been a member of the union leadership since 1960. In 1980 they convinced me to give up my work and to become a full-time union functionary. First, I had to go to a special union school, and after I returned I was nominated as vice-chairman of the factory union leadership [BGL].

I quickly realized the hopelessness of our situation, and when the AGL [departmental union leadership] chairman in the department in which I used to work stepped down for health reasons, I decided that it would be better to be chairman in a department I really knew well than to be second in command in a structure in which I couldn't change anything anyway.

But today I also find myself in a situation in which I don't know where to go. Our unions are defunct; the last thing we are supposed to organize is the elections for the factory councils. I am not going to be a candidate again, however. I am too old for all these changes, I can't relearn everything again, I guess that's a job for the younger ones. I have done my duties, and now I can go. I can't retire yet, so I have to figure out some way to survive over the next five years. Maybe I can work as a machinist again, but I've been out of that for more than 10 years now. Well, I've just got to try something.

You see, I only joined [the party] because they worked on me for such a long time. But my basic beliefs came from my experiences in World War II. My family was bombed out three times. My mother died of typhus, and my father was a POW for many years. I got to know this whole misery. So my ideal was socialism, and never again war. I don't really know what happened to it, but the idea, I think, is as good as ever.

Doris C: [Born in 1934, she began her apprenticeship on 5 December 1949 as a lathe operator. Since they did not yet have cranes at the time, work got too hard for her and she was subsequently employed as an assistant engineer. She later finished school in evening courses at the factory and started a special course of study in the economics of mechanical engineering. She was employed in the field of technology from 1953 until 1990 and active in the unions since the time of her apprenticeship. She finished her study in 1972, after which she became a member of the AGL. She was particularly involved in "women's politics, because this was still an area of much unfairness." She became a member of the party in 1976, shortly before her son was arrested for refusing to get divorced from his wife who had angered the party by fleeing to the West.] I immediately wanted to leave the party again. It was a very, very hard struggle for me. I was supposed to become AGL chairwoman, and they told me that this would no longer be possible due to the arrest of my son. I blamed everything on the Stasi. The party, I thought, stood for ideals that I fully supported. So if I had left the party then, I would have betrayed those ideals and acted as if the Stasi was right in claiming that my family and I were unreliable people. Furthermore, I thought that I can do much more for my colleagues if I stay in the party.

I finally left the party in December of 1989.

In 1986 I became chairwoman of the AGL in the department of technology. Now I will be released into early retirement. It's not easy; I have to find some place to work in order to survive. But where is an old person like me supposed to find one now? I simply can't take away a job from a younger person who needs it even more than I do.

Maria C.: [Born in 1940, worked continuously in the same factory from 1954 to the present as an industrial photographer.] I was never a member of the party, but I once was very active as a member of the FDJ [the party-run Free German Youth Association]. I have been an active union member in my work collective for decades.

Was it a problem not to be in the party but to be a union member?

No, not at all. There were always a set percentage of token nonparty union members.

Leonhard B.: [Born 1948, began an apprenticeship as machinist in 1965.] I was always pretty much in sync with the goals of the party. I was born into a so-called "red family." My father was a mayor. I always had a positive attitude toward socialism. During certain times I was a full-time employee of the state apparatus and the unions, in the council of districts [Rat der Gemeinden].

[He joined the party in 1967, after he had finished his apprenticeship, and left the party in 1978 in opposition to the obligatory duty of party members to participate in the "Factory Fighting Groups."] I had always thought that this did nothing but steal our time, making us crawl around in the fields and play war. This whole institution may have made sense in the early sixties, but not today. And only because I refused to participate in this nonsense—I like my weekends, I had a family—they confronted me with the option "party and fighting group, or nothing." So I chose nothing. They argued with me for over a year; it wasn't easy to get out of the party at the time.

Still, I have been shop steward in the brigade ever since I joined it.

Rudi E.: I am assistant chairman of the factory union, born in 1938. We started out poor, my father got killed in the war. After the war my mother was active in the antifascist renewal on behalf of the small folks. First, I learned boiler and tank work, then I studied engineering. For 12 years I worked as a construction engineer of coal-operated energy plants, before I started here.

I joined the party when I was 19. I would define myself as a critical socialist. I experienced the limitations of this system at the workplace. For two years I was departmental union chairman. But somehow not until the Fall of '89 did I begin to see certain things that finally did away with this damn discipline we all had; I have to admit this very frankly.

I don't really know whom to blame; somehow we were all part of this system; it's very hard to delegate responsibility. There were very few like Hans Modrow; he was definitely an exception. I think if all of us had taken more responsibility, things could have turned out a lot better. But after the Fall there was really no point in remaining in the party, so I left in December.

■ *Let me begin by asking you all a question concerning the open letter of*

29 September 1990 that you sent to the chairman of the Free German Union Alliance and member of the Politburo, Harry Tisch. This letter, which is signed by thirty union members of your factory and which is very critical of the party and the union leadership, is the only letter from workers that became public during this critical period. Tell me how you came to write this letter, and whether you know of more documents of this kind.

Doris C.: The only reason this letter became known and had some effect at all was that some of us had contacts in the West, so it was published over there. Otherwise, it would have disappeared where hundreds of other letters have disappeared before it: in the trash. I know of many other people who wrote letters that were even more outspoken and aggressive than ours which made it to Harry Tisch's desk but were never answered.

Please try to explain this to me. I have been in numerous factories by now, in Berlin, in Leipzig, in Magdeburg, and most members of the work force at those places told me repeatedly that there was nothing one could have done. . . .

Maria C.: . . . Nothing was possible because our letters disappeared in the trash. . . . Colleagues have been trying to get heard for quite some time by writing letters. I personally know this from numerous cases.

It really started after the elections in May of 1989. I remember that the day after the elections I accompanied our enterprise director, our factory union chairman, and the party secretary on a tour through the factory during which they congratulated certain colleagues who had been elected. The official results were not yet known.

I just remember that colleague W., or rather then comrade W., had asked "do you already know the results?" Both the enterprise director and the party secretary replied, "Well, we've been to about three polling stations, and in each case the outcome was about 10 to 15 percent no-votes." [Traditionally, results ranged in the upper 90 percent consent, and the elections in May were the first in which it was later proved that at least 10 percent had crossed out the party slate. The party, however, still claimed in the aftermath of the election to have won about 98 percent support.] I was flabbergasted by this response, and so was comrade W. But when we went home the same evening and read the newspapers, the official result was still 98 percent.

Did any of your colleagues participate in the organized attempt by the opposition to send out election observers to all polling stations?

Maria C.: Yes, of course. And later they tried to tell us that the absentee ballots had all been in the party's favor, and this is how the high approval rate could be explained. Of course, we did not believe a word—in fact, we were outraged—and that's when open resistance began.

Rudi E.: Something else that started at the time was that protests took place on every seventh of the month in Berlin, which was the day of the month in which the elections had been held. This was largely organized by church people. But in any case, it was an opportunity every month for people who were dissatisfied to come together. And then, of course, we had this wave of emigrations that picked up tremendously after the vacations had begun.

Let us return to all that in a moment. I would like to know a bit more about these protest letters that fellow workers were writing. Who started all this? Were these individual people, or did you openly discuss these matters?

Maria C.: In our case the entire departmental union leadership organized and wrote the letter and then talked to all the workers in the department about it. We told them what we wanted to do, then sent the letter off after having made some copies for ourselves—one of which we sent to West Berlin, where it got published, and that's why they had to react to it. . . .

. . . Earlier you were talking about other letters as well. . . .

Maria C.: . . . Yes, but written by colleagues from other departments and other factories. . . .

Rudi E.: . . . Yes, from other places. In our case this whole thing was triggered by this letter of 29 September. We immediately informed the chairman of the plant-wide union, and he immediately went to talk to all shop stewards and came out in support of their views. . . .

Leonhard B.: . . . But we should also mention that some of these letters and petitions were posted in individual workshops, and in most cases the supervisors of those departments insisted on these documents being taken down or tore them down themselves, so it's not as if we had not tried to draw attention to our problems earlier. . . .

Rudi E.: . . . But it's simply not true that we had previously published anything in such a form, all we did before was to write internal bulletin board news sheets. . . .

Maria C.: . . . But that had only to do with the repressive measures we had to deal with, the fact that they could find out where a letter or such had been duplicated or copied. I had to give a precise account of every sheet of paper I had used. It's only that this particular letter made it to West Berlin and caused such a scandal, with the security police and the Central Committee involved—they would have liked to tear us to pieces. . . .

Bernd K.: . . . But it is a bit too narrow only to look at this one letter; this whole process had started a lot earlier. . . .

. . . I totally agree, I just wanted to understand the circumstances of this one

*letter and your earlier claim that many such letters had been written by workers
from other enterprises. I have not yet come across an enterprise in which people
told me about writing open letters and such. . . .*

Maria C.: . . . You know, let me tell you this story: comrade [Günter]
Schabowski, party district secretary of Berlin, came to see us, shortly
before Harry Tisch came to see us as well, and he gave a talk in which he
admitted that he received sacks full of letters like the one we had written,
the only difference being that none of the others had ever been published.
He was saying this in the context of calling our decision to send the letter
to West Berlin "an outrageous act." But he did admit to sacks full of letters
and petitions. . . .

. . . Written by individuals, union representatives, whole enterprises?

Maria C.: . . . By individuals, groups, entire enterprises, cooperatives,
and so on. . . .

Rudi E.: . . . And not only from Berlin, but from all parts of the
country. . . .

Bernd K.: . . . Many people also wrote anonymous letters, because they
did not dare to stand up openly to the party. . . .

*. . . Well, this is why I keep coming back to this point. Writing a letter or
petition of open criticism does not exactly represent a small "aside" in the context of
the former GDR. Many citizens and colleagues in the factories have continuously
told me over the last few weeks that "what you have to understand is that there
was nothing we could do, the whole system was too repressive, we could not defend
ourselves," and so on.*

Rudi E.: . . . Well, there were numerous ways and means to carry your
dissatisfaction all the way to the top. The real question was whether such
actions had any results. If you limited yourself to a certain prescribed
format, they accepted small doses of criticism, sometimes even responded
to it by coming to your workplace. But they never openly discussed how
many complaints they had received, what the problems were all over the
country, and how many people were pissed off. Only when they were
about to drown did they begin to admit some of this. Since we were a
major enterprise which also served some kind of "showcase" function, we
frequently had the likes of Mr. Krenz or Mr. Schabowski show up at our
place to show off about their contacts with the "base." We always asked
them very tough questions, but they simply lied to us, or once again put us
off. Our colleague K., for example, at one point asked Harry Tisch
whether he had any privileges, and he responded, "my only privilege is the
car I am allowed to drive in my position." This, of course, was a huge lie,
as we later found out. In other words, they always lied and cheated; they
talked water and drank wine.

Leonhard B.: Take Schabowski, for example. He frequently came to see us at the workplace; he always left the impression that he was genuinely interested in what we were doing, in what our problems were. He actually talked to us, listened to us, so we were foolish enough to think that he could perhaps be a positive force. But later, we always realized that although he had talked to us, nothing ever happened. They completely ignored our problems, and he was a very good example of that.

Doris C.: Just look at our monthly reports. In my position as AGL chairwoman I had to write these monthly reports, answering preformulated questions, and in the last part of the report we were asked to write about the atmosphere and opinions of colleagues at the workplace. I had made very critical remarks since the fall of '88, the time when things began to fall apart. We had deep suspicions that our factory union leadership did not pass on these reports; we had a lot of ugly conflicts about that, yelling at each other and such. We simply thought that things could not go on like that . . .

Rudi E.: . . . You see, we were one of those enterprises that was supposed to report directly to the party. . . .

Doris C.: . . . And then we had joint meetings once a month, called "political arguments"—we called it "red-light treatment" [Rotlichtbehandlung]. All the plant union leaders and the bigger departmental union sections, like ours, were invited to these meetings, and there we began to stand up officially in August of 1989 and protested against the current situation. . . .

Bernd K.: . . . And you have to keep in mind that this was all before everything began to change; we still had to face Stasi harassment. . . .

Doris C.: . . . We stood up and made a lot of noise. At the time, I still tried to calm my colleagues, because I still thought that we would get some kind of response. In October, when everything began to turn upside down, they sent a commission from the Central Committee to us. . . .

Bernd K.: . . . What we did at the time was revolutionary; some of my colleagues don't even know about that. We had another one of these party instruction meetings, and at the end of the debates comrade F. said, "OK, let's adjourn until next time in four weeks." I could not believe it. I stood up and said "I do not agree that we should simply end at this point, carry on as if nothing has happened, that we are simply put off like this again. The situation is so tense that we should, right here and right now, write up certain demands and send them to Harry Tisch." Of course, this meant revolting against our highest official boss, but I immediately had everybody behind me. So some of us got together and formulated a text. We accused our union leadership of incompetence in dealing with our problems, and of corruption. We wanted a new, democratically legitimized leadership. . . .

Doris C.: . . . In September I had already stood up, after they had given us another one of those primitive political arguments and then wanted to prevent any discussion about it, and said: "This cannot be true. We came here to get arguments and facts for our colleagues, in order to be able to discuss matters with them. We have so many problems, and we do not receive any answers here, and all you do is prevent any discussion." And then things blew up. We never received an answer, which is the real reason why we wrote this open letter in the first place. We were outraged at that point. . . .

Bernd K.: . . . I just wanted to say: why did this revolution happen so peacefully? It could only happen so peacefully, not because so many people came together on the streets, but because the whole system was so rotten, was so finished at that point, that everybody, even in the party, all the way up to the central leadership, must have realized that things could not continue like that.

I would really like you to tell me, with some specific examples, what exactly the problems were and how you reacted to them.

Bernd K.: I brought along a monthly report from 20 September part of which I would like to read to you. It was written by me directly to the district union leadership, not via the factory union leadership. "The rank-and-file workers of XXX continue to be worried and angry about the current political situation in the GDR. Despite the fact that we have demanded it for a long time, the media still does not openly report on the reasons why so many of our colleagues have decided to leave the country. On the contrary, the media still reports about 'a broad-scale action perpetrated by the class enemy.' The term 'reform' is still interpreted as synonymous with a 'departure from socialism'"—which is, of course, something that nobody wanted. What we really wanted was to change socialism, but not to get away from it. . . .

Doris C.: . . . That is something we really did not want. . . .

Bernd K.: . . . [continues reading] "It is certain that the 'class enemy' will make use of every weakness in our system in order to prevent the further development of really existing socialism. But all children in a socialist system have already learned in school that revolutions cannot be exported"—what I was trying to say here was that things have to develop internally; you cannot export it. I had to write it like that in order not to go too far for them to be able to digest it. "Our organization, the FDGB [Free German Union Alliance], has always valued the free exchange of opinions. But now I have to assume that the only opinions that reached our leadership were those that fit into their understanding of really existing socialism. That is precisely how we got into the currently existing situation in the first place. There is no doubt in my mind that we can only master the current problems if we openly point out the problems and openly discuss them in public. All of us together have to work step by step in order to find solutions we can all live with. Every day that we ignore certain opinions, or even repress them, is one day too many. This is not just my opinion, or the opinion of the Western media, it is the opinion of the vast majority of all working men and women, whose representative I am. Sincerely Yours, and so on."

So this is what I wrote to the district union leadership. As a result of this letter, I was ordered, together with my BGL chairman, to the union headquarters for a so-called "cadre discussion" two weeks later. They told me that they did not understand the world anymore, I had always been such a good functionary. What had happened to me all of a sudden? . . .

Doris C.: . . . Which is nothing compared to what most other people had to go through. . . .

Bernd K.: . . . Yes, right. This went on until I finally said, "This is enough. You have talked for an hour and a half, now it is my turn. If you do not realize what is going on out there until they [East German workers] begin to break your windows, just put on your coat and go to the factory with me. We'll go through any shop you like, and you can talk to any colleague you like, and you can ask him about his opinion, and you can repeat that as many times as you want. And if you then find out anything other than what I wrote, you can accuse me of being a liar or whatever." This was, of course, also quite risky for me. . . . Political issues were still considered to be items that were too hot to handle.

Rudi E.: We have to keep in mind that we are talking about processes here. In August the big wave of emigrations via Hungary and Czechoslovakia began, and they brought things into the press, such as that people were "abducted by Western agents," and "these are the methods the West is employing". . . .

Doris C.: . . . We had a lot of big laughs at the time about all the ludicrous stories they were making up. . . .

Rudi E.: . . . About people who had been drugged and did not wake up until they got to Vienna. You have to imagine that such things were on the front page of the official party newspaper. They were actually trying to convince us that the West was employing such methods in order to worsen the situation in our country. Of course, we usually found out, as most people had already suspected, that there was no truth to such accounts. But what I was actually trying to point out was that this was their method of telling us that we should not worry, and that we could easily live without those people. We were not supposed to "shed a tear" for those who went to the West and stayed there.

Doris C.: The straw that finally broke the camel's back was Honecker's statement that "we are not going to shed a tear for these people." We were simply outraged, everywhere, young people and old people alike. This statement was just impertinent. Every evening we saw on Western television thousands of young GDR citizens who had fled to the West German embassies or had made it across the border in some way, and then this comment "we are not going to shed a single tear." Actually, that helped spark our letter to Harry Tisch. It was just outrageous; I can't tell you how we felt. . . .

Rudi E.: . . . And back then we still trusted Harry Tisch as somebody who was concerned about our problems, and as somebody who would listen. He had always acted as if he was "close to the people." . . .

Let me ask you at this point: do you mean that your dissatisfaction did not get to the point where you thought that something had to change until mid-1989?

Doris C.: No, the dissatisfaction had been there for a very long time. . . .

Rudi E.: . . . It just vastly increased during 1989. . . .

. . . But what was your dissatisfaction all about? Can you give me examples?

Rudi E.: Well, for example, the election fraud in May 1989. . . .

Doris C.: . . . But before that, the whole issue surrounding permits to visit relatives in the Federal Republic on the occasion of funerals, weddings, confirmations, and so on. Many people never got a permit, so quite a few tried to get out for good. There were many protests here. It was so arbitrary; it pretty much depended on the official you were dealing with. One person got a permit; the next did not.

Rudi E.: Actually, it was pre-decided at the workplace whether somebody received a permit or not. . . .

. . . You mean the party secretary in the factory decided?

Rudi E.: Well, sort of. It started with the workplace supervisor, then it went to the department supervisor, from there it went to the party cadre office, so you already needed three signatures from your workplace. . . .

Doris C.: . . . And then it was totally arbitrary as to how many days they allowed you to go. Then, all of a sudden they changed the law to say that you could only visit relatives in your immediate family, so a husband could not get a permit to visit his wife's aunt, for example. This happened to a good friend and colleague of mine. His reply was that if I am not going to get this permit, I am going to apply for emigration. So we had this meeting with factory supervisors, party secretaries, and the secret police people. I had to attend as AGL chairwoman. I told them, "Please don't do any harm to this man. He has been working in this factory for more than 30 years; he's been a good worker as you all know, and he's been a shop steward for a long time. Isn't he right to be mad?" I said "you can't just change the law any way you want to." All they said was "we have to make our decisions exactly according to the law," and I said, "This can't be true. Are we not a democratic society? How can you pass laws against the people? It just cannot go on like this. If you have to make your decisions according to the law, then you just have to change the law." After that, my friend came into the room, and at least we could prevent repressive measures being implemented against him. But a bit later he fled the country anyway. . . .

Rudi E.: . . . We took a personal exception to all that had happened. . . .

Doris C.: . . . Yes, exactly. So this is just one of many examples of what was driving us crazy. . . .

Bernd K.: . . . Well, and in March, shortly before the elections, they changed the law again, because there was just too much pressure. So then the number of travel trips increased again, and people could see with their own eyes, could make comparisons. You have to understand how completely we were walled in; very few people had been allowed to travel and to see for themselves what the West was like. And those who were allowed usually did not talk about it much because they did not want to risk their chance of getting a permit again. . . .

Doris C.: . . . And sometimes people simply did not believe what they told us after they had returned. Or people were accused of just wanting to bitch and complain about the GDR when they told us how things looked in the West, when they conveyed such golden pictures of the West.

How much and how openly could you, and did you, discuss such matters in the workplace?

Leonhard B.: In the shops we discussed these things a lot.

I guess one thing I still don't quite understand is that there was such a debate about this. After all, you could all receive Western radio and TV, so you should have had a pretty good impression as to how things looked in the West, didn't you?

Doris C.: Yes, everybody watched Western TV. . . .

Bernd K.: . . . But you simply could not imagine the dimensions of it all, the technological level, the availability of consumer goods. I do not want to talk about the social conditions in the West. But whereas we had to wait for an apartment or a house for more than 15 years and had to pay these incredibly overpriced amounts for certain goods, or simply could not get certain basic goods or had to wait for them forever, it was just mind-boggling, at least to me, when I went over there for the first time.

I just want to tell you how we experienced these things. Of course we watched Western TV, saw Western advertisements, and such, but the reality of it all just blew me away. When I went to a home appliance store in the West for the first time, I walked through the aisles and just mumbled to myself, like a senile old man, "This can't be true, this is unbelievable, I must be dreaming." They had all the things I had been trying to get at home for years, and not just in one kind, but in hundreds of variations. I can't tell you how I felt. The same was true with grocery stores. We never had to go hungry in the GDR, never, but we had to stand in line for cheese or meat, and often had no selection, and certain things we just never saw. And if you then went to KaDeWe [located in West Berlin, one of the largest department stores in Europe with one of the best-stocked food departments in the world], you just thought you were on another planet.

Rudi E.: I think the main thing is that we were never exposed to any of this. We were walled in, things were kept away from us, we were lied to. And then, all of a sudden, we realized things could also be done or organized differently, and that's when it all began, when we began to rethink everything. After Honecker had been to West Germany in 1987, there was hope again, and more people were allowed to travel, from some 400,000 before to some 1.5 or 2 million per year afterward. But that way, people could get their own personal impressions, and that had to have some consequences sooner or later.

Let me put it in a provocative and oversimplified way then. Why couldn't one say that, in the last analysis, the gap in consumer standards and the desire of the GDR citizens for more consumption has led to the Wende?

Doris C.: No, no, not at all. . . .

Leonhard B.: . . . No, I would not put it like that at all. Of course, this question of consumer items plays a certain role, but it was not the key issue. You see, we had people in the GDR who also had everything. In fact, as we later found out, some of the party hacks had far higher living standards than anything we had ever suspected. Or, for example, if somebody had a dacha, and his neighbor turned out to have everything your heart could desire, all Western stuff at that, well, then you knew, first of all, this guy is probably with the Stasi and, secondly, he could therefore get everything he wanted.

Over the years, more and more people found out that there were those who had no problems acquiring anything. I met a construction supervisor once who told me that they were sometimes asked, for an extra 1,000 Marks a weekend [about the average monthly income of a worker in East Germany], to leave their real jobs and build houses for functionaries, mostly with Western material.

So you are saying it was more a sense of injustice than the desire for consumption?

Leonhard B.: Yes, precisely. There was just an incredible degree of injustice everywhere.

Rudi E.: This injustice was really quite unbelievable. Some people had everything and hence did not give a damn about what common folks at the bottom of society had. Nothing has changed on that level over the last few years. . . .

Leonhard B.: . . . Of course it has—it has gotten considerably worse. . . .

. . . Well, as you have been told many times, and as many Western critics believe, social injustice is far worse in the West. . . .

Doris C.: . . . Yes, yes, but there it did not touch me, it didn't make any difference to me. But here, with a socialist government, claiming to be just dyed in red, always ready to quote Karl Marx, and then acting like this, that just drove us mad. And it got worse and worse; after a while, they did not even make an attempt anymore to cover it up, like they had previously done, and they got increasingly excessive in their consumption trips.

Of course, we had to find out sooner or later. It was, for example, just a year ago that I found out that they had special stores in which all the functionaries, from the lowest-ranking Stasi officer all the way up, could buy stuff. But later we came to know this.

And, you know, the election in May was decisive for a lot of people, because we simply said to ourselves that most governments in the world that receive 10 to 15 percent no-votes would kiss their own feet. After all, what government receives 80 to 85 percent support? But that they even had to lie about these 10 to 15 percent—we were really deeply upset about that. So more and more people went to the church, not because they liked the church, but because they were seeking protection in the church. Women my age all of a sudden ran to church on every 7th of the month, lighting candles and all, simply because we no longer knew what to do with our bottled-up anger. All of those double standards, all of this arbitrariness came to our attention after a while, even though we used to say to ourselves "there is nothing you can do anyway." This attitude we had deeply internalized. We deeply believed that there was nothing we could possibly do. An individual can't change anything anyway. And if we had tried as a group, we immediately would have been treated like criminals.

But this election fraud just pushed things beyond the breaking point. After that, a lot of people just thought: "It doesn't matter anymore. Let them come, let them accuse me of crimes, let them arrest me, I just can't take it anymore. I will no longer say 'yes' to all this."

When you say there was "nothing one could do anyway," how did things go in the factory, at the workplace? Did you have specific work-related problems as well, and could you talk about them?

Doris C.: Oh yes, we talked, we copied things or wrote petitions ourselves that we posted in the shops, but usually these things were immediately torn down again. There was an incredible atmosphere in the shops; people were totally fed up. . . .

Rudi E.: . . . Of course, there was always fear that they would punish you individually. . . .

. . . So there was widespread fear that if you took it too far, if you complained too much or talked about your complaints with too many people, then . . .

Doris C.: . . . You certainly tried to check out very well with whom you were talking, but you could still never be certain that one of them was not a Stasi informant. But we still began to risk it, because we just felt too stupid carrying on not saying anything. Until this very day we are not sure as to who exactly was a Stasi informant. . . .

Bernd K.: . . . There were so many who had been blackmailed by the Stasi in one way or another and who fulfilled certain duties for them, as informants, as errand boys—it could be your colleague, you never knew. . . .

Doris C.: . . . You know the term "niche society," I suspect. My son, for example, was put in jail in 1976 because he refused to get divorced from his wife who had fled to the West. I was not allowed to become AGL chairwoman because of that. In '78 they [the East German government] deported him to West Berlin, and after that my husband and I were no longer allowed to go fishing on the Baltic coast. We had been very keen anglers, but after that they did not let us go there anymore, because it was a border area. We were also not allowed to travel to Yugoslavia, China, Cuba, or anywhere else. And they did not let my son visit anybody in the GDR. He was not even allowed to attend his grandmother's funeral.

Well, and one result of all that was that I could not go out with my husband anymore, not to a restaurant, not to a bar, or anywhere else. As soon as he had drunk two or three beers, he would begin to bitch and complain terribly about the communists. I have to add here, of course, that I was in the party; I had just recently joined, shortly before my son got arrested. I had simply figured that I could do more for my colleagues if I was in the party. I had known all along that things were going wrong, but somehow I had always thought that Erich Honecker did not know anything about that.

I wrote petitions to Erich Mielke [national director of the security police], I wrote petitions to Honecker, I wrote piles of petitions throughout all those years. I always received the answer that "according to section so-and-so, we are not required to provide you with an answer to your request." But talking about "niche society," we had a little dacha, and this is where we met over the weekends with friends, that is where we talked and complained and got angry. And that is exactly how every other GDR citizen did it as well. Everybody had a niche in which he sat and privately complained.

Or when they asked me in the factory to take over the chair of a departmental union leadership. Whenever we had the so-called AGL instruction meetings, the union members approached me in all openness with their complaints, and I always tried to pass it on to the plant-wide union leadership, and I wrote these ominous monthly reports. But nothing ever happened, and our anger about that just built up over the years. And then this election fraud. I wrote to them that "if your claim is true that everything was done correctly and legally, why don't you just put the voting slips on the table and publicly count them?"

What is surprising to me about all of this is how long you continued to invest trust and hope that you could change something by appealing to official organs or party functionaries.

Doris C.: Yes, you are absolutely right about that. But you have to understand the basis for this, which was our work. We all had work; in fact, we did not know any unemployment. Families with a lot of children were supported. We had a comprehensive child care and kindergarten system. We had a decent educational system for everybody. All of this was very well-established, nobody had to live in poverty or great need, everybody enjoyed a sense of security, had enough to eat, a place to live, and clothes to wear. Basically, we always got everything we really needed. . . .

Everybody always bought everything he could get his hands on, whether he needed it or not, and then we exchanged things among ourselves. We had a lively barter economy going. It usually took quite a long time to get what you needed or wanted, but you almost always got it at some point. In that sense, we were all pretty satisfied, and that's why we did not have this blazing dissatisfaction around here. We swallowed a lot and protested a little every once in a while. Let's put it that way. . . .

Rudi E.: . . . The real disputes and discussions only occurred in small private circles. . . . You see, in the Soviet Union something was happening, something good was happening, but not here. . . .

Let's talk for a moment about the status of the worker in a GDR factory like yours. How would you compare your previous status as a worker in the GDR to a worker in the FRG in terms of your rights, your security, your space, and so on?

Doris C.: I think our status was a lot higher than in the West. . . .

And, for example, nobody was actually ever fired, because for every person we fired we had to employ three so-called "Asis" ["asocials," a derogatory term widely employed by East Germans to refer to alcoholics and people who were presumably unwilling to work]. We always tried to keep the people, a policy which was, of course, very advantageous to those colleagues who had problems—even though it may have been terrible for the factory. It was the duty of the brigade to do anything necessary to cure a colleague from alcoholism, or whatever the problem was. We were supposed to house him, if necessary, to accompany him on his way home, to talk to him about his problems, and so on. Nowadays these people will simply be fired and nobody gives a damn about them anymore. They will now just go down the drain. This is the kind of humanity we previously had here. . . .

Rudi E. . . . We do not want to exaggerate, but there was a kind of community and support network that we are currently in the process of losing.

It is true that the productivity was really quite low. We had a lot of patchwork in the factories, much was only solved through extra shifts, which cost more and ate away the financial substance of a given enterprise. . . .

Bernd K.: . . . The whole production process was just very badly organized. Often we had to work on Sunday, with all the extra payments and benefits involved, and on Monday we just stood around because a certain part was missing, so we couldn't continue to work.

Leonhard B.: What we also experienced a lot was that they invested millions in setting up some new shop, and as soon as work was completed, the whole thing was already outdated again, or nobody needed it anymore. So many rank-and-file workers began to wonder whether we had idiots organizing our production. We constantly asked ourselves "don't they, can't they comprehend what is going on?" If we as workers understood that things like that should not happen, one would assume that someone who went to college should be able to grasp that as well.

Bernd K.: But I would not label all of our directors "idiots," because they had to follow certain regulations as well. . . .

Maria C.: . . . It just developed that way. If people now claim that we did not have the right people, I can only say that is total b.s. The problem was the party. If a young person came right from the university and said to himself, for example, I will never join the party, he could as well have just given up immediately, because he had no chance of making it whatsoever. The absolute most a person like that could achieve was to become department supervisor, but even that would have been an exception.

So all of those people basically sat down in the corner and did not do anything. They were, of course, not motivated, thus did not further qualify themselves, did not show any interest. This was a terrible situation.

People obtained certain positions because of their party affiliation, and not because of their competence. So frequently we said to ourselves, "This guy became department supervisor? I can't believe it, he is not qualified at all." Naturally, this led to a very widespread dissatisfaction among our colleagues. . . .

Bernd K.: . . . But we rarely managed to speak up about matters like that. . . .

Maria C.: . . . Some colleagues, of course, also exploited this situation. People sometimes worked on something for five days that should have taken them no more than a half-day. I would have fired people like that; even ten years ago I would have fired them. But, of course, nobody ever got kicked out. . . .

Bernd K.: . . . You see, we really employed everybody; we really did not have any unemployment. So the attitude toward work was not always very good. . . .

Maria C.: . . . The wages were low, but at least we all had work. . . .

Peter R.: (another worker, who joined our circle late, intervenes) Yes, everybody had a security. Nobody really had to do anything; they could all goof off. Material was not available either; nobody could get kicked out; productivity went down, particularly in comparison to the highly industrialized Federal Republic. . . .

Maria C.: . . . Yeah, but that wouldn't have been necessarily bad, except that people should have never seen all the things they have on the other side, because then, of course, they wanted to have them as well.

Well, now they are unemployed and receive unemployment compensation in the West. Isn't that nice? . . .

Well, let me ask you another question then. You mentioned earlier that you would have liked to continue some form of socialism, and that "good things" were only happening in the Soviet Union. But what about Solidarność in Poland, a movement that was generated by workers, that was not antisocialist, at least not in its main currents, and that had already in 1980 come to the conclusion that reform could not be achieved with this kind of party? They opposed the "leading role of the party" and thus were struggling for their own independent organization. It seems to me that this had no . . .

Rudi E.: . . . effect in the GDR whatsoever. . . .

Leonhard B.: . . . The relationship between Germans and Poles plays a large role in this. In our view, and we get constant proof of this, the Pole is simply not as diligent as the German. So there was a widespread opinion they did not want to work anyway, so that is why they started all those strikes and so on. We had quite a few Poles at our factory whom we could talk to . . .

Doris C: . . . And who were very good workers, very diligent . . .

Rudi E: . . . Yes, but then they were only sending us the best they had . . .

Leonhard B: . . . Anyway, so it was probably a misjudgment on our part . . .

Rudi E: . . . Solidarność was probably a step in the right direction, but we did not see it and could not accept it as such at the time.

Well, I still don't quite understand how your discontent . . .

Rudi E: . . . For years, for decades we had great admiration for Erich Honecker, because he had been in a Nazi concentration camp for 12 years, because he had to go through many hard struggles in the early years of the republic, and he had to fight hard against big names such as Ulbricht before he got control of things.

So there first had to come a time, in terms of the economic situation and in terms of the desire for more freedom, in which the need for change could be awakened and developed, like through the Helsinki process. This took a very long time here. At first, I did not articulate my unwillingness to participate in this system anymore; I just realized a slowly increasing anger because I could not travel, because I could not get certain things, but I still did not know what exactly caused all these problems.

Maria C: In March of '89, that is, still before the elections in May, we had a party delegation conference here. At one point, a young engineer stood up and asked, "How could you have banned *Sputnik*," this Soviet dissident magazine. He, as a young party comrade, was supposed to recruit people for the party, and people frequently responded to him: "We are certainly not going to join a party that even bans a Soviet magazine. You can't even explain to me why they have done this, what the rationale behind that was." So, he continued, "I have no credibility with people anymore; they simply make fun of me, ridicule me now." Then he demanded some explanation as to why *Sputnik* had been banned, and the party leadership more or less simply ignored him. And then I remember well how somebody who had never read *Sputnik* himself jumped out of his seat and yelled, "So tell us, what is this *Sputnik* all about, why can't we read it, what's so dangerous about it? I want to see it." So what you can see here is that there was increasingly vocal discontent even at the base of the party. . . .

Bernd K: . . . Many people also left the party during those months. . . .

Maria C: Of course, this never surfaced in public, because they were still too scared of doing that, but it was there nonetheless. And people began to get more elaborate in getting around some restrictions. *Sputnik,* for example, was read more widely after the ban than before. Somebody somehow got it in West Berlin, brought it back with him, and people either copied it here or passed it around.

Leonhard B: . . . In fact, *Sputnik* got known because of its ban. . . .

Maria C: . . . But above all, the Soviet press releases, particularly concerning Gorbachev and his speeches, were read around here. You would not believe it. Everybody began to show interest. Prior to Gorbachev, nobody had ever looked at a Soviet newspaper, but since then the papers sold out quickly; we passed them around, talked about them. We had an incredible desire for freedom of the press. . . .

Rudi E: . . . Too many things had just been taboo. You could not read about them, much less openly talk about them . . .

Maria C: . . . We said at party meetings that we must publicize everything, that only if we admit our own mistakes can we learn from them and grow. They were so incredibly frightened that they could be toppled if all the things they were doing became public. . . .

■ BÄRBEL BOHLEY, artist, founder of New Forum; "mother of the underground" (a Stasi appraisal); "mother of the revolution" (the popular appraisal). ■ *"There had never been a pastor who said—for instance, on the occasion when they were called to the ministry of the interior concerning the preparations for the peace workshops— 'I will only go there if these women can come with me!' The pastors always went there by themselves, and then they told us what the officials had told them, or told us what we should and what we should not do, what was considered to be a touchy issue, and so on. In that sense, the role of the church was very regulating, very confining."*

In the Fall of 1989, Bärbel Bohley was the best-known voice of the East German revolution. She was the initiator and founder of the largest opposition group, New Forum. For a short period of time, Bohley's historical role and her public reputation coalesced; she could be seen almost daily, as it were, on television and radio news programs. At the time of this interview, however, the 45-year-old Bohley, painter and sculptress, had once again been pushed into the background by the resurgence of "normal politics." Her political ideas had clearly fallen out of favor.

In her entire adult life Bärbel Bohley had pushed herself and others to speak up, to talk to one another, and to become active instead of complaining about "others" and thereby absolving themselves of responsibility for the depressing nature of life under one-party rule. Her vision was deeply egalitarian and, as such, was democratic in ways that were significantly in advance of the political realities common to both existing systems of governance, East and West. As she exclaimed at one point: "We must determine our own future ourselves."[26] Predictably, Bohley had never found a comfortable place within a society run by the party.

But what she considered to be the "fast-paced, cutthroat consumer culture" of West Germany did not seem likely to provide a more hospitable environment for her. Again, her political vision, and also her very personal vision, could not find space to grow. "Our self-determination is being denied to us, in different ways, by both political systems."[27]

For much of the eighties she had been considered the "opposition personified" in the GDR—selfless, courageous, and candid. After her last arrest in the spring of 1988, she was deported and unwillingly spent a half-year in Great Britain. She returned to the GDR at the first opportunity granted by the authorities—in effect, returning to a land where those in power regarded her as a pariah. Her willingness to shoulder this burden, to accept a daily life of police surveillance and harassment, earned her immense credibility among the East German population. To a degree that is true for few other people in the GDR, Bohley can actually claim to have been active in the opposition for more than ten years. After her arrest following a publicly staged protest against a new military conscription law for women in 1983, the secret police invented a new derogatory term for her, one she could, if she wished, wear proudly today. The Stasi called her "the mother of the underground."

But it is hard to visualize Bärbel Bohley engaging in such self-promotion because she is the kind of political activist who is extremely unlikely to make a political career either within the context of one-party rule or of

26. Bärbel Bohley (ed.), *40 Jahre DDR . . . und die Bürger melden sich zu Wort* [Forty Years of GDR . . . and the Citizens are Speaking Up] (Frankfurt am Main, 1989), 9. My translation.
27. Ibid.

Western-style politics. As many political friends and foes can attest, she has always said and done what she really believed in, regardless of the consequences. She never wanted to be a celebrity—indeed, she frequently avoided media attention in favor of a few quiet moments in her studio or among friends.

One such instance is particularly telling. In the midst of the East German revolution, two reporters of a major West German television network had driven an executive limousine to the opposition-occupied House of Democracy in East Berlin in order to pick up Bohley for a prime time news program. This was done on short notice—that is, without having taken the precaution of notifying her first. It was planned that she would discuss the meaning of the revolution and the best future course for East Germany with former chancellor and honorary chairman of the West German Social Democratic Party, Willy Brandt. When the network representatives finally located her, she simply replied: "Gentlemen, this house is full of interesting and articulate people. I have other plans for tonight"—and walked off, to the utter astonishment of the two Western TV reporters.

The woman with whom I sat down in a small office of New Forum in Berlin seemed exhausted by months of strenuous organizing efforts. I could detect none of the fervor and hope she had demonstrably exuded. "My place is in the opposition," she remarked at one point with experientially confirmed conviction. Ever since her public reaction to the opening of the Wall on 9 November 1989, she has, in fact, lost much sympathy even among various members of the opposition. She had called the opening "premature" and told government and people alike that "they seem to have lost their minds." Like almost no one else in Germany, East or West, she realized right away the dangers to authentic and enduring democratic forms implicit in any sudden and unprepared clash between the two social systems. While her initial fears concerning a precipitous Western takeover proved to be remarkably precise, such unpopular accuracy turned out to have disastrous consequences to her political position within the opposition.

In the aftermath of East Germany's revolutionary autumn, and at the moment this interview took place, the ideas she had fought for had been crushed so thoroughly that she seemed to have given up even on many of those who had previously stood by her side. Within the world of the opposition her story is unmatched in poignancy. Elements of this are visible in the section that follows, and become clearer on pp. 292–303 and pp. 360–62.

■ *I actually wanted to ask you a little about your own political development in the beginning, but since you are so hard-pressed for time. . . .*

. . . I would not talk about that anyway. . . .

Can you recall at what point, and why, you came to the conclusion that things cannot go on like this, something needs to be done, and it cannot be done through the party. . . .

. . . I had never been a member of the party. I always considered parties to be a corset that I did not want to put on. Earlier, I worked as a departmental committee chairperson in the Alliance of Artists, which was also a kind of political work for me. This committee decided who would be admitted to the Alliance—which was not easy at all, among other things because it was somewhat exclusive, being the only structure that existed for artists.

And then, of course, this committee was always consulted if someone had applied for a trip to the West. So the work in this committee was really quite political. I always tried to help those artists who had previously had no opportunity to exhibit over there, or to exhibit at all. So this was primarily what I did.

The new conscription law of 1982, on the other hand, had directly and immediately to do with me because it stated, for the first time, that women could be drafted for certain military duties. So this was the incentive for me to found the group "Women for Peace."

Could you describe for me how exactly you did this? I have noticed time and again that there is considerable confusion among Westerners as to what was possible in the GDR and what was not possible in terms of free speech and political organizing.

Well, you see, the habit of writing petitions was very widespread in our country. So I wrote a petition concerning this new draft law. It was essentially a personal letter in which I stated that I did not agree that it was at all necessary to mobilize women for military service as well, particularly considering the worldwide military situation.

On the contrary, I told them that we should *decrease* the number of military personnel. I wrote this during a time when the debates concerning the Nachrüstung [the U.S.-Soviet arms race in Europe, particularly in Germany] were going on all over. My main argument was that the tension, or conflict, between the two political camps would only be heightened if women were included as well.

So I protested against this new law. And then I knew three other women who had also written personal petitions, and we all had received these meaningless answers. We all thought that we could not accept that, and began to look for other women who would join us in our protest. This is how we got together about 150 women—a complete novelty for the GDR. Nowhere before had people, and particularly women, organized a political group like ours outside of the church. . . .

We basically thought it was terrible enough that all men were drafted, and now it was finally up to us to do something. This is also why we did not want men to write any petitions on our behalf. It had nothing to do with us viewing this problem from a female perspective, but rather with the fact that this new law explicitly concerned women, and that was why women should raise their voices. Of course, there was also a tactical consideration: men had always been criminalized much more easily, they had been the ones who had been labeled "instigators," and so forth. So we came to the conclusion that we should do this on our own. . . .

Every woman in our group had the feeling that this was definitely an issue about which we had to speak up. There wasn't even much fear among most of us; in fact, most weren't scared at all. . . . Pretty quickly, however, the members of our group were massively harassed by the Stasi. Some even quit. About 40 women stayed with it, and they did not fold under this pressure—they did not retract their signatures. So these women continued to meet, and this is how the group Women for Peace got founded.

Our main concern was really the demilitarization of the GDR. We wanted to fight against the militarization of the entire society, such as premilitary training in the schools, for example. Every one of us had children. We were all women who had already finished their education and who had kids of school age. . . .

Throughout our work it was important to us to make clear that we were a group which worked outside of the church. Early on, we had ascertained that the church played much more of a regulating role than a liberating one. The church represented, in essence, the mediator between the two social pressures, one from the top, and one from below.

Could we explore this a bit more, if possible? Could it also be said that various Protestant pastors played a very supportive role for the opposition, and that there were many debates and struggles going on within the church as well?

Well, yes, some of them did support us, but I have to say that they basically—and that, I think, applies to all of them—never succeeded in establishing a direct dialogue between the state and those various opposition groups, which, of course, was not really a matter of concern to them. What they did was to talk to us, and then they ran to representatives of the state and talked to the state. There had never been a pastor who said—for instance, on the occasion when they were called to the ministry of the interior concerning the preparations for the peace workshops—"I will only go there if these women can come with me!" The pastors always went there by themselves, and then they told us what the officials had told them, or told us what we should and what we should not do, what was considered to be a touchy issue, and so on. In that sense, the role of the church was very regulating, very confining. . . .

What about later activities by Women for Peace? Aside from your early actions, such as the petitions you wrote in response to the new draft law and this spectacular action you staged on Alexanderplatz,[28] I was not able to find out much about your group. What did you do after 1983?

Well, we always actively participated in the so-called Peace Workshops, and we organized so-called "Night Prayers" in the Resurrection Church [Auferstehungskirche]. We had a good contact with a female pastor in this church, and she had given us permission to use the church for these night prayers. Usually, a number of people showed up for this, and not only people from within the church. This was very important to us.

And then there were those groups which did thematic work on all kinds of issues, and we frequently participated in some of them. And we began to have increasingly close contacts with the women at Greenham Common [outside the U.S. air base] in England, and with the Greens in West Germany. . . .

If I may interrupt for a moment: I understand that you went through some extremely difficult times because of those contacts. I guess one English peace activist visited you and was later caught and strip-searched at the border, and they found protocols of conversations between her and you, which was followed by your arrest, yet you were released relatively quickly due to pressure from outside. Could you describe this for me?

It wasn't so much pressure organized within the GDR, but rather really pressure from outside. At this time the disarmament conference in Stockholm was going on, and all the people we knew just began to exert quite a bit of pressure on the GDR government.

It's really not true that there was much solidarity within the GDR. People were still too scared.

But as far as I can tell, this seems to have been the first time that this kind of pressure was consciously used in order to get someone out of jail. . . .

28. The main square in downtown East Berlin. On 16 October 1983 Bärbel Bohley, Ulrike Poppe, and 30 other women, all dressed in black, marched to the main post office on Alexanderplatz to send off their declarations to "refuse any military service." Five women were arrested. Bohley and Poppe barely escaped Stasi agents.

... That's right. ...

... Something that was to play an ever larger role in later activities—to create some security for people engaging in oppositional activities in the GDR by generating a certain inevitable publicity. Is that right?

Yes. The really new element in all of this, however, was that Ulrike [Poppe] and I wanted to be released into the GDR. Until then, if people had been arrested for oppositional activities, they used these six weeks or so in jail as a sort of intermediate station before they were expelled to the West. Our case was the first case in which the state could not take that route. On the contrary, they had to abandon the preliminary proceedings against us and subsequently had to release us in the GDR, and not deport us. I think that was very encouraging to a lot of people. ...

But outside of Berlin, it seems to me, this strategy was only used very late in the day, because people did not know about it. Frank Eigenfeld [founder of New Forum in Halle], for example, recently told me that they did not make any efforts to use outside contacts for their own security until 1988. Before that, they had always acted according to the understanding that outside contacts should be avoided at all costs, because it would alienate people, unnecessarily heighten the tensions, and involve unpredictable risks. So they continued to write petitions. ...

The problem, of course, was that it was much more difficult in the GDR to establish these contacts [with Western activists or the Western media] than was the case in East Berlin. Here, we had the press around all the time; here, we had the border; here, people from the West came over. Hardly anybody from the West ever went to Halle. It has a lot to do with the locality: such contacts in some remote city or town would have been much more conspicuous, and therefore also much more dangerous.

I see. Was this problem widely debated among oppositionists? Could you tell me a little about the particular elements of this debate?

There was always quite a bit of serious conflict surrounding this question [of how much and when to make use of the Western media]. Many groups in the GDR simply refused to have any of these contacts. We in Berlin, on the other hand, were convinced that nothing would work without these contacts, because only with their help could we generate some publicity. Without publicity, in effect, our activities might as well not have happened.

Without publicity, your activities became nonevents; the Stasi could see to it that no one heard about these activities, is that right?

Yes.

All right, what then were the main arguments of those who were opposed to using Western media?

Well, the main concern had always been to initiate a dialogue with the state, and they did not want to threaten or scare the state. They thought it would be extremely harmful if an issue came out of the Western press first. That would give the appearance that the opposition in East Germany was made up of cold warriors allied to the "other side." Therefore, it was thought by many in the opposition that we should undertake every conceivable effort to talk to representatives of the state first.

On the other hand, we discovered early on that they would only talk to us if they were under some kind of pressure. I mean, *of course* they were not willing to talk to us voluntarily.

A slightly more general question: It has been my experience with other social movements that those people who stand in the limelight of media attention and who make up the leadership of oppositional organizations are usually the ones who are quoted and to whom most sustained attention is given afterward. Yet, of course, there is almost always a very active base at work in those movements, people who sometimes quite literally make up the movement, but people about whom we hardly ever hear anything. On the other hand, most commentators and many leading spokespersons of the opposition itself have said that there was little else to the "movement" in East Germany than a few small groups that were mostly organized by intellectuals. Furthermore, these different groups had very similar political ideas and pretty much limited themselves to efforts of public information on the one hand, and a few spectacular political actions geared toward the Western media on the other. But the attempt to recruit, or at least establish links of communication, to larger segments of the population has, according to this line of argument, never taken place.

That's correct, it hasn't really.

Well, what I don't quite understand about that is that it seems to be quite obvious if people limit themselves to such a narrow frame of activities, they will find themselves pretty much "on their own" in times of political change. . . .

. . . There were many reasons why it happened that way. It isn't as if we did not try to create a public space, or some form of publicity. We wrote open letters concerning various topics; we tried to contact all sorts of people, and so forth. But internal pressure to act simply did not exist, and when it did come to exist among certain individuals, most just tried to leave the country. They applied for an emigration visa, or tried to get out some other way. People did not feel the pressure that they had to become active politically. We just simply have to say this. The West always represented the apparent escape from misery, so to speak. . . .

What was really important was contacting people before they had made up their minds about having no other choice than to leave for good, and to say, "Why don't you join us and help us change the country from within?" We did have people who joined us that way, but there was still this continuous trickle of people leaving for the West. . . .

One question I always ask has to do with Solidarność in Poland. From the perspective of many Westerners, this seemed to be something that could have had a great appeal to East Germans, perhaps even in terms of trying to emulate it. Here we had a movement of workers who managed to generate—largely on their own—the largest working-class movement in history. Furthermore, their demand for an independent organization was not only unprecedented in the Eastern Bloc, it also addressed the heart of the problem of all states under one-party rule. What was your reaction to this?

It must simply be stated that our situation was entirely different. You cannot compare the GDR with any other East Bloc country; it would simply be wrong. The GDR always played a special role. We were always better off than any of the other socialist countries. We always had family and friendship contacts with the West. Our view was much more focused toward the West. We also never perceived ourselves as an occupied country, like the Czechs, the Poles, or the Hungarians, because we always thought "it serves us right. Why did we have to start World War II? So now we'll just have to put up with the Russians." In other words, our situation was really quite different. It was pretty clear that something like Solidarność would never be possible in the GDR.

You mean primarily because of the existence of the Federal Republic of Germany?

Yes, absolutely.

In other words, socialism was not possible in the GDR because of the existence of West Germany, and it was not possible in West Germany because of the existence of the GDR?

That's exactly right. . . . You simply cannot talk people into anything. There is much more to the task of altering conditions of life than that. Solidarność in Poland had developed out of the pressure of existing conditions, and one simply has to see that this kind of pressure did not exist here. What we had in the GDR was a different kind of pressure, one that was not even detected until much later, until it suddenly burst open like a valve, when people just wanted to get "over there," when they made clear that they wanted what people in the West have. And that, as events have shown and will show even more clearly in the future, is not enough. . . .

3 THE MANY MEANINGS OF "REFORM"

■ KLAUS KADEN, Protestant pastor, and a central facilitator within the church for the opposition in Leipzig. ▮ *"So the result was what the result had to be: the groups portrayed themselves as if they had been banned from speaking out. They began walking around with bandages across their mouths. You have to imagine this: across from the pastor, on the opposite side of the church, facing the chancel, stood some two-hundred young people with bandages across their mouths, holding banners saying 'Stop the church hierarchy' or 'The church people are the same as the ones outside.'"*

Numerous members of grass-roots groups in Leipzig had suggested that I should talk to Klaus Kaden because he had proven to be one of their most supportive and knowledgeable contacts within the church. Kaden was born in 1951 in a city called Chemnitz, later renamed Karl Marx Stadt, and in 1990 returned to its original name. He summarized his youth with considerable economy and clarity: "I grew up in a Christian household. My parents were simple people, my father a worker, my mother a housewife. I had four siblings. Ever since I was thirteen I wanted to become a pastor. When it was time to take the final exams of the 'Abitur,' however, I was rejected for political reasons, because my parents believed—and I agreed—that it was not acceptable for me to join the communist youth organization FDJ and to go through the Jugendweihe [the SED's secular version of confirmation]."

Interestingly, Kaden was the only Protestant pastor I had interviewed during the summer of 1990 whose participation in the East German civic movement was religiously motivated. Whereas many others had become Protestant pastors primarily because of their political aspirations—aspirations for which they could not find any space in the GDR other than the church—Klaus Kaden had become acquainted with oppositional political activism merely through his position as parish pastor. While he remained supportive of a variety of groups, his personal inclination seemed to point more toward the goal of "catching up" with the West—a goal symbolized, of course, by re-unification[29]—than it did toward exploring new democratic and egalitarian terrain.

In the following interview, Kaden cogently reveals the wide range of social grievances and resulting political aspirations among members of the civic movement—a diversity that was indicative not just of the opposition at large, but very much reflected the debates within the church.

The driving momentum of the grass-roots groups emerges as a connecting thread in this interview. We learn, for example, that one of the first large-scale public protests in Leipzig was aimed not at the party, but at recalcitrant church leaders who were—inappropriately in the eyes of the grass-roots groups—impeding free expression within the growing opposition movement. In this manner, Kaden helps to identify and clarify some of the sequential building blocks which undergirded and made possible the revolution of 1989. The interview took place in Kaden's pastoral residence next to the Michaelis Church in Leipzig.

■ I sort of slid into all these political debates right away. I moved into this house and started my new job in November 1987. About the same time what we called the "Working Circle Environment" at the youth parish department had invited people for a discussion about the retaliatory actions of the Stasi increasingly employed against the emerging opposition. The discussion took place in January of 1988 at the "Umweltbibliothek," an oppositional café/library/workshop within the parish of pastor Simon in Berlin. You probably know that members of this initiative were arrested, precious printing equipment was confiscated, literature was destroyed, and so on. And it just so happened that on the very same day the Working Circle had invited opposition activists to this discussion, the arrests of the illegal demonstrators at the Karl Liebknecht/Rosa Luxem-

---

29. There is an important difference between "unification" (Vereinigung) and "reunification" (Wiedervereinigung), since the area covered by the two respective Germanies is a result of World War II, that is, the combination of the two has never existed before. Thus, in a strict historical sense, there was nothing to be "reunified." Within the political debates in East and West Germany concerning the question of (re)unification, one could distinguish the traditional "right" from the traditional "left" according to their use of these terms: the right consistently spoke of "reunification," whereas the left went out of its way to avoid what was considered a "revanchist" terminology, and thus only used the word "unification."

burg commemoration had taken place—Krawczyk and others. [Stefan] Krawczyk was a singer/songwriter and had, not long before, performed at the Michaelis parish along with other dissidents.

The Michaelis Church was a place that had always opened its doors for such difficult events. So, in my function as official organizer of this discussion—as director of the youth parish department, I was officially in charge of the Working Circle Environment—I was suddenly right in the middle of all this. Since about 100 people were arrested at the demonstration in Berlin, not only the usual 50 or 60 insiders showed up for this discussion meeting, but also about 400 other people. We had to go into the church, the cold church. Well, of course, this was a very controversial assemblage, a very hot event. Immediately, the Stasi showed up everywhere. A debate or discussion about what had happened never took place. Instead, what happened for the first hour were general denunciations of the system of the GDR. Prominent in these denunciations were the so-called would-be émigrés [Ausreisewillige]; they had come from all over the country. . . .

It was at this huge gathering that I—for the first time in my life—said something publicly on behalf of the opposition. My critical remarks were mainly directed at the would-be émigrés. I warned against any heated action sparked primarily by those who merely wanted to get out and for whom using almost any means to achieve this goal seemed justified. So I spoke against having a public demonstration, vigils and such. To me, at least, it was very important that I gave this little speech because that way I was able to experience for the first time in my life what it means to get a very negative response for no other reason than having made some cautious remarks. While some people applauded my speech, most yelled at me "you pig" and other terrible things like that. It was quite educational for me.

Could you elaborate on this a little? Are you saying that the majority of those present were would-be émigrés . . . ?

Of the ones that were vocal, yes. They listed all of the things that were terrible and bad in this country; then they talked about what really happened in Berlin, and then they proclaimed that something had to change around here. But, as would-be émigrés, they of course described the possible means to achieve some changes in such extreme terms that I began to worry that those who really wanted to change something in the country, from within the country, that if they went along with this they would be throwing themselves directly upon the sword of the Stasi. That, of course, I wanted to help prevent.

In other words, you are saying that the kinds of demands and ideas were so, as you call it, "extreme" because the would-be émigrés were basically just searching for ways to speed up their emigration?

Of course, that's exactly what they were trying to do.

I inquire into the details because many of the people who had participated in the demonstrations in Berlin claim that the only reason they were subsequently released was precisely because of the efforts to make this public, because of the vigils and the demonstrations?

This may well be. There are a number of dynamics at work here. I was just referring to Leipzig. Some of those who had been arrested in Berlin did not want to get deported, others wanted precisely that. But this is not how it was in Leipzig. Perhaps we should also keep in mind that two students—I think they were theology students—made a proposal on the same evening to organize and invite people to memorial services at the student parish. And this is what happened on the very next day. They organized daily memorial services for all those who had been arrested, and they organized a so-called "contact telephone" [a hot line] which people could call in order to find out about events and protests and so forth.

I admit that my response to this idea of holding memorial services was deeply skeptical. Also, I would not have taken responsibility for such activities in my position as youth pastor—for that, I was not yet acquainted enough with the entire situation. I did not know what to expect yet, and I did not really have any colleagues at my side who could have helped me with that. I pretty much had to take over the youth parish department on my own. It was a very complicated situation at first. In any case, that's how the daily memorial services developed. They grew in size from day to day. Unfortunately, more and more would-be émigrés began to join them as well, because they had heard of Bishop Stolpe's remarks that "the church can help would-be émigrés"—a statement which he quickly withdrew a few days later.

You have to keep in mind that people who had applied for an exit visa were treated very badly: they had to wait up to five years for an official response; their children were not allowed to go to a post-secondary school; teachers were fired from their jobs—all in all, it was a very tough position to be in. It was really the pressure of the would-be émigrés, particularly in Leipzig, that brought about the peace prayers and led to all these political activities. Of course, the grass-roots groups supported this process, they gave it a particular content, and ultimately pushed it forward, there is no question about that.

Is it correct that all the ones who had been arrested were released as a result of these memorial services, some released back into the GDR, while others were deported?

Yes. What happened was that pastor Führer from the Nikolai Church came to one of those memorial services in late February—the place was totally crowded at the time, it was almost impossible to get in—and said, "Why don't you continue those services at the Nikolai Church?" He said his church "was open to everyone," and that "this is clearly an important issue"—all this after intense intra-church debates as to how much of this should be allowed to take place under the roof of the church [the Nikolai Church was not only very big, but it was the most centrally located of all the Leipzig churches]. The almost-institutionalized Monday Prayers at the Nikolai Church, every Monday at 5 P.M., had existed since 1982. But the Peace Prayers were not started at the Nikolai Church until after pastor Führer had invited activists to come to his church in February of 1988. Until then, the Monday Prayer had been a very small event, which had originated in response to the first Peace Decade in 1981. So all of a sudden, not only 5, 10, or 15 people showed up to the Monday Prayers, but about 400 or 500, steadily growing. And after the people who had been arrested were either set free or deported, there was no reason to have daily memorial services anymore. So all those who had come every time— I would call them a "fan club for political change," two-thirds of them, I guess, were would-be émigrés—thought that the church could help them. I had hundreds of pastoral conversations with would-be émigrés in those two and a half years. Some actually turned out to be in terrible situations, while others seemed to have been sent by the security police. For most people it was their first contact with the church.

What happened during those Monday prayers at the Nikolai Church— inevitably, I guess—was a growing polarization between the majority of would-be émigrés and the minority of people in the grass-roots groups [Basisgruppen]. They were united only in their goal, namely that this system had to be reformed or abolished.

Can we clarify that? Is it not a big difference whether I think this system should be reformed or whether I think it should be abolished?

Well, yes, I agree. Most of the grass-roots groups initially spoke just of reform, with the possible exception of the human rights groups. I myself said at a conference in September [1989]—and I earned a lot of disagreement for this—that I thought it was time to vote this system out of office by means of nonviolent resistance.

Before we come back to this, I want to try to clarify the basic evolution of the opposition movement, as a movement. May I ask you some questions concerning early developments toward opposition in Leipzig? You mentioned the polarization between would-be émigrés and political activists. Could you elaborate on that?

Oh, yes. Well, there were groups, two or three, that opened up for would-be émigrés, the group "Environmental Protection," the "Human Rights" group, and the "Justice" group. Some of them even initiated subgroups in which the would-be émigrés could concentrate on their problems, could organize and invite fellow citizens to meetings concerning their own issues. Some of this stuff was really hot. I remember the next-to-last Youth Day at which they put up this huge billboard on which were posted reproductions of interrogations, arrest documents, and such—wow, this was very hot stuff. I was always walking a very thin line, sort of a balancing act: on the one hand, I paid close attention and took care of the would-be émigrés as best I could. Every month I organized a meeting with about 100 to 120 people. In fact, this was the only parish in which a majority of the church leadership had allowed us, after long conversations with me, to use church facilities to meet. This was a crucial issue for me. If I may become religious for a moment, the gospel of Jesus Christ represented an immense life support for these people. We read the Bible together . . . it would be presumptuous to say that we did the same kind of work as Ernesto Cardenal, as the pastors of "liberation theology" who have set up schools for peasant children and so many other things, but it was similar. We had people who, for the first time in their lives, were holding the Bible in their hands, common people, but also intellectuals. And they reflected on their situation through the word of the Bible. Those were very happy times for me. Of course, we also talked about very concrete steps as to how people could be helped, people who had been turned down for the fourth time, what they should do, and such. It was a very important time. I saw this through until June of 1989 when thousands of would-be émigrés began to flee through the open border [between Hungary and Austria].

Let me see whether I understand you correctly: your work with the groups of would-be émigrés was mostly religious, and not so much oriented toward concrete support?

Yes, that's true. We did give legal support to the extent we could, however. Dr. Berger, for example, who was both pastor and attorney, gave us a lot of legal counseling—some people now claim that he had worked for the Stasi. I don't know whether that is true, it is certainly possible. He also gave a lot of personal support or advice. As you know, it was totally prohibited to seek help from the outside, such as from West German lawyers, or to go to foreign embassies. People who did things like that were immediately prosecuted.

This, then, was quite a balancing act—for the church—to provide help on the one hand, but not to go too far on the other?

Oh, yes, it very much was. I personally was under so much fire, both from the Stasi and from inside the church, that I decided in May to call Bishop Hempel in Dresden and to ask him whether he would support me if I continued this work. He immediately responded: "Brother Kaden, we agree with what you are doing. We would just like to ask you to keep it within the realm of the church." In this respect they did not have to worry about me. He continued by saying, "We understand that you have to do this, these people need help, and even if you end up with more than 100 people, we trust that you know how to deal with that." So this was of great help to me.

But this support did not really include the Peace Prayers every Monday at the Nikolai Church. These events created sort of an uproar every Monday in Leipzig through which the much-praised "good relations between church and state" were put under severe strain. The police, the Stasi, and, of course, the local party and church leadership had to come together every time "in order to resolve the crisis." . . .

So the Monday Prayers were already organized by the grass-roots groups before your groups joined them in February of 1988?

Yes, you could put it that way. In the beginning there were only about three or four of those groups, a Nicaragua group, a peace group, and an environmental group, and so on. It all started very small. But ever since the Karl Liebknecht/Rosa Luxemburg demonstration in Berlin in 1988, followed by the spontaneously founded memorial service groups,[30] which primarily consisted of people who were concerned with human rights problems, things got a lot bigger. . . .

But during this time we started to have severe internal problems. People who had a fundamentalist religious consciousness, like the ones in "Church from Below," for example, always caused a lot of tensions. Those groups had some very critical and outspoken members. They were particularly critical toward the church hierarchy, which sometimes made it very hard for the church leadership to build bridges of understanding.

We continuously experienced very difficult internal church debates about the Peace Prayers—as the point of political culmination—and about the problems surrounding the questions "What should the church be like nowadays? Who determines this within the church? And what would be an adequate contemporary reading of the gospel?" I was present

---

30. As specified in the introduction and elaborated upon on pp. 196–98, the use of the descriptive word "spontaneous" to characterize the origins of a new oppositional form is organically invalid. It merely suggests that the user of the term does not, in fact, know what the source of the innovation was or how it came to exist. Indeed, far from being "spontaneous," the memorial service groups were a conscious invention of, and organizing achievement of, the previously organized "grass-roots groups."

at a meeting between people from the grass-roots groups and the bishop. Jochen Lässig, a theology student who now plays a very important role within New Forum in Leipzig—I will never forget that—jumped up and asked the bishop, "Who gave you the right to tell us what is and what is not in accordance with the Gospel? You are in no position to do that." Oh, oh, that was the very first time in my life that I had ever experienced something like that, a person questioning the authority of the bishop in this way.

How did the bishop respond?

Actually, he responded very well. He said, "I heard what you had to say. It affects me a great deal, but you are right. All of us have to ask and pray in order to achieve clarity. But I must expect from you the very same thing; you have to question your standpoint just as much." Nevertheless, this was, I think, a watershed mark in the sympathy of the church leadership toward the grass-roots groups.

When did this meeting take place?

In October of 1988, after the disaster between superintendent Magirius of the Nikolai Church and the grass-roots groups in the Nikolai Church. Until June of 1988 the Peace Prayers had been organized and run by the grass-roots groups. In June the so-called Solidaristic Church, another one of those grass-roots groups founded by theology students and others, organized a Peace Prayer. I think this was the most extreme thing I had ever seen: for the first time the politics of the party and state leadership were criticized in such a clear and far-reaching fashion that virtually nothing good remained. They said, referring to the leadership of the country, "Those are the ones who are arresting and imprisoning us, who are shooting at human beings, those for whom the value of a human being equals zero if he is of a different opinion from them. In short, they are the ones who have to be abolished." And on top of that, they had invited a hard-rock singer. His name was Caesar, an incredible kind of guy. He wore leather, was standing in the chancel and doing a kind of hard rock with political lyrics. Well, it couldn't get any more drastic. It certainly had nothing to do with a "prayer" anymore. They had overstepped the boundaries and had clearly pushed it to a breaking point.

I have to admit that even I said to Jochen Lässig afterward, "This cannot go on like this. I can't assume responsibility for this kind of thing; this no longer has anything to do with a religious service." You see, it was very important to us that we *actually* had religious services in the church. This was not only important in symbolic terms, but also in our relationship to the state. Besides, I think we owed that much to our beliefs and our reputation.

We had a lot of disputes over this question. Many of the members of the grass-roots groups did not want to see it that way. But, of course, we as theologians had to insist on that. We decided that we had to assume more responsibility for those Peace Prayers, that the church had to get involved more.

What happened then, unfortunately, was that Magirius—entirely on his own—wrote a letter to the groups during the summer break [of 1988] in which he notified them that as of August, the end of the summer break, the church leadership of the Nikolai Church would assume complete organizational responsibility for the Monday Peace Prayers.

This letter, of course, fundamentally undermined the role of the grass-roots groups while strengthening the authority of the church hierarchy. I understood why he had written this letter, because the church leadership *did*, ultimately, have to take responsibility for whatever happened within the walls of their church. In the end, they would have received a beating for something they had not been responsible for. This was always a very difficult issue. Yet the blatant authoritarian manner in which Magirius wrote this letter was so hair-raising that I also clashed with him for the first time. He could have, instead, at any time called an extraordinary meeting of the synod committee for grass-roots groups, and could have openly discussed the matter. But he chose not to do that, for reasons I was never able to understand.

So the result was what the result had to be: the groups portrayed themselves as if they had been banned from speaking out. They began walking around with bandages across their mouths. You have to imagine this: on the opposite side of the church, facing the chancel and the pastor, stood some 200 young people with bandages across their mouths, holding banners saying, "Stop the church hierarchy," or "The church people are the same as the ones outside."

This was a very tough time, a very mean spirit threatened to invade the church. Later, they occupied the altar, people from the grass-roots groups who wanted to talk to the many present who did not know what was going on. Many of those in attendance thought the Peace Prayers were going to be prohibited, because that's how the grass-roots people were portraying it, simplistically so. Unfortunately, the mistake was made—which, again, was largely due to Magirius—not to play out this conflict openly, even though that would not have been a problem at all. All one would have needed to do, after the Peace Prayer was over, would have been to ask all the people interested to stay and discuss the matter openly.

Well, of course then the grass-roots people could have brought out their big guns and things could have gotten very messy. In any case, Magirius instead gave the sign after the prayer for the organist to play a finishing tune, and one of the grass-roots people stormed up there and turned off the juice for the organ. You can imagine what kind of a stir this caused. It was an extremely difficult situation.

On that very day, for the first time, people read a public statement in front of the church, namely the statement of the grass-roots groups concerning this whole issue. So for the first time ever, a public protest happened out in the open. People began to realize that one can also stage a protest not only inside the church, but also in front of it. It is very interesting to look at how all of this worked itself up.

To pursue this a bit further: since Magirius, as the person essentially in charge of the Nikolai Church, had made the decision that from now on the church should be fully responsible for the Monday Peace Prayers, was that supposed to mean that a certain pastor should be chosen each time to conduct the Peace Prayers and be responsible for them, or was it supposed to include a certain censorship, a prior decision as to what was possible and what was not?

For about six months or so, the grass-roots groups had nothing further to do with the organization of the Peace Prayers. Instead, they were solely conducted by pastors, or by theology professors. Those people gave a sermon, a few songs were played, and that was it. There was, however, the possibility of passing on information. The groups could go to pastor Führer as the chairman of the church presidium of the Nikolai Church in case they had something hot—if people had been arrested again or something like that—and they could ask him to pass this or that information on to the participants in the Peace Prayers. Führer, of course, could then decide whether to pass on this information or not—so that was the censorship. This continued until about April of 1989. Somehow I was always in charge of the Peace Prayers when it got very difficult—it wasn't my choice, it simply happened that way.

It became most extreme when the grass-roots groups decided not to go to the Peace Prayers anymore at all, or only in order to disturb them. I was, however, very impressed by the fact that they did not decide to organize an alternative Peace Prayer, but rather that they found the strength to go to the synodal committee and to negotiate with the church presidium.

In April the grass-roots groups once again received permission to conduct the Peace Prayers, under the one condition that they would have to find a pastor, any pastor, who would be willing to be responsible in the last instance for the content of the Peace Prayer. So now it was up to this pastor, whoever he or she might turn out to be, to meet with the church presidium one hour before the Peace Prayer and to tell them what was planned and find out whether they could agree with that. We did not have to show them our sermons or anything—something I would have rejected—but we did have to come to some sort of mutual agreement. We really tried hard to give the whole thing a proper face. . . .

You mentioned that some groups, like "Church from Below," used the church "in order to push their own agenda," as you have put it. What do you think about that? Isn't this indeed necessary in a country which was totalitarian, or at least authoritarian?

Oh, I did not say this with a critical intent. It couldn't have been any other way. The church has a damned responsibility to provide this kind of space. But you should also not idealize it. One could not claim, for example, that these people cared much about our ideas or our headaches. They basically behaved like elephants in a china shop, and if the landlord ever said, "Folks, we have to pay a little more attention to our guidelines on this matter," well, then all hell broke loose.

I saw myself as a "black cassock" [Schwarzkittel]—this is what they called church pastors. I always tried to mediate, and I would claim that I was more on the side of the grass-roots groups [than on the side of the church hierarchy]. But I also never severed the connection to or gave up my responsibility toward my church. This was always very important to me, and it helped me a great deal to make it through this time without much harm. Otherwise, I would have also needed to go into politics, or I would have had to resign altogether and would, today, be angry about "all the others," and would rise like a Phoenix out of the ashes, blame everything on others, and act as if I had brought about the turnaround [die Wende].

I was asking this question for another reason, because I was quite surprised to find out that not only people from outside "made use of" the church, but that, in fact, some present-day church dignitaries entered the church essentially out of political motivations, and not out of religious motivations. There are pastors out there who openly call themselves "socialists."

Let me tell you quite frankly, there are more people under the roof of the church, and particularly among the pastors, who are harboring PDS [Party for Democratic Socialism, the successor party of the communist party] thoughts than I would like and more than I had anticipated. Those left-liberal people, mostly coming out of the '68 revolution, people who went to college at that time, they all came out of this movement.

I remember it well from the theological seminary. Even though that movement pretty much ended in 1971, such people played a very decisive role for quite some time. They were talking about a theology that was basically socialist. You didn't even need Karl Marx for that; you could get it right out of the New Testament, for example, with the Sermon on the Mount.

But what happened next on the official level was what we call "the restoration" [of 1971], when the whole church, and not just socialists within the church, suddenly conformed to the official line. The church in East Germany agreed, as you know, that it would be a "church within socialism."[31] They could hardly have conformed more. This was partly due to the various privileges we received. The party said, "If you bring in Western money, you will be allowed to construct buildings. And if you behave correctly, your people can also travel freely."

We in the church were clearly a diverse bunch of people. But on the other hand, one should not be malicious or naive about that in retrospect—our playing along was absolutely necessary because otherwise nothing would have happened in our church anymore. We had to build new churches, we had to establish contacts with the outside. But the state, of course, really played cat and mouse with people in the church.

What people exactly are you referring to? Everyone in the church, or some more than others?

People who had long made up their minds that socialism was the only real alternative to capitalism, and not only as an idea or as an ideology— something I could have respected, because the West or the Federal Republic certainly did not look like the real Kingdom of God to me either; too much is missing there as well. But also, to me, these were people, some of them, who were simply afraid of the party; they did not want to push what they said they believed in—democratic socialism—because if they were really serious about that, they would have to go over and join us in the opposition. They kept a very low profile out of fear of being exposed to themselves, of discovering whether they themselves were really wheat or chaff.

I see. This dilemma, or tension, however, seems to have existed in every sector of society, even in the party itself. In this respect, what do you think of the reform communists, people like Hans Modrow and Wolfgang Berghofer [mayor of Dresden]?

I think they were obedient servants of a merciless party discipline— certainly persons who deserve respect, who even showed some backbone in some ways. But still, they were obedient servants nonetheless. Berghofer simply overestimated his own abilities, thinking that he could be-

31. See note 21, p. 83.

come the "big boss." As for Modrow, I think he is a very tragic figure. You see, everybody who had any position within the old Honecker regime was deeply implicated, everybody. In this respect it doesn't help much if you have lived like a normal average person with a two-room apartment and a GDR-made car, like Modrow. They all had to push through decisions that greatly limited human rights, that deeply affected the well-being of East German citizens. And unfortunately, they did this to the disadvantage of most ordinary citizens. Therefore, they have to go. Ultimately, these are problems they have to come to terms with themselves—we can't do that for them.

Before leaving this basic subject concerning the tensions generated everywhere by one-party control of social life, a final question: Besides the anxieties that a police state generates among oppositionists and among its own apparat, there is, it seems to me, the more general anxiety that pervades society as a whole—among people who elect not to be active politically. In such situations, external events can provide a galvanizing impetus of some kind. For example, the appearance of Solidarność in Poland. Yet there seems to have been virtually no positive response or reaction to Solidarność in the GDR, that is, the Polish movement did not so much spark hope as it seemed to help generate certain resentments. Furthermore, there seem to have been almost no contacts between dissidents outside the party and reformers inside the party in the GDR. Please correct me if I am wrong, but this seems to distinguish the situation in the GDR from the other Eastern European nations.

You have to see one thing, of course, which is that we were, ever since 1981, cut off from Poland. Honecker had come to this agreement with Jaruszelski to abandon visa-free travel between the two countries. For about five years, one could only get into Poland under very difficult circumstances. It was almost more difficult than traveling to America. Therefore, we could not establish any illegal contacts with Solidarność; it was simply not possible.

I also have to say, of course, that the much-praised German-Polish friendship had never really materialized. Quite the contrary. It seems to me that the resentments against Poles were even bigger in the GDR than in West Germany. So, while the average GDR citizen somehow took note of the existence of Solidarność, all they officially heard about the movement was that it was criticized as "antisocialist." Not one positive side of Solidarność was ever reported in the official channels. Lech Wałęsa was not even mentioned at all during the first four or five years; he simply did not exist. He was a nonperson. Even when he was supposed to receive the Nobel Peace Prize, that was considered to be "the workings of imperialist forces." . . .

But wasn't that only the official side?

Of course, but the people did not know much more about the whole thing, except for what they got from Western TV. . . .

It was my understanding that radio and television stations from West Germany could be received in most East German homes, so it would appear as if a great many people must have heard rather extensive reports about what was going on in Poland at the time. Am I mistaken about that?

No, that's right. But as far as I can tell, there was nobody who tried very hard to get in contact with Solidarność. I don't know what the reason for that was. Maybe it had to do with all the old resentments against the Poles, some of them perhaps unconscious, having to do with not being able to accept that the Poles invented something that was better than what we had and we were not able to pull off. And, of course, the same is true with Charter 77 in Czechoslovakia, and many other things. People had internalized the terrible experiences of how the Prague Spring was crushed in 1968 to such an extent that little was possible. Any contact had to be conspiratorial, and if they [the party] ever found out, the repercussions were always quite severe.

What about the psychological dimension of the Solidarność experience? Regardless of whether one likes the Poles or not, the fact is that they managed to generate a mass organization that was fundamentally challenging the state and the party; that they created their own independent institution. Why, do you think, didn't this motivate or encourage people in East Germany?

Well, let me put it this way. I don't think the GDR citizens had the necessary confidence in themselves to pull off something like that. I also think that since the early eighties the Stasi net was so strong that it could effectively suffocate any beginning in this direction.

The Stasi was very good in conveying to the GDR citizen that they were quite capable of obtaining any information they wanted to, so people were scared. I think people were considerably more scared in East Germany than in Poland.

The other factor is that we were much better-off. After all, the Poles did not wake up either until they were about to drown. Most of the time it works like that: a popular upheaval has ideology only at its head; the real pressure comes from being hungry. Pressure comes from being hungry and from having to lead an undignified life, and that is certainly not what we had. We were pretty well-off.

Ever since the early eighties, practically everybody could travel at least once a year. You could apply for a passport—and you had to be super-nice if you did; you had to turn into a sycophant. People began to think about going to the elections again; they thought about how to be a "good citizen," because otherwise they might forfeit these fragile travel rights, and so on.

It was this kind of mentality. Terrible. It may be that there is something typically German about this. I do not know. When it comes to one's purse, or to certain kinds of advantages, people's conscience immediately took second place. It was just hideous.

And I think the way people were raised in this society contributed a great deal to that. This society rewarded opportunists and sycophants. They were the ones who moved up. This is also the reason why we never had any party ideologues who turned radical, like Yeltsin in the USSR, capable of saying that something fundamental had to change. Sure, we probably had a few in the party as well, but none of them were real ideologues. They all enjoyed their goodies, wanted to tinker a little with the economy, or just wanted to lead a good life and make some money. But you certainly did not find any committed socialists or Marxists. . . .

All right. To return to the subject of the evolution of the popular opposition, you said that after April of 1989 the grass-roots groups began to get active in the Monday Peace Prayer again. Did this also signify a change in composition and content, away from the would-be émigrés and toward the issues of the grass-roots groups?

Yes, it definitely got more political after April.[32] It was made very clear that "we want to change something in this country." And it was a fortunate coincidence that at the same time the so-called "conciliatory process" began here in a very positive fashion. The church produced a lot of papers, first "Studies of Concern" [Studien der Betroffenheit], and later "For Peace, Justice, and Preservation of the Creation" [Für Frieden, Gerechtigkeit, und Bewahrung der Schöpfung], the latter one being, interestingly enough, very decisive in articulating the ideas of the Wende.

Particularly concerning the question of justice, many wonderful things were said and written. Superintendent Ziemer from Dresden and others—also in cooperation with the Catholics—really managed to do some ground-breaking work in this respect.

The entire process got started at the "Düsseldorfer Kirchentag" in West Germany by Carl Friedrich von Weizsäcker [brother of the president of Germany, Richard von Weizsäcker]. But particularly for us in the GDR, this provided an official protection that allowed us to finally speak

32. On 5 April 1989 the Polish round table between the Jaruzelski regime and Solidarność announced an agreement for free elections to the Polish parliament, to be held in June of 1989.

up about some of the catastrophic conditions in our country, such as problems concerning the environment, justice, the extent of democratization within society. We debated all of those issues very openly.

What was the third factor: the opening of the border between Hungary and Austria, or the local elections in May?

The opening of the border came a little later. Much more significant at this point were the [official] elections in May. During the period leading up to these elections, many grass-roots groups founded subsidiary "election-observing groups." Many of the would-be émigrés participated in those groups. Their goal was to take part in the vote-counting process at all the polling stations. Previously, we had not been allowed to participate in the election committee—another one of those outrageous facts that we had just swallowed. Actually, we did not begin to realize until after the Wende the dimensions of what they had done to us, how many rights we had given up, even though most had been guaranteed constitutional rights. It's very strange . . .

I see. Are you saying that the momentum behind oppositional activities surrounding the official "elections" had built up to such an extent that it politicized people—educated people—especially inside the movement itself in finding ways to throw off the fetters of oppression? That everyone was discovering just how many fetters there had been, how totally the party and the Stasi had invaded and taken control of people's psyches?

Yes, precisely.

This is extremely helpful to me since the details you are providing do so much to illustrate in detail how autonomous political activities create "consciousness." Since the dynamics are so important, could you provide some details about what happened after the May elections in Leipzig? You had the controversy surrounding the street music festival in June, and the controversial Alternative Church Day in Leipzig in July . . .

Many things happened after the elections, which revealed beyond a doubt that the party had been cheating—it was clear election fraud. They "improved" the results by up to 20 percent. People knew. We had a lot of "no-votes" in Leipzig.[33] There was a lot of grumbling going on. People had become very aware of what was going on. There was simply no longer any legitimacy for this party, for this parliament, or for this local leadership. . . .

33. East Germans had to vote on a party slate—that is, a choice existed only between preselected party functionaries (either members of the SED or of one of its satellite parties). "No-votes" refers to people who crossed out the entire ballot, thereby stating their opposition to these kinds of election procedures.

The time leading up to the Church Day was full of very heated debates and controversies. As you know, the Church Day congress is an autonomous laymen's consortium, independent of both the state and the official church bureaucracy. The consortium, of course, wanted the Church Day to take place, and their approach was one of seeking compromise with both the state and the rebellious grass-roots groups. They basically wanted the event to take place and did not want anybody to stand in the way of this.

But then they made the mistake of creating a barrier for the grass-roots groups, right from the start, which the groups, in turn, simply could not accept: of the roughly 68 grass-roots groups in Saxony, only three were to be allowed to participate in each of the three basic topics of the conciliatory process: Peace, Justice, and the Preservation of the Creation. Of course, the grass-roots groups withdrew, said that they could not condone such limitations, and got Christoph Wonneberger [a progressive Protestant pastor] and his church presidium to help organize this "Alternative Church Day" [Statt-Kirchentag]. The grass-roots groups were joined by many active members from various parishes. They must have had hundreds of participants. . . .

Did Wonneberger run into any difficulties because of his active support for the Alternative Church Day?

Yes, there were quite a few tensions. But the great thing about this man is that he always made it sound very casual: "Well, if these young people want to organize something on their own, don't you think that we can provide some facilities for them?" or "Don't worry so much about the consequences. Why don't we give them a chance? What can go wrong anyway?"—that's just how Wonneberger is. So his church quickly turned into the center for the Alternative Church.

The most conspicuous thing that happened during these days was an action by about 200 young people who, in response to the events in China, carried banners through the 60,000 to 70,000 official Church Day participants with the word "democracy" painted on them in German and Chinese. They did this during the end of one of the big events there. Some of the stewards wanted to stop them, but most of the organizers fortunately said, "Why don't we let these young people go ahead and demonstrate." The Stasi circled with helicopters over the area, taking pictures in order to be able to identify the ones who were taking this public stance in favor of democracy. The whole event was well-staged for dramatic purposes. They had these long white ribbons, making a chain by holding each others' hands. So, in this way, the Alternative Church Day paid a visit to the official Church Day and confronted them with some of the real problems, and this was welcomed by quite a few.

This event was organized by the people from the grass-roots groups who had organized the Alternative Church Day?

Yes, people who said that although they were not allowed to participate officially, they were still going to try to make a statement there.

Before that time two other things had happened. First, on 4 June, we organized the so-called "Pleisse memorial march" [the Pleisse is a river that runs through Leipzig]. The purpose was to save—well, actually, that's an exaggeration, to fight for the "cleaning up" of—the Pleisse. We published an illegal little brochure exposing the extent of pollution in the Pleisse. We spent a lot of time and energy on that. The young people worked really hard, day and night. We also organized a documentary: pictures of pipes spewing toxic waste into the Pleisse, and so on—fantastic exhibition.

The Stasi went completely berserk. I myself was followed around by Stasi cars and constantly observed. They knew exactly what we were doing, but they did not yet do anything about it. I was the official organizer of the event; I had to negotiate with the police, who ultimately refused to give us a permit for the march, with very fishy justifications on their part, and I protested against that. I was, in effect, ordered to stand up in front of the several hundred demonstrators whom we thought would gather in front of the church [actually several thousand showed up] and tell them that we had no permission for the march and that we should, for now, refrain from going ahead.

You can't imagine this, about 400 Stasi people, shoulder to shoulder, standing in front of the church on that day. In the adjacent streets they had numerous trucks full of riot police, and, of course, a lot of regular People's Police officers all over. Our plan had been to have a sermon and meet at one church, then peacefully march along the Pleisse, and to have a final rally at another church. So we decided to cancel the march, and let people go from one church to the other in groups. Why not? But the police still could not refrain from interfering. They arrested people, threw them into trucks, and so on.

The bishop as well as the superintendent intervened later on the same day and managed to clear up a lot of the charges against us. I gave my big speech, and I guess most people could somehow accept it [that the march was canceled], but it was also made very clear by practically everybody that this was the very last time that we would accept something like that. We made very clear that things were stinking to high heaven around here, and we were no longer going to let our future and our children's future be ruined by some idiots in the government—things would not and could not go on like this. All of this was expressed very clearly, so clearly, in fact, that we had a huge controversy at the district council a few days later.

On that occasion, I protested against the way we had been treated by the officials. I told them quite explicitly that I was here for negotiating talks, and not for taking orders. I said, "Be more careful in the manner you talk to me. All we want is to talk about the problems. We are not marching in the streets because it's fun, or in order to aggravate you, but because the conditions around here are stinking to high heaven. Don't you understand that? Don't you see how this entire city is quite literally falling apart?" These sycophants did not have any real power; they always had to ask Berlin first. It was just terrible. Worst of all was the city administration. They intoxicated themselves at one lavish reception after the other, while the whole city around them was collapsing. It was so bad that later on I could not tell anyone about this "conversation" I had with the party hacks. If people had known how stupid and incompetent these bureaucrats were, at the same time acting as if they were the biggest and strongest, they would have taken to the streets much earlier.

Here, you seem to be agreeing with a number of others who have told me that people should have moved into opposition activities much earlier, that people should have tried to make use of the rights they did have. Is that view valid in your opinion?

Yes, definitely, but it entered absolutely no one's mind to demand such rights, to sue for such rights, because we all knew that if we dared to say anything they would get us—that was the mentality of the GDR citizen. If you criticized somebody for not speaking up in those days, you instantly received the response: "Well, you know very well that we could not have said anything; they would have immediately arrested us." This was an ever-present fear somehow; it permeated all walks of life, this haunting fear that you could be arrested at any time, right off the street. The Stasi heard everything, knew everything, were everywhere, and everybody knew that.

It wasn't as if we walked around like crippled creatures all the time, but as soon as it got political, one had to watch out, one had to be extremely careful. This is also what broke us, at least a great many of us.

What you just said contains, perhaps, an interesting contradiction. On the one hand, you argue that people should have made use of their rights much earlier, and, on the other hand, you state that the risks or dangers were very real, that it had less to do with the mentality of the GDR citizens than with actual dangers and repercussions, in other words?

Of course, there was a real danger, but nevertheless I criticize all of us for having done way too little for much too long. . . .

You are saying more would have been possible without asking people to become martyrs?

Of course. For example, if we in the church had begun to say in the early eighties, when the first major confrontations with state power occurred around here, "enough is enough" [bis hier und nicht weiter], things could have turned out very differently. I guess the Protestant church is just a priori rather unpolitical. But of course that is not a viable stance in a country in which people are oppressed, a society in which they have been robbed of basic human rights. So this is the very point where my critique applies—also to myself.

I know it would not have made any sense to take to the streets, but it would have made quite a difference if we, as religious dignitaries and functionaries, had spoken out more clearly and openly, naming the people who stole our freedom and who held the key to our freedom. Much too little of that ever happened.

I do not blame myself as much as some others, because at least I dared to do a number of things others did not. But still, I am also to blame, because I also did not take it any further—that is, far enough.

None of us went to prison and were released as possible spokespersons of the reform, like Václav Havel or others. Now we have to come to terms with the consequences. We have to look at what happened to us, as individuals *and* as a church.

I can still see Bishop Hempel at the Pastor Day, shortly before the Wende, on 5 October 1989. He was a nervous wreck and got very upset about the question of whether or not the Peace Prayers should be prohibited.

Particularly in Dresden, this was a very critical time, and some people argued that the events in Dresden could easily turn into a bloodbath. The bishop came out in favor of continuing the Peace Prayers, but he got very distraught about people giving him a big hand against Magirius. About two-thirds of them had been in favor of continuing the Peace Prayers; in fact, they wanted to expand them. So they gave him a big hand as if they wanted to say, "You [the bishop] have won." He apologized for that later on, because he believed in the idea of "church unity" and the whole affair was very embarrassing to him.

At this point, the church hierarchy in Dresden finally and at long last realized that this whole process was coming down to basics [es geht ums Eingemachte]. The question was not any longer whether we should organize a Peace Prayer or not, or whether we could stay out of the whole controversy or not. The time when we could have kept out of it was long past. Now we had to see this thing through. From now on it depended on our trust in God, whether we trusted our Lord that he would continue to govern the hearts of people with nonviolence. We certainly could not have imagined at that time that this state would collapse as easily as it did just a little later.

In retrospect, I can only say "thank God" that we had a few people here in Leipzig, and elsewhere, who managed to come through by overcoming the caution of the church hierarchy.

■ SEBASTIAN PFLUGBEIL, physicist, leading environmentalist, and nationally prominent opposition activist. ▮ *"What we engaged in was open, relaxed and nonexclusive. We succeeded in sustaining that for many years. We were what one might call 'experimenting in democracy.'"*

Though agreeing with people like Klaus Kaden about the nature of life in the GDR, Sebastian Pflugbeil never seemed content to express his views through political alternatives that could be described as "already existing." He conceded that his ideas might be considered "somewhat idealistic," yet he maintained that the real problem with East German society had to do with people "simply following some colorful flags" instead of taking any initiative themselves. "Our parents have already done that kind of 'following the lead,' and we have also simply gone along for the last 40 years."[34]

A physicist by training and probably the most preeminent environmental expert within the opposition, Pflugbeil was one of the thirty founders of New Forum. In the "government of national responsibility" formed under Prime Minister Hans Modrow, Pflugbeil became minister without portfolio for New Forum.

I first encountered Pflugbeil's name in an article about the East German opposition in the *New York Times* in November of 1989. He was quoted describing the opening of the Wall as "an act of desperation" by the communist regime, "a blow aimed at the people's movement." As East Germans were suddenly, for the first time, allowed to go West, Pflugbeil worried that "they will now stay out of politics." Why? Because there was much reason to fear that "the small amount of national identity that

34. Quoted from an interview conducted 26 October 1989. Rein, *Die Opposition in der DDR*, 21, 22. My translation.

developed over the last two months would be drowned in West German chocolate."

A little over two months later, Pflugbeil offered another memorable evaluation, this time in *Der Spiegel*, the largest political weekly in West Germany. He said: "We have once again come to the point where the powerful decide, and we will have to fall in line behind a brass band of those who determine what the world will be and what will become of the children." For reasons I wanted to try to understand firsthand, his fears seem to have come true with remarkable speed and completeness.

I interviewed him in his well-appointed and spacious East Berlin apartment. Pflugbeil is a relaxed, rather quiet person, whose responses are cautiously yet sharply phrased. Much of his hope and energy, fueled by the revolution, had apparently been drained, according to his own account, by months of tireless work, constant setbacks, and the obvious general failure of the revolution to provide anything vaguely resembling what Pflugbeil and his friends had sought. He seemed to have accepted defeat for the time being, and, like 16 million of his fellow citizens, was now trying to cope with an environment that had radically changed in a breathtakingly short period of time. Shortly before I left his home, he quietly remarked, almost as if it was not meant for my attention: "We have helped give birth to a child that quickly turned into a rather ugly creature." The sheer speed of this process seemed absolutely unprecedented in history. It is a subject to which it will be necessary to return.

■ I was born in 1947 and grew up in a small town called Greifswald. My parents were church musicians. Because of their close association with the church I was, from early childhood on, treated as a minority. I never participated in the Young Pioneers, and when I went to school I did not become a member of the FDJ.

I survived this situation rather well in the small university town of Greifswald, however, because there were quite a few critical people and older people who had no association with the FDJ. Actually, they wanted to have nothing to do with the government of the GDR. So we were not the only ones with different ideas. But we were always a minority.

You seem to have had no problems getting into the university despite the fact that you had not played along. . . .

Yes, I really did not have too many problems with that—I was extremely lucky in terms of timing. During those years it was a lot easier than later on. During my course of study I participated actively in the Protestant student parish, something one could perhaps call the beginning of my political consciousness. On numerous occasions I later on tried to apply the kind of broad and critical thinking I had [acquired] there to state organizations and institutions like the Free German Youth. . . .

After I had graduated I joined the Academy of Sciences. One of the first things I initiated there was the founding of an FDJ chapter, something we actually managed to pull off. What this meant was that we had founded this FDJ chapter before it was installed from above, so we subsequently enjoyed many years of relatively free political debates within our FDJ organization. In fact, our FDJ chapter functioned very similarly to the student parish.

When you are referring to "us," whom do you mean?

Well, people who more or less thought alike, people who were interested in political and professional debates, but who were not at all interested in the usual kinds of dogmatic and narrow sham debates going on in most mass organizations and parties. What we engaged in was open, relaxed, and nonexclusive. We succeeded in sustaining that for many years. We were what one might call "experimenting in democracy." Of course, eventually our chapter was also killed from above. . . .

I would imagine that it must have been rather difficult under then-existing circumstances to find like-minded people.

Again, we had pretty advantageous circumstances. I, for example, began my professional life at a time when there was a glut of natural scientists in the GDR. The state had estimated its needs for natural scientists according to West German figures, and they had not taken into consideration that there would not be enough jobs for all those people.

The industry, at the time, offered almost no research jobs, and the positions within the university were quickly filled. So they did not know what to do with us.

Many of my fellow students could only find employment as "product quality controllers" in the toy industry, or similar jobs like that. Most of them ended up doing jobs which had little or nothing to do with their training.

I was lucky enough to get a position in the Academy of Sciences, doing basic medical research. Most of the people there were pretty lively, people who had not yet become resigned, and who were very interested in lively debates. . . . Of course, I immediately got the reputation of being a troublemaker there as well. Even at the academy, people with dissident ideas constituted a clear minority.

What kinds of issues did you debate or fight over at the academy?

The first and foremost issue was to implement some continuing *studium generalis,* that is, education in the broadest sense with a clear political emphasis. The purpose of that was, among other things, to test the limits of what was possible. We began to read Rosa Luxemburg, for example, which they could only accept with great reservations. . . .

We sparked an amazing amount of movement within the academy simply because we initiated things ourselves instead of waiting for things to come down from above. We simply tried to decide on our own what to do and what not to do. The older members seemed to really like that kind of initiative. But that also did not last very long.

I later became part of the regular staff of the institute, despite my reputation. In political terms I quickly began to concentrate my work within the antinuclear arms movement, which started around the early seventies and lasted until the time of the deployment of new generations of missiles in both East and West Germany in 1983/84.

To this very day I am the "uncle" to whom people come if they want to find out how nuclear bombs or missiles actually function, what they can do, how dangerous they are, and so on. If people needed literature on this issue, they usually came to see me. We later expanded our political work to the intrinsic connection between nuclear arms and nuclear reactors. In other words, if one does not want nuclear reactors either, one has to deal with the entire question of how to develop a national energy policy without dependence on nuclear reactors.

Those are the kinds of topics I have been dealing with for years now. And to the extent I could, I always tried to disseminate my findings to the general public as much as that was possible. Particularly over the last few years, one had a number of possibilities to do that. All of them, however, took place under the auspices of the church. The church was, in effect, the only place in the GDR where one could meet and communicate freely.

To do work within the realm of the church, of course, was not very difficult for me due to my prior connections there. I knew many people, I knew how the church was organized, and I knew what kind of language one had to use within the church. . . .

After Chernobyl I wrote the first comprehensive and detailed paper available in the GDR about the consequences of the use of nuclear energy, with a particular focus on the specific problems in the GDR. . . .

For many years critical debates were pretty much confined to the realm of the church. . . . There were, of course, advantages and disadvantages to this relationship. A disadvantage was that one sometimes had to discuss for months certain issues with church officials, such as how to phrase certain things. I sometimes had endless arguments whether this or that was going too far, or should be put in a different fashion—all debates with people who did not know anything about the subject matter, but debates one had to fight out in order not to run into any trouble.

The advantage was that my studies, when they appeared under the auspices of the Alliance of Protestant Churches, immediately received "diplomatic" importance. They were thus much more difficult for the state to contest, even though they [state and party functionaries] got very angry about the fact that someone had, for the first time, laid things out in such a clear fashion.

One should also keep in mind that it was very difficult, in most cases even impossible, to publish anything outside the realm of the church. . . .

I was somewhat surprised, when I first began to study dissent and opposition in the GDR, by the large number of oppositional groups which never seemed to have managed to create a cooperative network among themselves. My first impression was that the reason behind this multitude of groups primarily had to do with personal animosities, and not so much with different ideas or goals. Is that correct?

One reason for that might have been that it had always been very difficult to communicate with one another. There were very few opportunities for printing anything, telephones were routinely tapped, letters were read by the Stasi, and so forth. So, for purely logistical reasons, most groups remained confined to small-scale local work.

Another reason was that many of the stalwarts of these groups were quite pigheaded. They did their own things without being affected much by what was happening around them. You know, people who tried hard not to be pushed around by the Stasi, by the church, or anyone else—which is precisely why they were the stalwarts.

In other words, they were the most courageous, the most daring. . . .

. . . Well, yes, but beyond that pigheaded people, as a type, are very difficult to bring together under one roof. What you get are a lot of tensions and animosities. When you have a lot of clubs, so to speak, you also have a lot of club leaders.

But you are right, in programmatic terms, in terms of ideas and goals, we all had very similar points of view. . . .

Let me ask you one more question about the precise difficulties you had in terms of communicating with like-minded people in the GDR. One thing I learned, to my surprise, was that there was an assortment of "contact telephones" one could call, at the Umweltbibliothek in Berlin, or at pastor Turek's church in Leipzig, for example, in order to receive information on what was going on, whom to contact, and so on.

Yes, this functioned relatively well in situations of acute crises. Whenever we had heard, for example, that some people had been arrested, one could find out specifics about who had been arrested and where with the help of these contact phones; about what was planned in terms of how best to respond; who was organizing something in solidarity with the arrestees; and so forth. For such purposes, communication was organized stunningly well.

But when it came to problems or debates of political substance, when the issue was, for example, how to come up with a new concept for the economy or for a national energy plan, these communicational links did not work well at all. Instead, you had these typical "insider circles" of a limited few who regularly met, all of whom knew each other well. Attempts in this direction were completely dependent upon the individual efforts of a few people. We virtually never reached wider circles of people.

Most people, it seems to me, were interested more in having informal meetings, in planning certain political actions, or in distributing fliers, and such.

What about all those different grass-roots groups which were initiated within the realm of the church, in Berlin, in Dresden, in Leipzig, and many other cities across the country? In your opinion, were these groups engaged more or less continuously in political work concerning issues such as peace, the environment, human rights, and so on?

It is true that within those grass-roots groups things worked pretty well for quite some time. They got many things done; they organized a number of important events, such as "Peace Concrete" [Frieden Konkret, a national meeting of grass-roots peace groups that was organized for six consecutive years].

All such events were very significant in that they helped to establish some rudimentary forms of communication between different groups and people. But it was also quite obvious how severe the limitations of these groups were. They represented the beginnings of a movement, but they were still far from representing anything like a coherent agenda for a different society.

■ GERHARD RUDEN, leading activist of the Initiative for Peace and Human Rights, parliamentary candidate for Alliance 90, municipal director for environmental issues in the city government of Magdeburg. ■ *"It felt like some sort of personal liberation."*

Some of the essential dynamics of social movements—in East Germany as in all other East-Central European countries—are brought clearly into focus by Gerhard Ruden, though I was fortunate even to discover him at all as a possible source. Some five weeks into my historical search for the roots of dissent, and for people who could tell me about the emergence of oppositional groups, I visited the medium-sized city of Magdeburg. There I encountered the director of economics of MAW, the largest industrial instruments plant in Europe with some 7,000 employees in Magdeburg alone, and some 11,000 others scattered across the GDR. I had a long conversation with Mr. H., in which he told me about previous mismanagement and the looming danger that his plant would go under in the near future. With the coming of the currency union with the Federal Republic of Germany, Mr. H. feared, the former GDR would necessarily lose all contracts with their Eastern neighbors and the Soviet Union. None of the Eastern Bloc countries were able to pay in "hard" Western currency.

But since this influential East German executive could not help me unearth oppositional activities prior to the Fall of 1989, either inside or outside his plant, the interview with him is not included in this book. What he did tell me, however, was that "there is a Mr. Ruden, a very courageous man, who I believe has been politically active in Magdeburg for a very long time. I think he is now municipal director of environmental issues in the city government."

I proceeded to city hall and inquired about Mr. Ruden, and was sent to his office on the third floor. Mr. Ruden was in a conference at the time. So—another fortuitous accident—I began to talk to his personal advisor, who turned out to be a West German Social Democrat, civil servant, and expert on environmental questions from Düsseldorf. He had been assigned to "help out" Mr. Ruden in setting up his administration in Magdeburg. "At least there are some positive signs of support from the West," I thought to myself: someone who had come not in order to "take over," as was usually the case, but rather in order to help out and facilitate.

My meeting with Gerhard Ruden took place that evening in the recently opened office of New Forum. A man of about 45, a construction engineer by training, Ruden had been one of the candidates of Alliance 90 for both state and national parliaments. In both efforts he had been narrowly defeated.

Again, I was deeply impressed by the patient, sensitive, open-minded, and candid approach that Gerhard Ruden, like many other dissidents, brought to our discussion. No subject, however distressing, appeared off-limits. His story sketches another vivid portrayal of how an "average citizen" in the GDR began to make a difference by exploring ways to make his private opposition effectively public. He was among that growing band of East Germans who could no longer bear the prospect of being asked—after the opportunity had passed—"why didn't you try to do something?"

■ My political activities started within the realm of the church. I am a Protestant Christian. Since about 1979 our pastor began to talk about problems concerning the environment, and I quickly became very interested in that particular topic. We started with little things, riding a bike instead of taking the car, or collecting household garbage. But we also debated the more global aspects of these problems.

The other important problem, of course, had to do with the accelerating arms race. We organized meetings, seminars, and things of that kind in the Sankt Michaels parish.

Our Protestant pastor, Kretschmann, as well as pastor Bohley, a brother-in-law of Bärbel Bohley, and pastor Tschiche were the most active pastors around here. Pastor Tschiche, I would say, was by far the most revolutionary person within the realm of the church, at least in this area. He constantly had quarrels with the church hierarchy. He had started a peace initiative as early as 1983 under the auspices of the Protestant Academy. Two years later, he was thrown out of the academy with his peace group. After that, the peace group moved to pastor Bohley's parish, and there I joined them in 1985. So that was the initial seed for any kind of peace activity in Magdeburg. It was a very lively, very active group. . . .

Our first activities were not very spectacular. Initially, we merely tried to enter some kind of communication process with the official state organs, such as representatives of the district council, of the city council, or of the factories. We actually managed to initiate dialogue with representatives of one plant that was particularly interesting to us: the Energie Kombinat, the plant that was mainly involved in building the nuclear reactor near Magdeburg. We basically attempted to convince them that nuclear energy was too dangerous to pursue. Of course, this was perhaps a bit naive on our part, but we thought it was worth a try. . . .

The next thing we organized was a seminar on human rights issues [in 1988], which was a pretty spectacular event at the time. We mainly discussed criminal justice procedures in the GDR. Actually, we wanted to write an alternative criminal law, but we ran out of energy and time. The revolution, you see, sort of got in our way [laughing]. . . .

How much did you know about the numerous activities in various other cities in the GDR throughout the eighties?

Well, I knew of some of the groups, such as the Initiative for Peace and

Human Rights in Berlin [founded in 1985], whose Magdeburg chapter I joined in 1989. We also knew of people like Bärbel Bohley, or Vera Wollenberger, and, of course, we knew about pastor Rainer Eppelmann. . . .

A sort of network throughout the GDR began to be created with Frieden Konkret, an event that took place every year. . . . They actively attempted to create a network among all those disparate groups across the country. Frieden Konkret was also by far the most spectacular event related to peace activities that happened every year in the GDR. . . .

Our main contribution to Frieden Konkret was a programmatic paper in which we wanted to use moral arguments in an effort to force the church to provide space and support to the grass-roots peace groups who tried to organize within the church. . . .

You see, the church had an attitude of sympathetic distance, or, if you like, distant sympathy to the work of the peace groups. The bishop once got very interested in our work after representatives of the state had paid him a visit and had told him: "Herr bishop, you have people in your church who engage in dissident political work. We expect you to stop this kind of activity."

Their understanding had obviously been that the church was organized like the party or the state, where Honecker could tell the last comrade in the province exactly what to do and what not to do. So they thought the bishop could also tell a grass-roots group like ours what to do and what not to do. Of course, the bishop realized that this would not be possible with us. But he came to see us anyway, and inquired politely as to what kinds of activities we had planned, how we perceived our role, etc. He also asked us whether we could please inform him before we engaged in any public activity, because, as he put it, "wouldn't it be sad if I had to find out through the secret police what you were up to?" We agreed to that. But most of our activities were so extemporaneous, usually in response to some kind of event or happening, that there was usually no time to discuss matters with him beforehand.

I have to say, however, that the church never really held a grudge against us for being so refractory. It is true, we did not pay excessive attention to all the conventions and rules, and none of us were regular visitors to church services. In fact, we were an extremely mixed bunch in terms of our ideological backgrounds. Quite a few atheists were in our group. We had representatives of every age bracket, from 16 to 74, and we had socialists and conservatives—really quite a cross section of society. . . .

You see, we all knew each other in Magdeburg. Everyone who was active in any kind of oppositional political activity did so within the realm of the church. We all had some loose contacts with one another. If nothing else, we met when the church managed to organize a Peace Sunday, which they used to do quite frequently. Unfortunately, they stopped doing this in the last few years before the revolution. Those were wonderful events which took place in the cathedral. All the groups—Third World groups, peace, environmental, women's groups—all presented themselves and their material on little tables. So that was always a wonderful opportunity to get to know people, to exchange material and information, and to make contacts. . . .

I think the last Peace Sunday was organized either in 1986 or early '87. But after that, the church hierarchy was just so scared, they stopped doing this. . . .

I felt very relieved to have found this group. It felt like some sort of personal liberation. The work within the group moved me, affected me so much—it is hard to describe: to have finally found a group of people who seriously dealt with some of the very issues of survival facing humanity. Not only when we actually met, but also during all other parts of my life, I was constantly trying to do things "for the cause." What we were trying to do, you see, was to create a movement.

I began to use a lot of my work time trying to establish contacts, trying to obtain information, and so on. The work in this group quite literally began to take over my life. More than that, it began to *be* my life. My daily job simply could not compare. You see, one could easily sit out one's job on one's left buttock within this so-called socialist society. I used my telephone primarily in order to make calls that were related to our political activities. With a little skill, one could easily spend a large portion of one's own work time on such political matters. . . . My work environment was quite ideal for doing oppositional political work. You might say that this was "socialism" at its best. . . .

How many people were active in your group?

Actually, not all that many, about 12 who regularly showed up. But out of those 12, only four or so were really active, organizing events, writing petitions, and such. . . . It just required a lot of courage. Like when we wrote a letter to Honecker—to sign something like that took some guts. The fear among the population in the GDR was so strong, and so pervasive, that people sometimes asked me in utter astonishment, "How can you dare to do that?" . . .

In one letter we wrote to Honecker we accused him of always saying the same thing in his annual New Year addresses, of always making the same promises without ever doing anything to live up to them. Not surprisingly, we routinely got replies from some of his cronies that said absolutely nothing—replies that inadvertently supported our underlying point, of course. . . .

The last large event that took place before the revolution had to do with the local elections in May of 1989.

Grass-roots activists in virtually every city in the GDR had organized something on the occasion of this election. How did that happen? Was there some sort of nationwide plan, or at least some communication throughout the country?

No, unfortunately we did not manage to pull that off. It was certainly what many of us had hoped for. I think at the next election we would have succeeded in coordinating our efforts nationwide, in finding a GDR-wide strategy of how best to push the state to its limits. . . . A long time before the elections, in the fall of 1988, we had already written letters to the party district leadership concerning the next elections. Actually, it was a letter of demands. At that time we had already stopped requesting things politely. After all, if one did that, nothing ever happened anyway.

I remember that throughout 1988 we had an ongoing discussion about how best to write letters to the authorities, how best to obtain a positive result without getting creamed. Should we continue to write these rather submissive "shake hands" letters, or should we be a little more forceful? We reached the conclusion that we had offered our cooperation long enough; now it was time to make demands, to demand those basic civil rights that one should actually be able to take for granted anyway.

So in the fall of 1988 we stated very clearly "we demand closeable voting booths; we demand that the party of a given candidate is written right next to the name of the candidate; we demand that the name of this candidate has to be marked," that is, active voting rather than the usual passive voting [where one only crossed out the names of the candidates one did not want to be elected].

After that, we were invited to the district leadership. We were greeted by the secretary of the district leader. . . . He approached us in a very rough, "class-struggle" kind of fashion. Obviously, he wanted to impress us, to influence us, to force us to reconsider our position. He came straight out saying, "The primary goal is to maintain the power of the working class. You can say about that whatever you want," he told us, "but the question of power has been resolved in the GDR by the working class and its representative, the Socialist Unity Party." It's incredible how they talked to you.

In any case, shortly before we were about to leave again, I casually remarked to him, "You know, I am not as uptight as you seem to be about this question of who holds power. The SED has held power for forty years now. Might it not be time to give someone else a chance?" Wow, talk about uptight, his reaction was more than just uptight. They began to exert all sorts of pressure, not only on me, but also on the firm where I was currently employed, and, of course, on the church. For instance, they told members of my parish that "the person who runs the peace group in your parish, Mr. Ruden, plays a very subversive role in this group. He tries to exploit it for his goal of undermining the power of the working class."

After that, they scheduled another meeting, not only with me, but also with my employer and the church leadership, with the obvious purpose of reprimanding me severely and, ultimately, silencing me. They talked down to us, or rather yelled down to us, just like the security police. To their utter dismay, however, most of the others they had summoned supported me, and thus there was not much they could do to me after all. . . .

But, however much our activity upset the party, there is also no question that all these grass-roots groups caused quite a few stomachaches for the church hierarchy over the years. Nevertheless, during this local election they, too, realized that they should support us, that there were extremely good and competent people in their ranks who had drafted these election complaints, and who had organized all the protests as a result of the blatant election fraud we had revealed. Somehow the church had to realize that we had gotten more done than they had, despite the fact that they had all those experts, lawyers, and such, and we were just self-organized small groups with no funds, little support—little of anything, in fact. We were the ones who put our fingers right on all those blatant injustices, who came right out and dared to call a spade a spade.

You see, the state and party people did not stop at violating their own laws. The way they had prepared the elections was not right, the way the actual election process took place was full of violations, and on top of that they had obstructed our rightful attempts to oversee the election process. They actually kicked us out of most of the polling places. . . .

So, they had undermined themselves to such an extent that they could not, logically, prevail in a conversation with us, no matter how they tried to cloak it in the language of class struggle. They were bankrupt.

■ ANDRÉ BRIE, vice-chairman in 1990 of the Party for Democratic Socialism, successor of the East German communist party. ▮ *"Our most disastrous miscalculation was to believe that reform could happen with, and from within, the party."*

A tall and slender man in his early forties, André Brie is known for his dour facial expression, a characteristic that did not improve with the coming of revolutionary changes in the Fall of 1989. In many ways he appears as a rather typical representative of the upcoming (middle-aged) generation of new party leaders in the PDS: a dedicated communist intellectual, too critical and outspoken to have risen to top leadership positions under the old guard, yet also too committed to "the cause" to consider leaving the party. It became evident in the manner he conversed with me that Brie was extremely troubled by the events that had occurred during the previous year. He was still very much engaged in the struggle of coming to terms with his own role in all of it.

Despite this inner tension, he seemed, for a while, to relish the chance for an engaged conversation with a Westerner, allowing himself for a moment, as it were, to step out of his daily tasks as PDS vice-chairman, and to reflect upon the unexpected changes that had radically transformed both his country's politics and his own personal life.

What follows is a complex and troubled account by a person engaged in a desperate and deeply contradictory search for ways to retain the socialist dream in the face of its 40 years of distortion in Eastern Europe. It is revealing to discover how exclusively Brie's attention was and remains focused on people who sat atop the party that sat atop society. It seems as if everybody else—whether considered by the party as agents of a progressive historical role or viewed as a major obstacle—remained part of an abstract and undiscovered "mass of people." It is interesting to learn, for example, that "workers" were not included in his list of potential constituencies for the reorganized socialist party. Such a denouement obviously represents a major deviation from the classical communist script in which "the proletariat" is "the only true revolutionary subject," and thus, one assumes, the primary political constituency to which the party should direct its attention. But, in terms of twentieth-century history, this stance does not, in fact, represent a noticeable deviation from the political vanguard model first formulated by V. I. Lenin. "The working class" was part of the rhetoric that rationalized elite party rule, but as worthy participants in a "new socialist society," workers were almost never in the conscious range of vision maintained by the party's intellectuals.

Thus, what Brie seems to have in common with his colleagues in most any other party, East or West, is a deeply internalized elite concept of politics. Advocates from across the ideological spectrum have perceived, and continue to perceive, "ordinary" citizens as inherently lacking both "necessary competence" and the "proper consciousness" to participate in the political process in any meaningful fashion—public rhetoric to the contrary notwithstanding. The rationale has a similar ring, East or West: since we live in a "hard world" of "tough political choices," more often than not "the people" just cannot be trusted. The revolutionary dynamics in the GDR somehow took a "wrong turn," in Brie's remarkably candid phrase, because "change did not emanate from the top."

The sober truth that hangs over the following interview with Brie is the pervasiveness of intellectual closure, not only within the whole of society, but within the ruling party itself.

■ I think the fact that my father had been a Jewish-communist émigré in Great Britain played a very significant role in my biography. He returned to Germany in 1946, while his parents, his sister, and his grandfather, who was also a communist, remained in Great Britain. His family did not want to return to Germany because virtually all their relatives had been killed in Nazi Germany.

In any case, my father's first position in the newly founded German Democratic Republic was state chairman of the FDJ in Mecklemburg. In the early fifties, however, he was dismissed from this position and even arrested for a short while during one of those communist witch hunts in connection with the activities of the Fields [the reference is to Noel H. Field, an American communist who was accused of spying for the CIA—a virus planted by the CIA itself, as was later discovered].

Even though he was rehabilitated later on, this "break" in his career contributed decisively to the fact that he continued to be a highly critical person. And, also, his children were able to learn firsthand about the cruelties of Stalinism at a time when virtually no one talked about that in the GDR yet. Our father always tried to raise us in a very critical and open-minded fashion.

Later on, he became a diplomat, so for stretches of time we grew up abroad, particularly in China and Korea at the time of the Vietnam War. Of course, that also shaped my political ideas and my subsequent professional orientations a great deal. . . .

In 1971 I began to study foreign policy at the Institute for International Relations, a course of study that was certainly very much geared toward training elite cadres for the diplomatic service of the GDR, but one that was necessarily also a program of high quality and depth. . . .

Many friends and I had had first experiences at this time with getting disciplined by the party and the state apparatus. What I am about to tell you is probably very hard for a Westerner to understand, because you come from such a radically different culture. Most of the things which resulted in disciplinary actions taken against us, and which thus required a certain amount of courage to undertake, sound absolutely silly nowadays or must seem absurd to someone from the West. . . .

Let me give you an example. In 1973 we were supposed to study Lenin's piece "The Renegade Kautsky," and some of my friends thought that, in order to come to a fair assessment of Kautsky, it would be necessary to read some of his own writings. I was assistant party secretary at the time when a campaign started against us claiming that such a request represented "doubting comrade Lenin." I fully supported my comrades, however, and thus got caught in the ensuing whirl of events.

Let me just characterize for you in what ways this debate was conducted back then: the whole affair happened five years after the Czechoslovakian events of 1968, so they couched our request in terms such as "this is reminiscent of the debates at the universities in Prague in 1968," or "this represents the invasion of the counterrevolution"—they would not even talk to us on any level other than such blatant slander.

While we had initially received the unanimous support of the entire class of '71, the entire class just as unanimously caved in a couple of days later. After that, we also gave up and ultimately caved in as well. You see, they had made it very clear to us that we were risking our entire training, even though we really did not understand what all this stir was ultimately all about.

At the time, I accepted the consequences and handed in my resignation and dematriculation, but an old comrade persuaded me to tear up this document after a very tough conversation. He thought the whole affair had been completely silly, and told me that we should not respond to this kind of silliness.

What was important about all of this was that the four people who were mainly involved in causing this affair to take place did not fall apart as individuals, or break apart as a group afterward. Rather, we became even more critical. It was a sort of an emancipatory process for us. But, on the other hand, I have to admit that it also led to more conformity, slave language, much more caution. . . .

I joined the party in 1968. I had just turned 18. . . . My two party guarantors [one needed two guarantors to be accepted into the party] were both old communists, both Jewish. Whether to join the party or not was simply never a question for me. It was only later that I thought that I had not been mature enough, but back then it was the logical route to take. . . .

Since you joined after the events in Czechoslovakia, do you remember how you had experienced the Prague Spring?

I remember very well that I was deeply troubled during the entire summer of 1968. I can also recall having a highly ambiguous response. On the one hand, I was fascinated; it was something that I suspected was right, but that was as far as it went. On the other hand, I had, of course, deeply internalized all these party clichés concerning "unity" and "to-getherness," and I was concerned about a chasm opening up between Czechoslovakia and all the other socialist nations.

I was also extremely vulnerable to the propaganda conducted at the time in the GDR. So when the Warsaw Pact nations marched in, I even felt a sense of relief. I was worried that a further deterioration of the situation would lead to the Czechs breaking from the Warsaw Pact and out of the socialist camp. The whole situation seemed to have gotten out of hand. . . .

Back then, the main question we were debating, one that we would debate for the following 17 years, was whether reform, some kind of new start for Eastern Europe, was possible without the Soviet Union. We did not think so at the time. . . .

Well, after my studies, I began working at the same institute [Institute for International Relations] as an assistant. My field of work concerned the Federal Republic of Germany in general and disarmament issues in particular. . . .

Disarmament probably represented the only topic within the social sciences of the GDR which allowed one to say anything critical at all about the existing society. I had a number of opportunities to publish, and, within the context of security and peace questions, I was able to address some of the more fundamental philosophical questions concerning all of society. But as I said before, all of this was, of course, presented in a kind of slave language, all very halfheartedly.

In 1977 the same four people who had been involved in this controversy in 1973 wrote a paper together in which we made—with much arrogance and ignorance, and unfortunately without any attempt to reach the pub-lic—an attempt to clarify our positions regarding the condition of our society in the areas of politics, economics, and ideology. These papers essentially took a position that would, a decade later, become known as perestroika and glasnost.

It was not that we were able to do that because we were so well-informed or so outstandingly intelligent, but simply because these things were already in the air. Ever since the events in Czechoslovakia of 1968, and perhaps even earlier—perhaps as early as the building of the Wall in

1961—the societies of Eastern Europe were developing in a direction that had to be blatantly obvious to everyone who possessed a healthy common sense. And you have to keep in mind that these events were discussed everywhere, even in the GDR. . . .

Our vantage point was the Biermann affair [the best-known dissident political songwriter who was expelled from the GDR in 1976]. . . . The controversy surrounding Biermann represented a deep and decisive break for many critically minded supporters of socialism in the GDR. All the hopes we had nurtured since 1971, hopes that under Honecker a slow process of reform would be set in motion, were shattered. . . . Well, and then we went through a number of years in which the critical attitude we had developed produced little of spectacular quality. On the lower level of the party, it was possible to discuss things absolutely without constraints; on the medium level, this became considerably more difficult; and on the higher level, nothing happened at all.

I was on the higher level within the university for a while and could pretty much say whatever I wanted to, but only under the strict precondition that nothing leaked out, a precondition that I accepted at the time. From today's perspective I have to say that this probably represents the most disastrous mistake or miscalculation on the part of all critical reformers within the Socialist Unity Party during these years: we all thought that a process of reform was possible with, and from within, the party.

In fact, all of us should have left the party, in 1985 at the very latest, and should instead have frontally attacked it. We need to realize that very clearly. . . .

Well, and after '85 with Gorbachev, things quickly intensified. Initially, we had hope—something that continued to discipline us and keep us quiet—that change in the GDR would now become inevitable as well. But by early 1987 at the latest, when the party leadership took a clear position against the Central Committee speech by Gorbachev in which he said that "we need democracy like we need air to breathe," these hopes completely disappeared.

But then there was another factor that helped to keep us patient and quiet a little longer: the assumption that this completely overaged and senile leadership would, in view of the clear and dramatic deterioration of the situation in every area, be replaced with younger people soon. Everyone knew that the economic situation, for example, had badly deteriorated, so we thought it could only be a matter of months until the old guard would finally be replaced.

There was one last factor that kept many of us disciplined, but one that should not be rejected out of hand. All the other factors may have had to do with cowardice, with mendacity, with miscalculations, but not this one. Precisely because the situation had so dramatically deteriorated in the GDR—and by that I mean not only the economic situation, but also the pressure from the outside and the tangibly growing degree of dissatisfaction among the population—we figured that if already existing resentment and anger about this situation were to break out from below, there would be neither a future for the GDR nor a possibility for a renewal of socialism. So we thought change would have to originate from above, and then could be responded to from below. If change did not come from above, there would be no prospect of renewal, but rather things could only move toward unification. As today's situation proves, this was a very justified fear. . . .

We thought that if change happened the same way here as it had in Poland in the early eighties, the GDR would simply cease to exist. Here, we only had a chance if reform could be implemented quickly and radically. I have to qualify this assessment from today's perspective, however, by saying that I do not think that the chances for this renewal still existed in the eighties.

As the economic situation kept getting worse, the support among the population for the socialist idea broke apart and cynicism set in instead. One could have detected that, could have clearly seen that back then, but I simply underestimated the force of this dynamic.

In retrospect, I do not think that we had a chance to turn things around substantially and to move toward a new beginning, neither in '85 nor in the beginning of the eighties. In comparison with the West, we had fallen behind too far; the domestic consensus was already undermined too much. The last real opportunity had been with Czechoslovakia in 1968. . . .

Just recently, I wrote in an article that opposition and reform should really have been initiated right after 14 August 1961 [the day the Wall was built].

You were talking about the consent of the population toward the idea of socialism, and the fact that this consent declined and ultimately disappeared. Did that consent, in fact, ever exist in the GDR after 14 August 1961?

Yes, at least among a substantial portion of the population. Of course, another portion, whose existence was always either ignored or denied [by the party], never supported the ideas of socialism, and this other portion was not small.

So how exactly do you explain this gradual decline of consent among certain sectors of the population toward the idea of socialism?

The GDR increasingly fell behind [economically, compared to West Germany], and people began to realize how small the capacities of this society were in terms of innovation. This was not only significant in quantitative, materialistic terms concerning people's standard of living, but even more so in qualitative terms.

One issue that became increasingly important to most GDR citizens was the question of whether one could travel 'or not. Throughout the entire Helsinki process, questions surrounding democracy and human rights were pushed to the forefront of political debate, not only as something people were hoping for, but as something that was increasingly perceived as absolutely necessary for the development of a modern society. . . . We had serious deficiencies in this area. Then the ultimate disappointment came when many people began to realize that our leadership was determined to prevent perestroika in the GDR. You see, perestroika symbolized great hope for us in the party as well. Millions of people suddenly began to read the speeches of the general secretary of the Soviet Communist Party, Mikhail Gorbachev.

At the time when things began to appear increasingly hopeless [around 1988], I participated in a project under the auspices of Humboldt University, something my brother and Dieter Klein had helped to initiate. The purpose was to think about a modern form of socialism.

In May of 1989 we published our first results, that is, quite some time before the Wende. But we were only allowed to print 200 copies, which in turn were only discussed internally. The whole thing was largely suppressed, but people made about 2,000 illegal copies. In the fall of the same year this document played a large role among the people of New Forum, the Green Party, and other groups of the civic movement.

After May of '89 we continued to publish our work. And when things came to a breaking point in September of '89, we wrote a position paper to Honecker. We were pretty scared about doing this. I was probably more scared than the others. Unfortunately, I was also the one who toned down the whole thing because of my fear. One tragic result was that we did not send it until October, even though the paper had already been finished in September. I was the one who prevented us from sending it out earlier. I thought we needed to collect signatures from key people inside the party before we sent it out.

Well, this whole process wasted fourteen precious days, because some just could not make up their minds. . . . Why did I force the others to wait until we had some signatures? Because for the second time after the *Sputnik* ban in 1988, I went through the same trauma I had first experienced in 1973.

You see, after the *Sputnik* ban, I had demanded that my local party organization write a collective open letter of protest to the Central Committee. At first my request was unanimously accepted. But in the course of the following five days an amazing barrage of pressure came from the Central Committee. Central Committee members came to our party organization, and within days all the members of my party organization caved in.

The director of our institute told me that the end of my university career, my dismissal as a teacher, and my expulsion from the party were demanded by the Central Committee unless I wrote a so-called "self-criticism."

This edict was handed down over the weekend. I was in West Germany at the time, and when I came back I found out that I had lost absolutely all support from my friends at the institute. So I discussed the matter with the few remaining friends outside, some of whom were critical voices in the Central Committee itself. . . .

I thought about whether I could survive as a writer, and came to the conclusion, "No, I cannot." There was only one publishing house that might have continued to publish my work after my expulsion; the others would have no longer even touched anything written by me.

So in the end I caved in as well [he is very moved].

Can you be more explicit? [he wipes away a tear]

I was simply scared of not being able to work at all anymore.

The same thing had just happened to a friend of mine, and I had voted against his expulsion from the party, which was now also used against me. So I bowed before them again, something which I now regret a great deal. Of course, I had no clue that everything would change as quickly and dramatically as it did just a few months later.

May I ask you what this "bowing before them" exactly involved? What did they want you to do, and what did you do?

I had to write a five-page self-criticism. It was extremely humiliating. I maintained my position that I thought it was tactically wrong to ban *Sputnik*, because I thought that we should debate these issues rather than suppress them. But I dropped all my other principal points, and instead completely caved in. I was in turn excluded from the party leadership at the institute, disciplinary proceedings were started against me, and my travel privileges were taken away from me. But they let me stay at the institute.

I was supposed to get tenure as a full professor that same year, but in September they told me again that this was out of the question now. But at least I could continue to work.

The point, of course, was not so much to punish me, but rather to establish an effective warning to the party organization and thereby to pacify the party membership at a time when the entire country was about to boil over.

This was only successful for a very short time, however. Within eight weeks we began to have open debates, yet, once again, with this despicable understanding that we keep everything among ourselves.

What I was really trying to explain to you, however, was that all of those experiences led me to be extremely cautious concerning this document we wanted to send to Honecker, and that's why I first wanted to collect some signatures. I certainly did not want to run full speed into an open knife again. But this fourteen-day delay turned out to be very harmful, a crucial loss of time for the cause of party reform. . . .

Let me take you back in time once more. Earlier you mentioned that open and critical discussion was possible among the lower echelons of the party, or at least was not usually followed by repressive repercussions. Why, then, could you not also attempt to establish contact with people outside the party who were interested in some kind of a socialist alternative, as was done more or less successfully in Poland, Hungary, Czechoslovakia?

There are many aspects to this. The first has to do with the process of self-discipline. Even critical members of the party had deeply internalized the belief that we could not move without the Soviet Union, and that the GDR was in a unique situation, since any kind of national identity was completely missing.

Also, the GDR was the "outpost of socialism" in Europe, and it certainly never got a break from the West. We were caught within a kind of confrontational form of politics that did not emanate just from the GDR or the socialist countries, but one that emanated at least as much from the West.

And then there was a conscious strategy employed by the party leadership to allow critical discussion in small circles, as some kind of necessary outlet. We were, in turn, usually calmed down by that and pleased about how "critical" we could be within these circles. But on the whole we functioned within a public sphere in which communication simply did not take place, a public sphere, furthermore, that was limited to the party.

The universities are an example of such a party-controlled public sphere. But wherever there were attempts to expand this sphere, to communicate with other sectors of society, disciplinary measures set in with brutal force. . . .

When I wanted to give an official talk within the church, for example, it was either prohibited or I had to ask for permission at the highest level. . . . People who went on to establish such contacts anyway were usually expelled from the party. Or communication happened only on the highest level, as in the yearly meetings between high-ranking party officials and high-ranking church dignitaries. But that pretty much defined the limit; more was not allowed.

The consequence was that contact between critical reformers from within the party and interested people from without almost never took place.

Another reason for that, of course, was that people who organized under the umbrella of the church tried to protect themselves. They didn't necessarily trust party people due to their experiences with the security police, with informants, and the restrictive policies of the party in general.

In other words, people and interest were there, but contact did not take place because of fear of repression?

Yes. Contact was either established clandestinely and got nowhere, or, if it was done publicly, the involved party members were immediately expelled and forced into the same trap as all the other nonparty oppositionists.

In other words, your understanding continued to be that change could only come out of the party?

Yes.

Therefore you wanted to stay inside the party and use whatever possibilities came up to change things from within, rather than take the risk of establishing contacts with people outside?

Yes, exactly. I remember clearly that one of the most effective arguments for me, one which party members used concerning my writing of political satire, was "with this you endanger your opportunities as a party member, your opportunities as a faculty member at the institute." I had established numerous international contacts through my work, so I took this argument very seriously. I even began to write political satire under a pseudonym. . . .

■ INGRID KÖPPE, independent activist, recruited to the opposition movement. New Forum representative at the Central Round Table, delegate to the Berlin city parliament, Köppe subsequently became a member of the new united Germany's national parliament. ■ *"The Stasi targeted in advance the people they figured would demonstrate. At this point I was not even able to make it to the demonstration, because they followed me around from early in the morning. I could not believe the time and energy they spent on each single person. I thought 'how many Stasi people must there be if they can do this with every single one of us?' "*

In the words of an admiring colleague, the well-known oppositionist Sebastian Pflugbeil, "Inge Köppe came out of nowhere. An extremely intelligent, very articulate and capable advocate, she quickly assumed a leadership position within the opposition." This happened despite the fact that, in Pflugbeil's words, "no one had known her before."

The interview with Ingrid Köppe took place at the "Red City Hall" in East Berlin, where she had recently begun to serve as an elected member of the (East) Berlin city parliament. Her short hair, sharp blue eyes, and self-assured, straightforward manner give her an energetic, almost boyish expression. Similar to many other East German oppositionists, further-more, her conduct and appearance struck me as pleasantly casual and almost effortlessly candid. Here was a person who had made history, who had helped to bring down the one-party state, who had participated in the Central Round Table; but here, too, was a person who acted as if she had not played a prominent role in these events, as if she was still virtually unknown to her fellow citizens.

Köppe's political views, however, no longer seemed to be in demand outside of Berlin. Though still very much engaged in trying to preserve some of the achievements of the revolution, she no longer could envisage much of a political future for herself. And yet, several months after this interview, she became the domestic policy spokesperson for Alliance 90/Greens in the newly established German-wide national parliament.

As it was early in the morning, we ordered two cups of coffee from the huge city hall cafeteria, and began to talk about how she grew up and what, exactly, had caused her to question "the system GDR," even though she had never been exposed to anything else. Köppe was born three years before the Wall was built.

■ ... What was probably very important in terms of my childhood was the fact that my parents always put great emphasis on independence. You have most likely encountered this issue in other conversations as well: either there was this counterinfluence [the parents] to the school, or there was not. Both my parents and my grandparents stressed the importance of independence and self-reliance, which, of course, on numerous occasions led to big problems in school for me. . . .

Most of my youth was very normal, however. I was a member of the

Young Pioneers, of the Free German Youth, and so on. One learned quickly and easily to conform to certain norms; that was more or less a political necessity, particularly in such overtly political subjects as Staatsbürgerkunde [civics], where you knew exactly what was expected of you. One always knew what kinds of answers they wanted to hear, and usually one just played along. Of course, everybody had a few occasions where she or he showed some resistance.

I finished school in 1976 and started to study pedagogy in college. This was another one of these examples of how the party regulated our lives: I never wanted to study pedagogy; I actually wanted to work somewhere. But at the time it was required that everyone who had passed the Abitur had to go to college afterward. They told us that we were the "elite of the future" and stuff like that. . . .

Of course 1976 was this famous year in which Biermann got expelled, in November. It was common at the time for them to circulate a resolution that everyone was supposed to sign, saying that you fully agreed with this measure. I refused to sign it, for a variety of rather down-to-earth reasons. First, I could not sign something without knowing about Biermann, without knowing exactly what had happened. This was, by the way, a very common thing around here, that people just did what was expected of them, without giving a thought as to what it meant, as to what the background was. But I also did not sign because I knew some of his songs, and I thought it was ridiculous that he was banned from performing or circulating any of his stuff. Of course, it was also clear to me that expelling somebody could never be a solution. . . .

Were there any debates about this, among the students for example?

Yes, but they had nothing to do with substance, you know.

You mean, nobody tried to get the texts written by Biermann, or to talk about the political dimension of his deportation?

No, not at all. Within my circle of friends we did some of that, but not at the university. On the contrary, some of my fellow students said to me, "This is stupid. Why don't you sign," or "Sign it so that it will be illegible."

What do you suppose was their reasoning behind saying that? Was it that they thought you should play along in order not to lose room for maneuvering?

Yes, but also a deeply internalized belief that one just had to do what they asked you to do, that one couldn't simply refuse to do that. In the aftermath of my refusal to sign I had plenty of so-called "conversations" with faculty members, to which I was summoned time and again. I also had my first contacts with the Stasi.

During this time, "politically subversive graffiti" appeared throughout the city, and the Stasi tried to implicate me in this action, even though I had nothing to do with it.

I subsequently dematriculated myself, which was a very difficult procedure, because actually no one was allowed to do that. When we began our training as teachers, they told us that we would not be allowed to drop out. Since they desperately needed new teachers, you could not get kicked out, regardless of how poor your performance was. In the end, I got myself a physician's statement to the effect that something was wrong with my vocal cords.

After that I was not able to find any work for quite some time. What I had not known at the time was that they had a so-called "cadre file" on everyone. Whenever you applied for a job—it didn't matter what kind of job—they requested your cadre file. So, even though my interviews always went extremely well, after they had consulted my cadre file they were somehow never able to offer me a job. So it took quite some time before I was finally able to find a job as a librarian's assistant. I even managed to get back into the university, which was extremely rare for someone who had once been through a story like this. Usually they denied any further education to people like me. . . .

You know, low-key political debates were always going on. For example, I was director of the library I worked at later on, but you could not, in this position, decide on your own what books to order or put on display. Instead, they told you what you had to do. So at the time of the Nachrüstung [debates surrounding the arms race in the early eighties], we increasingly had to order military literature. I worked in the children's library at the time, and we had to order things that were just not fit for children. . . .

. . . Was this during the time in which the party made a general large-scale effort to militarize education throughout society?

Yes, exactly. Of course, you could protest against that in various ways. For example, I always stored away military literature immediately after we had received it. Sure, there were possibilities to do a few things like that.

We also regularly received instructions about what kinds of events we should organize, among them, at the time, an increasing number of military preparation courses, which I always simply refused to schedule. Another ludicrous thing was to form a guard of honor whenever the party received visits from foreign state representatives. Whenever this happened, the members of "state cultural institutions" were called a couple hours ahead of time and then ordered to some place for the purpose of forming a guard of honor. Most people obediently succumbed to that as a matter of course, you know.

I sometimes think about that these days. Back then, so many people were involved in activities like that, and now they act as if it never happened. If more people had resisted things of that sort, who knows? I went twice [to the guard of honor], and after that I refused to go again. I said "this is a waste of work time, I'd rather do something meaningful during this period." You could do that—nobody could force you to participate. The only disadvantages one could suffer had to do with being denied certain extra payments or things like that.

This was also during the time when nuclear missiles were deployed [in both West and East Germany, 1983–84]. The reasoning of the GDR leaders had been that they needed to do this in order to defend themselves against the NATO forces, against the NATO re-armament decision [Nach-rüstungsbeschluss]. And, like all other issues that concerned everyone, it was never publicly debated. Slogans appeared all over the place, but no debate. This whole development had a great effect on me.

During this period the first grass-roots groups began to appear in the churches. Even though I had always known about these groups, I never participated because I had not had any previous contacts with the church, and thus somehow thought it would have been dishonest for me . . .

I understand that a number of people without any prior church affiliation joined these groups. Is that correct?

Yes, I guess different people just had different attitudes toward that. I also went to some of the events they organized, but I never joined any of their groups.

Instead, some of my friends and I began to write and produce flyers concerning the arms race—under circumstances that are probably very hard to imagine for someone from the West. We did not have any of the material we needed, no computers, copy machines, or printers. We thought that we might be able to do it with ink pads. Of course, it was rather conspicuous to go out and buy a lot of ink pads, so we ended up buying children's picture ink pads, until we had enough together. We made the rubber stamps ourselves.

As you can imagine, this method turned out to be too complicated after a while. So we changed our method. I was developing my own photo-graphs at the time, so we figured we could also draw up something, take a picture of it, and then develop it ourselves. What we did was take a piece of glass, write something on it and then photograph it. But again, we did not yet have the kind of markers in the GDR with which you can write on glass. I can remember so clearly when I got the first one of those markers from someone in the West—you know, this marker was so important to me—and now you can get this stuff all over the place, it's just hard to believe. . . .

We started with these activities in 1983, and in some ways we anticipated many of the thoughts that came up later with Gorbachev. It was a very exciting time for us.

The task of getting our flyers distributed was at least as difficult as the task of producing them. We thought hard about how exactly to do this. We finally tried to do it all in one day, putting it in people's mailboxes, trying to avoid being seen by anyone. We produced and distributed about 2,000 of these flyers, which was quite a few at the time.

What did these flyers say? What was your intention?

We had different texts, all written by ourselves. One flyer was a reminder of the history behind World War II; one contained the suggestion that one of the two sides [West or East] should refuse to go along with these ever-expanding cycles of the arms race. . . . Much was directed toward initiating actions we thought individuals could engage in on their own. So we didn't just deal with big politics, but rather tried to remind people of their personal responsibility to protest and resist. . . .

I tried to stay informed about what other activists were doing, but even though I saw that a lot was going on in the churches, I always felt that this would never reach a broader public. Within the safe walls of the church people could live out their resistance without it ever reaching anyone else. So it was our explicit attempt to make something public, even though we did not quite succeed in that either. . . .

I was active myself in the peace movement in West Germany at the time, and I remember that after they had voted to deploy Pershing IIs and Cruise missiles in West Germany, the peace movement pretty much went down the drain. We had been defeated, and we didn't know where to go next. What did you do in the aftermath of that?

Well, the first major thing that happened here was a sudden flood of emigration. My partner left for the West, for example. This whole era was very depressing to me because I lost a lot of friends, one after another. It was always such a final thing. You knew that if someone left, that would be the end of any normal relationship. OK, you could write letters, and we always promised each other that we would see each other again in Prague or somewhere. But still, everyone who left represented a terrible loss to me. I can't even describe it; it was just terrible.

Of course, this got worse over the years, and it went on for a very long time. Again and again, some friend told you that she or he was going to leave. I could usually understand their reasons, because at least my friends did not leave for the Western consumer society, but rather because they had tried many things to change this country from within and had failed, and thus had given up and had decided to leave. It was extremely depressing for those of us who stayed.

Were these people who had officially applied for an exit visa, or people who tried to escape in some other way?

Both. One friend, for example, just tried to get to the other side, which they called attempted escape from the republic [Republikflucht]. I could understand him too. You see, after having lived right next to this Wall for so long, you developed this overwhelming desire just to walk right through it, and that's exactly what he tried. We had spent the evening together, and afterward we walked along the Wall and he suddenly said, "I'm going to try to get over there now," and that's exactly what he did. He was arrested, spent some time in jail, and was subsequently deported. . . .

You said at some point that you always talked openly among friends and fellow students, and some resistance had always been possible. So far I have conducted about 40 interviews with people from Berlin, Magdeburg, Erfurt, Leipzig, and so on, different people from all walks of life, and I have received widely divergent answers as to what was possible before one got into serious trouble. Of course, there is a predictable tendency in these interviews that those who have resisted at some point accuse those who never resisted of not making use of the possibilities for resistance that were available to everyone. Just to give you an example. Rainer Börner [a 31-year-old socialist, currently PDS chief of staff], claimed that discussions at the Free German Youth were absolutely open, anyone could freely speak up, and that claims to the contrary are gross falsifications. Others tell me: "Look, there was practically nothing we could say or do without risking far-reaching repression." How would you describe the degree of freedom to act in the eighties?

I am sure that this was, in fact, very different for different people. Among other things, it was always dependent on the specific officials who evaluated your activities. You could, for example, have professors at the university who made considerable efforts to create their own courses so as to provide some space, or others who, if they had the slightest suspicion, gave you bad grades or wrote reports about you. One's experiences concerning this were, therefore, certainly very different. Yet, there is no doubt that there was room for resistance . . .

. . . Such as refusing to give a signature?

Yes, for example. Another factor is the question of how much people had already conformed to the whole system, the extent to which they were still capable of thinking independently or coming up with any kind of opposition. And, of course, it had something to do with fear, or courage, whichever way you want to put it. There were many things that have just recently been revealed about the Stasi that no one had previously known about, but everyone had known all along that you could be severely punished for acts of defiance or resistance. You learned about that in school, so that at age ten, I think, everyone knew this. I am sure this fear was very significant. Interestingly, people lost their fear only after they had been punished. It was the same thing with the Stasi. Only after we had our first contacts with them did we lose some of our fear. But out of this deeply internalized fear, many restricted themselves right from the beginning and instead tried to meet what they perceived to be the general expectations of the state or party rather than come up with their own thing.

How would you describe the development and the changes of your relationship (or lack thereof) to the state and the party? Most people told me about slow processes of breaking away from the party and the state. Most people seem to have supported the idea of the GDR somehow, or at least they thought that socialism was a good idea and that things could perhaps be improved through the party, even though there were many apparent problems. But, over time, these problems increased in number and could no longer be ignored . . .

I do not belong among those who ever thought about joining the party. Today, I would even go so far as to say that I would and will never join any party. Of course, I knew people who joined with the argument that they wanted to change something, but it was clear to me early on that this could not and would not work—perhaps because I had experienced it with some of my colleagues, for instance when they told me that they had gone to a party meeting, but were not allowed to talk to me about it.

So I think I had a very skeptical attitude toward the party very early on. They did try to recruit me once, when I had just finished my Abitur, but that was more a matter of course. I told them to forget it. They never approached me again after that.

And my attitude toward the German Democratic Republic, well, if you want to put it in the simple categories of "socialism" and "capitalism," I always thought that socialism was more humane. But, of course, the way we experienced socialism here had little to do with what I associated with socialism—if only because one was not allowed to travel freely.

I once traveled to Mongolia, because there had been this open spot with the state-run Youth Tourist [the party-sponsored tour agency]. It had always aggravated me a great deal that Youth Tourist claimed that everyone could travel to the West with its tours, even though everyone knew that only selected people were allowed to go. So one day I went to their offices and said, "You claim in the newspaper that one can travel everywhere with you. So what about it?" They stuttered around for a while and finally said that this was probably not an offer which was meant for me. I responded that they should not put such things in the newspaper then. But I continued to go back there, and at one point I told them that I did not want to travel to the West, but that I would like to go to Vietnam.

I think I got on their nerves so badly that they finally decided to offer me a trip, a group tour to Mongolia. This was the very first time that I really got out—I had been to Hungary and Czechoslovakia before, but that was different. Those big airports, seeing people from the West who knew exactly what to do, how to behave, and feeling very stupid because you did not know.

At the same time, I had this wonderful feeling about seeing another part of the world. I always knew that I would return [to the GDR], but I just wanted a chance to travel, to get to know other countries. Not only did I feel personally deprived, I also thought that this would have helped this country a great deal. I had always been interested, for example, in how Western libraries were organized. One could perhaps have learned a lot. Instead, only the so-called travel cadres were allowed to travel, and they never told you anything when they returned. . . .

Was the official line of the SED—namely, that they also wanted a different kind of socialism, but could not yet build it because of "imperialist encirclement" and hostile capitalist forces—at all convincing for all those who considered themselves to be some kind of socialists as well?

No, not at all. Being imprisoned, for example, was always proof to me that the leadership was scared. I experienced this feeling of being imprisoned very severely. There were times when you did not think about it, but often it was very depressing. Particularly here in Berlin, like taking the S-Bahn [above-ground commuter train] to Pankow, where you ride alongside the Wall for a very long stretch. I always noticed that it got very quiet in the train during this stretch, that people suddenly interrupted their conversations and just stared at the Wall. And after the Wall had passed, they began to talk again.

Or when colleagues or friends ever got a chance to go over there and then talked about it afterward, telling you about their shocks.

I was afraid to apply for a trip to the West because I feared they would turn me down since I was not "one of them," and with that I wouldn't have known how to continue living here, because this would have meant—at least that's how we perceived it—that I would be forced to accept the thought that I was imprisoned for the rest of my life. If I didn't apply, at least they could not turn me down, and there would be no concrete proof that I was permanently stuck in East Germany. . . .

Before I ask you about the developments in 1989, I would like to probe your reaction to a few events before that time. First, let me ask you about Solidarność, the first democratic mass movement in an Eastern European country. . . .

. . . Yes, we were continuously worried that our troops would get orders to march in, numerous battalions had already been ordered to the border region between Poland and the GDR. For a time, I was really afraid that we would see the same thing happening as in 1968 [when Warsaw Pact troops, East Germans among them, invaded Czechoslovakia].

Did the experience of Solidarność, nevertheless, provide some kind of hope?

Oh yes, absolutely. But on the other hand—I have just recently thought about this in the context of the currently rising hostility toward foreigners—that time might have been the beginning of hostility toward foreigners in East Germany. Many people said that the Poles were on strike simply because they did not want to work. Somebody once said, "The Poles would rather die for their country than work for it." It was quite sad.

Unfortunately, I have frequently encountered this attitude. It seems almost as if critical intellectuals, with varying emphases, were intrigued by what happened in Poland, while the East German working population was rather hostile. . . .

This may have even worked itself out on a psychological level: envy that the Poles had managed to pull off something like that, that they had defended themselves, and at the same time thinking that "we are the dutiful citizens," and "breaking the norms like that cannot be right." It was completely unprecedented to have strikes in a socialist country, particularly strikes of that size. . . .

The next thing I would like to ask you about has to do with 1985 and Gorbachev's rise to power in the Soviet Union. What was your response? How did you and your friend feel about this?

Well, it was a spark of hope. For me, Gorbachev very much represented a confirmation of many things I and many of my friends had thought all along, whether it was his statements concerning peace or human rights, or just his commonsensical and logical approach to things.

To what extent did you harbor hopes that this would have an effect on the GDR, and if so, how?

We had quite a few hopes, which explains why it was all the more incomprehensible to us that while the Soviet Union had always been portrayed to us as the great example we should follow—after Gorbachev, this rapidly changed. They banned the Soviet magazine *Sputnik*, and they banned a number of Soviet movies.

So all of a sudden our leadership created this distance from the Soviet Union, all the way to banning a variety of things from there. At the same time, I thought that they could not possibly keep that up for very long; they could not afford to isolate themselves from the entire socialist bloc.

Did this affect your position toward the possibilities of change in the GDR?

Yes, definitely. First of all this represented a confirmation of my own position. And, of course, it signified a great hope that change would eventually take place in the GDR as well. But I had never given much thought to how exactly this [change] would have to take place.

Many people now say, for example, that they had thought that change could or should emanate from within the party—that was never a scenario I had in my mind. Furthermore, one could notice that individuals were already in the process of changing in response to what was going on in the Soviet Union. All of a sudden, the news about the USSR was found to be extremely interesting, while previously anybody who had shown a sympathetic interest in the USSR was frowned upon by her/his peers.

You mean the Soviet Union all of a sudden became an attractive place?

Yes, exactly. Suddenly, ordinary citizens in the streets showed a great deal of interest about what was going on over there. . . .

Could you describe for me how you experienced this period between 1988 and 1989? Did you know what was going on in other places around the country, and did you ever perceive some kind of discernible break after which you realized that change of some sort had to happen?

. . . The most decisive experience for me, and I think for many others as well, had to do with the elections in May of 1989. You got the clear impression that something fairly big was going on.

After the elections we had monthly demonstrations against the party's election fraud, every 7th of the month. I participated in the first one, on 7 June. We had planned to deliver a petition to the People's Assembly, but the demonstration never got off the ground because many of us, myself included, were arrested.

When we arrived at our prearranged meeting place, there were Stasi people everywhere. We never really got together, except in little groups. So we tried to communicate with one another and decided individually to try to make it to the Marien Church in order to proceed from there. But when we got to the church, Stasi people were again all over the place, preventing anything resembling a march from coming together. We subsequently met in the Sophien Church, after hours of walking around.

Again the church was surrounded by the Stasi. We debated whether we should abandon trying to get to the People's Assembly anyhow, and subsequently some of us tried, but we did not get very far. . . .

First, they surrounded us, police in uniform as well as in civilian clothes. Ostensibly, they gave us a warning to disperse, but I never heard that. And then, for the first time in my life, I had a firsthand experience of a brutal police action. Most of us got terribly beaten. About three of *them* approached every one of *us*. One of the guys who arrested me was particularly brutal. He kept on beating me, and when I finally managed to say, "Don't you realize that I'm a woman," he just replied, before hitting me again, "It's your own fault. Nobody told you to be here."

This whole affair scared me a great deal, but on the other hand I thought "there were about 130 of us, that's quite a lot."

I was in detention until the next morning. The whole affair had made it on the radio, and when we found out that the public knew about our arrests, it became pretty clear to us that we were fairly safe. What happened, of course, was that all of us were put under constant police surveillance after this point.

The following month another one of those demonstrations was planned—7 July. During the run-up time for this one, the Stasi targeted in advance the people they figured would demonstrate. So I was not even able to make it to the demonstration because they followed me around from early in the morning.

I could not believe the time and energy they spent on each single person, so many people for just one individual. I thought: "How many Stasi people must there be if they can do this with every single one of us?"

Early in the morning I found a letter in my mailbox asking me to come to the employment agency at noon. I knew, of course, that the employment agency and the Stasi worked together. So I called and told them that I already had other plans for today, and then, of course, they asked me, "Well, what kinds of plans do you have?" And then I realized that a carload of Stasi people was parked in front of my house. When I left the house, they began to follow me around, wherever I went.

What was especially awful about this was that I had long planned to go to the cemetery and visit my mother's grave this same morning, and they actually followed me all the way to the grave. Afterward I met with some friends, and we tried to get to the demonstration by commuter train. A few stations before our destination we were pulled out of the train and were told that we could not go any farther. So we said, "OK, we will go back," yet they continued to follow us. I asked them how long they were planning on doing this, and they said they did not know. It was a very hot day, and so we decided to go to a lake with a nude beach. This was totally ridiculous; we took off our clothes, and the Stasi people were standing right next to us, and when we went swimming, they sat on the beach with their suits. It was quite something.

During the summer it became more and more obvious that something would have to happen. . . .

You are referring, I take it, to the vast number of people who began to leave the country for good and who crowded into the Western embassies in Warsaw and Prague?

Yes. It is probably hard for you to imagine how terrible this was for us—all these pictures of how people ran away. It was simply awful. Yet it simultaneously became obvious that something big would happen soon, simply because this could not go on very long; the country couldn't survive much longer under these conditions. Then I heard of the founding of New Forum [on 12 September]. Two days later, I went to one of the contact addresses in Köpenick [a borough of East Berlin] I had heard about.

The founding of New Forum became public knowledge very quickly. I myself went to see Bärbel Bohley. I signed the New Forum founding statement and asked her what I could do to help. One funny thing that happened had to do with this man who said, "Well, I don't know what you can do, but you could baby-sit some of the children." I said, "What? Baby-sit children?" And he replied, "Well, yes, children of people who are doing other things." Anyway, I told him that I'd much rather be doing "other things" as well. The alternative that was initially given to me was either to look after children or to work on a computer, until somebody said that they still needed further contact addresses, so I organized one for Köpenick. That was a very important experience, because I got to know so many very different people. Hundreds showed up.

PART II
"DEMOCRACY—NOW OR NEVER"

Slogans from the East German Revolution,
October–November 1989

We are the people
Liberty—Equality—Honesty
The 'Leading role' belongs to the people
The people lead, and the party limps behind
The party needs a people—no people need a party
Imagine socialism—and no one runs away
Take off your uniforms—join us! (aimed at East German riot police)
The GDR is the sum of all *that* which could have been prevented
Workers of the world—My sincerest apologies, Karl Marx
We will live tomorrow like we demonstrate today
Democracy—Now or Never

Media headlines, October and November 1989

Pressure from Below Grows (*Der Spiegel*)
Decline of the East (*New York Times*)
Victory for Freedom! (*Berliner Zeitung*)
German Revolution Impresses the World and Changes Europe (*Stern*)
The Wall Comes Down as East Germany Heads for
Democracy (*Manchester Guardian*)
West Germany Poised for Leadership (*Washington Post*)
Freedom! (*Time*)   Is It Possible? (*Newsweek*)
East Germans Agree in Rejecting Goal of Reunification
(*Manchester Guardian*)
With Open GDR Borders, a New Era Begins
(*Frankfurter Rundschau*) Reunification Next? (*New York Times*)

■ Any outsider trying to understand the emergence of the East German revolution is confronted, first of all, with a basic informational problem. Because East Germans had literally led a walled-in existence for almost three decades, few outside observers could pay any systematic attention to their lives, and even those who had so endeavored had run into great difficulties obtaining reliable information about ongoing social life in the GDR. As Western scholars and journalists could readily attest, access to dissident sectors of the population had been severely restricted by the communist police apparatus. Almost everything that passed as "news" was filtered information that contained no concrete evidence of the authentic social life of East Germany. The party's censorship provided only self-serving announcements from the top of society. Ironically, this limitation harmonized rather well with sanctioned views about politics in the West. While Western commentators and politicians had seized every opportunity during the past two decades to dwell on the allegedly ubiquitous disaffection of citizens in the "Honecker prison," virtually no outsiders had paid much attention to what East Germans themselves had to say about the specific power relations in which they were caught. There were many difficulties surrounding this fact—difficulties of discovering actions in the first place, and then difficulties comprehending these actions, once discovered. For example, most Westerners scarcely imagined that grievances of East Germans could grow out of frustrated aspirations that were anything other than "Western" in substance, such as the desire for what Sebastian Pflugbeil called an open "experimentation with democracy." It was, in the deepest sense, a conceptual shortcoming that emerged from perceptions about the normal rhythms of politics in a world—East and West—that is not accustomed to seeing decisive political choices being made outside the oak-paneled citadels of decision-making at the top of society. Yet, as most everyone acknowledged, the tumultuous events of 1989 did not have their origin at the top.

This fact brings into focus an abiding dilemma: if the revolution did not originate at the apex of society, how was one to discover its origins within a walled-off and unstudied population? The challenge, here, was essentially one of locating previously unknown evidence of experiences and aspirations among East German citizens. This has been the purpose of Part I.

At the outset of Part II, it is appropriate to return to a subject alluded to in the introduction of this book—namely, the ingrained tendency of observers from every ideological corner to see popular risings such as the one that occurred in East Germany as "spontaneous" happenings. The utility of this description is, quite obviously, to provide a causal explanation for social dynamics which, in the absence of concrete evidence, are not otherwise comprehensible. In the specific case of 1989, the logic of this rationale played itself out this way. After Gorbachev had effectively withdrawn Soviet support for the communist hard-liners who ran East Germany, and after thousands upon thousands of people had begun to flee the country for good, the population was retrospectively seen to have arrived at the sudden conclusion that "enough is enough." For too long, it was argued, had they silently suffered from totalitarianism.[1] They therefore elected to "stand up" and fight for change. It was all quite spontaneous, an overnight collective resolve that more or less magically appeared out of the bowels of society.

The fundamental implausibility of this explanation became apparent as soon as I began to interview the actual East German participants in the revolution. Their responses easily contradicted such a line of reasoning. Far from being spontaneous, the revolution had been building for years. Ever since the 1970s, increasing numbers of East German citizens had begun to talk in earnest about a variety of possible reforms that were quite distinct from mainstream Western understandings of desirable change. Indeed, the more I inquired into the causes of the East German revolution, the more I encountered specific roots whose origins reached far back into the unique social fabric of postwar East German history. One concrete manifestation of an emerging organized opposition in East Germany—decisive to any understanding of the revolution yet routinely overlooked—was the growing number and diversity of local grass-roots groups. By the summer of 1989 an estimated 600 such groups existed throughout the country. All of them consisted of people who had found ways to overcome their private resignation, of people who had decided to come together with like-minded fellow citizens in order to address the central question of "what, specifically, can we do to bring about change?"[2] Only by completely ignoring these rich experiences—indeed, whole ensembles of experiences—could the events of 1989 be seen as "spontaneous."

1. One can, of course, only speculate on what terms such as "totalitarianism" or "to suffer" might conceivably mean in this context. For one, there is the problem—as all social historians know—that "suffering" itself, that is, the existence of deeply felt grievances, does not in and of itself generate any specifically coherent forms of social activity, much less a social movement or a revolution. Furthermore, in such generalizations it remains unclear what specific grievances one is referring to, and what specific acts (or nonacts) they may or may not have generated among different sectors of society.
2. Michael Arnold, New Forum founding member in Leipzig. Personal interview, 12 July 1990.

We have already become familiar with the most crucial efforts in early oppositional movement-building. But it is difficult to continue putting in place these building blocks of popular insurgency without first rehearsing the coverage of the East German revolution that was, at the time, available to interested recipients in the West. In conducting such a review, I also seek to reestablish for the reader the kinds of portrayals that generally came to circumscribe Western understandings of East German events.[3]

Western reporting about changes within East German society did not begin to appear, for all intents and purposes, before the summer of 1989—the moment when outside commentators first picked up on scattered reports about "unrest" in the GDR. Throughout these months the ailing leadership busily prepared for the fortieth anniversary of the "socialist worker and peasant state," which had formally been founded in the Soviet-occupied territory of Germany on 7 October 1949. As members of the most highly industrialized society among the nations in the Soviet sphere of influence, East Germans had managed to create a system that did not know poverty, guaranteed full employment, provided comprehensive national health care and free education for everyone. On the other hand, the price of this remarkable reconstruction of the war-torn country had been high: consumer items had always been scarce, and everything beyond the necessities of life was difficult to obtain. The entire social infrastructure as well as the natural environment had long been in a process of grave deterioration. Furthermore, political freedoms had been severely curtailed. Travel to the West was impossible except for retirees, travel cadres in the party, and a few chosen others.

Throughout the eighties, according to Western media coverage, East German citizens had increasingly suffered from this state of affairs. The country's leadership, however, did not respond. On the contrary, despite perestroika and glasnost in the Soviet Union and clear signs of reform in neighboring Eastern Bloc countries, East German party leaders sternly held to their hard-line course. An oft-quoted statement came from the chief party ideologist Kurt Hager: "There is no need for us to change our tapestry just because our neighbors are doing so."[4]

Yet a growing number of East German citizens no longer seemed to

---

3. In no way is this summary intended to be some kind of substitute for a full account either of the East German events or of the various portrayals that were written about them. The point is not to write an ersatz history at this point, but rather to recall the quality of the accounts that flooded the West during the Fall of 1989.

4. *Neues Deutschland*, 10 April 1987.

agree. During the summer of 1989, news began to trickle out of East Germany indicating increasing dissent at the bottom of society. Two general kinds of evidence materialized: a blossoming variety of public protests and—in some ways even more ominous—ever larger numbers of people trying to leave the country for good.

Then, in August and September, one could learn about numerous oppositional groups and two oppositional parties that were officially (and illegally) founded. At the same time, tens of thousands of citizens decided to leave everything behind and escape via Hungary, Poland, and Czechoslovakia. Thousands of others began to take their complaints to the streets. Something was going on at the heart of East German society, something that could scarcely be ignored any longer.

The state and party leadership, however, decided to do just that. Erich Honecker, 77-year-old general secretary of the Socialist Unity Party and thus "first man" in East Germany since 1971, epitomized the calcified thought processes of the aged leadership when he addressed a gathering of discontented workers in Erfurt. He denounced all criticism of the state as "reactionary" and proclaimed, in slight alteration of an old German proverb, that "socialism in its course will neither be stopped by ox nor horse."[5]

During the same tumultuous summer months the old guard seemed determined to let nothing interfere with the fortieth anniversary festivities to be staged in front of cameras and the world's political leaders on 7 October. In what was portrayed as an "obvious embarrassment," party leaders were forced, for the second time in a single week, to grant exit visas to 7,600 East German refugees who had previously stormed the West German Embassy in Prague. During those same days, East German police forces were arresting and beating many of those who had decided not to escape, but rather had elected to stay and fight for changes from within the country. The party and state leadership seemed willing to pay any price—however contradictory—for peaceful and orderly anniversary celebrations.

Once again, the "embassy squatters" were put on sealed trains that would take them from Czechoslovakia to West Germany, thus carrying them through the very East German countryside from which they had just

5. Quoted in *Die Tageszeitung,* 15 August 1989. The German original reads: "Den Sozialismus in seinem Lauf hält weder Ochs noch Esel auf." Just a few months prior to 9 November, Honecker doggedly asserted that "the Wall will remain in place for at least another hundred years."

successfully fled. On the first occasion, on 30 September, thousands demonstrated along the tracks as the train passed through. Indeed, hundreds made attempts, often almost suicidal attempts, to climb aboard the train. The second time, on 3 October, large police units sealed off the grounds alongside the tracks throughout East Germany, a move that again generated violent confrontations between police and demonstrators. To East Germans from all walks of life, the Western readership was informed, it became agonizingly obvious that the party's strategy was to ignore all signs of discontent and to proceed as if everything were in the best of order.

And yet, to the consternation of the party's remote leadership, tens of thousands of citizens did not go to the official party rallies on 7 October. Instead, throughout the country—in East Berlin, Leipzig, Dresden, and numerous other cities—they either stayed at home or took to the streets in enormous protest demonstrations. In some cities, official rallies even had to be called off, while more than a thousand "unofficial" marchers were arrested, interrogated, beaten, or otherwise mistreated.

Yet people came out to march again the very next day. This outpouring of energy from below appears to have "so stunned" the party that top district functionaries in Dresden abruptly agreed on 8 October to *negotiate* with opposition representatives. As numerous observers correctly pointed out, this was an absolute first in the forty-year history of one-party rule.

The tumultuous events that ensued were told along the following lines: Far from caving in, party leaders in Berlin on the selfsame day unequivocally announced their determination to suppress, if necessary with force, any and all further public demonstrations. Yet on Monday, 9 October, Leipzig witnessed the most massive demonstration yet seen. About 75,000 demonstrators came out to participate in the traditional Monday Peace Prayers—at least three times as many as had demonstrated the previous Monday. After short services that were held simultaneously in most inner-city churches, the protesters proceeded to march peacefully around the loop encircling downtown Leipzig. By all accounts, it was an eerie moment. The level of fear among participants ran high. Since the East German leadership had recently congratulated the Chinese government for its "successful" suppression of the democracy movement in Bejing, many marchers worriedly asked themselves, "Will there be an East German Tiananmen massacre"? Almost everyone expected some kind of crackdown.

Yet, nothing happened. As the marchers lit their candles and chanted "no more violence," the large contingents of "People's Police," "People's

Army," "Factory Fighting Forces," and secret police either stood by, silently watching, or quietly withdrew. A few even began to talk to demonstrators or bystanders and voiced their resistance to the orders they had initially received to shoot, "if necessary," at peaceful marchers. Support for the party's hard line, it turned out, was rapidly melting away in the party's own ranks. Even the district party leaders had, at the last minute, opted for a peaceful resolution of the conflict. Perhaps worst of all for the top party leadership in Berlin, a growing number of veteran party members actually participated in the demonstrations! For different reasons and with different goals, a growing number of citizens, party members and nonparty members, intellectuals and workers, Christians and atheists, political activists and the "silent majority," had come together to oppose openly what was increasingly seen as the common enemy: the aged general secretary Honecker and his cloistered Politburo that ran the party.

The four weeks following 9 October saw a myriad of activities on the part of both the party leadership and the rapidly forming opposition. Amid negotiations, petitions, marches, and organizing meetings, Honecker resigned under pressure on 18 October; the Monday demonstrations in Leipzig grew from 160,000 on 16 October and more than 300,000 on 23 October to almost 500,000 on 6 November. Meanwhile, another 24,000 citizens had fled over the Hungarian-Austrian border in October alone, and the party trade union leader, Harry Tisch, resigned because of growing opposition in the factories. Newly elected general secretary Egon Krenz thereupon flew to Moscow to seek Gorbachev's support. One apparent result was the party's abrupt decision to grant amnesty to all political prisoners.

On 4 November the biggest rally in German history was held in East Berlin—some 1 million participants. On 8 November the party officially recognized New Forum and, on the same day, the entire Politburo resigned. One (now famous) day later, the district party secretary of East Berlin, Günter Schabowski, announced that unrestricted travel to the West was immediately to be granted to all citizens. Twenty-eight years and two months after it had been erected, the Berlin Wall no longer was a wall.

To all appearances, the party had decided to open the Wall for much the same reason it had been built in 1961: to stop the flood of East Germans escaping for good.[6] The massive exodus signaled an unambiguous rejec-

6. In 1960 some 200,000 people left the GDR, and by 13 August 1961 another 155,000 had fled to the West. See Karl Wilhelm Fricke, "Opposition und Widerstand," in Alexander Fischer (ed.), *Die Deutsche Demokratische Republik* (Würzburg, 1988), 122. These

tion of the party dictatorship, one with potentially lethal consequences for the state. The GDR could not continue to exist if large portions of its primarily young and well-skilled work force fled into an unknown future rather than stay.[7] And, perhaps even more significantly, the one-party state had also rapidly lost control among the majority of those who had elected to remain. Thus, in a badly orchestrated and ill-prepared press conference, the party announced what few people had even considered a serious possibility: the opening of East Germany's borders to the West. With this move, it was widely understood, the party gave up the single most important instrument of power it had employed over the preceding 28 years. Germans in East and West, it was said, "were the happiest people on earth" that day. Communism was dead. To all appearances, the West had won the Cold War. But how East Germans had managed to arrive at that point, or, for that matter, what their complicated reactions to this sudden turn of events entailed, was effectively drowned out by the drumbeats of victory in the West.

Yet the revolution had also created what was frequently referred to as a "power vacuum." As East Germans quickly realized, the problem of where to go from here, the question of how to fill such a "vacuum" had suddenly become the central political issue of the day. Not only did the eventual outcome appear astonishingly open-ended, but there was the open question of who would participate in the search for an answer. It was a striking historical moment: radically transformed conditions and no one in a position "to take over." Where to go from here?

While Western reporting once again searched for answers at the top (only this time more in the West than in the East), most East Germans would probably have agreed with New Forum member Frank Eigenfeld who described this period as "the most exciting time of my life." Along with the party and the Wall, long-settled beliefs concerning the common modes of day-to-day politics under one-party rule simply collapsed in the face of a newly assertive population. Many besides Eigenfeld expressed a "sense of regained hope," an expectation that "finally, we can make a difference." What seemed most important to those who had been instru-

---

numbers were not surpassed until 1989; more than 225,000 East Germans had escaped by 9 November 1989. *Der Fischer Weltalmanach—Sonderband DDR* (Frankfurt, 1990), 142.

7. According to an internal document by the Ministry for State Security (MfS or Stasi), 67.7 percent of the emigrants over 18 were skilled workers, and another 16.5 percent had received some form of professional training at the college/university level. In Armin Mitter and Stefan Wolle (eds.), *"Ich liebe euch doch alle"* (Berlin, 1990), 82–92; MfS, ZAIG, Nr. 3933/89.

mental in bringing about these monumental changes, however, was what one interviewee called their "great desire for democratic experimentation." One of the most revealing examples of the depth of intention within the opposition was the way New Forum organizers responded to the 200,000 (incredibly diverse) people who flooded into the organization within the very first days of its founding. Far from being alarmed by this absence of ideological cohesion, organizers such as Ingrid Köppe relished the challenge: "There was very little that people previously had in common, other than their opposition to the party. That's why we tried to build a sort of replica of the entire society within New Forum, to set up groups dealing with literally every aspect of the organization of a society. The intention was to generate a new model of society, to see what could be done differently. Of course, nobody took into consideration that we might not have any time for all of this."[8]

It is difficult to overstate the cultural and therefore political significance of this fundamental sea change in consciousness. As the interviews in the following pages reveal, established political certainties toppled from one day to the next—and with escalating magnitude and meaning.[9] The very ground rules on which East German society had been established were collectively redefined. This, then, was the revolutionary moment—literally the time when the structure of society became altered. From Leipzig to Berlin to Rostock, ordinary East German citizens held demonstrations, wrote manifestos, organized meetings, thronged to rallies, and set up countless "round tables." They did this locally, regionally, and nationally.

8. See Part II, chapter 7, p. 321.

9. The centrality of this often overlooked dynamic has been considerably heightened in visibility by the extraordinary events of August 1991 in the Soviet Union. It is now much more widely apparent that the transformative structural changes in the governing hierarchy of the Soviet Union rest upon and are a direct outgrowth of organic changes in the self-perception and the social relations of Soviet people. Clear as this relationship now seems, it nevertheless must be added that outside analysts of the "Soviet revolution" are much more preoccupied with studying competing political leaders or with interpreting the structural changes of Soviet governing institutions than with this underlying and much more broadly significant reality. "The people" stood up to the tanks and decisively contributed to the complete failure of the military coup. For this they receive due credit. But how this stunning turn of events had come to be possible, and what all this meant for the creation of a "democratic civil society," was largely drowned by debates concerning the relative importance of leaders such as Gorbachev or Yeltsin, or the global political dimensions of a possible disintegration of the Soviet Union itself. As Soviet citizens left the barricades and mass demonstrations, they once again disappeared from view. Like their compatriots in East Germany or Czechoslovakia, they are now also in imminent danger of disappearing from "history."

In short, citizens filled the civic vacuum of the one-party state with concrete acts. These acts, diverse and decentralized as they were, pointed in bold new egalitarian and democratic directions. Perhaps most importantly, they raised the fundamental questions of power: who should have it, how much, and under what conditions? Every step of the way through these tumultuous autumn months, more and more East German citizens began to act on their own.

The pace of events accelerated beyond everyone's expectations. Again and again, what had seemed impossible just a day earlier suddenly happened, and, within another week, this recent "impossible" development had become so widely recognized, so commonplace, that it quickly became understood as "normal." In September of 1989 the mere idea of instituting round table discussions between the opposition and the government, for instance, would have been dismissed as utterly inconceivable. In November, however, round tables were being set up in virtually every community, and by December they had already become an integral part of East German politics. The longer that people were exposed to this process, the more they experienced themselves being active participants who could alter society, the more clearly the barriers to further change came to be weakened. As Sebastian Pflugbeil put it in his summary retrospective on these tumultuous events: "Change began to take place because people began to act as if they were free to act. At first, there was an immense buildup of tensions toward the government, but then everything became very exciting. . . . We had the best chances to begin something completely new."[10] It is only in this context that we can understand, with Eigenfeld, why this was "the most exciting time of my life." To activists in the opposition movement, most everything seemed possible during the moment of revolutionary opening.

In the midst of all these tumultuous events, old forms of deference and self-censorship melted away. If it was possible to topple one of the most stable communist police states, if one could overcome all those limits, why acquiesce to new limits? Why be supinely content, for example, to confine one's hopes for a "good society" within the limits of West German achievements? Why not think about democratic routes to break through the social constraints of both the capitalist and socialist systems?

It is impossible to exaggerate how greatly subsequent commentators everywhere seem to have lost sight of this seminal problematic that lay at the heart of the East German revolution. Neither party functionaries nor

10. See Part II, chapter 4, pp. 306, 313.

dissidents in the organized opposition had ever focused much political attention on life in East Germany "after the party," or, for that matter, on life "without the Wall." Such scenarios had usually been relegated to some distant future, if not dismissed as downright fanciful. Life in the GDR beyond one-party rule had just not been on the agenda of normal discussion. But when the suffocating control of the party suddenly vanished, a new world of possibility opened. Michael Arnold, founding member of New Forum, explained: "We felt as if we could go back to the drawing board and start from scratch again."[11]

And to the drawing board they went. One factor, quickly forgotten yet incontrovertible, was that unification with West Germany had not been an issue at the outset, much less an energizing force for mass demonstrations and public demands. "No one had talked about unification before the Wall came down," confirmed Ludwig Mehlhorn in a conversation that paralleled many others I had. "Nor," he added, "did many people seem to have wanted it at the time."[12] Yet the events of 9 November forever al-

---

11. Personal interview, Leipzig, 11 July 1990.

12. In fact, with the exception of self-interested proclamations by the West German government or by West German alliances of refugees from the former eastern territories of the "German Reich," virtually no one had questioned the reality of postwar separation anymore—a conclusion supported by most of the scholarly literature on postwar German history. See, for example, the recent volume by J. F. Brown, *Surge to Freedom: The End of Communist Rule in Eastern Europe* (Durham, N.C., 1991), in which the author argues that "the vast majority of the Federal Republic's citizens, despite their paying lip service to reunification, and despite the fact that the goal of German unity was enshrined in their constitution, were content to relegate this issue to the dim, distant future" (p. 128). As a common social and cultural ground between Germans East and West began to disintegrate, the reference to "one people" increasingly degenerated into mere cold war rhetoric. A prominent German philosopher correctly captured this phenomenon when he asked "who had really considered possible something like reunification—and who would have wanted it?" Jürgen Habermas, "Der DM-Nationalismus," in *Die Zeit*, 30 March 1990, 62–63. My translation.

Commenting on the question of unification, Richard J. Evans, German historian from Great Britain, suggested that there was no greater a basis for unification between the two Germanies than a case for unification between West Germany and Austria: "German national consciousness no longer exists even in the sense in which it did, within limits, between 1871 and 1945. There is no fundamental reason why a linguistic group such as the Germans should need to be united under a single state, any more than that the same principle should be applied to other linguistic or cultural groups, such as the English-speaking nations." Richard J. Evans, *In Hitler's Shadow* (New York, 1989), 102. See also Claus Offe, who argued that "the new nationalism in Germany today [spring of 1991] is not . . . the nationalism of an emotionalized *Volk;* in fact, a large part of West German

tered the debate. As a Western journalist correctly observed: "It was at once East Germany's chance and its tragedy that, unlike in Poland or Hungary, the boundaries of social self-determination and national self-determination were not the same."[13] Within days of the opening of the Wall, organizers of the largest opposition group, New Forum, expressed their concern that the party leadership had probably opened the border merely to relieve pressure on the government and to distract attention from a serious restructuring of society. Oppositionists like Sebastian Pflugbeil now feared that their achievements and democratic hopes would "drown in West German chocolate."[14]

Reform energy was dwindling, opposition members feared, as another 100,000 East Germans took permanent leave as soon as the border opened. They followed some 200,000 who had already fled during the previous three months. Amid the euphoria (for some) and the frustrated consternation (for others) that attended such events, a leading member of the East German opposition, Ulrike Poppe, was plunged into deep resignation: "The little bit of independent culture, political enthusiasm, and engagement that we had mobilized is rapidly disappearing."[15]

Less than two months after East Germans had forced the party to relax its suffocating grip over their society, one that had previously seemed virtually unshakable, it became obvious that there would, in fact, be *no* "East German" future as such. Rather, it became clear that the revolution that had brought about the sudden collapse of one-party socialism would speedily culminate in the end of the German Democratic Republic itself. As the nation began to dissolve during the months following Germany's first peaceful revolution, virtually crumbling under the burden of both internal failures and relentless Western pressure, the wide range of newly assertive voices effectively disappeared from the political center stage. Somehow the hopeful moment of almost unlimited possibilities had given way to an abrupt closure. The long-sought and self-generated opportunity for expanded discussion seemed once again obliterated.

During the very weeks that millions of East German citizens continued to pour into West Germany as visitors, West German politicians and

---

citizens expressed reservations about reunification that were of a cost-conscious nature. Instead, a calculated and moderate 'elite-nationalism' exists which dramatically sets the sensible stage for a hurried-up process of economic integration." *German Politics and Society*, no. 22 (Spring 1991), 21.

13. Timothy Garton Ash, *The Magic Lantern* (New York, 1990), 74.

14. See Part I, chapter 3, p. 161.

15. Personal interview, East Berlin, 18 July 1990.

businesses bulldozed their way through the Wall and into the matrix of East German society. Little of anything was in place to guard East Germans against this sudden emergence of West German economic and political predominance, or, for that matter, against the awe and confusion inspired by their own first trips to the West. As New Forum founders Bärbel Bohley, Jens Reich, Sebastian Pflugbeil, Reinhart Schult, and others pointed out in an open letter published two days after the fall of the Berlin Wall, the party's order to open the concrete barrier at this point had been as self-serving and undemocratic as had been its order to build it: "They did not ask you then, and they did not ask you now."[16] As a result of this party decision, the authors feared, East Germans might lose any voice in the process of building a new society. Herein lay the agony of all those who had broad dreams of egalitarian and democratic reform—that is, dreams for social reconstruction beyond that which had been achieved in the highly stratified societies of the West.

The fact of the matter was that the public unveiling of their concerns in the open letter—accurate as these concerns may have been—brought on a political calamity. Amid the popular rejoicing and a deeply felt sense of victory over the party, the open letter of the activists had little immediate context; the founders of New Forum appeared to be taking a stand against the hopeful tide of existing events. The letter thus proved to be a strategic disaster for its authors. As a result, the gap that had begun to open between most leading opposition intellectuals and the majority of the population widened—perhaps irretrievably.

Be that as it may, the fears expressed by virtually all prominent oppositionists turned out to be extremely well-founded; their gloomy predictions soon proved to be precisely on target. The open letter had warned fellow citizens against the imminent "selling out" of the GDR to Western interests in ways "that will turn us into the backyard and source of low-wage labor for the West."[17] As another New Forum member with connections to the party phrased it (in the apparently deeply internalized language of flamboyant party rhetoric): "West German corporations will now ride like tanks over the East German landscape, crushing its sovereignty and social achievements, and leaving behind mass unemployment and bankrupt enterprises." The irony surrounding this impassioned judgment was that it came to be immediately dismissed as old-time party verbiage,

16. "The Wall has Fallen," New Forum. Signed by Jens Reich, Sebastian Pflugbeil, Bärbel Bohley, Reinhard Schult, Eberhard Seidel, Jutta Seidel. Document in author's possession.
17. Ibid.

when it was, in fact, a prophecy that soon described the East German reality.

Observers in the West, however, gained little sense of the deep ironies and serious choices confronted by East Germans in the midst of their revolutionary moment. One could find little more than snapshots from a distance, featuring faceless masses of indistinct people or short sequences of actions that seemed to have emerged from nowhere. On occasion, one might have been fortunate to stumble upon a "zooming in" news feature, briefly focusing on individual people, covering the "human interest" side of dramatic events. Yet even such reports were routinely transmitted out of context, providing nothing but refracted clues derived from our—and not their—experiences. Short-lived, sweeping, and confidently presented as they were, few media accounts grappled with the unique agonies and antagonisms that had been an inherent part of the 40-year history of the GDR. What became visible was a multitude of cameo portraits framed by abstract generalizations. Remaining buried was the intricate mosaic of very specific human perceptions and aspirations that had made it all happen in the first place.

Perhaps nothing about East Germany's revolutionary autumn has been more difficult to imagine—that is, to take seriously—than the range and depths of objectives of the growing East German civic movement— objectives that had emerged from a self-propelled sequence of events that, in turn, had opened up an immensely enlarged public space. It was in this arena that the civic movement flourished, where democratic ideas flowered, where popular activity took practical political form. By the time Western-style politics had successfully occupied the entire political land- scape of East Germany, these objectives had effectively been pushed out of public sight, and thus out of democratic public consideration. In the end, they were either ignored entirely, or they were simply dismissed as chimerical.

But this moment in history is too important to be buried in so unwitting a manner. The interview sections that follow focus intently upon this submerged reality.

4 STRUGGLES WITH
SELF-CENSORSHIP: DECIDING
HOW MUCH TO SEEK

■ LUDWIG MEHLHORN, prominent oppositionist, expert on East-Central Europe, founding member of Democracy Now.[18] ■ *"What we were desperately trying to do was to create space in which people could help change the country instead of leaving it."*

In Part I, Ludwig Mehlhorn explained the various complications confronting opposition activists who wanted to step out of their isolation and carve out "a bit of free space" within East German society during the 1980s. In this part of the interview, he poignantly addresses what he perceived to be the dynamics behind the escalating changes that took place in the GDR between spring and fall of 1989. In so doing, Mehlhorn appeared slightly at sea when musing about who specifically should have been "reached" or "recruited" among the East German populace in the opposition's effort to build a social movement. Who were "the people"? Did they include nonintellectuals? If so, how should one go about establishing meaningful lines of communication between different sectors of society? It should be noted that Mehlhorn, like virtually all other dissident intellectuals in East Germany, tended to slide over social terrain which was essentially unfamiliar to him. In such cases, he instead tended to invoke terms of description that were as broad as they were highly elusive, ascribing certain qualities to groups such as "workers," or simply "the citizens of the GDR." Interestingly enough, this habit of thought was to prove even more widespread among a number of his fellow oppositionists, as some of the following interviews will show. In one such telling state-

---

18. For background information on Mehlhorn, see Part I, chapter 1, pp. 76–89.

ment, a highly prominent spokesperson of New Forum in Berlin once told me, "You know, people were simply not ready for a real democracy." Not surprisingly, I was never able to ascertain what exactly he had meant.

It may also be noted in passing that Mehlhorn here places himself among the many commentators who, almost off-handedly, employed grand generalizations to cover sensitive factual areas where no facts were known. Events in these areas were simply characterized as having happened "spontaneously." The term appears in this interview on four separate occasions.

Despite such conceptual difficulties, it is necessary to emphasize that Ludwig Mehlhorn provides in other ways an incisive evaluation of the factors that contributed to the collapse of one-party rule. He also draws vivid comparisons to other East-Central European countries, and successfully communicates to an outsider the magnitude of the social challenge that had suddenly confronted the relatively small number of emerging nationwide opposition groups.

■ *If I understand you correctly, you talked about a "first phase" in which you began to engage in some kind of organized political work, and you also tried to define the possible goals of such an attempt, and then you talked about a "second phase" in which you more or less tried to spread the word in an attempt to broaden your base. What followed after that?*

Well, the third phase began in 1989, not in the fall, but already in the spring, during both our preparations for the May local elections and our responses to the elections. We tried to run independent candidates, which meant that we had to approach official state organs directly. Of course, they immediately turned down our request.

Numerous groups tried to step out of the realm of the church at the time in order to build a nationwide oppositional network. There was also the attempt in March 1989 by the Initiative for Peace and Human Rights [IFM] to organize themselves nationwide. Our group made attempts in this direction as well. None of these various efforts found much response among the population, however. Apparently the situation was simply not yet ripe. There was not a mass public yet that would have supported such attempts.

Not until the Fall of 1989 did we reach that point. Public statements or appeals of the kind made by New Forum later on in September had been written and published before, but at earlier points in time such appeals had not yet received much of a positive echo, certainly not the kind of overwhelmingly positive response the New Forum appeal later received.

Why didn't you merge with New Forum in September, since Democracy Now was very similar in its positions? And how, in general, do you explain that so many different groups were founded during the Fall of 1989?

There are many different causes behind that. We had come to an agreement within the opposition—that is, after the May elections and the brutal repression of those who had publicly protested against the crackdown on the democracy movement in China—that a collective initiative of some sort was absolutely necessary at some point. But we had also come to the conclusion that we should wait for that until after 7 October, until after the fortieth anniversary of the GDR, because that was a kind of sacred cow to the communists. The simple calculation behind that was that we did not want to cause any unnecessarily brutal repression. So that had been our arrangement as of June 1989.

That was an agreement within your group?

No, no, that was an agreement among all groups.

Just in Berlin or nationwide?

Well, at least among the important people of all groups—including the members of the Initiative for Peace and Human Rights, Rainer Eppelmann, us, and the people who later founded New Forum, such as Bärbel Bohley and others. But then a number of things happened that tremendously speeded up the whole process of change in the GDR. The first noncommunist prime minister was elected in Poland, and then the Hungarians opened their border to Austria and masses of GDR tourists fled for good. In short, we had a situation all of a sudden in which many people said, "We can't wait until after 7 October. We have to respond now; otherwise, we will be left behind by the rapid developments occurring all around us." We thought that we had to make our positions public as soon as possible.

And then, of course, it was difficult even on a technical level always to reach some prior agreements among all groups. Besides, there were personal rivalries between certain people that we apparently could no longer keep the lid on. All of these dynamics resulted in the formation of various different organizations.

In other words, the causes were more personal than they were political?

Yes. It just so happened that New Forum had more or less arbitrarily selected a group of people without others knowing anything about it, and they published this appeal, this founding statement in September. Others were subsequently offended by that and thus started their own circles, such as Democratic Awakening. We too had our own little tradition. The Initiative for a Social Democratic Party was organized at the same time as well. They essentially tried to reinvent a social democratic party, to pick up the thread of the long historical tradition in Germany. I had strong reservations about that at the time, because such an attempt would not only dispute the communists' legitimacy of power, but it would also delegitimize its own history. After all, the SED not only perceived itself as the legitimate heir of the communists, but also of the social democratic tradition. So I thought that such an attempt to reinvent a social democratic party was bound to fail, and I think one year earlier it would, in fact, have failed dismally. But through September and October, the whole system proved to be more shallow and defunct than anyone had expected it to be. Absolutely no one could have suspected or foreseen how weak the whole apparatus had suddenly become.

You see, we had certainly not expected that the party was still able to create a new ideological push forward, that a genuine political and productive performance could still emerge from the old structures of this system. But we had calculated their ability to suppress any organized opposition not only to be much higher, but to be virtually intact.

Let me ask you again about these summer arrangements within the opposition. Did these arguments include the opposition movement in Leipzig, since we hear so much about the opposition having originated in Leipzig?

Sure. We had numerous contacts with friends in Leipzig. But what happened there was still pretty autonomous. Leipzig acquired a much larger base for oppositional activities within society throughout the year 1989, perhaps even earlier than that. In Berlin we never quite succeeded in reaching larger sectors of society, such as workers, for example. In Berlin the opposition was pretty much confined to intellectuals. In Leipzig, on the other hand, the whole thing was more open. . . .

. . . You mean, the groups were more open toward including nonintellectual circles as well?

Yes. . . . One should not forget, of course, that the situation in Leipzig was fundamentally different from the one in Berlin. I guess that is particularly difficult to understand for someone from the outside. In fact, the situation for the opposition in Berlin was completely different from anywhere else in the GDR, be it in Leipzig, Dresden, Rostock, or what have you. Just the fact that we had West Berlin right next door, and that most Western journalists were working in Berlin, and that we could, with their help, get certain news items to the West, and that West German TV was constantly stationed in Berlin. All these things made it very different for us.

I see. In other words, there were much better conditions for oppositional work in Berlin?

Yes, absolutely. The barrier of repression was much lower in Berlin; you could do a lot more in Berlin because the party leadership was much too worried about creating an international scandal. It was much more difficult for the opposition movement in Leipzig, for instance, to get anything out to the Western media. So there is no doubt that conditions in Berlin made it much easier for us.

But why was the opposition in Leipzig so successful then, or, the way you put it, even more successful than the Berliners in reaching wider circles of the population?

[Long pause] I have a very hard time giving a final answer to that. But there are numerous factors that might have played a role in this, such as the historical formation of the two cities, particularly the history of the last forty years. Berlin, in general, was always very privileged over all the other cities in the GDR—which is, by the way, true with all capitals in each and every dictatorship.

Hitler had invested a great deal in building up Berlin as the Reich's capital, and the communists did the same thing. Berlin was the capital of the GDR, and thus we received all these extra funds and privileges. The infrastructure of Berlin was never allowed to collapse like it did in all other cities of the GDR. You had to see certain residential areas in cities like Leipzig to fully appreciate how much more people had to suffer there. The supply of virtually everything was generally worse anywhere else outside Berlin. This also had something to do with the close proximity of West Berlin. The provinces have always tried to rebel against the center— efforts in which they usually did not succeed. There was a general frustration in the country toward Berliners. Even within the opposition, the Berliners occupied this peculiar position of being told by others: "Well, it's easy for you to complain, but wait until you see what our situation is like."

There were also certain oppositional traditions that played into this. . . . I think people in Leipzig had more of a conscious memory of protest, because they had experienced it more often than we had, like in 1968, when they staged large-scale protests against the demolition of the University Church in downtown Leipzig. . . .

In Berlin, on the other hand, the last large-scale public protest had taken place in June of 1953. Leipzig was also not as deeply compromised as Berlin was during the Nazi regime. Berlin was the capital of the Nazi movement; in Berlin the whole disaster had started, all the Nazi centers of power had been located in Berlin. Leipzig, in contrast, had been more of a trade center of international stature. I think it had perhaps been particularly humiliating to the inhabitants of Leipzig to have experienced this dismal deterioration of their own city, and it had also aggravated their sense of frustration toward the center, Berlin.

So those are all ingredients that one would have to take into consideration and evaluate. And there is one more element that I forgot to mention, which is the catastrophic ecological situation in Leipzig, which no doubt also boosted the willingness of the people of Leipzig to participate in oppositional activities. . . .

What I'd be interested in finding out from you at this point has to do with the sequential steps people go through from being passive to becoming dissenters in their own mind all the way to overcoming their barriers of fear and committing public acts of dissent. It is my understanding that people have problems and grievances virtually all the time. Yet grievances in and of themselves, however severe, cannot explain the appearance of public dissent, much less of any kind of organized opposition or even of a popular social movement. In other words, what do you think had happened at this particular moment in time that increasing numbers of people were willing and ready to do something, to stand up and step outside of the narrow boundaries of what a friend of mine calls "private insurgency"? You said earlier that the small organized opposition had decided not to move until after 7 October, but that you were forced by subsequent events to move much earlier. Why?

That was sparked by Poland and Hungary. GDR citizens were suddenly leaving in masses. You probably remember the pictures of the West German embassies in Prague and Warsaw, and the speechlessness of people who had remained in the GDR, their utter inability to grasp this or to know how to respond to such developments.

On the other hand, the opposition simply had to respond to those events if it was to take its responsibility as an opposition halfway seriously. The way we did respond, of course, was to call for the building of a large-scale movement which would bring about the fundamental transformation of the country. What we were desperately trying to do was to create a space in which people could help change the country, instead of leaving it. And yet we were probably still too late, even though we went ahead with our plans earlier than we had initially agreed upon. At least, we were not very well-prepared. We were only a few people, small circles with small numbers of participants. Overnight we basically faced the problem of giving some structure to the sudden enthusiasm, the sudden protest energy of hundreds of thousands of citizens.

We needed to give this oppositional energy not only a program, but also an organizational structure. And that was simply not possible to achieve with the meager means that were available to us at the time. We were not at all prepared for that. It was way above our abilities in virtually every respect. We had nothing in terms of possible sites of organizing effort—other than our private homes and a few spaces within the church. We did not have, for instance, a communications network that could have functioned independently of a few individuals.

So, in other words, you would say that what generated the "revolution" in the GDR was at no point an organized social movement?

No, certainly not. It was a spontaneous expression of dissent by masses of people. It was definitely initiated to a certain extent by organized oppositional groups, but those groups which had existed prior to the Fall of 1989 never succeeded in placing themselves at the head of this popular enthusiasm. I have to say this self-critically. Not even as late as 9 November were we able to provide leadership for the people. Things were happening on the streets, but not in any organized fashion. It really was spontaneous mass enthusiasm, and also an enormous willingness to take immense risks, particularly when you look at the 70,000 or 80,000 who demonstrated in Leipzig [on 9 October] when things were still extremely dangerous.

In retrospect, one has to add, however, that even those people only represented about 5 percent of the population. The vast majority of people still sat behind their curtains and, at the very most, occasionally dared to peek through them in order to see what was going on outside. Nevertheless, the number of people suddenly on the streets was way too large for the small organized opposition to handle. There was simply no way we could have provided much of a structure for them.

Do you see any differences, however slight, in the degree and form of organization between places such as Dresden, Leipzig, or Berlin? You said previously that it was more of an intellectual movement in Berlin, whereas Leipzig had a broader-based civic movement, including workers.

Well, the whole thing also happened more spontaneously in Leipzig and Dresden than it did in Berlin. I think even prior to the Fall of 1989 people there had more willingness to participate in spontaneous oppositional actions, while in Berlin we based our work more on words, on the power of words to convince people through discussions, through the dissemination of our journals, and so on.

Others, again like the Leipzigers, also engaged in more symbolic actions, such as when they set up a symbolic voting booth on the marketplace shortly after the polling stations had closed during the elections in May. The point was to provide an opportunity for all those people who had either voted "no" or had not voted at all to drop a note to that effect. Of course, the police intervened, and the whole thing turned into a very emotional event.

In Berlin, things like that never took place. I think one reason for that was that we did not have a geographic center in Berlin. I mean, tell me where the center of East Berlin is?

How would you evaluate the significance of outside factors such as the opening of the borders in Hungary, the election of the first noncommunist prime minister in Poland, or even the role of Gorbachev? Some historians would even argue that one has to understand Solidarność before one can attempt to understand what followed in the wake of Solidarność, because ultimately Solidarność made somebody like Gorbachev possible in the Soviet Union. . . .

Yes, I think one could clearly show that Gorbachev is, at least also, an answer to Solidarność. In other words, Gorbachev understood that the system had to be opened up, that it had to be democratized, that the old command structures had to be taken apart if the whole economy was not to collapse entirely. And in this sense the experiences in Poland with Solidarność helped a great deal to initiate the thought processes behind perestroika and glasnost, and to give them credentials as something that was simply necessary. I think we could find an abundance of proof for that causal connection. If you read some of his speeches, or analyze his Poland visit in 1986 or '87, it becomes obvious that his political ideas are very much a response to Solidarność.

What about other outside factors, such as the wave of emigration that took place in the late summer and fall of 1989? Some people even argue that ultimately it was this wave of emigration that forced the SED to its knees and initiated what came to be called the East German revolution?

I don't think one can view any of these factors exclusively. I think all of these factors helped each other along. At the bottom of events in the GDR lies a mixture of numerous factors. It is true, however, that the rapid acceleration of events in the Fall would not have taken place had the Hungarians not opened their borders. But on the other hand, it would also never have been as peaceful a transformation had those various opposition groups not already come into existence. Had this minimum of a program and an organizational structure not existed, there is no doubt in my mind that the events of the Fall would have led to a violent confrontation with the state.

When I said that these structures were completely insufficient to deal with those masses of people who suddenly took to the streets, I meant to criticize our own structures. But on the other hand, things would have been much worse had those few structures not been in place either.

When people argue in favor of one exclusive factor that brought about this transformation, you can safely assume that there is some political purpose behind that, such as either minimizing or glorifying the role of the organized opposition.

■ KLAUS KADEN, Protestant pastor, reformer, and the church's contact person for grass-roots groups in Leipzig.[19] ■ *"At that point in time it was the very most we could have imagined: a reform and democratization of the existing system, even though most people in no way identified with this system. But everything else was simply inconceivable, everything else would have meant war."*

Unlike all the other Protestant pastors I interviewed, and certainly unlike the vast majority of opposition activists from any sector of East German society, Reverend Klaus Kaden's dedicated activities within the East German civic movement were fed from the very beginning by his desire for the two Germanies "to be one again." The following, I believe, best represents the range of arguments for unification that increasingly came to dominate the internal political landscape in East Germany. After the party had effectively collapsed as an ongoing political force and no viable home-grown alternative seemed capable of taking its place, the reasons for unification with West Germany here invoked by Klaus Kaden were largely adopted by what probably represented the majority of East German citizens. Whether or not one considered the West German political and economic model a "good choice" was no longer a decisive or even relevant consideration. The controlling point was that a growing number of people perceived it as "the only choice." As even the newly elected chairman of the restructured communist party, Gregor Gysi, conceded in late January 1990, "the question of unification is no longer 'if,' but merely 'how.'"

■ *We talked about the Monday Peace Prayers at the Nikolai Church in Leipzig, about the would-be émigré groups and the more explicitly "political" grass-roots groups. You also reflected upon the activities surrounding the May elections and the Alternative Church Day, and you commented on the Pleisse Memorial March. All these things date back, as it were, to the time prior to the Fall of 1989. What was the long-term significance of all these events?*

All these events quite simply prepared people for the shock in July/August when the Hungarians opened their borders and people began to emigrate by the thousands.

You see, even though the citizens of the GDR never had much money, they always tried to travel as much as they could, even if it was only by hitchhiking, with a sausage in one's pocket. So, during the summer of 1989, many citizens already had a visa in their hands, and others just tried to get to Hungary illegally. It was simply terrible. It got really bad during this time.

In Leipzig especially, so many people had already left. Everyone knew somebody who had fled, and so everyone had to confront him or herself once again with the question, "What am I still doing here?" There was absolutely no hope. The city was in ruins, and the big shots up there told us that we were not supposed to "shed a tear for those who had left." I remember this so vividly, I could have crushed my television set when they made those statements that "we can easily live without those few hundred people." Just terrible. This was the first time that I lost all hope.

The next thing was the Monday Peace Prayer on 4 September. This Monday happened to coincide with the Industrial Fair in Leipzig. So, as always when the fair was going on, they had to show some restraint because the international press was there with their cameras. Of course, the Stasi people were still present everywhere.

In and of itself it wasn't a very significant peace prayer that Monday; it was not even very critical of the party or anything like that. They discussed the problem of large-scale emigration, but nothing else. But after the meeting was over, hundreds of people gathered in front of the church. Some of them were members of the justice group, and some others unfurled banners, demanding freedom in general and freedom to travel in particular. The Stasi people immediately tore them down—pictures that went around the world, as you know. And then it suddenly tipped over again, and hundreds of people began to chant, "We want out, we want out."

This was very shocking to the activists in the grass-roots groups. They had struggled so hard all summer long for people finally to take their fate into their own hands and to fight for changes *in* the country instead of leaving it. But here again the majority of those present were moved by only a few would-be émigrés to chant "we want out." These people could have already left through Hungary. This was a very big shock, for me as well.

I remember standing right next to the president of the church assembly, Reverend Auerbach, and I said, "Brother Auerbach, now we have to make up our minds as to whether we take to the streets or whether we turn our backs on these wounded and shattered people."

What did you mean by "turn our backs?"

To stay within the church and to let them fight it out alone with the state. I just knew that the time had come where the decision would be— had to be—either them or us. I have a very vivid memory of all those activists from the various grass-roots groups, how utterly disappointed they were as they stood on the sidelines watching this sudden development. They had taken so many risks, and here these people were yelling "we want out, we want out." And this was what went around the world—as if we did not have other problems.

But, of course, the peace prayers continued, and every Monday more and more people showed up, until we had at least 70,000 on 9 October, despite the most severe kinds of repression and most extensive forms of intimidation exercised by the party. As you know, they had used their whole arsenal of threats prior to 9 October, telling people they would use, if necessary, guns and tanks to repress the demonstration. And still, more than 70,000 people showed up. We have to keep in mind that this was about half the population of Leipzig willing to risk their lives.

What was the significance of the would-be émigrés at that point?

None. They played absolutely no role anymore: 4 September was their last public appearance, and after that they were gone, completely insignificant. After that, "the people" came. Already on 11 September the people came, and emigration played no role anymore. . . .[20]

Every Monday the police encircled the entire area around the church. It was really terrible; everyone felt that this could not go on much longer. Every Monday we had "crisis meetings," the bishop had to come, and so on.

After 11 September, the bishop also began to participate in the Monday Peace Prayers—that is, incognito. He just wanted to see everything, wanted to experience this, but he never wanted to come in his official position as bishop. I thought this was great, just amazing. He was later accused, I think very unjustifiably so, of having had secret dealings with the state. I think that we should be very grateful to him. On 9 October he literally ran from one participating church to the other and everywhere conveyed his message of nonviolence and encouraged people by saying, "We are on your side."

And then there was this appeal by Kurt Masur[21] and others, who said that they would make every effort to seek a peaceful solution. People in the

20. A decisive event occurred between 4–11 September—the public unveiling of the founding statement of New Forum on 10 September. With its exclusive emphasis on reform of the GDR from within, this political manifesto successfully transcended the parochial objectives of the émigré groups.

21. Kaden is here referring to the open letter by Kurt Masur [director of the Leipzig Symphonic Orchestra] and three local party secretaries [Kurt Meyer, Jochen Pommert, and Roland Wötzel] calling for a "peaceful dialogue" between citizens and party in order to prevent a violent confrontation on 9 October. See also n. 20, Part I, chapter 1, p. 74.

churches responded with a standing ovation after this letter had been read to them, despite the fact that this letter stated, among other things, that "we support the reform of socialism." You see, at that point in time it was the very most we could have imagined: a reform and democratization of the existing system, even though most people in no way identified with this system. But everything else was simply inconceivable, everything else would have meant war.

It came differently, and many people were very happy that they could finally get rid of this system, that they could finally be part of this "one people" again. We had not been "one people" for such a long time. We had only been the "bad cousins" of a great people. We were the ones who had to pay for these two ill-fated wars that we had begun and lost. In other words, we could finally be Germans again.

This had nothing to do with chauvinism. On the contrary, it was the scream of a repressed people without identity. Of course, there were people who wanted to exploit this, like the far-right Republicans, but they had no chance whatsoever, not one.

I think you have opened up a very fruitful question for discussion. Isn't it still far from obvious whether those hundreds of thousands of people who said before and right after 9 November "we are the people," and who carried banners demanding "democratic socialism" and an independent East German future, were the same people as those who later on said "we are one people" and who demanded unification?

I think in most cases those were the same people. Unfortunately, to my great dismay, speeches were not given until late November at those big demonstrations. Twice I went to city hall demanding that the mayor and the representatives from the districts should speak. People were sitting on Karl Marx Platz at the end of October and sang a few songs—we didn't know many songs, so they even sang the "Internationale."

Everybody was waiting for someone to say something, and some were screaming—we did not even have bullhorns—"what did they say over there," or "what statement did these people read, we can't hear anything," and so on. It really would have been necessary for someone to say something over a loudspeaker or so. But somehow nobody wanted to do that.

At first, no one from the churches said anything outside the church either. . . .

Let me just say this: the members of the grass-roots groups were also of many different opinions concerning this question of East Germany's future course. A little more than half a year ago, even church superintendent Friedrich Magirius was still praising, clearly and explicitly, socialism as "the only good alternative to capitalism." And the other superintendent here, of course, had a very different stance. He was not exactly a "German nationalist," but he clearly stated his complete and total rejection of socialism. He felt that socialists had a very different understanding of human nature. All of which is to say that there were very many different perceptions and ideas out there.

For me, on the other hand, a dream was coming true right from the start: I had always wanted to experience, during my lifetime, our people becoming one again. That had been my dream ever since I had been a child. I never had any relatives in the Federal Republic, or anything, so I did not have some kind of personal interest. To me, it had just been a catastrophe that we had been separated like this, which had always meant to me that I had no identity. I was never able to identify with this system, with the political entity called the "GDR." . . .

Of course, and I admit it, there were many other people who felt very differently about that, even within the church.

I heard that there were a lot of conflicts in November and December between those who demanded unification, those who waved black, red, and gold flags, and those who were interested in reform, in democratization, and an autonomous East German path into the future. Is that correct?

Yes, that's true. I think the reason behind this polarization between those two groups mainly had to do with pragmatic reasons: the latter group wanted reforms without having noticed that this country could no longer be reformed. The economy had collapsed, the infrastructure was destroyed, and the people no longer saw any purpose behind making any efforts within this system. I don't think they would have accepted another "experiment." . . .

But on the other hand, the question immediately popped up as to "who can help us now?" The Russians could not, the Poles could not, none of our other neighbors could. But our big brother, the Federal Republic, he could. The big brother had always maintained that "we are brothers" and that "we want reunification." All those GDR citizens who had always been West German citizens after eight o'clock [the time the major West German shows started on television] were, of course, well aware of that. They had deeply internalized this . . .

. . . Excuse me for interrupting at this point, but this sounds to me a bit like an explanation that is shaped and justified by what happened afterward. I am not convinced that some of these dynamics were quite that obvious at the end of 1989. For example, wasn't it very much an open question as to what should be

considered an "experiment?" What actually happened was interpreted by many opposition activists as more of an experiment than the attempt to find some kind of third way, that is, something between socialism and the West German model. I am also a little suspicious of those claims that the GDR is completely dilapidated, as if the GDR had absolutely no chance on its own. After all, as you yourself have said, in comparison to other East-Central European countries, and to many less-developed capitalist countries, conditions in the GDR were relatively good, weren't they?

But look at the price we had to pay for that . . .

. . . I agree completely. But there are many people who would argue that the price may now get very high for most GDR citizens as well.

No, I don't agree. What the price will be this time around is still an open question. Let me just give you one example. If you were to estimate what it would cost to get the road and railroad system at least close to Western European standards, you would come to the conclusion that it would cost at least 700 billion Marks [about $400 billion]—and that does not include any of the necessary airports. And then, in comparison, look at the roads and railroads in Czechoslovakia—they have done a much better job over there. Leipzig alone requires an estimated 40 billion Marks in order to get the infrastructure back in shape, just roads, irrigation, sewers, gas pipelines, and other basic things like that. There is no way we could have afforded that. This is precisely the kind of price we paid; this is why we made relatively good money while everything else was going down the drain. It would not have taken much longer and this situation would have resulted in a total catastrophe. . . .

True, I cannot judge how things are in Poland, Hungary, and so on. Perhaps we could have pulled it off, one of these days, with a lot of hard work, taking up loans, and so on. Nevertheless, the opportunity for a quick solution was right next door, and it was the wish of most people finally to be free and rich again, just like the big brother in the Federal Republic. In my opinion it was the very combination of terrible disappointment with this system and the immediate help offered by West Germany that determined the eventual outcome of this revolution. . . .

Let me try to explain. So many horrific things we had not known anything about were disclosed—no one had known about Wantlitz [a secluded and guarded section of Berlin in which high party functionaries lived in considerable comfort], or about the various machinations of a Schalck-Golodkowsky [a confidant of Erich Honecker who allegedly managed large GDR investments in capitalist firms and also helped engineer large-scale arms trades]. Week after week, one catastrophic revelation after another, all the way to their support of terrorism. We had not known any of this. It was a terrible shock and disappointment to realize what kind of system we had been part of, to find out how things had really been. . . .

And in this situation there was only one entity that offered help, and that was the Federal Republic. The imposing figure of chancellor Helmut Kohl himself came to Leipzig and promised the people, "We will never let you down." Only then did things begin to speed up so much.

At first, we thought unification could perhaps take place in 1993 or '94, but suddenly they were planning for an immediate currency union and unification by the end of 1990. And still everybody was thinking: "How are we even going to keep the people until then? They are running away in hordes." As late as April [1990] thousands daily left the country for good. So we got to a point where it became simply impossible to calculate things in a normal fashion. We could not possibly have engaged in another experiment at that point. We just had to realize that we immediately needed a social and currency union, then political unification, and after that we would see how we could pull off things together . . .

. . . But isn't that an incredible experiment as well?

Yes, but with a fantastic partner.

All right. But one argument that has often been made was that one could also have negotiated with this partner, as partner among partners, so to speak. Yet the East German government was not being taken seriously anymore. Wasn't that a problem—that your negotiating position was being terribly eroded?

What kind of result could a stronger GDR position have produced? March was the most sobering moment [he is referring to the first free elections]. I had not considered it possible that the Greens and Alliance 90 [an election alliance of three major opposition groups] would take such a terrible beating in Leipzig. . . .

On the other hand, one should also not make the mistake of glorifying the people who brought about the Wende. They made a lot of mistakes as human beings, they displayed a lot of arrogance vis-à-vis people who thought differently. The worst thing for me was that the left, which had only received a very low percentage of the vote [on 18 March 1990], simply did not understand—or if they did, they did not want to accept it— that most GDR citizens wanted to make sure, they wanted to finalize unification. . . .

The left is no more capable of democracy than the far right. They do not understand that if you want to establish a parliamentary democracy, or something like that, you necessarily have to go the long way through the institutions. . . .

Let me just say this: if you look at our previous economic performance, our economic conditions in general, we represent a clear-cut failure on this side of the divide. And, whether we identified with this system or not, we are all responsible.

In the West, of course, everything is running full steam right now, very successfully so. It is not so much that they are different people, but they are certainly far more successful; thus, the whole world envies them. And suddenly we had the chance to go together with this big brother. . . . Sure, we are not real partners. Of course, they annexed us. But this is the only chance for us to recover, politically as well as economically.

■ FRANK EIGENFELD, biologist and founding member of New Forum; HARALD WAGNER, mathematician, pastor, and founding member of Democratic Awakening.[22] ■ *"I was close to a total collapse. . . . It was the most exciting and interesting time in my life."*

Most of the prevailing arguments in the West as to what had made the East German events possible can be seen as falling into three main categories: first and foremost, that a totalitarian and badly functioning system simply caved in soon after the USSR under Gorbachev stopped providing for its security; second (and closely related to the first line of reasoning), that some sort of "natural" urge toward Western-style capitalism had reached dimensions which could no longer be controlled by the East German leadership; and, finally, that the ever-growing wave of emigration, made possible by the existence of the "other" German state and—since the summer of 1989—exacerbated by the open border between Hungary and Austria, began seriously to threaten the day-to-day functioning of East German society.

As the interview sections in chapter 3 have revealed, all of these factors undoubtedly helped provide some of the preconditions for the East German revolution. But it has become equally evident that they cannot, by themselves, explain any of the specific dynamics behind the rapidly unfolding events of 1989. Above all, such arguments sidestep completely the critical role of the organized opposition, and they conceal as well the driving motivations behind hundreds of thousands of East German citizens who decided to commit dangerous public acts of defiance in the presence of existing state authority. In short, conventional explanations, remote and abstract as they are, leave the East German people out.

22. For background information on Eigenfeld and Wagner, see Part I, chapter 1, pp. 35–54.

After Ludwig Mehlhorn rendered a more general account of the overwhelming organizing problems that surfaced in the Fall of 1989, and Reverend Klaus Kaden presented his reasoning in favor of a Western-dominated unification process, as we have just seen, I asked Frank Eigenfeld and Harald Wagner, as founding members of New Forum and Democratic Awakening, to describe in more detail the complicated emergence and growth of an organized opposition during that fateful year. I asked them in particular to shed some light on the doubts and agonies that suffused this process. Their answers provide vivid examples of a most fundamental problem with which everyone who tries to organize an oppositional force has to cope—in East Germany or anywhere else.

Indeed, as almost all of the following interviews make evident, opposition activists were continuously confronted, day after day, month after month, with this particularly difficult problem. We may call it the central problematic underlying the very idea of popular politics, affecting all self-generated attempts to create an actually functioning "civil society" or democratic polity when one is confronted with the layers of hierarchy that exist in all modern societies. This central problematic facing all oppositionists is: if they do not push the existing state apparatus, they may end up in historical irrelevance. The corollary problematic is that if they push too hard too quickly, they may get obliterated by the powers that be.

Virtually every opposition activist, and even a number of reformers in the party, had painfully experienced the results of "pushing too hard." They had been arrested, beaten, interrogated, indicted, and incarcerated.[23] But the party's most effective means of preventing the emergence of an organized opposition in the GDR had been the weapon of exile; hundreds of activists had been expelled to the West over the years. Equally dismaying, however, were the consequences of not pushing at all; things remained the same, the level of resignation and cynicism rose, and many citizens opted, in the end, to apply for emigration visas or tried to get out some other way.

In short, for every individual member of the opposition much was at stake at every turn, at every stage of this decision-making process that determined what one did or did not do at any given moment. What might have appeared as obvious or logical in retrospect involved, before the fact,

---

23. Janusz Bugajski and Maxine Pollack nicely captured this phenomenon in the book *East European Fault Lines* when they wrote: "East Berlin periodically eases pressures for emigration and attempts to deflate the civil rights movement by granting 'amnesties' for prisoners of conscience and issuing exit visas to persistent 'troublemakers'" (Boulder, Colo., 1989), 135.

very difficult, very problematic, choices. Under such conditions, it was often difficult for East Germans to decide what was "radical" and what was "moderate," what was "effective" and what was merely "romantic," who was helping the oppositional cause and who was, in fact, hurting it.

What follows can only be described as an intense, if tolerant, argument between two oppositionists, an impassioned conversation that serves to highlight how open-ended, confusing, and debatable popular politics inherently are. In this sense, this conversation can be seen as a harbinger of what a "democratic" argument might look like in a functioning democratic culture.

The energized debates within the opposition essentially grew out of the frantic search for realistic political strategies within an environment where everything was in a drastic state of flux. This flux had a kind of centrifugal quality—away from the ossified reality of organized life under the party, but toward something new that was neither foreseeable nor even clear as a goal. As this early period of political incubation was abruptly cut short by factors beyond the control of the reformers, the internal debates within circles of dissidents began to explore the possibility that they had brought much of the failure on themselves through self-inflicted errors. Though Frank Eigenfeld and Harald Wagner argue at length in the following pages over some of these conceivable shortcomings, I could not help but wonder about the inherent relationship between social marginalization on the one hand and sectarian quarrels that seemed to be fueled by marginalization on the other. These disjunctures also help to emphasize the oft-overlooked fact that the quarrels themselves had now become marginal: for reasons beyond their ability to influence, the train into the future GDR had already left at the time these oppositionists were still debating the best way to get to the train station.

■ *Obviously there has been much speculation about who exactly brought about the transformation in the Fall of 1989. Numerous commentators have argued, as you know, that the revolution would have never happened without the pressure of a growing number of would-be émigrés. I have heard that they pretty much dominated all the groups until about June/July, when it first became possible to . . .*

Eigenfeld: . . . Well, actually it was quite risky to get out via Hungary before November of 1989. First of all, one needed a visa, and then it wasn't all that easy to get to Hungary, but even if one succeeded in taking those two hurdles it was still far from simple to get across the border from Hungary to Austria. . . . Many took this route, but the majority [of those who wanted to get out] stayed and waited for a better opportunity.

This is how the situation appeared to me: the would-be émigrés knew very well that publicity was helpful. Every time when there was a trade fair in Leipzig, for example, they staged a spontaneous and spectacular action. At the time of the fall trade fair in the beginning of September, demonstrations in Leipzig were, in fact, still dominated by those people who chanted "we want out." . . .

During the weekend of 9–10 September, of course, we met in Grünheide to write the New Forum founding document. The initial plan had been to wait until after 7 October [the fortieth anniversary of the GDR] for any kind of national political initiative. Our still rather naive understanding had been that it would hurt our cause if we pushed the state too hard too quickly. We continued to carry around some kind of "consideration" for this state. . . . We also continued to hope that one of these days they would have to recognize us and respond to our demands. We thus wanted them to have time to celebrate the fortieth anniversary before we confronted them with New Forum.

Somehow such considerations were pushed into the background during the discussions in Grünheide, however. It just did not seem to make sense to wait any longer. We also thought that it might be difficult to bring together all of us again a month later.

We had no idea what many of the consequences of our meeting would be. So, at long last, on Sunday, 10 September, we decided to go public immediately. We had already finished the text, there was nothing else to do, so why should we wait? The only other thing we discussed was the formal application for official recognition of New Forum, an idea that Rolf Henrich [former party member, lawyer, and dissident] had brought into the discussion. His point was that according to existing law we had the legal right to register as an already existing organization. So on Monday the 11th we made this text public, and on Tuesday each of us went to our respective local office of the Department of the Interior with this text and applied for official registration.

The Western media of course knew about this, so the whole initiative became public very quickly. And during the following Monday demonstration the chants of the participants had already changed from "we want out" to "we are staying." I do not want to claim that this was an immediate first consequence of our appeal. On the other hand, we had stated very clearly in our appeal that we wanted to address all those who wanted to *stay*, all those who wanted to fight for a transformation of the *existing* society—in short, all those who wanted to achieve a dialogue between party and people and sought a meaningful debate about all the problems that the party had previously kept the lid on. And the outcome was simply that people began to demonstrate for political change rather than for the possibility of getting out. Of course, I don't know for sure what went on in the minds of people who demonstrated in Leipzig, but the chants and demands literally changed in the course of one week from "we want out" to "we are staying."

Wagner: Just a little correction. Even on the previous Monday there was a little group that had already chanted "we are staying." In fact, the demonstration split up over that point. The would-be émigrés, who constituted by far the larger group, went in one direction, while the others, a group of about 80, said "we are staying," "we demand human rights," and so on.

But I completely agree that the New Forum Appeal was of great significance. I believe that 11 September [the publication of the New Forum founding statement] will be remembered as a day which was at least as important as 9 November [the opening of the Wall] for the changes in East Germany . . . the things that this appeal brought out in a lot of people were simply unbelievable . . .

Eigenfeld: . . . Yes, this whole period was the most exciting time I have ever experienced in my life. During the same night we had returned to Halle I myself printed copies of the New Forum Appeal. . . . Of course, we didn't have any adequate equipment, but a friend of mine owned an old wax printing machine. You see, we were not allowed to use the church printer anymore—the Stasi had already arrested me on numerous occasions because I had used it for making copies of the "Umweltblätter" [an oppositional samizdat journal] or of various commemorative services. The church leadership had consequently prohibited me from using their equipment again. But, as I said, I knew of one printing machine that was not known to the Stasi. . . . I asked my friend who owned this machine, and he was very excited about putting it to use for this purpose.

Somehow I knew that if we began to disseminate this appeal among the people, change could not be prevented any longer. For that reason, in fact, none of us had even expected to make it back home. We all thought that the Stasi would intercept us and that we would most certainly get arrested . . .

. . . So the idea was that everybody would go home, find a place to copy or print this appeal and begin handing it out among as many people as possible . . .

Eigenfeld: . . . Yes, exactly, to spread it among the people as quickly as possible . . .

. . . So how did you do that, whom did you ask and what channels did you use? The church, for example?

Eigenfeld: Well, yes, also the church. But, generally speaking, we tried to make use of any conceivable route to get it to the largest number of people possible. So we printed it on Sunday night—we had written a little addendum to the effect that we were addressing all those who wanted to stay in the country, and that they should contact us. . . . Whoever supported the project should come to us and sign. Beyond that, we were also seeking official recognition.

So on Sunday night I printed 2,000 copies of the appeal and distributed them on the next day. At that point we didn't specifically select people anymore, but rather simply handed it out to anyone we could reach. That's how it all started. From early in the morning until late at night people came to see us and wanted to sign, 200 to 300 people a day, ten at a time sitting in the hallway waiting. This went on for months—until November, to be precise.

We didn't have an office or anything else. Not until early November did we set up a provisional office at the Georgian parish. . . . We just had to get out of our private apartments. People came from dawn until into the night, there were constant discussions going on, and I was close to a total collapse. Yet it was the most exciting and interesting time of my life. Some people came, for example, and told us "you shouldn't even know who I am, but I think this is extremely important, and I am going to sign, no matter what." People from all sectors of society showed up at our doorsteps. I also received a huge pile of support letters at home, mostly signed copies of the original appeal. . . .

Wagner: . . . May I say something disturbing at this point? It was a moment of great pain for all the others when your appeal became public, because we had agreed that if something like that was initiated, we would do it together. That's what everyone had agreed upon . . .

Eigenfeld: . . . But that wasn't quite true anymore . . .

Wagner: . . . Well, that's exactly the question now: who is lying here, Bärbel Bohley or Ehrhart Neubert [pastor, leading representative of Democratic Awakening, later MP for the Social Democrats]. You can really limit it to those two people. . . . The question is why at least half the opposition, the people of Democracy Now, the Social Democrats, and we from Democratic Awakening—a group that might have never come into existence had it not been for this exclusion; we might have turned into "Democratic Forum" or something like that—why all of those people were not included. That was a bad thing, I think there is no doubt about that. Some of us were in terrible shape after this . . .

Eigenfeld: . . . Well, yes. But the causes for this development can only be found much earlier . . .

Wagner: . . . No, I don't agree. Some of the earlier disagreements were completely independent of the question of why our efforts did not lead to a combined, to a unified, opposition. You see, Neubert was clearly instructed by us to talk to Rolf Henrich and Bärbel Bohley and to make arrangements [for a common initiative]. And he claims that they had promised him that this common initiative should be launched on 1 October, and here they were making it happen on 10 September. Meckel and Böhme [leaders of the Social Democrats] were promised the same thing, and, of course, we were all there on 1 October. So the question is really who is lying . . .

. . . If I may interrupt at this point. Is it correct that all of these opposition groups you were talking about already existed in some kind of embryonic form during the summer, and the idea was that some kind of combined effort should be started on 7 October?

Wagner: Yes, they did already exist as groups of people who knew each other and who had done political work together, in a few cases going back quite some time. You have to realize that opposition activists were oppressed in the most severe kinds of ways. It was not at all farfetched when people began talking about internment camps. We found whole Stasi lists of opposition activists to be arrested and interned in time of crisis. Even the execution of oppositionists was, according to the documents we later found, seriously considered.

So this is precisely why it would have been important to get together all 300 or so people who were seriously committed to such an initiative, and not only the thirty that came together for the founding meeting of New Forum.

Eigenfeld: We really have to look at the prehistory of this, even though I can't quite recall all the relevant facts for this either. . . . The whole question of forming some kind of organized national opposition did not really come up until Bärbel Bohley returned from her exile in Britain in August of 1988. . . . The journal published by the Initiative for Peace and Human Rights, *Grenzfall,* had not been published for quite some time at that point, and in September 1988 it appeared for the first time again, and she had a piece in it that was entitled "We Need an Organized Opposition in the GDR." She argued that we had reached a point in the GDR at which our efforts should take on a different quality. She wrote that everything we had done so far did not suffice, because it had always remained among small circles of people, because we never managed to grow much. . . . She also stated that most grass-roots efforts had, until then, been dominated by the issues and problems of the would-be émigrés, and that those were issues we could neither control nor influence, and thus should stay away from.

It was only after this article had appeared that we began to engage in the first serious discussions about establishing a real opposition, about building a real oppositional organization. Ever since that time, the question of how to organize played a decisive role at all meetings of the Initiative for Peace and Human Rights.

In the spring of '89 Ibrahim Böhme [first chairman of the East German Social Democratic Party after its founding in the Fall of 1989, later accused of having worked for the secret police] had already had the idea of founding a Social Democratic Party. Even though Böhme also attended the Summer Academy of '89, however, he never mentioned anything to that effect. And yet, at the end of August, they had their organizing meeting of the initiative for a Social Democratic Party. . . .

Wagner: . . . But the question remains why these groups of people did not come together despite explicit prior arrangements to do so. . . . Some later claims concerning all this just seem very fishy to me. . . . But whatever the truth may be, the majority of us were under the clear impression that there were definite arrangements that would include all of us . . .

. . . *Neither one of the two of you were personally part of any prior consultation after the Summer Academy?*

Wagner: No, but that is really not the point. When we sat together in our respective groups, of course we did not make arrangements for every member of each group to talk to all the members of other groups. Rather, we chose people who would take over certain tasks, such as communicating with the other groups. Like all the others, I also had my area of responsibility, which was to organize Chemnitz and Leipzig, but my task was not to create communicational links to other groups. . . . The best-known representative of Frank's group [Initiative for Peace and Human Rights] was Bärbel [Bohley]. An effort on her part to establish some combined organizing structure would thus have been very important . . .

Eigenfeld: . . . But that didn't work . . .

Wagner: . . . Not even to speak of towns such as Chemnitz or Dresden. To this very day they are asking themselves, "How did we end up with so many different groups?"

In Berlin, of course, things looked very different. If Rainer Eppelmann doesn't get along with Bärbel Bohley . . .

Eigenfeld: . . . But that's exactly what came out of all of this . . .

Wagner: . . . Things got so messy and complicated in Berlin. But still . . . on 1 October we again went to Seidel's and Pflugbeil's, and everyone basically supported a combined effort. We all agreed that in such a decisive situation personal animosities should not define our common political efforts. . . . That's where the first outline for Alliance 90 [a later coalition of three major oppositional groups formed for the elections of March 1990] came from, a concept that unfortunately lay dormant until the elections of March 1990.

It had always been our unequivocal intention to combine all the different oppositional activities. We figured we should simply not send Eppelmann and Schnur, or Bohley and Henrich, but rather some of the many people who could get along with each other and who could work together, just so that this movement would not fall apart. . . . Somehow it kept falling apart anyway, which is something we should seriously reflect upon within the current situation . . .

Eigenfeld: . . . But, you see, there were those previous personal contacts . . .

Wagner: . . . Yeah, but just think about it: it is simply unbelievable that a GDR-wide opposition could not come together just because four people did not like each other . . .

Eigenfeld: . . . But that's exactly what happened; it was simply a reality. Wolfgang Schnur was never seriously considered because of the previous experiences all of us had had with him; Rainer Eppelmann was not included, and Edelbert Richter just had bad luck because he was in the Federal Republic at the time . . .

Wagner: . . . At the time, but what about before . . .

Eigenfeld: . . . Well, he was invited, but he was on the other side at this point. And when he returned, he was completely taken aback that we had gone ahead without him . . .

Wagner: . . . Yes. But again, there were many others you could have included. We had simply always expected that you would do this together with us—not just with Edelbert Richter, but with us as already existing groups . . .

. . . *Where did the list of the 30 initially come from? Who came up with the names on this list, and who invited them? Why were others not included?*

Eigenfeld: Katja Havemann [wife of the prominent communist dissident Robert Havemann who died in 1982] and Bärbel Bohley essentially wrote up this list. Practical reasons played the main role in coming up with those 30 names. The initial idea had been to initiate something that would take effect in November, that is, to make prearrangements that would be discussed at some later point with a larger circle of people. We did not know at the time we met on 9 September that we would make this public as soon as the 11th. This whole thing had a certain internal dynamic . . .

. . . *But wouldn't it have been totally logical at such a point to contact other people as well . . . ?*

Eigenfeld: . . . Yes, but at that point it was already too late for that. If the appeal is supposed to be made public the next day, there aren't many people one can contact in the meantime. . . .

 . . . *Of course. But even without the benefit of hindsight, wasn't it completely obvious that either one manages to contact the others as well, or one does not go ahead with it at all . . . ?*

Eigenfeld: . . . Yes, except that we thought it made sense concerning the initial steps if the group was not too big. Thirty was already the maximum, even in terms of available space . . .

 . . . *But, realistically speaking, wouldn't you still have had the alternative of waiting a week and trying to inform the others about what you had come up with . . . ?*

Eigenfeld: . . . But that option was still available. At the point we made this appeal public it was totally insignificant whether 30, 20, or five people had initially signed, it in no way precluded that everyone could still sign, everyone could still have supported it . . .

Wagner: . . . Except that you should have taken into consideration the vanity of people. That someone like Eppelmann does not simply climb aboard an initiative founded by someone else was pretty obvious, particularly since everyone knew that something collective was planned.

It may be, looking at it in retrospect, that nothing much would have been different. But at the time it was very sobering among all the people concerned . . .

Eigenfeld: . . . But you also have to consider the following. There was an invitation for the 24th of August in Leipzig for the purpose of creating a common oppositional force. And it was our hope that, even though we had already made public the appeal of New Forum, that it would still be possible to establish a kind of common ground . . .

Wagner: . . . That wasn't even ruled out. Edelbert Richter and I from Democratic Awakening, as well as people from the Social Democrats, clearly stated in our press releases that it was quite possible that we would found two contrasting movements on the common basis of the New Forum Appeal, namely the SDP, that would evolve into a Social Democratic Party, and Democratic Awakening, which had stated that it wanted to be a civic movement directed at gaining parliamentary power. But New Forum did not go along with that. They said that they would "not write a program," that they would not create any established structures. . . .

I believe it was correct to give ourselves [Democratic Awakening] some structure. Yet even at the point when we offered some kind of alliance— New Forum as the basic platform, and the other two movements as parts of it—we didn't get any positive response.

Eigenfeld: Yes, but I also think that the other groups expressed a kind of pride at that point which was not necessary. . . .

Wagner: The problem was that Bärbel Bohley said "we should not create any institutionalized structures," and with that kind of stance she was about as wrong as one can get.

Eigenfeld: . . . But that was also a much-disputed issue. I myself had argued time and again that establishing some organizational structures was necessary. After all, we had explicitly stated that we want to take over political responsibility. My argument had always been that we should build a New Forum group in every city and in every district in order to include all the forces that were out there. And, clearly, some structure was necessary for this . . .

Wagner: . . . But that was the idea of a segmented structure that would never have been sufficient. . . . We had always stated that we thought this was a good start, and we would help you in that. But, we also argued that we need to build, in addition to that, an organizational structure that would allow us, if need be, to sit down with [the head of state and communist party leader Egon] Krenz for negotiations *the very next day*. We needed, in other words, an organizational structure that was authorized to enter negotiations on behalf of people at the grass roots.

Bärbel Bohley and Rolf Henrich, of course, possessed nothing but self-assumed authorizations—legitimized by you because they were your figureheads. They had never been democratically elected in any way. At no point had they thus been democratically entitled to speak for New Forum in negotiations with the government or with anyone else. They spoke, in fact, simply as individuals . . .

Eigenfeld: . . . But back then everything was still illegal . . .

Wagner: . . . Yes, but we could have already known that we necessarily had to run into those kinds of problems. . . . The point that made me so angry was that people acted as if this all-leveling grass-roots democracy would be capable of substituting for a parliamentary system in the attempt to bring down the dictatorship. That was an illusion, and we could have known that all along. What we needed were specific people who were democratically responsive and who could say, "As of today we take over" . . .

Eigenfeld: . . . But back then we didn't yet think that far ahead. In retrospect, this may be easy to say, but everything was still illegal at the time . . .

Wagner: . . . I can remember very well that we said this at the time.

Eigenfeld: One thing was already obvious at the time we met in Leipzig on 24 September. Those forces that had brought about the creation of New Forum had already generated quite an effect . . .

Wagner: . . . Just think about what you are saying here. Simply because you took the initiative a bit earlier—contrary to previous agreements with us, that is—you now say to us "what do you want?" You are saying "by going public, we are the ones who have the population behind us, so who are you, you others, who do not have that support?" When in fact this only happened because you single-handedly did something early [in creating New Forum] that all groups wanted to do together.

I can remember this line of argument very well. Bärbel Bohley said, "We are thousands, how many are you?" It is true, Democratic Awakening had only organized some 100 people, but that was still a very insidious argument for you to make.

Eigenfeld: I still thought that it would be possible, even after the appeal of New Forum, that we could all come together under the umbrella of New Forum . . .

Wagner: . . . Of course, you are right in saying that unjustified pride played some role in this too. But there are also many people whom you simply can't accuse of that. . . . Yes, pride also played a role, but mostly we are talking about justified political considerations.

I overheard a conversation between Bärbel Bohley and Edelbert Richter in which she told him: "Edelbert, you are the only person who is democratically minded, the others are all puppets, very authoritarian."

Eigenfeld: Of course, you cannot eliminate these personal animosities. I also regretted this. I have always maintained that for such large-scale political struggles one has to subordinate one's own personal feelings.

Those things that happened in the Fall of '89 weigh very heavily on us to this very day. . . .

I see an important qualitative difference between New Forum and all other groups, in that New Forum became very popular because it was the group that brought about a lot of changes. In the consciousness of people these changes occurred because of the existence of New Forum. That is, the name New Forum did not exist and subsequently caused something, but the name New Forum was the result of this development. All the other groups that made a name for themselves later on were not as much a part of this.

In short, to put it very bluntly, New Forum made history, and its name evolved out of that, while the other groups had a name and merely *wanted* to make history. That is why the name New Forum had a different kind of value for people than a name like "Democracy Now."

Wagner: Again, I fundamentally disagree. I think you are vastly over-estimating the significance of a name like New Forum.
We have collectively made the revolution possible. And if we had stayed united, we could have had much more of an impact later on.

■ RAINER EPPELMANN, prominent oppositionist, founder of Dem-ocratic Awakening, minister for disarmament and defense.[24] ■ *"I now carry out a function in which I can very well influence things . . . right in the middle of the government."*

The Reverend Rainer Eppelmann of Democratic Awakening was one of those prominent dissidents in the East German civic movement whom some held responsible for the fact that a unified, GDR-wide opposition alliance never came into being.

Eppelmann was the driving force behind the founding of Democratic Awakening[25] in October 1989, that is, after New Forum and Democracy Now had already been established. Ironically, while Democratic Awakening was the only large opposition group that made initial references to a "reform of socialism," it was also the only group which quickly tried to establish close ties to conservative forces in West Germany. After the group's first chairman, the attorney Wolfgang Schnur, had been revealed as a secret police agent, Rainer Eppelmann was elected as his successor and became the principal engineer of this sharp political turn away from the rest of the organized East German opposition.

In the remaining section of my interview with him I focus on this seemingly contradictory development, one that was rejected by the vast majority of Eppelmann's former friends, and one that not only raised questions about his personal credibility, but, more importantly, about conceivable positions for East German opposition members within radi-cally transformed conditions in general.

■ *I would like to ask you a question from today's perspective. It has become evident that those who previously fought together in the dissident community of the GDR have now gone off in many different political directions. Despite this, many of your former "comrades in struggle" seem to be particularly critical of*

24. For background information on Eppelmann, see Part I, chapter 1, pp. 55–67.
25. The group, and later party, is called "Demokratischer Aufbruch" in German, which could also be translated as "Democratic Start" or "Democratic Departure." I have chosen here to adopt the most widely used English translation.

your *conduct. Many people I have talked to have difficulties comprehending your current political trajectory. Keeping this in mind, I would like to ask you to try to put yourself back into the early to middle 1980s again and tell me what your political ideas concerning the future of the GDR looked like at that time?*

Just like most of my friends, I did not think—and here I am consciously using a term that is not usually part of my vocabulary—about "reunification." That was simply not part of my thinking. What we were trying to do was to turn East Germany into something else, into a society that would seem attractive to us, that would seem humane to us, a society in which it would be fun to live, in which one would be able to fulfill oneself. If my evaluation of the entire situation is correct, those were the predominant ideas of the opposition until November of 1989, with only very few exceptions.

The very first voices stating that we needed one German state again came out of Democracy Now in the late summer of 1989—from people like Konrad Weiss. The closest that Robert Havemann or I came to such ideas involved the withdrawal of all Allied troops [a demand that was part of the Berlin Appeal, 1982], or the realization that the idea of the Allied powers to cut apart Germany in order to make Europe safe had actually turned into its opposite. Europe has not become safer, but rather less safe. There are more weapons deployed here than ever before.

But our own thinking had not yet reached the point at which we said, "Let us overcome the separation of Germany in order to overcome the separation of Europe." We did not reach that point until the Fall of 1989. The furthest we got was to think about demilitarization and perhaps some kind of confederation [between the two Germanies].

In my opinion, all of this drastically and decisively changed on 9 November 1989, even though some of my friends—or rather former friends, as I unfortunately have to call them—have not yet realized that. When I think back to the first platform of Democratic Awakening, we were still talking about "societal alternatives," and that was meant very honestly . . .

. . . *Well, actually you were still talking about "different forms of socialism." In fact, you were the main initiator of the only oppositional group that was still explicitly talking about "socialism." . . .*[26]

---

26. In an earlier interview, shortly before the founding of Democratic Awakening, Eppelmann told reporters that "the reform-socialist impulse informs our program because for some members of our group . . . participation was only possible if we preserved rather than rejected what is positive in socialism." In the same interview he stated that "we firmly believe that the further development of the GDR into the next century is not conceivable without the SED." *Die Tageszeitung,* 3 October 1989.

. . . I am willing to admit that that's true, at least about 80 percent true. But you have to realize that about 20 percent of this was because of fear or tactics—after all, this still happened under Honecker—and we figured if we wanted to have any chance of reaching the public as a party or a movement, instead of continuing to work in hiding. . . .

. . . But aren't we dealing with issues here that go way beyond the question "autonomous GDR or reunification," that is, questions that have to do with political substance, political direction? Here we have you—a friend of Robert Havemann and many others like him—who, later on, ends up with the Christian Democrats. Independent of the questions surrounding reunification, this is a rather astounding development, isn't it? It certainly represents a political path that differs substantially from practically all the others with whom you used to work . . .

. . . That's right. But perhaps it has to be that way.

I do not mean to evaluate it; I would just like to understand it . . .

. . . I understand. I will try to explain it to you. I have always belonged to a minority. Aside from what I have told you so far, I could tell you other stories, like when we burned candles in front of the American Embassy, or when I created one of the first peace circles in the Samariter Parish. . . . When the Protestant Church initiated the Friedensdekade [Ten Days of Peace] in the early 1980s, the Samariter Parish was the only parish that actively participated every day for the entire six years this event was organized. We frequently staged big events, such as concerts with Stephan Krawczyk [dissident singer/songwriter], or lectures by Stefan Heym or Rolf Schneider [critical, reform-minded authors]. These were events attended by some 2,000 to 3,000 people. Within the realm of peace and human rights activities, the Samariter Parish definitely made a name for itself throughout the GDR. . . .

After the Berlin Appeal and the activities surrounding "Swords to Ploughshares," numerous peace circles were founded all over the GDR, at first exclusively under the roof of the Protestant Church. Not until 1989 did these activities go beyond the church. They all started at zero, and in '89 I think we had more than 500 peace circles, environmental circles, human rights circles, Two-Thirds World circles . . .[27]

As I understand it, the first attempt to go beyond the realm of the church was

---

27. East German activists did not speak of the "Third World," but rather of the "Two-Thirds World" in order to avoid the prioritization implicit in "First" and "Third" World and in order to signify that at least two-thirds of the world population live at "Third World" standards."

undertaken not by your group but by the Initiative for Peace and Human Rights in 1985 . . .

. . . Well, that's true, but it was a small, rather marginal group. All the others grew in size much later . . .

. . . But those people at the Initiative for Peace and Human Rights were also the people with whom you used to work, weren't they?

Yes. Then you probably also know that I am still friends with some of them. It's not true that everybody says "Eppelmann is the traitor."

I did not say that, but they say other things about you . . .

. . . Well, maybe they say "traitor to his own convictions." All the things they have accused me of make me a bit sad, because I have to ask myself, "What is the significance of 10 to 15 years of common life, or at least of common political struggles, if people do not even try to talk to you once they don't understand you any longer?" That makes me very sad. A woman like Katja Havemann who puts an announcement in the newspaper, stating that "I am ashamed for you, Eppelmann" did not make a single attempt to talk to me before. To this very day, she does not know, at least not from me, why I am doing the things I am doing. . . .

I would like you to explain it to me. As your first explanation for why you took this particular political route you mentioned that you had always been a political outsider, a part of a minority. But being a member of the Christian Democrats now seems to be the very opposite of being part of a minority. Secondly, this issue of being a minority does not yet say anything about your motivations or convictions . . . ?

. . . That's right. I have a program, a program I have had for a long time, and one that I continue to have to this very day. Broadly speaking this program has to do with freedom, humaneness, and tolerance. I always had my difficulties with people who thought they were in possession of the whole truth, regardless of what political or ideological corner they came from. Every form of infantilization, of taking away people's rights to make up their own minds, makes me very angry. This probably goes back to the fact that my father was a very authoritarian and hot-tempered person. So this kind of political self-righteousness has always sparked resistance, and ultimately action, in me. And then, at least since the mid-1960s, the question of how to transform the country I was a citizen of into something more peaceful was looming large in my mind. I really think that I was a pacifist, down to my bones, and I think I still am. I continue to support, for instance, the very valuable motto "swords to ploughshares," and I have very concrete concepts as to how that can be achieved.

And, let me also say this, ever since the day when I decided to become a conscientious objector and to refuse armed service in the fall of 1965, all the way until the end of 1989—so for at least 24 years—I have not lost sight of this goal. . . .

I am sure it is not everybody's thing to go to jail, but I would say today that those eight months I spent in jail were very important to me. Later on, one thing happened after another. But everything had to do with the goal of removing all weapons of mass destruction from Germany, from Europe, and preferably from the world. For 24 years I suffered for this goal, I fought, I complained, I demanded, I moaned, and I prayed.

And then, due to the changing political circumstances in the GDR, I was asked in the beginning of March whether I wanted to try to put into reality my goals of the last twenty-four years. And I said "yes."

I have just recently tried to explain this to a colleague of yours who was asking me about my reaction to the latest press campaign in which it is claimed that I am a "world champion in acquiring arms." I told him that this really hurts. I can understand if people say that even 221 million Marks for weapons are 221 million Marks too much. Generally and basically speaking, I would agree, particularly if you consider that these 221 million Marks could help children and adults not to starve to death. So if somebody wants to beat me up for the 221 million Marks that I have spent on arms, I would say "OK, beat me, I deserve it." But if you look at all of Europe, I at least stand at the end of a chain of people, and all those who came before me and continued to spend billions for weapons should be beaten up first. If I compare 1989 to 1990, I have to say that I am a "European champion in disarmament."

To return once more to current political developments and your claim to be part of a minority: one thing I still do not quite understand, something about which I have asked many people, is the fact that there was not just one civic movement in East Germany, not just one political organization in the Fall of '89, but rather at least three, namely New Forum, Democracy Now, and Democratic Awakening. I received many different answers as to how this split came about, but it seems pretty obvious that it had something to do with personalities. Bärbel Bohley, for example, told me that she would never have worked together with Eppelmann.

This sentence upsets me a great deal, if I may say so. I could not say something like that to anyone. Just to give you some arbitrary examples: I say "du" [the informal form of "you" in German] to Gregor Gysi [chairman of the Party for Democratic Socialism] and Hans Modrow [former communist district party secretary in Dresden, prime minister from December 1989 to March 1990] just like I do with Lothar de Maizière [chairman of the Christian Democratic Party, East Germany, prime minister, March 1990 to October 1990] and Rita Süssmuth [Christian Democrat, president of the former West German parliament]. It is very important to me that there are people in all factions of the People's Chambers with whom I have a good relationship, and they with me.

The sentence you just cited from Bärbel Bohley, I just find appalling. First, in general terms, because there is no alternative to talking to one another. And secondly, because we are talking about a woman who signed petitions that also carried the names of Gregor Gysi, André Brie, and others, in which she invites her political friends to a political demonstration co-organized with the new version of the old party apparatus, the PDS. That is, she is engaging in political activities with a party about which she should know—if she has not totally repressed it—that 80 out of its 100 members are still old Stalinists . . .

. . . I was actually asking you a question about yourself. . .

Yes, I just wanted to point out the difficulties I have with such a position. But back to your question. It was my understanding, and I could name witnesses for you who could verify this version, that by the summer of '89 there were a number of people who thought "now it is time to found a party." I had already toyed with this thought during the fall of 1988. At that time I went to see a high-up church dignitary and asked him whether the church would be willing to protect me if I were to found a Social Democratic Party. But instead this man almost fainted and advised me not to do it. And when I talked to a leading person of the West German SPD—in February 1989, again long before anyone else did so—about what they would think of me founding a SPD-East with some political friends of mine, his jaw dropped, and he said he would have to ask the other presidium members of his party and would let me know later on. I am still waiting for an answer.

But like I said before, the tendency toward such a thing grew during the summer of '89. First came Democracy Now, then the predecessor of the SPD, the SDP. So it became increasingly obvious that something had to happen in this direction. At that point I came together with Bärbel Bohley, Ulrike Poppe, Erhart Neubert, and . . . (pause)

. . . Edelbert Richter . . .

. . . Yes, that's right. So I met with these people at a church meeting of the Union of Protestant Churches. In the meantime, I had told six or seven friends of mine that we should secretly meet somewhere during the vacations and talk about whether it would make sense to found a party now. I had talked to Passauer, Wolfgang Schnur, Rudi Panke, two people from our parish, Erhart Neubert, . . .

242   Democracy—Now or Never

. . . Not Schorlemmer?

Yes, Schorlemmer as well, and Edelbert Richter. We came together in Dresden and decided to go ahead with it. But at this church meeting in Berlin I found out from Bärbel Bohley that she had, together with some people whom I did not know, and together with this lawyer from Eisenhüttenstadt, whose name I forget . . .

. . . Rolf Henrich . . .

. . . Yes, exactly, that they had similar ideas. So I said, "Let's do something together." Bärbel Bohley replied: "Sure, let's do that." I already knew that we would meet on 20 August, but Bohley said, "No, we are not going to meet until September." So I said, "OK, then we cannot organize a joint meeting until you have met, so let's do that in the second half of September." I thought it was good to have two groups come together separately at first and join later. This way we could generate more ideas, because otherwise we could perhaps only come up with one concept.

You did not have any contact with the initiative for a Social Democratic Party at that time?

Not at that time, no. So our group met in Dresden, and I said, "Let's not engage in any activities yet, because Bärbel Bohley and others may join later on, and Bärbel Bohley has promised me that we'll arrange a joint meeting once their group has met." Well, when I came home on 11 September I heard it from the media: they had not waited for a joint meeting with us, but rather had gone ahead by themselves. I think that they wanted to be the first ones and did not want to organize anything together with us. So they went public with their thing, and we felt pretty cheated.

I heard from some of the thirty people who attended the New Forum founding meeting that they had not planned to go public with their founding appeal two days after they had come together. They also told me that the composition of the group had to do with logistical reasons, that they wanted to have people from all over East Germany, and that this is why they did not contact everybody, because they could not possibly gather 300 people . . .

. . . Well, that's interesting, but it does not address my problem.

I know, but their argument behind it was that this did not at all preclude a joining of forces after their meeting, because after all they just wanted to create a collective movement open to everyone . . .

But if we just assume for the moment that I am not lying, then this was clearly not in accordance with the agreement that Bärbel Bohley and Rainer Eppelmann—made in front of witnesses—had with each other. At least that's my opinion. She could at least have called me and said, "Rainer, you have to come immediately . . ."

. . . So you were not informed at all?

No! This declaration, "we are founding New Forum," came as a total surprise, something that never should have happened. On the contrary, Bärbel Bohley should have told me: "We have a concept. Do you have one as well? If so, let's come together as soon as possible and start a joint initiative." But that did not happen.

Let me see whether I understand you correctly. Does what you are saying mean that there was absolutely no reason in terms of political substance, in terms of political goals, to create different groups, but rather that this happened because of personal differences?

It all could have been one organization. I chose seven people at a time when we still had to be on guard constantly against the secret police. What that means is that our initial thoughts about this followed a typical GDR pattern: what we were doing was conspiratorial—you could go to jail for that—and so you first contacted people whom you knew well and whom you could completely trust.

In this context I would like to ask you a more speculative question concerning your assessment of certain events. I was told by numerous people from all three political groups that it was not yet clear at all on 9 November that unification with the Federal Republic was inevitable. Rather, they argued that it might have been possible to maintain the sovereignty of East Germany within some kind of confederation with West Germany, that is, if only the opposition had remained together and had been willing to take power in order to carry out different political concepts.

I totally disagree with that assessment. The opportunity to "take power," to put it that grandiosely, only existed from mid-October until 9 November. From the day of Honecker's fall from power and the taking over of power—which was already no real "power" anymore—by Egon Krenz, through 4 November, when 1 million Berliners demonstrated here, until the early evening of 9 November, the power in this country was lying in the streets. Thus far I am in full agreement. And it is also true that there was no active group determined enough to pick up this power. I am not sure in retrospect, however, that if such a group had existed, the consequence would not have been that we would have experienced our own version of a Tiananmen Square.

You see, . . . even today it is not quite clear how this system, which we all thought was very strong and powerful, could suddenly collapse like an old, decrepit house. I think it had something to do with the psychological effect of the party leadership finally realizing that if they picked up guns against their own population, they would stand against millions. They had realized that they would not only face a small group of courageous oppositionists who wanted to take over power, but rather millions of citizens. I believe in the end this is what prevented a bloodbath here.

I think—"he who has ears shall hear, he who has eyes shall see"—that it was all over on 9 November. I admit that I had not realized that on 9 November either. I did not realize that until December, when I saw how people reacted. It was finally clear to me during the election campaign.

I also have to say that all of us, including myself, vastly underestimated one thing: the influence of Western television on the political consciousness and the political conduct of East German citizens. We knew that there was a tremendous longing for the West, that 85 to 90 percent of the GDR citizens received their information from the West—whatever they thought about it. But the political structure in the minds of the vast majority of GDR citizens—in terms of the society and in terms of political parties—was exactly the same as in the Federal Republic. That, I believe, we did not realize. With the opening of the Wall, with the arrival of top politicians from West Germany, it was all over. Joe Schmoe from Nowheresville never had a chance against Helmut Kohl, Willy Brandt, or Oskar Lafontaine.

Maybe we would have had a chance in a "political Greenland," but not with 16 million people who during their lives had seen Kohl, Brandt, and Lafontaine at least 150 times on the evening news. And they had never heard of Joe Schmoe from Nowheresville . . .

But they had heard of Eppelmann, for example, or Konrad Weiss . . .

. . . I think you are overestimating that . . .

. . . *So something like the development in Czechoslovakia was not possible in East Germany because of the existence of West Germany?*

I would not even dare to make a specific claim as to the reason why Eppelmann is known in the GDR and in the Federal Republic (long pause), but that is probably only true since the election campaign. That means—and one should make note of this—since February or March of 1990. And please remember, the Berlin Appeal was 1982, the candle event was in the fall of the same year, thousands of events. Thousands of people came to see the Blues Masses, and all they did was hear my name and forget it again afterward.

It is probably true that there was a kind of "scene" in which I was pretty well-known. Perhaps I was even known a little beyond that among politically interested people. But until the end of 1989 I would not even have dared to claim that one in two GDR citizens had heard of me.

Let me ask you two short final questions. The party you are chairman of— Democratic Awakening—is a completely different organization from what it was at its inception just eleven months ago. Most of its founding members have already left. What keeps you with Democratic Awakening, and what do you say about all those who have left, people such as Edelbert Richter and Friedrich Schorlemmer, both Protestant pastors like you, but people who did not go along with this turn toward Western-style conservatism?

Well, I can understand their conduct—Edelbert Richter is now MP for the Social Democrats. I am sorry that we can no longer deal with each other the way we used to. I am not sure to what extent that has something to do with hurt feelings or a bad conscience. After all, we did not beat up on each other, or accuse each other, and I only found out later on that he had left.

Let me just say something provocative. I am not sure whether my friends, or I should say "former friends," . . . have not taken the easier route. It has not always been easy to stay with Democratic Awakening because, and I am very willing to admit this, it has undergone a different political development than I envisioned at the time when I asked people: "Do you, or do you not, want to participate?" This was also agonizing to me. But I was a Protestant pastor for 15 years, and in no way was everything in my church always to my liking either.

During these 15 years I learned not only something that concerned my political activities, but my entire life: if I want to change something I have to stay with it, and cannot leave it. Escape can be egotistical conduct, or it can be absolutely necessary if I do not want to drown or die. But if there is something I care about in a given community and its future, then I cannot just leave simply because something is bothering me. Otherwise, the community will stay the same, and I will no longer be able to influence its future direction. . . .

I now carry out a function in which I can very well influence things. I can do something for 16 million GDR citizens, not just in a newspaper article, but right in the middle of the government, or in coalition negotiations. So if I take all that into consideration, I dare say that I have made the right decision. I also have to say that the whole process developed very differently from what I had anticipated. There were many factors which I could in no way influence, such as 9 November [1989] or, if you want, 15 and 16 July [1990], the days of negotiations between Kohl and Gorbachev.

I would be a naive dreamer, to put it mildly, if my understanding of the entire situation had stopped changing in September 1989. If I tell you that at least two things happened since then that have changed the world, then I hope that they have also changed my insights and what I think needs to be done now. . . .

For many years I have tried to change things with words, and now I have the unique chance to translate this into effective political action. It would have been inconsistent with myself had I not taken advantage of this opportunity. After all, it is not a coincidence that Prime Minister Lothar de Maizière did not ask me whether I wanted to become foreign minister, or minister for labor and social affairs, but rather asked me "do you want to be minister of defense"? And I replied "no, not minister of defense, but certainly minister for disarmament and defense."

One last question. How would you, as one of the "insiders," describe what happened in East Germany: as a revolt, a revolution, or a Wende?

If you understand revolution to be something that fundamentally changes existing relations—political and economic relations—then we have to call it a revolution. If you mean by revolution that the people are different today from what they were yesterday, then it was not a revolution.

■ CORNELIA MATZKE, opposition activist, founding member of the Independent Women's Alliance, Leipzig.[28] ■ *"The question simply became 'do we want to risk our lives' "?*

It seems prudent to provide a bit of complex background material to familiarize the reader with the political perspective that Cornelia Matzke brought to the East German opposition movement. While Rainer Eppelmann represented a rare exception among members of the East German opposition because of the relative ease with which he moved into Western-style parliamentary politics, Matzke appeared to distance herself altogether from any kind of broad political involvement. Even before the dust of the revolutionary upheaval had settled across East Germany, she had concluded that she had all along been struggling for goals shared by only a small minority of East Germans. Like many of her friends and colleagues in New Forum or Democracy Now, Matzke seemed to take the course of events following the opening of the Wall as sufficient evidence that "most East Germans" wanted nothing but more "consumption" and better "travel opportunities."

Whenever I came across such vast generalizations—and members of different sectors of East German society were routinely characterizing each other within such generalizations—I began to inquire about specific

28. For background information on Matzke, see Part I, chapter 1, pp. 67–75.

examples, about details and explanations. Usually I did not receive answers that went beyond unsubstantiated abstractions. On the other hand, I learned a great deal about the preconceptions and prejudices that members of different social groups harbored against one another. In Matzke's case, however, I was particularly surprised to encounter such an array of aloof answers. She had proved to be extremely perceptive concerning the traps of a gender-prejudiced language, for instance, but apparently did not entertain the possibility that similar types of group prejudices might also be imbedded in words that connote class differences among East Germans. What, in fact, did it mean if a lathe operator asked for betting living conditions and expressed his wishes for the future in terms of "materialistic goods?" It required no more than a tour through any industrial plant (not to mention coal mines) in the GDR to realize how working conditions, the organization of production, and the quality of goods had undermined the very dignity of those who had to earn a living, day after day, and year after year, on the shop floors of East Germany. Unfortunately, it seemed as if citizens who had never been exposed to such conditions were virtually incapable of deciphering the very language of rank-and-file discontent.

While reviewing my interview tapes, I found that almost everyone with whom I had talked—intellectuals, workers, party members, activists, and bystanders—frequently used the reference "they" when explaining why things had developed differently from what one had hoped for. Until the Fall of 1989, "they" had usually referred to party and state functionaries. But as the party collapsed and the state apparatus began to disintegrate—in short, at the very moment the common enemy had disappeared—"they" began to refer to anyone who did not share their own view or, even more dismissively, anyone who had committed or failed to commit some act and was now to be blamed for having "messed things up." Grandiose abstractions began to fill a void that actually pointed to earlier failures in communication and pointed as well to an underlying lack of sustained understanding of one another that haunted the GDR opposition movement. An organized large-scale movement which could have provided space for the emergence of such communication had simply never materialized. The reason, historically embedded (and, perhaps, unfair) as it was, illuminates a baneful truth: the civic movement itself was a casualty of time not available, or, rather, time not granted.

Having said this, it is only fair to emphasize the thoughtful and courageous role that Cornelia Matzke played in the politics which helped liberate East Germans from a life circumscribed by the severities of a police state. Few if any activists in East Germany were more experientially equipped to discuss all of the fears and nagging doubts surrounding the question of whether one's political activities were not, in fact, "risking one's life." Beyond this, Matzke also vividly expressed her frustration in the face of all the obstacles standing in the way of getting women's issues on the agenda. In this, too, she stood in the forefront of cultural innovation and change.

Yet when Matzke talked about citizens from sectors in society alien to her own immediate social environment, one heard words and phrases that did not convey a sense of "real" people with widely different biographies and highly complex aspirations. These "others," in short, did not seem to have a wide range of individual identities, but appeared merely as faceless abstractions.

■ *How did you experience the period between August and November of 1989?*
I was kind of vacillating between doing more within the country and leaving it for good. All of my friends were in this position. We were simply not sure whether it could ever be more than hopeless martyrdom to get involved more openly and actively. It was a very difficult time. . . .

I think many of us would have left as well if nothing had happened until the end of the year. And, don't misunderstand me, not because we ever wanted to leave. Somehow we all felt responsible for this absolutely desolate country.

Let me ask you as someone who perceives herself to be "on the left": did you ever think that socialism in the GDR could be reformed, perhaps along the lines of what was happening in the Soviet Union, or at least that the opposition could be more decisive in determining the future political course, as perhaps it was the case in Czechoslovakia?

Yes, absolutely, that was our goal.

I am asking because you said earlier that you were thinking about emigrating because of how little, if anything, was possible in the GDR. So why did you think that it was more difficult to achieve reforms in the GDR than, for example, in the Soviet Union?

There were many reasons for that. But before I say something more, it is important to point out that what was going on in the Soviet Union was decisive for the entire movement; otherwise nothing would have ever happened here. So this was the basic event. And it was simply terrible how the GDR leadership responded to these openings and changes in the Soviet Union, high-ranking party functionaries like Kurt Hager saying, for example, "just because our neighbor changes his tapestry does not mean we have to do so as well."

And then, the way I see it, we never managed to generate the kind of large-scale oppositional movement in the GDR they did, for example, in Czechoslovakia with Charter 77. I had a friend with Charter 77 in Prague, and from what she told me they had a real movement, not just a few people here and there.

I don't quite follow you. As I understand it, the number of people actively involved was in no way larger in Czechoslovakia than in the GDR, at least not in the beginning. Am I wrong about that?

Well, I don't know, it certainly happened on a more continuous basis [in Czechoslovakia]. They did not have new people over and over again; instead, they had a stable core of people who had been doing oppositional work for years. In the GDR, on the other hand, whenever someone dared to come out and voice her/his complaints, they were expelled [from the GDR]. In one way or another, our network was destroyed time and again; we never had the chance to build a stable oppositional structure. In Czechoslovakia, sympathizers could pretty much always concentrate on the same people, which was never possible here.

But isn't it very problematic, then, in this context, if GDR oppositionists toyed with the idea of emigrating—in other words, helping to disrupt any possibility for continuous work? Wouldn't the logical decision have been to say, "We will stay, no matter what"?

Well, yes, after all we did stay. For most of us, the question of emigration was not a serious option until things got very bad, as they did, for example, with the Tiananmen Square events in China. The way the GDR leadership responded to that—Krenz immediately visiting the Chinese Communist Party, congratulating them for their swift and determined actions—made it simply unclear what that might mean for our work in the GDR. The question simply became: "Do we really want to risk our lives?" Besides, all of the ones who were in one way or another part of this oppositional movement were also asking themselves: "Who are these GDR citizens? Do they really want us to fight for some kind of change or reform?"

What kind of an answer did you come up with? You as a physician probably had contact with many people from all walks of life. What was your impression concerning what people thought and wanted?

Consumption. And that was the really depressing part about it. You see, the nice thing about this country called the "GDR" before the Wende was that we all had something in common with each other, something about which we all agreed, which was complaining about the leadership. But the reasons why people disliked the system were very different. I always felt very strange when I realized that all that seemed to matter to people was the possibility of unrestricted travel. You see, there are people who don't have the money even to consider traveling. I always thought there should be more reasons than just travel restrictions for people to disagree with this system.

And if you pushed people a little on that question, they came up with material things—that they had to wait more than 10 years to get a car, that there were so many things one could not get, that nothing was working right, and so on. What people were concerned with were mostly material things. So I came to the conclusion that what I was doing, what I was fighting for here in the GDR, well, I was ultimately doing it for myself. It was impossible to want to achieve something for others.

One simply had to make this decision for oneself, saying, "For the following reasons I reject this system, and therefore I am fighting for a different system by myself." And you also had to make up your mind whether this was important enough to you even to accept being jailed for it, for example. But, in any case, one had to do it for oneself, not for someone else. Of course, I guess, this was still an illusion to some extent, for it is important to receive some acknowledgment from a wider group in society. For this reason, I guess all of us continued to see it in a larger context.

This, of course, is a very complicated issue that touches on all sorts of questions. Let me just ask you about something that seems relevant in an immediate sense to me: If we assume for the moment that the people of the Soviet Union, Poland, and Czechoslovakia are not completely different from East Germans, how do you explain the initial broad-scale popular agreement with Gorbachev's reforms in the Soviet Union, a massive popular movement like Solidarność, and the seemingly widespread support of the civic movement in Czechoslovakia? Wouldn't it make sense to say that all these people were concerned with much more than the mere expansion of their consumption opportunities?

Well, of course, in terms of the protagonists, those who try to create or maintain an ongoing movement, things other than mere consumption are important. But those people always compose merely a small minority . . .

Perhaps. I was just inquiring about this because you stated earlier that you ultimately had to fight for yourself because "the others" were ostensibly not interested in the same kinds of goals anyway?

Yes. You see, you had asked me about my contacts with patients, and that, in fact, gave me the opportunity to listen in on what other people, not only the ones I knew as friends in the opposition, had to say. It was quite clear that they wanted something different from what I did. I would have had to close my ears and eyes to believe they wanted the same things I did.

Besides, later developments have clearly proven that they wanted something else: they wanted the West German Mark and material gains. It really was a very small group of people who wanted other things, who thought about establishing another kind of political system.

What do you mean by a "small group?" New Forum, for example, received far more than 200,000 support signatures?

Well, yes, but New Forum was initially perceived to be a group mainly opposed to the existing leadership . . .

In other words, you believe that the only thing people had in common, and the reason behind their initial support for New Forum, was their collective opposition or rejection of the party and the government?

Yes, that definitely represented the main motivating factor. We all shared a hostile attitude toward the government. But when you began to ask, "why are we opposed?," then this unanimity quickly collapsed. People seemed to have very little else on their minds other than consumption and travel. They didn't worry, for instance, that once all of us were allowed to travel freely, some of us might not be able to afford it any longer because by that time we might be unemployed and poor. I just think people saw this promise as some sort of "freedom," and forgot about everything else. . . .

The common ground was opposition to the party, which accounts for why we had so many people at one point. "We below" against "you at the top." And it was not even clear who those "at the top" really were, or what that meant, because so many of us "below" were also implicated in one way or another. . . .

Let me ask you once more about what you previously called "your thing," by which you meant women's issues. Did this play much of a role in your political activities during the time before the Wende? You did not found a women's group, or something like that?

No, I did not.

How did this emphasis develop in your own mind?

Well, when I went to the contact address of the New Forum [in the first week of October] to sign their petition and offer my help, I told them that I would like to set up a contact address for women who would like to work in a women's group. I had already tried a number of other issues, such as environmental and economic problems. But, first of all, I had always run into problems with the men in these groups. Secondly, I figured that all the other issues were pretty much already covered anyway, so why not do something that I could do on a very personal basis, something that no one had tried so far. . . . A few other women had also shown interest in establishing a women's group, and then I convinced some of my female friends, and so we got a small group together. The first thing we did was to write a proposal for a program and to publicize the fact that we existed. We just wanted people to know that we were out there, and give them some ideas as to what we wanted to do. . . . I was interested in political work in general, and particularly in finding out to what extent gender was a decisive or determining factor in the struggle for power or domination. Through the gender problematic, one could think about all the dynamics in society in a way that was very different from what we were used to.

When you were talking about power, do you mean that you wanted a fair distribution of power among men and women, or did this also include questioning the way power functions as an ultimately male-dominated concept?

Well, actually both. First of all, we had some rather basic things on our agenda, simply because we wanted to be understood by everyone. One of those was a quota system within New Forum, and in politics in general. This demand, by the way, ultimately represented the breaking point in our cooperation with New Forum.

One other important item was to maintain the economic independence of women, that is, secure their opportunities to work and, at the same time, their access to socially guaranteed child care facilities. These were topics that came up time and time again.

Another example had to do with pacifism; that is, the point that women should not come under the control of the military as well, that they should not serve in the military. A friend of mine with whom I had started our contact address was supposed to deal with the more practical side of what we might do, and I was in charge of the more theoretical questions. Right from the start, we thought it would be a good idea to split up work like that, to create different groups along those lines, mostly because we thought that a lot of women would probably show up wanting to participate. She also came up with ideas like building a women's center, an office which would provide legal advice to women, and things of that kind. Afterward, we advertised our group by displaying our program and ideas at the New Forum office, and women who were interested in our kind of work began to contact us. . . .

You began to set up meetings and to organize working groups?

Yes. First, we had a number of smaller meetings, and then we scheduled a large meeting at the Trinitatis Church in November. This was supposed to be a sort of founding meeting, and at that point we already had about 100 women. We called ourselves the Women's Initiative Within New Forum. We had very pleasant and very open discussions at this founding meeting. I think similar things happened in all the larger cities in the country. I was the contact person between our group and New Forum, and in this position I also participated in the national coordinating meetings of New Forum.

Why and how did this break between the Women's Initiative and New Forum come about?

There were numerous reasons. First, we had a number of women who wanted to be members of the Initiative, but not of New Forum. And then, on 3 December, the Independent Women's Alliance [UFV] was founded. In January we had a national delegates' conference of New Forum in Leipzig, and when we were debating New Forum's program and statutes, the question of whether or not to have a quota system turned into an important debate.

Unfortunately, I was not a regular delegate at this conference, because I had been among those responsible for organizing the whole event. . . . And one of the complicated issues that came up early on was the usage of language, that is, whether we should always use he/she and generally try to get rid of all sexist references. Many people did not understand the importance of that at all. They resisted the whole discussion quite a bit. . . .

And then this debate about a quota system came up after I had proposed a motion for a 50 percent quota. Today I would do this a little differently, because at the time this was asking for too much of most participants. Today I would probably propose a 40/40 quota, with the remaining 20 percent being open. That would just make it a lot easier. . . . We had many speakers who were hiding their sexist views behind a gender-balanced use of language, and at the same time professing not to know why all of this was such a big issue.

In any case, we did not succeed. We even had a disagreement among the women about this proposal; in fact, the majority of them were also against a quota system, mostly because they were not feminists. So this motion of mine was probably not a very intelligent move, politically, at the time.

The women's group had a very conflicted attitude toward New Forum right from the start. . . . We constantly had to explain and defend the legitimacy of our group, and the importance of women's issues in general. We just got very tired of having to do this over and over again. And most of the continuously repeated discussions were on such a superficial level. There was never any depth to these debates, simply because the significance and complexity of women's issues were not at all on the minds of most people. You see, we began to realize how deeply this ignorance was anchored in our society. Forty years of life in the one-party state were 40 years that effectively interrupted the emergence of an awareness about women's issues.

5 THE CONSTRAINTS
OF A PARTY-CENTERED
PERSPECTIVE

■ HANS MODROW, last communist prime minister in East Germany, parliamentary spokesperson for the restructured communist party, now called Party for Democratic Socialism.[29] ■ *"Once you have gone through the experience, you will subsequently have a changed relationship to it."*

The timing of this interview was probably the most fortuitous of any conducted in the course of researching this book. At the time of our conversation, former Prime Minister Hans Modrow was still the leading parliamentary representative of the truncated remains of the Party for Democratic Socialism. The fact that he had motivation to grant me an interview was evidence of his drastically changing status, similar to that of a whole generation of former high-level policy-makers who were rapidly being pushed into the background.

Modrow came out of a parliamentary session and squeezed me in before meeting the ambassador to Angola. It was apparently important for him to rectify "widespread misunderstandings" about the party and its reform wing. On a personal level, he seemed at pains to dispel all doubts concerning his democratic intentions and his openness toward the opposition during the process of transformation in the GDR.

As the following pages make evident, Hans Modrow undoubtedly helped shape events in decisive ways. He was the first high-ranking party official to formally negotiate with the opposition; he helped to avert a bloodbath in Leipzig on 9 October; and he was instrumental in bringing about improved relations between the party-controlled government and

29. For background information on Modrow, see Part I, chapter 1, pp. 89–96.

the opposition at the turn of 1989/90. Yet events had largely passed him by. It was my sense that he had begun to realize this at the time of my interview with him, and that he thus wanted "history" to record his deeds in a proper context.

■ *What concretely motivated you to assume leadership within the reform wing of your own party (which, I presume, in the end also resulted in your becoming prime minister), and at what specific point had you decided on this course of action?*

My becoming prime minister had nothing to do with it yet. There were two factors in the background of my becoming prime minister. The first had to do with [first secretary] Egon Krenz's visit to Moscow in early November, when he met Mikhail Gorbachev, who mentioned two names as possible candidates: Willy Stoph and Hans Modrow. He probably mentioned Stoph because the Soviet Union had long perceived him as a partner, even in the era of Erich Honecker. They apparently also believed that he could, together with Krenz, do the work for some time to come.

But then, secondly, the party rank and file forced Stoph to step down, whereas Honecker simply passed on his posts into the dutiful hands of Krenz. At least this is what happened at the Central Committee meeting on 18 October [1989]. Honecker handed in his resignation and suggested Krenz as his successor. . . .

Initially, Krenz was under a lot of pressure, first from Gorbachev, who had asked him what he thought about including me, and, secondly, because the list he had proposed concerning the new Politburo had been rejected.

I had clearly stated that no one should be on the list for the election of the new Politburo who did not personally declare that he was willing to work for a newly elected leadership. . . . After all, Krenz's list revealed that he was still acting under pressure, and not out of conviction [concerning the reform process]. . . .

Over the last eight weeks of interviewing participants in this reform process from all walks of society, it has become very clear to me that it was decisive for people that Krenz came first and then you. That is, if you had been perceived as the immediate successor of the old regime and there had not been this "transitory figure" Krenz, whom nobody trusted and through whom everybody had lost hope that fundamental change could in fact happen with the party, then the overall situation would have developed very differently. In other words, if so much hope had not been lost in the Krenz interregnum, then, when you came to leadership, more genuine change—and strictly speaking East German change—might have been achievable. What is your evaluation of this today?

Well, first of all, strictly speaking, I did not succeed Krenz, which of course was my problem as well. I too saw a chain that was Ulbricht—Honecker—Modrow, when in fact, again strictly speaking, it was Ulbricht—Honecker—Krenz, that is, the line of first secretaries. The line of prime ministers was Grotewohl—Stoph—Modrow.

During this process of transformation, it became increasingly clear to everyone that the leading role of the party would disappear. I was therefore suddenly in a position [he laughs] where I was literally forced into an independent stance from the party. And that, of course, also began to show in my understanding of my relationship with Krenz. In fact, it had immediate consequences: after I got elected to the Politburo during this transitional phase, I made it very clear that I did not consider myself responsible to this Politburo anymore, but that, instead, I would only be responsible to the government. I also stated unequivocally that I did not expect to receive any more decisions from the Politburo that could in any way limit my position as prime minister.

Initially, however, the power to govern was transferred to Krenz and the state council on 18 October, and therefore he was quite independent until 13 November [when Modrow was elected prime minister by parliament], that is, for about four weeks.

In this context it is necessary, for instance, to analyze very thoroughly how the opening of the Wall on 9 November came about. For, if I ask myself about this event today, I come to the clear conclusion that the decision to open the Wall should have been a decision supported by both governments [East and West]. Both governments should have come to this decision together. Only then would we have had the possibility of a two-state coexistence over a certain period of time that would have made possible the slow growing together of the two states. Only then would Kohl's 10-point program and my initiative [concerning a slow confederation process between the two Germanies] have had a chance. . . .

But what is happening now—and history will ultimately provide an evaluation of this—is a hasty and botched bringing together of parts that don't fit, and the burden of this process is being shouldered almost exclusively by the citizens of East Germany. We are now experiencing things that could have been very different, in spite of the open borders and such. If only we had acted a little differently . . . , but it seems people would not have allowed that anymore. I guess they simply had a different understanding of what should happen next. History will be the judge.

So how did this decision to open the Wall on 9 November come about? To this day there seems to be a lot of confusion about this question, particularly since

[Günter] Schabowski [party district leader of Berlin, and member of the Politburo responsible for announcing the opening of the Wall] did not seem to know himself what he was doing...

At least he did not *think* about what he was doing, even though he had a note with him [from the Politburo concerning the new travel regulations], and he also had taken part in the decision...

You were not part of that?

Even though I had been nominated to the Politburo, I was, at that time, not yet part of the decision-making process. Only after 13 November did I begin to participate fully; before that I still had my duties in Dresden. . . .

Would you agree with me that the decision concerning 9 November signified a desperate attempt by the party leadership to hold on to power?

Not completely. With one reservation. It also exemplified the fact that they had become incapable at that point of responding to the situation in a fashion that was at all constructive. They were simply in a panic. That is the real explanation. Out of this panic emerged a kind of action that could have, once again, resulted in a bloodbath. All it would have taken was one of those unprepared border control guards to become panic-stricken and start shooting at people pushing through the checkpoints.

Did the party leadership ever consider closing the borders again after 9 November?

No, that was completely out of the question. All the meetings I was part of, including the ones with Kohl, did not bring up this issue. It was simply unrealistic. If anyone harbored such thoughts . . . no, it was just too unrealistic. All the consultations we had were directed toward meeting with Kohl and settling the preconditions for this so-called travel law, which was of major importance. Underlying the whole affair was a stupid assumption that clearly shows the narrow-mindedness and the lack of understanding of the whole thing: people always thought we would have a thing called a "travel law," something that we should then simply have applied unilaterally. That was plainly stupid thinking.

In fact, we were confronted with a formal political act [opening the borders] that should have involved, and been carried through by, the governments of both countries.

Before I ask you a question about the Central Round Table, let me ask you a question concerning 9 October. As you know, there is much speculation that the party leadership had planned to suppress the demonstrations in Leipzig with brute force. Yet this did not happen. Why not?

You have to take one thing into consideration. If you look at the exact sequence of events, on 8 October you had Dresden, and with that, the transition toward nonviolence. Berghofer [mayor of Dresden] and I took responsibility for this development back then. I did not talk to anyone in the central leadership about this. Bishop Hempel (whom I knew quite well), together with superintendent Ziemer, offered to take the step [of entering peaceful negotiations with the opposition]. They wanted to talk to the demonstrators and said that some kind of mutual consent should be found, and I agreed to that.

Out of this, the "group of 20" emerged on the same evening. Thus we had established the first example in East Germany of how one could settle a confrontation like that peacefully.

The reaction on the 9th [in Leipzig] involved Masur [director of the Leipzig opera] and the three respective district party secretaries. But the 8th had preceded this. There were also phone calls on the 9th. I talked to Horst Schumann, for example, who was the first District Party Secretary in Leipzig. I offered to contact Bishop Hempel who could, I figured, win the cooperation of the church in Leipzig as well. And then the Berliner Central Committee and the church leadership were also contacted.

Did you do that?

I made those arrangements with the Berliners, and I asked for support in taking this nonviolent route. The role of the church in Leipzig differed from one church to the other as well. While Ebeling [minister of the Thomas Church] took this strange position not to open the doors of his church, Magirius [superintendent of the Nikolai Church], of course, had his doors wide open.

What was decisive, however, was that we had taken the first step in Dresden.

But it is true, isn't it, that there was a decision by the party leadership, signed by Honecker, that the demonstrations in Leipzig should be suppressed by all means, if necessary by brute force?

I do not know the specific details of this case, and I do not want to give an interpretation that I cannot verify. The only thing that I can say is that I tried to influence things in a nonviolent direction by bringing in the leadership of the Saxonian church and by asking them to lend the same support to Leipzig as they had given to Dresden.

Let me ask you a question concerning the Central Round Table, Herr Modrow. For an outsider the round table seemed to be a very promising project. I was told by Rainer Börner [chief of staff of the party], and André Brie [vice-chairman of the party] about the interesting dynamics concerning the interaction between the party delegation at the round table and other factions in the party. Apparently there was very little communication between the party leadership, the party-controlled government, and the party group at the round table. Furthermore, they said that the cooperation among the party people at the round table was also not what it could have been.

Of course, everybody has his own understanding of these dynamics; my understanding is obviously slightly different. . . . First, there were certain signals that a round table should be formed. These signals also came out of the church. They were then conveyed to Egon Krenz in the party, and, hence, they initially had nothing to do with the government.

Krenz reacted quickly and spontaneously by showing his willingness to participate in the round table. Thus, the Socialist Unity Party did not block the creation of the round table, but rather was interested in the formation of the round table for the purpose of bringing together the different political forces. It was our initial understanding—and one has to take this into consideration—that the participants of the Central Round Table would enter discussions as two distinct formations: the communist party and its satellite parties on the one hand, and the civic movements on the other. But, for me, that also meant that the government would not attend the round table before the various civic movements evolved into something with which I could cooperate. As long as the members of the civic movement were not able to find themselves, but rather constantly fought and argued with each other—at least, that was my sense of it—the leader of the government had no place in all of this.

If, in my function as prime minister, my participation in a disorganized round-table process had the effect of undermining my potential capacity to play a constructive role for the society as a whole, then, clearly, I could not have continued heading the government. But still, from the third meeting of the Central Round Table onward, I always sent government representatives to participate . . .

But that was a demand of the civic initiatives, wasn't it?

We did not perceive it as a demand, but rather as an offering of admission to us. Our understanding was that we had been asked by the round table. For us it was not a question of standing against the round table, but rather acknowledging that the round table had realized that they could not do without the government, and that we would thus participate. That was our understanding.

The next thing, of course, was this famous demand of the round table on 8 January 1990 that I should be at their meeting "within one hour."[30]

---

30. The immediate reason for this demand was the statement of the government's deputy for the dissolution of the secret police at the round table, Peter Koch, that he did "not know

Previous to that, my first deputy, Mrs. [Christa] Luft, had been at the round table, my representative Lothar de Maizière had been there—in his capacity as party chairman of the Christian Democrats—and the usual government representative had been there. There had never been a vacuum between the government and the round table, but now they wanted the prime minister personally.

I would not have gone that day, even if pure coincidence had not come to my aid. But coincidence had it that I was already boarding a plane to Sofia at the time this demand reached me. In Sofia the last Comecon meeting to date was being held.

Therefore, objectively speaking, I could not have possibly attended this round-table meeting. But this question came up again on the 15th [of January 1990], and on the 15th I did go, even though I did not reach that conclusion until about midnight of the 14th. The reason is that I had to calculate how the citizens of this country would perceive my running to the round table at the request of Mr. [Reinhart] Schult [spokesperson of New Forum]. I felt that many would think that if I had followed an order to come to the round table within one hour, I could not be in possession of much authority anymore.

Yet I decided to go for the following reason, and I would like to say this: it was absolutely clear to me—and I think this was a certain problem— that the political influence of the round table was tremendous throughout the country. So if protests against the prime minister were to develop, emanating from the round table, the result would be a decline of my authority from the popular side. So I had to walk this thin line, not falling into either one of those two traps, and I thought that January 15th would do that for me. In fact, I got out of the January 15th round-table discussion with an increase in authority, and not with a decline.

At what point did you realize that the round table and the civic initiatives would have to be included in the government, and concomitantly, when and why did you decide to make the speech in February that came to be known as the "Germany, united fatherland" speech, a speech that caused a lot of confusion among political friends and opponents alike? Did you do that on your own, or where did it come from?

I had done this completely on my own.

But to your first question. First of all, I saw a chance for a wider

---

where the central data collection of the Stasi was located." Since it was one of the main goals of the round table to dissolve the Stasi, this statement was cause for some alarm among opposition members.

consensus following my January 15th appearance and my contact with the round table. I thought there was a definite chance. Secondly, I saw the necessity—that is if the country were to stick together—that these forces needed to be included. And thirdly, I followed the assumption that it would be good for the oppositional forces at the round table if they had the chance to participate in government for two months, thus having the chance to learn how to deal with certain things. And if you talk to people like Matthias Platzeck, or even Eppelmann, they will all tell you that it was no waste of time to participate in the Modrow government.

These were my thoughts: if we cooperated, then we should do it like this so that these new people could feel and learn what it means to govern. Once you have gone through the experience, you subsequently have a changed relationship to it. I saw this as my responsibility toward the round table.

And I want to say one more thing. I think it is too restricted a view if one always says "the government on the one hand and the round table on the other." You also have to take into consideration the role of the People's Assembly. If this cooperation had not worked out, we couldn't have done *anything*. After all, the People's Assembly represented the legislative body, and it was good that the round table respected that fact as much as the government did. In fact, we proceeded with legislative changes through the People's Assembly. Who else could have passed bills?

Wolfgang Ullmann [spokesperson at the round table for Democracy Now] was absolutely right when he said at the occasion of a People's Assembly meeting: "I speak in this acclaimed house and for the first time I actually have the impression that it is a house of the people." This was prior to March 18th; we sometimes tend to forget that. One has to put all these pieces together.

The round table was not the parliament; the round table actually had a good and intelligent understanding in that it did not question the relationship of the government and the round table to the parliament. I believe this is an important aspect of this peaceful transition. Whether it was a revolution, on the other hand, is quite another question.

Yes, but perhaps one comment on your "Germany, united fatherland" speech?

The concept for this speech developed on my trip to Moscow. When I was in Moscow on 30 January, we already brought along this concept that we subsequently made public on 1 February. We handed it to the Soviet delegation and discussed the matter.

You mean it was your understanding that no other political alternative was possible anymore?

Exactly! I was very conscious of that, and that's why it was necessary to talk about it. I also have to add that Gorbachev proved to be a very open partner for this discussion. So on 31 January 1990 we tried together to figure out how this could best be implemented.

Therefore, my only chance was to take personal responsibility for it.

■ WERNER BRAMKE, long-time party member, chairman of the history department of the Karl Marx University, Leipzig.[31] ■ *"The outcome of such a confrontation here could only have been absolutely devastating."*

Throughout the Fall of 1989 Werner Bramke, party member, socialist, teacher, and historian, seemed torn between two political stances which increasingly proved to be mutually exclusive. As with thousands of other comrades in both the opposition and the party, Bramke did not give up on "socialism" despite the fact that he had come to the conclusion that forty years of one-party rule had been a disaster. Unlike members of the opposition, however, Bramke for a long time continued to believe that "socialism" could only be realized through, or at least in cooperation with, the party. On the other hand, he was a rare exception among higher-ranking party functionaries in that he had consciously sought contacts with members of the opposition movement. Whereas someone like Hans Modrow did not begin communicating with opposition activists until tens of thousands of defiant citizens took to the streets, Bramke had, early on, been in touch with dissidents because of his position as chairman of the Karl Marx University history department in Leipzig. Yet his contacts beyond the party apparently remained confined to the "well-educated" strata of society. Again, it is worth pausing to observe the curious fact that Bramke, like so many other intellectuals inside and outside the party, displayed an immense psychological distance when the subject of discussion turned to nonintellectuals. When workers, for example, were found not to be acting in concert with the goals of intellectuals, they were quickly described as "narrow-minded" or "apathetic."

In this interview, Bramke tells of his visit to a factory in Fall of '89 and expresses "great dismay" at what he thought he had learned about the unresponsiveness of the workers. But he apparently did not realize that an organized visit of a party functionary, together with party plant supervisors and reporters from a party newspaper (whether they were "reformers" or

31. For background information on Bramke, see Part I, chapter 2, pp. 97–111.

not), could scarcely be expected to foster confidence and openness on the part of workers who had essentially been mobilized to listen to party dignitaries—of whom Bramke, of course, was one. Conditions on the shop floor, it seems, continued to be a rather alien world to intellectuals like Werner Bramke, whatever their ideological proclivities.

It is important to add in this respect that, to Western ears, the political dialogue in East Germany after the party had lost control was not always easy to interpret. Though there were a number of reasons for this confusion, most of them turned on the repeated use of certain key words— "freedom," "democracy," and "socialism"—that obviously had vastly different meanings for different people. Reformers in the party as well as most activists in the civic opposition movement initially expressed their hopes in terms of an "independent path" toward a "free, democratic, and egalitarian society." Some of them called this "democratic socialism," usually adding that what they meant was "the real socialism" or "socialism with a human face." Such a system, it was understood, would have nothing in common with the "deformed and corrupted" forms of socialism— those associated with Stalin, or, as of late, with Erich Honecker. But this terminology, so easy to come by, merely concealed the central problem: what was "real" socialism?[32]

Not only did I receive a wide range of answers to these questions, but the answers were invariably vague. For forty years no open public debate about these vital issues had taken place within East German society. The moment one-party domination began to crack, East Germans therefore set out with much enthusiasm to make up for this lost time. In a political context that was considerably more engaged and impassioned than anything I had encountered during recent times in the West, East Germans had begun struggling over the specific content of such fundamental social ideas, addressing, as it were, the whole range of basic questions concerning the organization of a modern society. Bramke was an engaged and articulate voice in this debate. His portrayal of how he perceived this process, and how he came to be an active participant, vividly recaptures the months of revolutionary upheaval in the GDR through the eyes of a party intellectual with diverse and often conflicting sympathies.

---

32. Only popular jokes of the time seemed able to provide a clear answer. Two jokes I frequently encountered in East Germany in 1990 went something like this: "Question: What is socialism? Answer: Socialism is a long and torturous road from capitalism to capitalism." Or: "What is capitalism?" Answer: Exploitation of man by man." "And what is socialism?" Answer: "The opposite."

■ *Since we have talked at some length about the developments leading up to the Fall of 1989, I would now like to ask you to describe your own trajectory away from the party and toward contacts with people in various opposition groups during this time. When exactly, and in what context, did this take place?*

I was in communication with people in the oppositional civic movement throughout 1989. I also had a pretty good relationship with students, and I knew of students who frequently participated in activities at the Nikolai Church. I had numerous conversations with these students concerning questions such as what *could* be done, and what should *not* be done. But my initial contacts actually date back further and have to do with the debates surrounding the *Sputnik* ban [November 1988]. As a result of this ban, I simply *had* to expose myself, because I had to stand up in front of my students and tell them what my own position was. There was no way around that. From that time onward, in fact, I had frequent contacts with people who were sympathetic to the opposition. So in October of '89 it was pretty easy for me to find a place in all the events taking place.

Did you ever participate in any of the Monday demonstrations?

Yes.

When did you participate the first time?

On 9 October. Well, actually, in the demonstration fourteen days earlier, but I remained on the sidelines that day. . . . I had a very strange feeling that first time [25 September]. When I saw what was going on, I felt sympathetic on the one hand, but on the other hand I was terribly troubled—all the contradictions I had long carried around with me suddenly surfaced. While I thought that nothing would change *without* demonstrations, it began to dawn on me that *with* these kinds of demonstrations we probably had to say good-bye to everything that one might call a "socialist reform movement" in the GDR. What I was seeing on this Monday evening was quite obviously going quite beyond just a "reform" movement. It was a movement against the existing structures, and thus against the existing state. So I felt this strange contradiction within myself.

Could you elaborate on this? If one demonstrates against the SED and against the kind of political order the SED represented, why did that necessarily imply a stance against some form of what you call "democratic socialism"?

It just began to become clear to me, and at the same time I began to get worried, that if these demonstrations grew in size and frequency—which was actually desirable—they would necessarily lead to an aggravated relationship toward the SED, and thus toward socialism. The tension-filled relationship people had toward socialism would just get worse. This is what caused my contradictory response . . .

But, in this respect, wasn't it at least as decisive how the SED *reacted to these demonstrations as what specific demonstrators demanded or fought for?*

Of course, you are absolutely right.

So do you think an open response, a willingness toward dialogue on the part of the SED, *could still have changed anything at that time?*

No. . . . The police had already shown such a level of hostility toward the demonstrators—and this is where the hostility came from, it was certainly not the other way around—that the gap between the party or the state and the demonstrators could no longer be bridged. This was in September.

It was different on 9 October. I said to myself that this demonstration simply *had* to take place. My only worry was that it would not end peacefully. But if it did, it would not matter anymore what happened afterward. At the very least it would lead to a "breaking apart" of the existing system, and that in itself would have to be an improvement. At that time it was not that important to me anymore whether socialism could still be saved or not. Sure, I still had some hopes, but I had also grown very skeptical.

But if the demonstration led to a confrontation with the state, one that could only have resulted in a civil war—and there was a very good chance of that on 9 October—then we would have experienced a terrible catastrophe, one that would have rendered all discussions concerning "socialism or not" hopelessly irrelevant. After all, one can easily imagine what would have happened here. The bloodbath that occurred in Tiananmen Square in China was far away, but here we lived at the very border between two world systems. The outcome of a similar confrontation here could only have been absolutely devastating.

My position on 9 October was thus very clear. I hoped that the demonstration would be successful and nonviolent, independent of any considerations concerning "socialism or not." What came afterward would always be better than mere stasis because of our fear that a reform of socialism might not have a chance anymore. But I did not reach this conclusion until 9 October.

It began to be clear on 2 October, when I heard of the first successful mass demonstration in Leipzig. As I said before, one week earlier I had still felt this tension inside between sympathy on the one hand and fear on the other hand that it was probably already too late.

Is it correct that the party, the police, and the Stasi tried to convey a very clear message prior to 9 October that anybody who participated in the 9 October demonstration would be considered an enemy of the state and should thus expect the most severe repercussions imaginable?

This is exactly how I understood it.

How do you explain the fact that you yourself and thousands of others dared to go anyway?

Well, I think many people did not perceive it that way. The demonstration on 2 October had already been a mass demonstration—there were different estimates, but I think 25,000 is realistic. Since the police had not intervened, there was hope that it could be repeated.

The movement had also generated a sort of "automatism" [self-propelling momentum]; it could not be stopped any longer. Many of those who were scared to go on 9 October said to themselves: "If we leave the movement at this point, everything may fall apart and all the hopeful beginnings, some of which have already turned into an avalanche, may be wasted." So most people felt they could not withdraw at this point; they just *had* to participate. But I still think that most people did not think that the state would use violent measures against them.

Obviously, many people who had never participated before joined on 9 October . . .

. . . Well, yes, the size of the movement had more than doubled . . .

. . . *And thus far my understanding from talking to various participants was that perhaps the very opposite of what you have just suggested may have been the case. I had the impression that precisely because everyone knew there was an imminent danger of violent repression, many people came to the difficult conclusion—after much deliberation—that they had to participate. I think there was a sense that otherwise they would be deserting those who would certainly go, and the whole movement might be killed as a result. What do you think about that?*

That may have been true for some people. But my impression from talking to many demonstrators before and after the demonstration was that the majority of those who had gathered here was hoping for a positive outcome and *did not* expect violent repression.

What kind of role did the celebrations—which had just ended a day before—surrounding the fortieth anniversary play? Quite obviously the leadership was determined to ignore all the problems in the country and, instead, went ahead with these pompous festivities at the same time thousands tried to leave the country for good and thousands of others took to the streets and demonstrated for reforms. Was that perhaps sort of the last slap in the face of all those who had still hoped for a positive response from the party?

Yes, that's absolutely correct. I was talking about an "automatism" earlier, and I think this was precisely what brought out those who had been hesitant so far. Many people figured that if they did not continue to push now—and the anniversary celebrations had proved that the leadership was no longer able to respond to the situation adequately—all the opportunities for change might be lost. So people knew if they did not do something then, nothing would ever move.

I am absolutely certain that these "horror celebrations" accelerated the demise of the regime quite considerably.

How did your own political involvement change after 9 October? Concretely, what did you do inside the party or inside the opposition in order to have any kind of influence on events?

It was a time of hectic activities. Within the party we at first pushed for a restructuring of the governing bodies inside Karl Marx University.

We had already scheduled a new election of the district party leadership for 24 October. The result was—and I think one can call it that—a "mercilessly critical reevaluation" of the past. It was a clear and total rejection of the kind of socialist model that had been operable for seventy years. All this happened within the days of intense debate between 9 October and 24 October.

For me, however, it was more important that I had joined the public discussion process. On 15 and 16 October, and the days following that, many conversations and panel discussions took place with hundreds of participants. In the Moritz Bastei, for example, we had a public panel discussion with 1,500 participants on 20 October. . . .

I participated in many of those panels. One of my incentives was to try to get the opposition groups officially recognized [oppositional groups were still considered illegal at the time]. . . . I had already demanded the recognition of the most important oppositional group, New Forum, on 14–15 October. . . .

I was also in pretty close contact with the three SED district secretaries who were part of the six-person group that issued the "call for non-violence" on 9 October. I consulted with them almost every day during this period. . . .

And, of course, I tried to be active within the university. Right after 9 October, student councils had been spontaneously formed, and in my department we had pretty good relations with those students, so we immediately not only recognized those councils, but in fact supported them. . . .

Twice I went into the factories, because there was a lot of apathy there, and I tried to call for the creation of grass-roots unions, in opposition to the old unions. It was obvious that you could not achieve anything through the FDGB [Free German Labor Union, the official party union].

Could you be a little more specific, because it is a bit difficult for me to imagine what exactly it means "to go into the factories"?

Well, once I just went to a factory with acquaintances of mine who worked there. The other time was actually more interesting, however. This was initiated by reporters of the *LVZ*[33] [*Leipziger Volkszeitung*, now independent, but at the time still a party newspaper] who had found out that nothing was going on in the factories yet.

Since we had seen very few signals or impulses from the factories, and since we had, above all, detected no self-organizing attempts by the workers against the old factory supervisors, party leaders and party-controlled Free German Trade Unions, we wanted to check out the situation in the factories and encourage the founding of independent unions along the lines of the Polish example.

We were greatly dismayed after our visit. Despite the fact that we had considered ourselves to be realists, we had probably held on to some strange notions concerning the "decisive role of the working class." In any case, we hoped that we could provide some impetus in this direction. A subsequent well-done report by the two *LVZ* reporters was also supposed to encourage attempts toward self-organization, both in the factory we had visited and elsewhere. I doubt very much, however, whether that helped much. . . .

Perhaps we could now talk about your own activities and perceptions between November of 1989 and March of 1990? When and why did you decide, in the end, to leave the party?

Between November '89 and February of '90 I tried to support the process of democratization in a number of different areas. In fact, I am surprised that I managed physically to get through these times. It was a time of frantic activities, and I worked an average of 15 to 16 hours a day. At one point we worked and organized, with few breaks in between, for 38 hours nonstop. The only reason some of us were able to keep this up was that behind all these activities was the hope that finally things we had long

33. The history of this newspaper would tell a great deal about the turmoils of German left-wing politics. Until 1917 the *LVZ* was the second most important social democratic newspaper in Germany. After the split of the Social Democratic Party into the Majority Socialists [MSPD] and the Independent Socialists [USP] around Karl Liebknecht and Rosa Luxemburg, the *LVZ* was a USP paper. In 1922, after the total defeat of the German Revolution, those two social democratic factions again merged into the SPD, and the *LVZ* became a Social Democratic paper again. The *LVZ* then existed until the Nazis took power in 1933, and reopened immediately as a SPD newspaper after the defeat of Nazism in 1945. Following the forced merger of the Social Democratic Party and the Communist Party in the Soviet-occupied territory of Germany into the Socialist Unity Party in 1948, the *LVZ* became an official SED paper. As the party-state collapsed in the GDR during the Fall of 1989, the *LVZ* was one of the first large party newspapers that continued operations as an independent daily newspaper.

been thinking about could be tested out, could be experimented with, and we did not want to end up having to accuse ourselves of not having tried everything possible.

Just to give you an example. We created a department council during this time which was made up of a one-third parity of all groups [faculty, students, and untenured faculty/administration], one in which all important decisions were first prepared and then decided upon. This council still exists, but it is the last one of its kind. . . .

At the same time, we tried to undergo the transition from regimented course work to the free choice of courses according to the Western model. To change and improve the content of the curriculum at the same time, however, was much more difficult. I was very surprised, in this respect, about the extent to which students and young colleagues were scared by the risks associated with these new freedoms. What they seemed to want was *both* the new freedom *and* the old security. . . .

Until January of 1990 I also spent a great deal of my efforts helping to restructure the SED or SED-PDS [as it came to be called after the party congress in December], within the university, in the district, and in Berlin. Before the extraordinary party congress took place in December, I saw some very good chances for a fundamental renewal of the party. In this respect, I thought it was merely of secondary importance whether the party would first dissolve itself and then start completely anew under a different name, or whether it would change under the old name.

It was during the party congress that I had my first serious doubts. Most of the endless debates were over procedural questions. . . .

The catastrophic miscalculations on the part of the SED concerning the dissolving of the Stasi, that is, the agencies for national security, in early January, and the very hesitant restructuring of the economy under the government of Prime Minister Hans Modrow further heightened my suspicions.

The point at which I lost the rest of my hopes for a fundamental restructuring of the old SED-PDS occurred at the traditional rally on 19 January 1990, commemorating the 1919 killing of Karl Liebknecht and Rosa Luxemburg. It was a rally with about 10,000 participants. I myself delivered one of the keynote speeches. During this rally one of the spokespersons of the civic movement severely attacked the SED of its long misuse of Rosa Luxemburg's name, and he was subsequently forced to end his speech because of a hail of whistles coming from the SED participants. At this point it became transparently obvious to me: . . . the solid basis of the party, all those long-serving members who had not stayed in the party solely for career reasons, but rather out of ideological faith and willingness to sacrifice—just like the old members in the KPD [German Communist Party] during the era of illegality under Nazism—stubbornly held on to the old party traditions. They were not open to criticism from allies within the left, and they were certainly not capable of helping to bring about a confederation of all the large democratic left movements.

So that was the point at which you finally left the party?

Well, not quite then. You had asked me earlier why reformers like me had left the party rather than attempt to radically change it from within. I can only speak for myself. Despite the very sobering experiences I told you about, I stayed in the party until June of 1990. . . . I was somehow still hoping that the renewal of the party would make some more decisive progress.

The reason I perceived the progress of renewal within the party as not sufficient up to that point was because I not only hoped for some kind of new party as such, but rather for a political party of an entirely different type, one not in the tradition of Leninism, but one that would throw off the burdens of the past without any tactical concerns and thus might be able to initiate a new democratic culture.

But instead, the PDS began to respond to the demands of political everyday life. . . . After 30 years of internal struggle with the apparatus and the many bruises I had received from that, this was simply not enough for me.

As it has become clear in this interview, I was wrong on numerous occasions in my life, but unfortunately I was not wrong in my realization that the chance for a democratic renewal within the PDS had been missed. In fact, the party never managed to come to terms with its own past.

■ ANDRÉ BRIE, vice-chairman in 1990 of Party for Democratic Socialism, the successor party of the old SED.[34] ■ *"It was the 'reality' of socialism that really put off people."*

Unlike activists in the opposition, most of whom expressed difficulties about "fitting" into any stringent organizational structure—be it a party or an oppositional group—André Brie, cochairman of the Party for Democratic Socialism and self-declared "reformer" inside the established apparat, had never known any environment for political work other than "the party." As evidenced in the previous interview section with him, Brie

34. For background information on Brie, see Part I, chapter 3, pp. 171–81.

always considered the party, despite internal confrontations and personal defeats, as his political home. It was in the party that he found intellectual stimulus, political friends, a job, security, and political support.

Like many other party reformers, such as Werner Bramke, Brie held on to the party throughout the tumultuous upheavals of 1989. But he was one of a small minority who doggedly continued to seek these qualities in the party right up to the time when the restructured CP, now called Party for Democratic Socialism, had already been relegated to political marginality. As will become clear in the following pages, Brie carried on the concept of "fighting for socialism through a strong party" for reasons that in many ways help explain why communist parties had such great appeal to millions of dedicated "socialists" for more than half a century in countries across every continent. It was a dream and a certain vision of a better, freer and more egalitarian world that seemingly compelled thousands of sincere people to stay with the party. Neither the revelations concerning decades of lies and corruption commonplace within the party hierarchy, nor the fact that the communist party "of a new style" had fallen far short of changing in ways Brie had hoped for, prevented him from becoming one of its leading representatives in the spring of 1990. The growing gap between their vision of a better world and the reality of actually existing socialism under one-party rule created the most startling tensions in people like Brie. Exposed here is a political custom, however, that can be found elsewhere across the ideological spectrum, that is, beyond the world of Marxism-Leninism—namely, loyalty to old ideas even after they have become ossified into inherited institutional forms. The following interview section, then, portrays a deeply troubled man.

■ *Let me ask you some questions about your well-known role as a reformer within the party and your specific ideas about how the kind of actually existing socialism of the GDR could be reformed. There are a number of issues that confuse me a bit. This morning I reread the document you had coauthored and which you sent to Honecker in October. You have mentioned on numerous occasions that there were still people who were interested in continuing "Project Socialism." The central question for me is, of course, what exactly did you mean by that? Reading some of the documents you have written, it occurred to me that many people would regard your concept of "socialism" as extremely abstract. In fact, I have noticed that, considering "socialism" abstractly, little difference is visible between your reform document and the public announcements of the old party on this topic. In short, it seems to me that as long as socialism is thought about in this form, no one could possibly know what it really means.*

A second matter concerns a related problem. You continued to base your ideas on the "leading role of the party," something that has been the central target of all the upheavals in Eastern Europe, including the Prague Spring 1968 and Soli-darność in 1980/81. Why did you hold on to that? Was that a tactical move on your part because you figured you could not yet push things any further in October of 1989, or does this still describe your political beliefs, and thus the program of the "new" Party for Democratic Socialism?

Well, as I tried to explain earlier, much in this paper was written in the belief that we could not yet go any further. My previous experiences played a large role in my continued caution.

You also have to realize that we were not the only ones who were cautious. All the oppositional groups were founded very late and went public with critical statements very late—even they were very cautious, staying in the background because they saw little room to maneuver. . . .

Secondly, in the study we had published in May of '89 we had in many ways already transcended this limitation. We wrote about a "need" for political plurality in the GDR, even though the whole study was phrased in an extremely theoretical and abstract fashion. It is true, we were hiding behind this theoretical terminology to some extent, but we were well aware of the need for a fundamental change of paradigms for quite some time. . . .

But the third reason was grounded in our belief that if the continuation of socialism was to have any chance in the GDR, then the process of reform had to be led—for a long time to come—by a strong Socialist Unity Party. That is why we had held on to the "leading role of the SED."

I remember well, after having read the founding statement of New Forum in September of 1989, that we thought we could support this paper in all of its details. On the other hand, we believed that New Forum would simply not be capable of leading this process. On the contrary, we believed that this process would quickly turn out to be uncontrollable, and would eventually be overrun by the frustration of large portions of the population. That much had already become very obvious.

Let's not be fooled by how this dynamic worked. Prior to the opening of the Wall the population was also demanding a reform of socialism, but that was largely because of an uncertainty among the population as to how far one could go. In reality, people had long been thinking about, and striving for, other things besides a "reform of socialism."

What about the organized opposition? It seems to me while some activists were using the term "socialism" for purely opportunistic purposes—like Eppelmann or Schnur in Democratic Awakening—most others were sincerely thinking about some kind of free and democratic form of socialism . . . ?

That is absolutely correct, most of those who were prominent within the opposition were demanding socialism. . . .

But then again, we understood "the leading role of the party" to mean something other than what the vulgar understanding of it was, also something different from what the party's understanding of it had been. We did not mean a leading role in *administrative ways*, but rather a leading role for the party in *argumentative* and *ideological* terms. . . .

But as far as today is concerned, not only were the conditions for socialist thinking fundamentally altered in this country, but I also believe that socialist thinking and socialist politics in general have to be fundamentally—and I mean *fundamentally*—reconsidered.

The central lesson in all this is that we have to make sure that there will never be so much as the slightest movement within socialist thinking in the direction of allowing anyone to have a "leading role," regardless of what leading force in society we are talking about. There is a basic need for plurality within every modern society. For example, we just *have* to come to a fundamentally different relationship with the old statement by Rosa Luxemburg that "freedom is always the freedom of the one who thinks differently." It's unfortunate, in this respect, that this valuable statement has been merely instrumentally misused by others. From a modern point of view, such a stance necessarily implies a need for both strong and changing oppositions—which would have to include even conservative forces.

Opposition needs to be understood as part of one's own interest. Only through the conflict of ideas, through the open exchange of political concepts, will modern societies ever be able to find answers to the many pressing problems they face. What we need is lively communication. One only hopes that other people view this similarly. I think even conservative forces have to come to the conclusion that if they have an opposition, they should not just tolerate it, but rather give it some room to operate, perhaps even let it contribute to their own politics. In other words, one should not just vote down the opposition all the time, but rather argue with it in a genuine exchange and competition of ideas, and then formulate one's own policies accordingly. It is a disastrous error to believe that one can dominate politics merely with majorities, be they communist, socialist, or conservative.

Let me expand my question a little then. I am still a bit confused what kind of "leading role" you actually have in mind. Much of what you wrote reminds me a great deal of the language the old party routinely used, the old Leninist vanguard model concerning socialism . . .

. . . But these papers were written for the old Central Committee, for

Honecker. We were still scared, and, besides, we were actually trying to reach him, to communicate with him in ways he would be able to understand. Our plan to get signatures from various party members for our appeal was not only meant to provide some security for us, but was also meant to get his attention. We were consciously using a kind of language that at least allowed some possibility for communicating with Honecker, despite the fact that we did not have all that many illusions about succeeding in this endeavor with him. At bottom, of course, this paper was actually meant to help *remove* Honecker.

The problem was that we all knew that none of the people in the Politburo were capable of initiating fundamental reform processes. On the other hand, we also knew that change could only come out of the Politburo. A putsch which would wipe out the entire Politburo was perhaps something that we hoped for, but it was simply unrealistic.

The dilemma, one of many dilemmas, was that change [toward a reform of socialism] could only come out of the Politburo, and there was no one in it who was comparable to a Gorbachev.

I am sorry, but I still have a few problems understanding what exactly you are saying to me. You mentioned previously that change could only have originated at the top, if at all, and not from the bottom, because otherwise . . .

. . . I only said that it was imperative that change came from the top as well . . .

. . . Actually, you said, "should originate from above," and the people should then have responded, which seems to mean that change should not have originated at the bottom, because, according to your own explication, the inevitable result of such a course would have been unification with the Federal Republic.

Yes, that's correct.

I see. And then you also mentioned that there was no Gorbachev-like figure in the East German Politburo. Is that not concentrating a bit too much on "passing personalities?" Is this perhaps an indication that you continued to hold on to some kind of elite concept of politics?

No, no, not at all. We cannot invest any hope in individual personalities, not even in Gorbachev, even though I still think he is an outstanding personality. All I was saying was that without such people this process could not have been initiated.

Throughout the eighties, reform-minded people in the party thought that Modrow could perhaps be such a person—due to his life-style, his modesty, the leeway he allowed artists, and so on. There were also rumors about disputes between him and several members of the Honecker-dominated Politburo.

The reason why we concentrated on individual persons as much as we did was that only "people" could have initiated a real reform process, one that would have included new people in leading positions as well as new political structures. On the other hand, we had realized all along that such a policy only had a chance if it was supported by the widest mass of people. There had to be a positive response from below.

For a long time I harbored many hopes and illusions about such a process. I always thought that such a process had the best chances in a country like the GDR. To some extent, I still think that was true. We had a certain "socialist consensus" here, including most of the oppositional intellectuals.

But I guess by late 1989 things had already moved along too far. We produced dozens of papers in the Fall of '89, torn between thinking that it was too late and hoping that there was still a chance, the chance for a "third way."

Well, let's talk about what you call "the bottom" for a moment. I noticed early on in my research that very little contact existed between intellectuals in the opposition and nonintellectuals in the population at large. Most intellectuals in the opposition, furthermore, claim to this very day that the vast majority of the population was not at all interested in any kind of socialism, or even in the continuation of some form of an autonomous GDR. Following this line of reasoning, the events between October of 1989 and the summer of 1990 confirmed that people were mostly interested in unification with the Federal Republic, in obtaining the West German Mark, and in improved consumption. I am still not very convinced by such claims. So let me ask you to what extent you knew about possible initiatives among the working population of the GDR and their attitudes toward some variety of what you call a "third way?"

And, following that, why does it appear as if nobody made any attempts to find out about the problems and hopes of the working population in order to create some kind of common, mutual political effort? I am asking you this question because I have always been under the illusion that a communist party would maintain good contacts with the working population—out of self-interest, if nothing else.

Difficult question . . . Over the last 10 years I gave an average of 50 to 70 lectures a year across the GDR. I thus had many opportunities to establish contacts and to find out about people's opinions. It was my impression that possible support for a third way had existed for quite some time. But I know I might also have been misled by my own impressions.

The topics I was talking about had to do with foreign policy and security matters, as well as more global topics, such as environmental issues. Yet we always ended up, virtually without exception, talking about domestic problems, like "what does all this mean for our own country, for economic or environmental policies in the GDR, or for the development of democracy in the GDR?" Many people obviously used these lectures and the following discussions as some kind of escape valve. In most instances we in turn discussed the nature of socialism. On the other hand, that could have been—and today I believe it in fact was—nothing but a vehicle which allowed people to discuss such matters at all in a critical manner. It may well be, in other words, that people's ideas were already on some other level, and perhaps they would have liked to express—if only given the chance—that they no longer wanted to have anything to do with socialism.

Secondly, the SED had about 2.4 million members, among them about 1 million workers. At some point they all went to party meetings, party training programs, and party schools called "schools of socialist work." At all these places people learned about "socialism," and they discussed politics with one another. But it was my experience that most people were simply bored by all of this. They attended without ever saying anything. I can only remember a few occasions where we had some lively debates. The huge wave of workers who immediately left the party in November and December of '89, on the other hand, were an indication that none of these lessons had been internalized at all.

And yet, thirdly, I am rather confident that the support for socialism among workers in the GDR was pretty widespread during the sixties, and perhaps even again in the early seventies. I think we could prove that. After the building of the Wall, for instance, a huge number of young people volunteered for the National Defense Army, even though we did not have a draft at the time. There was a tangible enthusiasm among large sectors of the population concerning the idea of building a better political alternative to the Federal Republic on German soil.

The SED itself, however, destroyed the ground for such support— consciously at that. The party leaders engaged in fewer and fewer efforts to create such a genuine alternative. Instead, they increasingly shaped their policies with reference to the Federal Republic. They focused more and more on material consumption, for example, even though that was the *only* area in which they could not possibly provide a better alternative to the Federal Republic. Or they increasingly forced people to remain isolated in the private sphere, in their dachas, or behind their TV sets— thereby individualizing them and turning them into real petits bourgeoises. With all that, I believe, the party itself effectively destroyed any possibility for a mass orientation toward socialist values or ideals.

Worst of all, they did all that merely in the name of maintaining power. They believed that privatized and petit-bourgeois-minded people would remain quiet. Of course, for quite some time it seemed as if they were right about that. But in the long run, this strategy could only lead to disaster.

Are you saying that this "selling out" of socialist ideals for the purpose of maintaining power represented a conscious strategy on the part of the party leadership?

Oh yes, absolutely. Kurt Hager [member of the Politburo responsible for cultural affairs] said in '89 that we had created a "new cultural sphere," the cultural sphere of the living room with a TV set. Or just look at our cities; there are no public places where people can communicate— yes, it was clearly a conscious strategy.

At times, people managed to break through this privatization, as in the case of numerous youth clubs. But even those were only allowed to exist because one thought that they would "quiet down the young."

You see, there were also economic reasons behind this policy. In their weekend dachas people could exercise all of the individual initiative that they could not make use of anywhere else in society; they could retreat into their own four walls and enjoy their privacy, which was endangered everywhere else in this society; and on top of that, they were also supposed to grow the vegetables that a mismanaged economy was unable to provide. So this was not only quite conscious, but it served all kinds of purposes for the party. . . .

After Gorbachev took over in 1985, there was once again hope among many people that things would get better. But again I am not sure in retrospect whether that was because people genuinely liked what Gor- bachev stood for, or whether they were just looking for any kind of outlet, for any kind of improvement. . . .

I guess the point is that one simply cannot separate the concept of socialism, that which you or I might theoretically associate with it, and the "reality" of socialism, that is, that which people were experiencing on a day-to-day basis. In fact, ever since the 1920s the concept of socialism has been defined by what the opposition called a "Stalinist reality," so people were correct in saying that this is what they perceived as "socialism."

It does not help if, as an intellectual, I say that this is not what socialism is all about; or when I talk about the roots of socialism in Christianity, in the Enlightenment, among the utopian socialists, or in Marx; or when I talk about what the international workers' movement has fought for. It was the "reality" of socialism that really put off people. On a day-to-day level they experienced socialism as highly inefficient, as inhumane, as contrary to their interests and life experiences. Based on such an experience, of course, it will require a very long time indeed before we may be able to recruit people to the socialist cause again. . . .

I think one can no longer work with the term "socialism"—it is destroyed, at least for quite some time to come.

I would like to take you back in time once more. In light of what you have previously said about what happened in October and November, how do you explain the sudden disintegration of the SED? And then, how would you explain how you yourself moved from being a member of the old party, to staying on during the transitional period, to currently holding the position of vice-chairman in the PDS? You said at some earlier point that all reform-minded people should long since have left the party, because the party had turned into a suffocating influence on any kind of positive development. Is the PDS really a different kind of party, and, if so, who are its current members, some 400,000 in number?

Actually, we now have about 350,000, down from about 2.4 million in the summer of 1989.

But let me say something about this sudden collapse. A couple of days ago I saw a wooden beam which was holding up a ceiling, and it looked completely intact. And when we wanted to put on a fresh coat of paint, we realized that there was nothing below the surface, the beam was completely rotten, eaten away over many decades by termites. It was literally hollow; there was no core left. The same thing happened to the GDR because of its economic contradictions, because of the immense frustrations that had built up over decades among the population. The appearance of total stability, artificially produced with the help of the security police, contributed a great deal to this overwhelming frustration. Through various repressive measures, the system always succeeded in preventing any meaningful debates from taking place. In fact, it was so effective that it rarely needed to resort to open force. In other words, not even the smallest conflicts were ever resolved openly. Instead, conflicts were pushed to a point where they became virtually unresolvable, without ever appearing in the open.

At the very moment the first brick was removed from this artificial edifice, the whole thing collapsed, because it had to collapse—particularly *because* of its seeming stability.

Had you anticipated this at all?

No. Over the last few years I had grown increasingly worried that the situation had, in fact, become unresolvable. But on the other hand, I probably belonged to the group of people who wanted to talk themselves into believing that there was still a chance for some kind of socialist renewal.

No, I certainly did not expect this to happen. That is one of the reasons why it could happen as it did: the party and the security police had lulled themselves—and us—into believing that nothing like that could ever happen. They were not capable of dealing with conflict. I think all of us were not capable of dealing with conflict. . . .

I would say that about two-thirds of the membership (mostly old people who have been in the party for many years) simply needed a political home. And the last third were people who in fact actively and critically fought for a new party. We even have people who have just recently joined, particularly intellectuals. Some have rejoined after they had been expelled at some point for their dissenting and critical views.

But we are far from having enough creative and critical people. Many party districts are still dominated by the old guard. We are in the middle of an extremely difficult process. After all, we not only wanted to become a functioning democratic party, we also wanted to achieve movement character, grass-roots participation, working groups, PDS initiatives, and so on. What we want is to create an open forum particularly for young people, for critical people, and for intellectuals. . . .

I had offered our new chairman, Gregor Gysi, my participation in the election campaign. So after the events of December and January, I came to the decision to stick to the party as the only chance of creating a socialist alternative in the future political spectrum of a united Germany.

I knew it would be a painful process that would require many years, many years just to come to terms with this terrible past, to replace the old personnel with new personnel, to change this disastrous apparatus, and to create a new program. You see, the SED had not really been a party, it was more of a "consent-enforcing machine." Therefore, the biggest problem for the PDS is to create an actually "functioning" party, one in which politics is articulated from below and is only coordinated from above. Currently, it still happens the other way around—the leadership formulates the program and then tries to sell it to its membership. . . .

6 WORKERS IN THE "WORKERS' STATE"

■ Joint interview with workers from Berlin[35] ■ *"The big political process proceeded rapidly, and the small-scale process of figuring out all the important details has not even started yet."*

Regardless of who I talked to during the East German summer of 1990, the opening of the Wall was not perceived as the kind of unmitigated "victory" alluded to in Western media accounts. As life in East Germany radically changed from one day to the next following the events of 9 November, the reactions of East German citizens revealed a complex web of deep yearnings and an intricate substructure of beliefs, all suddenly unleashed by this unexpected clash of the two German societies.

Some of the answers contained in the following pages may not appear as making much sense within the familiar range of discussion in Western culture, for they expose a range of (real or presumed) contradictions concerning people's perceptions and hopes that grew out of a uniquely East German context. Yet those very same voices in no way fit into the kinds of simplistic generalizations about "East German workers" routinely invoked by both East German intellectuals and Western commentators. An ear tuned attentively to these working-class voices picks up evidence of a world that is strangely absent from most political commentary. Here we encounter a web of experiences that is not only remote from Western sensibilities, but also from those of white-collar oppositionists in East Germany. The latter know—today—that a great opportunity was somehow missed, but precisely how remains unclear. Perhaps some important clues can be derived from the following interview.

35. For background information on this interview, see Part I, chapter 2, pp. 111–31.

■ *What was your response to 9 November 1989?*

Maria C.: I really think they never should have opened the Wall. It came as an incredible surprise when Schabowski presented us with this decision—to this very day I just don't like it.

All we wanted was to be able to travel. We wanted a passport. . . . We wanted to be able to go wherever we felt like, and for as long as we wanted, that's all. My vacation was only 24 days anyway, so I could not have gone for very long. We just wanted to have the freedom to make those decisions ourselves; that's what we wanted. Or just to go to West Berlin for a day and then come back. But this kind of open Wall, well, let me tell you, that is not what I wanted. And I also did not want to get rid of socialism. It is true, I did not want *this kind* of socialism, not one with the likes of Erich Honecker, but rather another kind of socialism.

You have to realize, we looked wide-eyed at Gorbachev, what he was trying to do in the Soviet Union. That came right out of our own hearts; that's what we wanted to happen here. We did not want these senile old men with their hunting lodges; we wanted young men who were willing to work together with all of us on something like glasnost and perestroika. . . .

Please clarify something for me, because I am getting a bit confused here, and perhaps all of you can help clarify my confusion. The fact is that in March 1990, during the first free elections held in the GDR, about 46 percent of the population voted for the Christian Democrats. . . .

Doris C.: Just look at what people voted for in Berlin . . .

Rudi E.: In Berlin we voted for the PDS and, above all, for the Social Democrats. . . .

Doris C.: Let me put it this way. The anger of the people was so great that they just could not see themselves voting for the PDS, even though Gysi [new communist party chairman] was very well liked. I know of many people who would have liked to vote for Gysi, but they just could not bring themselves to vote for the successor party of the old SED, so they voted for the Social Democrats. Unfortunately, not many voted for Alliance 90 [the coalition of civic movements, New Forum, Greens, Independent Women's Alliance, and Democracy Now]. I regretted that very much.

But a few votes like that do not really alter the overall picture, so let me ask you again: this whole development started much earlier—18 March is only, so to speak, the crowning moment of this process. Prior to 9 November, people carried placards at the demonstrations saying: "We are the people." There existed, it seems to me, a lot of political creativity. After 9 November, some people were suddenly saying: "We are one people," "Germany, united fatherland," or "Helmut, you are our chancellor as well . . ."

Doris C.: . . . Yes, but those were Saxons. The situation was different here. We had had experiences with West Berlin, until they put this Wall in our faces. And West Berlin was a lesson to us. We lived with their form of capitalism prior to 1961, right next door, with open borders. We knew exactly what was going on over there. . . .

I knew that West Berliners were exploiting us with their Western currency, that they bought our subsidized goods cheaply so that we could not get them anymore. I knew that thousands were going over there to work for minimum wages, because after they exchanged it for our currency, they still had more than anyone else. For all those reasons I did not want an open Wall.

Of course, you know what fellow Saxon citizens say to this. They say that the Berliners voted differently because they had always been better off than anyone else.

Doris C.: Well, in some ways that may be true. But wasn't it obvious all along what would happen after the opening of the Wall? West Mark and East Mark had to clash, and people began to work in the West, just like it was before the building of the Wall.

I remember those days very well. Somebody would sell tickets in a West Berliner movie theater, for example, and they would receive 200 West Marks for it, then exchange it 1 to 4 on the black market, and have 1,000 East Marks. That is more than a senior consultant would receive around here before 1961. That is precisely the reason why this Wall was built in the first place, because we could not survive under conditions like that. Our people left the country, and the West began to buy us up . . .

Rudi E.: . . . Today everything may look very different, but back then they had to build the Wall, because otherwise the clash between the two systems would have led to a disaster.

Things also improved around here after '61, until about the late sixties. But when this intensified competition with the West picked up in the early seventies, we just could not keep up.

Bernd K.: But you also have to take into consideration that we never received Marshall Plan aid. . . .

Maria C.: If the party had allowed freedom of the press and open public debates earlier, we would have seen a fundamental break with this kind of totalitarian one-party rule much sooner. It probably would have been a different kind of break, one that we probably could have agreed with much more.

You only have to look at the kind of unemployment we are now going to get—I am sure there were different ways to go from that.

Talking about ways you "could have agreed with much more," I would like to ask you a couple of questions concerning the time between October/November of '89 and March of '90. First, what did you think about all the people who suddenly stood in the limelight of political attention, namely, members of various opposition groups such as Democracy Now, Democratic Awakening, New Forum, or the Social Democrats? And, secondly, how do you explain the fact that this period symbolizes a development about which many GDR citizens told me "this is not what we wanted to happen at all."

Doris C.: That's absolutely true, nobody wanted this . . . [long pause, no one says anything]

On 4 November about 1 million people demonstrated in the streets of Berlin, probably the largest demonstration in German history. There seemed to have been some sort of organized power in the streets, in the hands of the people. Yet little of that seems to be left today; today we have a replica of West German parliamentary democracy here.

Doris C.: Maybe it's because all these Protestant pastors are running the government now . . .

Leonhard B.: . . . This is the way I see it. As we have pointed out by now, what we wanted was to get new people so that things would begin to function again . . .

What do you mean by "function again?"

Leonhard B.: Less arbitrariness and despotism, better organization, and the right people in the right places. We needed people who were competent, and not just members of the party . . .

Doris C.: . . . Economic progress, mostly, and freedom to travel . . .

Leonhard B.: . . . The tragedy is that things went backward instead of forward. We wanted a development within socialism, and not away from it. At least, I think that's what most people wanted.

Well, and when we took to the streets and such, we noticed over and over again that there were virtually no people who were capable of carrying out the kind of socialism we wanted. It was a big problem that all the positions through which one could have changed something were not filled with the right people during the first phase of this revolution. The senile old men were still sitting up there and continuing their mush. Only at the lower ranks did change actually take place.

All of this, in my opinion, pushed the cart so forcefully in one direction that it began to pick up speed by itself, and then it had to end up in the ditch. In the end, nobody could have implemented what we actually wanted anymore . . .

. . . Who exactly are you referring to when you say "we"?

Leonhard B.: Well, the people in this room, and then, of course, most other people in a similar situation. Most workers, I would say . . .

. . . I mean, after all there was a substantial portion of the population that publicly said "no more socialist experiments."

Bernd K.: Yes, that's true, there were those, but in much smaller numbers than the ones who wanted to hold on to socialism.

Doris C.: What you really have to understand is how fed up we were with people who held positions of authority for no other reason than that they were members of the party. . . . We could not get rid of these people during the first phases of the transition, and that, more than anything else, frustrated people a great deal. . . .

The same people who served Honecker for decades, as directors, supervisors, or managers, are now taking orders from the de Maizière government. And they are precisely the ones who are currently in the process of selling off our enterprises—I say *our* because that's what they really should be—to people from the West. And they sell it for little more than they would ask for a piece of apple pie, while we stand around like complete idiots and just let it happen. Once again we are saying, "What can we do? There is nothing that we can do."

Isn't it true as well that a lot of the energy that had flowed into demonstrating, debating, and organizing prior to 9 November now began to flow into the West?

Rudi E.: Well, that's true to some extent. Everyone wanted to go over there at least once, pick up his "greeting money" [100 Marks West for every East German visitor], and check out the place. But that only lasted for about six weeks . . .

Doris C.: It is true that Schabowski was very clever and successful in dampening the level of anger and frustration among the population, because right after the Wall had been opened it got pretty quiet around here. That's, of course, exactly what they had intended. They tried to remain in control of things, Krenz and Schabowski, that was their thing. I could have killed them for that. . . .

Peter R.: They should have organized this opening with us; they should have said, "We are planning to grant the freedom to travel. How should we do that?" Then, we could have kept the social security we had all enjoyed, but still could have lived the kind of unrestricted life we had always envisioned.

This pushing us around like children, this ordered repression, was just simply unbearable; it was so depressing. Every report you submitted to the union leadership or the plant management had to end with a "hurrah" to the party. We had to claim 150 percent success, even though everyone knew that this was a complete swindle. We were all part of this big lie; it was so frustrating, one could not really avoid it, as comrade, as colleague, as communist.

At some point we all began to say to ourselves, "Why, why does it have to be this way? These are my comrades, my colleagues. Why do I have to lie to them? Don't you understand, why, in God's name, don't you understand that?"

And then this valve opened, and we had so much hope that we could perhaps still save the whole thing. And then we got Egon Krenz, who had been fed the same shit, who *was*, in fact, the same old shit. Nothing, absolutely nothing, was possible with him . . .

Rudi E.: It's true that we had no new people who could have done the job, except, perhaps, Modrow. He was one of the first to realize and understand that something substantial had to change. I saw an interview with him on television in which he self-critically admitted how surprised he was when he realized how many people took his side after he found the courage to stand up for change in the Central Committee. So he said, "One should have started this process much earlier."

Leonhard B.: The opening of the Wall was also the opening of a valve. All the anger we had built up was gone at the moment we crossed the border. We had so much in our heads, new impressions and all. Everybody thought about all sorts of things, but not about the fact that we should now pay close attention to the political developments in our own country. So our chance really sort of slipped away. . . .

Bernd K.: I was born in Berlin, Schönhauser Allee, which is right next to where the Wall was built later on. After August of 1961 we suddenly could not even visit our neighbors any longer. So when I crossed the border on Bornholmer Strasse for the first time in more than 28 years again . . . [he can't finish, tears rolling down his cheeks]

Doris C.: . . . Many new groups—New Forum, for example—who had been active in the neighborhoods, in the factories, everywhere, simply disintegrated after the opening of the Wall.

An incredible number of young people simply took off to the West, stayed there for a couple of nights, came back, then stayed another couple of nights, and so on. The interest of a lot of people in changing things in the GDR simply disappeared for a decisive period of time.

I am afraid many people thought: "Now we have achieved what we always wanted, and the rest will happen by itself." So large portions of a necessary political potential were gone all of a sudden, simply gone . . .

Rudi E.: . . . And of course we were also not prepared for those politicians from the West who suddenly invaded our country. With this big show they put on, they successfully cajoled many of us into believing that their way was the only way of doing things. They promised us the West German Mark, they promised us the good life, and . . .

Maria C.: . . . When I saw the pictures from Leipzig, I was so angry I almost blew up. I could have gone to Leipzig and beat the shit out of them, with their placards and mottoes and "Germany, united fatherland."

I don't mind "Germany, united fatherland" in the long run, but, please, not so quickly. Just look at the relationship we had developed toward the West Mark: whenever I had two or three West Marks, I kept them in my pocket, brooding about how best to spend them, not really wanting to spend them at all because they were too valuable. Sometimes I got myself ten or twenty West German Marks from some senior citizens [allowed to travel to the West], paying six or seven East Marks for every West Mark, in order to buy something nice for my grandchildren at the Inter Shops [shops with Western goods which only accept Western currency]. The West Mark meant so much to us.

I knew that if the West Mark came to us, we would all go bankrupt. It couldn't have been any other way. We are simply not competitive with West Germany; we can't be. Every normal human being who goes into a store over there and looks at the goods they have, looks at how they are packaged, and then goes into one of our stores—of course, nobody would buy our goods anymore after they had the chance to get Western goods.

They all wanted to have the stuff that looks good, that is wrapped up in colorful ways. Starting with toilet paper, we are going to go bankrupt. I always said, "What is supposed to happen to our factories? They are all going to go under." We never stood a chance, whether it was toothpaste, fish, heavy machinery, or electronics. . . .

Doris C.: The way I see it, a lot of people are willing to go along with almost anything as long as they are getting paid for it. They will do anything if they can only get hard Western currency for it . . .

. . . *Well, but who are "they"?*

Leonhard B.: I guess that includes us. You see, you said earlier that people in the West claimed that GDR workers did not really work. In some sense that is true, I think . . .

Doris C.: . . . What do you mean, "in some sense"? I think you are burning a fuse . . .

Leonhard B.: . . . Wait, wait. On some levels we had people who shared their work with three others, as in the case of midlevel managers, engineers . . .

Rudi E.: . . . Yes, the whole administrative apparatus was just hopelessly inflated . . .

Leonhard B.: . . . But workers in the shops have, in my opinion, always worked hard. On top of that, their work required much more energy than in the West, because they had to make gold out of shit.

So now the opinion among workers in the shops is that "we have made certain for years that everybody is doing well." They now figure that a job in the West certainly could not be much harder, but it would pay three or four times as much.

People just want the same thing happening over here; they want the necessary changes to be implemented so that this incredibly oversized bureaucracy will be done away with and work can finally be organized in an efficient and competitive manner. Then we could also start paying decent wages around here. And it is exactly in this direction that nothing has happened lately. So a lot of colleagues have gotten tired and cynical and said, "You know what, do whatever you want to as long as I'll get some decent job again."

Nobody thought about what they could contribute so that changes would actually take place. . . . The big political process proceeded rapidly, and the small-scale process of figuring out all the important details has not even started yet. . . .

■ WOLFGANG K., newly elected trade union secretary at the second-largest heavy machinery plant (Magdeburg) in the German Democratic Republic. ■ *"Things could have been a lot better, but somehow we always managed."*

At the time of my appointment with Wolfgang K. on 2 August 1990, he had just been elected as the new secretary of the West German-based IG-Metall (Industrial Trade Union-Metal). We met in his new, spacious union office on the fourth floor of an administrative building which was surrounded by huge industrial facilities. The factory currently provided employment for some 8,700 workers, down from 11,200 prior to the revolution. He still seemed a bit ill at ease about his new environment— oak-paneled conference table, two telephones on an imposing desk, and a secretary next door busily fixing coffee for us. In other ways, however, he appeared to enjoy his new position, proud that he had been entrusted by his colleagues with the task of building a new functioning union structure in their plant. In any case, we got along well and spent more than three hours together. After our interview, he showed me around the plant, introduced me to any worker I wanted to talk to, and explained what he considered to be the main differences between his enterprise and a comparable plant in the West. He also confided in me that he did not see "much of a chance" for his factory to survive in direct competition with Western firms.

I found Wolfgang K. to be a man of clearly articulated ideas—with one notable exception. The way he talked about the old party and union structures, and particularly about "colleagues" who had made a living in those structures, was not only indicative of widespread confusion within East German society as to "what to do with former party functionaries," but also revealed the range of psychological as well as political complications surrounding that very question. Was every former "comrade" to be blamed for the current "mess"? If not, where should one draw the line? And what should be done with those hundreds of thousands of party functionaries who clearly seemed "responsible"? Those difficult questions obviously did not lend themselves to easy answers, as the following interview vividly illustrates. As a clear indication of Mr. K's confusion about this and related topics, the reader should pay attention to his constantly fluctuating point of reference—as exemplified by his use of "they" and "us"—when speaking of a wide range of very different people.

■ . . . Unfortunately, I have to say that very little happened here before the Wende. We pretty much had settled with what we had. We didn't know how to do anything about it. . . .

One exception in this factory was the steel foundry. They had a number of very courageous workers there who had written individual petitions concerning social measures for a long time. They had demanded safer working conditions, more breaks, better equipment, and such. They had also, on a number of occasions—after they had written petitions and either had gotten no response, a negative response, or had been threatened—publicly demanded that the union leaders should step down and be replaced by people who would seriously defend the interests of working people. . . .

All this got a lot more intense right after the opening of the Wall, of course. Masses of fellow workers withdrew their membership from the party, and a lot of open criticism was waged against the old union leadership, even against union people in our plant itself. In many cases things that were said were not justified. But I guess it was understandable that people then did revolt against everything that had to do with the old system.

Anyway, most of our colleagues left the party, and many really began to speak up. It was sort of a liberating moment. The pressure was gone all of a sudden. When you have been scared to speak up for such a long time, it just feels incredible to be able to say what you think. But still, much of what was said also kind of went overboard. . . .

The party management of our plant reacted to all this turmoil from below by issuing a decree that all political activities had to stay outside of the factory. In other words, since they could not stop us from speaking up any longer, and since they could not prevent us from organizing ourselves, they tried to make sure that we would at least keep our activities outside the realm of our workplace. . . . It was very ironic how they justified that: they said that politics and the workplace had nothing to do with each other. All of a sudden, we were workers with a contract who had to fulfill certain tasks within the factory, and outside we were citizens who could do whatever we pleased. Amazing to hear something like that from socialist party members. But then again, they had always taken the line that was most convenient, or most advantageous, to them. . . .

All this was quite despicable. Even the party secretaries in the factory, those who were really responsible for the incredible mess we were in, those who had actually run this joint, simply received "civil work contracts" after the Wende. You know, they all kept their jobs—new political leadership, the same people. I don't know. . . . Sure, it would have been difficult to replace everyone right from the start. But to do it like they did? They were responsible, yet they were never held accountable. They had made sure all right that they would not go under. . . .

In any case, by about March of 1990 the party structure within the factory had been pretty much dissolved. Unless one knew from earlier days, it was hard to tell who exactly had been in the party and who had not been. . . .

How did you and your colleagues respond to the old party leadership pretty much hanging on to their old positions?

Many colleagues of mine demanded that *everyone* who had played any kind of leading role in the party should be fired, including the ones in the unions. I have to say that I found such demands either very subjective or quite unreasonable. Some comrades in the party did a very good job, or at least they tried hard within their limits to do a good job. . . .

I know it is difficult to distinguish between those who are responsible, and those who were just in the party because they knew that they could not improve anything from outside it. Anyway, I believed that we could not simply say that someone was responsible for the whole mess just because he was in the party. I thought we needed to look much more specifically at exactly what people had been doing. . . . But, on the other hand, we were actually quite successful in preventing any kind of "reputational lynching." . . .

They [the old party plant management] started a new factory-wide newspaper in which some of these debates were fought out. They also demanded that the newspaper should "properly represent" the plant to the outside. I guess they were worried about their image, and ultimately about badly needed contracts. . . .

Yes, we did have some so-called "public meetings" at the plant—I think about three. That must have been between late November and December of 1989. . . .

I don't think that people from New Forum ever made any attempt to contact us, or to form a factory group of New Forum inside the plant, at least not that I know of. We did, however, have some New Forum sympathizers among our colleagues, people who on their own started a New Forum factory group. . . .

Who the Stasi people exactly were, what exactly they had been doing at our plant, and what happened to them after the Wende was never fully revealed. As far as I am concerned, they may still be among us. But I don't think that this will pose a large problem now. They are currently about as scared of us as we used to be scared of them. That's at least true for the moment; of course, that could change quickly again. . . .

What happened to the union is actually a rather sad story. As you know, the union was dissolved very rapidly, and there was really nothing to take its place at first. Now we have the West German union coming in. But in the beginning, our only representation consisted of the old departmental and factory-wide union leadership, even though there was no union to which they belonged any longer. . . .

It is true that a few of the shop stewards were replaced early on, those who had either lost their credibility or were for some other reason mistrusted among their colleagues. All of them were longtime party members. But most of the old guard remained in place, at least for the time being. And, as I said before, some of them were good people. . . .

But isn't it true that plant management, party leadership, and union leadership were all pretty much the same, that they were all under direct control of the party, and thus not very reliable representatives of their respective constituencies?

Well, yes, that's largely true. We never had much real representation within the old union. But you have to remember that the GDR was a "worker and peasant state," and that was more than just so many words. They always tried pretty hard to keep us happy. They knew that they couldn't do much if they did not at least have our quiet consent. They certainly did not want to experience another June 1953. . . .

But what you told me earlier did not exactly make it sound like there was much consent or support among your colleagues?

Yes and no. We all complained a lot. Lots of things were really going quite badly. Supplies were never sufficient. Some of the machinery was terribly old. The material we worked with was often not very good. And, of course, the party leadership always covered up all the problems with lies, lies, lies: no one believed their figures anymore. . . .

But, on the other hand, we were important to this state; without us, nothing would have worked. They needed us. And we got full employment—in fact, it was almost impossible to get laid off for any reason—we all had health coverage, and so on. You know, we never did too badly. Things could have been a lot better, but somehow we always managed. . . .

I have very little confidence in what is going to happen to us now. The role of our former union was much more significant within the then-existing system in the GDR than the role of the West German union within the West German political system. There is no doubt in my mind that workers and unions had far more rights in our former system. We are going to lose a lot—in fact, we have already lost a lot.

7 DEMOCRATIC VISIONS: A QUESTION OF SCOPE, A QUESTION OF POSSIBILITY

■ BÄRBEL BOHLEY, artist, founder of New Forum, "mother of the revolution."[36] ■ *"We never really entered a discussion process about possible alternatives."*

Among the East German oppositionists I interviewed, Bärbel Bohley was the only one who demonstrably lacked enthusiasm when talking about the revolutionary events of 1989. She seemed generally wary of providing answers about a period in East German history that, in retrospect, had left her profoundly disillusioned. Occasionally, she did not respond at all to my persistent inquiries. But when she did, her answers offered a sobering insight, I believe, into how a dedicated activist tried to make sense of a popularly generated revolution that had resulted in what she considered to be a clear defeat.

While Bärbel Bohley has not retreated into privatism, and wants to remain politically active, I clearly sensed that her experiences during the preceding year had broken something inside her. While other opposition activists like Ludwig Mehlhorn, Inge Köppe, or Sebastian Pflugbeil were no less disgruntled about the outcome of "their" revolution, they were obviously still (at the time of these interviews) in the process of trying to understand what exactly had happened. Bohley, on the other hand, seemed to have made up her mind that things "couldn't have happened differently." As a direct consequence, discussions with her were necessarily circular. Perhaps the best way for any Westerner to evaluate the following interview is to accept the fact that, in reading it, one is par-

36. For background information on Bohley, see Part I, chapter 2, pp. 131–39.

ticipating fully in the basic political dilemma that faced all members of the East German opposition: they wanted to be democratic and autonomous, but they were, in fact, quickly trapped by the existence of two Germanies.

■ *You have said on numerous occasions, and again in this interview, that you think that the East German population essentially wanted "the West." I would like to explain to you what kinds of difficulties I have with such an explanation, and then ask you some questions about that.*

What I considered remarkable and promising about the opening in countries like the GDR or Poland was the historically rare and, above all, self-generated chance for people to participate actively in the shaping process of their own country's politics. Here was an opportunity to transcend conditions in which citizens every four years or so merely vote for something (which they don't usually know much about) instead of being engaged participants in the political process themselves. One question I have is why this period of greatly expanded possibilities did not last very long in the GDR. And then, immediately after the Fall of 1989, political pundits again began to speculate about "the people," and about the ostensible fact that "they" did not want anything but the West German Mark and consumption. I don't quite understand how one can possibly squeeze the more than 1 million demonstrators in Berlin on 4 November 1989, or even the 100,000 marchers on 9 October 1989 in Leipzig into such a narrow and abstract category?

(long pause; no response)

Isn't it true that there were many different people with different perceptions and different problems, and that after November they all quickly found themselves in a radically changed political context in which the options were once again very narrow, this time between the Western model or something extremely unclear? If I am not completely mistaken about this, it might be very understandable that so many people voted like they did on 18 March 1990 [the day of the first free elections in East Germany]. But does that mean they uncritically wanted to copy the Western model . . . ?

. . . Well, no, of course not. They didn't even know it. (again, long pause)

I just talked to numerous workers in Magdeburg, for example, who told me that they had voted for the Christian Democrats on 18 March, but that they would certainly not do that again. They made it sound as if they voted in favor of beginning the process of unification, simply because that was the only path that still seemed viable. This is what I would like to ask you: it seems as if politically active intellectuals are very frustrated now, perhaps understandably so, because everything evolved differently from what anybody had envisioned. On the other hand, there were a vast majority of people who, by 18 March 1990, no longer saw much of an alternative, and who also strongly perceived a huge gap between themselves and oppositional intellectuals. They did not know who the activists in the opposition really were and what they really wanted. Some expressed fears in conversations with me that they did not want to be part of yet another experiment conducted on their backs again. What is your opinion about all this?

I simply have to say that the kind of pressure that existed in Czechoslovakia with Charter 77, or in Poland with Solidarność, never existed in the GDR. There were many reasons for this difference, including the failures of the Western left, which somehow had a desire to hold on to their illusions that "there is socialism in the GDR." There were very few people from the West European left . . . who had any contact with us over the years. The few contacts we had were merely personal. . . .

In this sense, what is happening in the GDR at the moment is not just because of the failure of "the people" or the failure of "the opposition," but rather is a failure that results from a particular kind of thinking, a "thinking in blocs," a thinking that conceptualized the two Germanies as belonging to two different camps. The Greens or the left in the West were caught in this thinking as much as we were. And, of course, this bloc thinking was strongest close to the Wall.

Could you describe a little how your own thinking developed over the years? When did you begin to realize that something drastic would have to happen, and how did your own ideas and expectations develop as to what was possible and what should be done?

The half year I involuntarily spent in the West [in Great Britain] was extremely important to me.

The premise of oppositionists in the GDR had always been: "We want reforms. We want to reform the existing society. We are not really an opposition." To be an "oppositionist" carried a very negative connotation; one was never supposed to be "oppositional." What most people said was "we just want to reform things, change things for the better" . . .

. . . You mean a "better socialism"?

Yes, exactly right, a better socialism. And I realized while staying in the West that we had to accept being in the opposition, that opposition is an integral part of a normally functioning society, and that a political opposition plays an important democratic role. . . .

I also believed that if we really wanted to be an opposition and really wanted to play a role at all, we needed to get out of the church. Over time I had come to understand the function of the church as an "extended arm" of the state, both in general and in terms of how they responded to me. They were softer, somehow, but that didn't change their basic function.

Besides, it increasingly dawned on me that the GDR was really an atheistic society, so something could have a substantial impact only if it came from outside the church.

Furthermore, it became increasingly obvious that it worried people if the same small group of oppositionists appeared on the scene time and again—which is, by the way, one of the incentives behind founding New Forum. We had to organize something that would show very clearly that people from all walks of life were participating and cooperating. We needed more people, different people, different concepts and ideas, and we had to be more open toward the rest of society. In 1989 the pressure everywhere got more and more intense. . . .

Because of my contact to Rolf Henrich [a lawyer and well-known dissident who was expelled from the party], the question came up as to whether we could not give this whole thing a legal framework that could provide some security for people by not initiating something "hostile to the state." . . .

Rolf came up with this idea about a "political alliance" because there was a law in the books theoretically allowing such alliances. The basic question had been: "Are we founding a party or an alliance?" And since my opinion had always been that we should try to form a civic movement, and not a party, and since there was no law in the GDR allowing for the formation of parties, we decided to form an oppositional alliance. We figured that would be less of a threat to the state. . . .

Fortunately or unfortunately—well, perhaps I should really say unfortunately—the founding document of New Forum appeared in public at the very same time the pressure was just incredibly high. If we had done this a year or so earlier, things would have developed very differently. It had been my expectation—and I remember having a bet about this with a friend in the West who thought I had just gone crazy—that we could have about 10,000 members at the end of the year [1989].

We simply had not anticipated at all that the whole thing would suddenly explode like it did [within four weeks New Forum had received more than 200,000 signatures].

This, of course, is also a pretty clear indication of how distant and alienated we actually were from the real problems people had.

I would like to return to this question of "distance" once more. But before I do that, let me quickly see whether I am understanding you correctly: between your departure for Great Britain and the founding of New Forum, about one year passed, and, except for the Initiative for Peace and Human Rights and the Women for Peace, no other organizations existed outside the church. So is it correct to say that your ideas concerning the need for an independent political organization originated, one from your agonizing organizing experiences in East Germany, and two from your exposure to a Western political culture?

Yes.

And then you were saying that you had always perceived the role of the church, as you had experienced it, as a corset . . .

Yes, but not only toward me. I think that the church was above all a regulating corset for the groups, at least in most cases. What I mean to say is that the church did not support or foster the emancipatory processes of the groups. They did not irrefutably stand behind the groups . . .

. . . You mean the church as an institution?

Yes, as an institution.

What about all those within the church who showed a great deal of solidarity?

Well, there were those. But, you see, no Protestant pastor had been arrested since 1982, for instance. If they ever took one along by accident, they immediately released him afterward. I think this is a clear indication that they did not consistently stand behind oppositional groups and their efforts.

But wasn't that a mutual problem? After all, many oppositionists consciously sought the protection of the church, because, understandably, the church provided some security for their work.

Well, yes. Of course, I am not talking about the whole church being arrested. But it really would have been a very positive signal if one pastor or another would also have been arrested on certain occasions, as when they jailed a number of conscientious objectors.

Could you give me some examples of people you were dealing with inside the church? Pastor Bohley in Magdeburg, I guess, is your brother-in-law. Or pastor Tschiche, whom you invited to the New Forum founding meeting . . .

. . . Well, Tschiche is someone who has always had problems with the church as well. It is true that these people inside the church who realized the problems I was talking about earlier also had severe difficulties, since they stood right in the middle between the groups and the church leadership. But I am really talking about the church as an institution, and not about a few exceptional pastors.

OK. Let us talk about the founding process of New Forum. I just recently had a group interview in Erfurt with Harald Wagner and Frank Eigenfeld. I still don't quite understand why New Forum was founded, why at that particular point in time, and with those particular 30 people who were invited to the founding meeting. Harald Wagner, for example, clearly accused you, and let me just quote him here, of having "broken your word" because there had been clear prior agreements that all the activists should be informed and included before anybody founded an organization. He also said that it was largely because of this betrayal that so many groups were founded later on, that is, that the opposition was not united. [see Part II, chapter 4, pp. 229–36.]

I continue to wonder how people can say things like that. I just don't understand. [long pause]

You and Katja Havemann invited people to this founding meeting of New Forum, is that correct?

Yes. There was no prior agreement about that. We invited those people, and most of the ones we invited did not even know each other. There was no agreement, with anybody.

I don't quite understand. Hadn't there been prior discussions among active oppositionists as to how to proceed and what to do?

No, these discussions had not taken place. That's why I really don't understand why people continue to claim the opposite. You see, Rainer Eppelmann approached me once and was talking about this thing he wanted to found. I neither responded negatively nor positively, but just told him that we had already made plans along the same lines, because we all agreed that something like an organized opposition needed to be formed. And then Mr. Neubert, later also a founding member of Democracy Now, talked to me and told me about the possible founding members they had for their project. And I replied, "No, I will not be a part of that. I will not cooperate with Schnur anymore, nor do I want to work together with Eppelmann." Those two were people whom I simply could no longer trust.

So therefore I told Neubert that I would not participate, and there were no more discussions with me on this topic. In other words, he received a clearly negative response from me concerning the Democratic Awakening project. You have to understand that it had become quite obvious to me over the years that it was completely absurd for us always to say that we were open for everyone to participate, knowing full well that such groups were infested with informants from the security police. . . . Always to act as if we all liked each other and there were no problems in such a context— well, I just realized that nothing positive would ever develop if we continued like that. You can only initiate a political group with people you can trust, or with people who at least give you reason to believe that they are trustworthy. And, of course, Wolfgang Schnur certainly did not belong in either of these two categories. Eppelmann had already mentioned a year earlier that he thought Schnur was working for the security police [it was revealed in March of 1990 that Schnur had actually been a Stasi informant]. It was just beyond my grasp how anyone could then start a project like that with Schnur.

But aside from Eppelmann and Schnur, why not include people like the later members of Democracy Now? Here, we have a number of people who had political ideas very similar to yours, people who had certainly not been working for the Stasi, people who could thus have been integrated in your New Forum project. Why didn't you do that?

Well, I just have to say that our starting point was very different. Our project was based on the premise that we wanted to do something that would really work, not something that would be bogged down for weeks or months with programmatic discussions.

You know, we sat down this one weekend, all 30 of us, and we collectively wrote this founding document. That is how it got started. These 30 people had a discussion beforehand, but they had not known each other prior to this meeting; at least nobody had known all 30.

Well, obviously you knew all 30, otherwise you could not have invited them . . .

. . . Yes, I did, but I was the only one.

So you more or less created the list of people who got invited?

Yes, I did. But this list was not put together according to who had already been active in the peace movement for the last ten years or so. Rather, my idea had been that we should have people from all over the GDR, from every state, with various kinds of professional backgrounds and various ages, as well as people who had already been active and people who had not yet been very active in any kind of oppositional activities. So, for example, we had Rolf Henrich who had been thrown out of the party because of his book, and on the other hand we invited professor Jens Reich who had never been in any trouble with the party. In this sense, it was a closed project—it was not a discussion process. It was more of a conversation with people who all thought that we should try something like that, try something concrete.

But hadn't you planned to go public with this project immediately?

That's what we did, one day later . . .

. . . I know you did. But had that been your initial plan?

Yes.

I am getting a bit confused. Both Harald Wagner and Frank Eigenfeld, among others, have told me that it was pretty much agreed upon among all the activists that you should hold off on such a move until after the fortieth anniversary?

That may have been true for Democracy Now or for Democratic Awakening; that I do not know. You see, Harald Wagner, for example, did not know anything about our project. Only the 30 people who had been invited knew about it.

So you had never debated the question of whether it might be better to wait until after the fortieth anniversary?

No. But I guess they had debated that question. The thing that Eppelmann had planned with Democratic Awakening . . . here we had seven parsons—you simply have to see it that way—who wanted to have me and Rolf Henrich in there as some kind of token gesture. I said very clearly at the time that I thought it was utterly absurd to found a thing like that.

First, they claimed they were initiating something outside the church, and then all they had were seven parsons leading it. None of them were really risking anything. The only ones who would have risked something would have been Rolf and I. And then to start something with people I cannot trust . . .

. . . Schnur?

Yes, and Eppelmann. That would have been really absurd.

Why Eppelmann, by the way?

Because he is much too vain.

But not because you thought he had worked for the Stasi as well?

No. It was because Eppelmann just had to nurse his neurosis concerning his public profile that I was not willing to found Democratic Awakening with him. What kinds of prior agreements he had with others I do not know, because I had never participated in any such discussions. . . .

Why, do you think, did New Forum and Democracy Now not immediately form some kind of alliance with one another? Did that have anything to do with different political ideas?

Well, no. What played a role in all of this was the sensitivity of the other groups. Since some of them had fiddled around in the opposition for years, I guess they simply had to quickly found their own groups. Basically, we were the first ones, and they could just have said, "OK, we are going to participate." But they did not do that.

And then our basic concepts were different as well. Democracy Now clearly stated in its platform that you could not be a member of another party as well. Our starting point was the exact opposite; we encouraged people to join, even if they were members of another party, because we wanted to be a civic movement that would transcend parties.

I know this from my experiences in the peace movement: if we had discussed these issues in great detail, it would have taken years, the Stasi would have known about it, and nothing would have ever come out of it. I simply did not feel like doing this any longer.

Did you consider it to be a problem that the opposition was split up in three or four different major groups?

For me this whole issue did not begin to turn into a serious problem until the elections for the Volkskammer [the People's Assembly]. That's when it turned into a problem. It actually had a lot to do with me. I just thought that out of this common history too much . . . well, let me see how I can say this. I thought we had to carry them along with us—those other groups, you understand. The main problem was that we created this alliance; this was really a big mistake . . .

. . . I don't understand. You mean the fact that you did create an alliance was a problem? Why?

Yes. New Forum should have stayed by itself. . . . I had never perceived the very existence of all these different opposition groups as some kind of problem. They had all contributed to the breaking apart of this monolithic bloc that had existed before. I had believed all along that we needed pluralism, and therefore we needed a lot of different groups and parties. So I did not consider the existence of various groups and parties to be a limitation or restriction. And, also, the oppositional groups *did* work together at the Central Round Table, whether the members were representatives of Democracy Now, the Initiative for Peace and Human Rights, New Forum, or the Greens. In some cases we even worked together with the PDS, or with the Social Democrats, or even with the Christian Democrats.

After all, everyone who was participating in this round table was interested in finding solutions to the problems at hand. And to some extent that worked pretty well. . . .

What if we looked at that from the perspective of the vast majority of the population. Wasn't it very confusing to be confronted with all these different small groups about which hardly anybody knew anything? I received the clear impression from talking to people across the country that it would have vastly increased the chances of the opposition, at least in the elections, if they had all been part of one and the same group. It must have been very difficult to find out, much less understand, where all these groups were standing.

Yes, I guess that's true.

Had this been a topic of discussions in your group at all?

Well, you see, we had been such a large group, we could not possibly think about issues like that. Within four weeks we received more than 200,000 support signatures, our telephones were ringing constantly . . . I just think that groups like the Initiative for Peace and Human Rights, with their fifty members, or Democracy Now, could have simply joined New Forum. Why not? It wasn't our problem that they did not decide to do that.

And I just have to say that if there was anyone who could have taken power at some point in October or November, it would have been New

Forum. For the other groups it would have been hopelessly ridiculous even to pose the question of "taking power." That was just not within their reach. The real question for them would have been why they had insisted on standing side by side with New Forum, as presumably equal partners, instead of saying "we are going together" with New Forum. . . . Most other groups were nothing but little debating circles, and it would have taken forever for anything to come out of them. . . .

Let me shift the focus a little at this point. It has been my understanding that you were more or less appalled by the fact that the Wall was opened on 9 November 1989, is that correct?

Yes, that's right.

Could you explain to me why?

It was really obvious to me right away that everything would happen exactly the way it actually did; there was not the slightest doubt in my mind about that.

You see, none of the groups, not even New Forum with its 200,000 people, had yet actually entered a real process of communication with the population. All these groups came into being in an explosion-like fashion, and they only emerged in "opposition to something." But what they wanted in its stead was really never debated.

Some civic initiatives, or some small groups like Democracy Now, were beginning to articulate what they wanted, because they consisted of people who had known each other for years. But a group like New Forum was really just a gathering of people at this point, we never even got to discuss any of these issues. We were busy trying to respond to the events happening around us all the time.

So your initial expectation at the time you started this project was that things would not change that quickly, but rather that you would have a lot more time for discussing issues and to getting beyond the "against something" to the "for something?"

We had discussed some of the things we all perceived as problems, and we wrote these down as topics of further discussion.

Democracy Now, on the other hand, had already made explicit statements as to where they wanted things to move. For us, the main point was to initiate a discussion process within the population. We did not want 30 people or so to stand up and to tell the population in which direction things should develop, or what should be done next.

Let me give you an example. It's quite clear that one cannot simply state that one does not want an expansion of individual traffic [as Democracy Now stated in their platform] in a society in which everybody was dreaming about owning a Trabant [the smallest and most affordable among the few and extremely hard-to-get cars in East Germany].

We thought that we should first outline the problems in order to get a popular discussion process going. After all, there had never been any broad-scale popular discussions on any issues in the history of the GDR. . . .

After you had received your official recognition as New Forum, did you try to establish contacts with members of the Socialist Unity Party?

Well, you see, a lot of members of the SED were in New Forum. We had a lot of party members coming to us because they had great problems with the party leadership. Those were also people who did not think that the GDR would collapse in this situation, but rather that it would break open, and then change. They did not resign from the party and become members of New Forum. Rather, they joined New Forum as critical members of the SED.

Did these people expect the SED to open the Wall, or, for that matter, did they anticipate that everything would collapse like a house of cards?

No, no one, absolutely no one had expected any of that. . . .

What about the time after 9 November? You said it was completely obvious what would happen . . .

. . . Right . . .

. . . *Yet you did participate in the political processes afterward. Didn't you have any hopes that things could conceivably develop somewhat differently, and if so, where did you see any chances or openings for that?*

One thing was absolutely clear: namely, that an incredible amount of work had to be done in all sorts of different areas. . . .

You see, capitalism is just a very alien world to us. We had heard about it in school, but we had never practically experienced it. I had experienced it a little in the half year I had lived in England, but I still knew nothing about the practical sides of capitalism. I had more or less watched it, and I had my questions about it. The ultimate question for us was: "Is corporate capital really so ravenous that it will only swallow up things, or are there people within the capitalist system who have realized that things cannot go on like that, that we cannot grow infinitely, that we have to think of fundamentally different ways to organize society if we take into consideration the environment, the Third World, and other problems like that?"

Well, soon thereafter we were forced to realize that they are, in fact, as ravenous as they had always been portrayed to us during our history lessons—that is, *at least* as much, probably even more so.

So this whole process of going capitalist was something I wanted to have a voice in. I had hoped that there were some entrepreneurs who under-stood that it could simply not go on like that, and that they would think this is a country in which we could develop something entirely new. But, unfortunately, this is not what happened. Entrepreneurs, I have dis-covered, are just too ravenous. It is as simple as that—or, if you prefer, as complex as that. In any case, it did not happen, or come close to happen-ing.

So you had already given up the vision of a different but independent GDR immediately following 9 November?

There were still numerous possibilities right after 9 November, like creating a confederation between the GDR and the Federal Republic of Germany, or having a fixed exchange rate between the two countries—all those things were still possible.

I was just wondering because you had said that it was completely obvious how things would turn out.

Well, in fact, I think it was—particularly because we—that is, the people of the GDR—never really entered a sustained discussion process about possible alternatives. We had never talked at length among our-selves about "something entirely new." And there you are.

■ SEBASTIAN PFLUGBEIL, physicist, leading environmentalist, and nationally prominent opposition spokesman.[37] ■ *"To the government, every citizen was—in case there was any doubt—'guilty by suspicion.' . . . We thought it would take many years to fight for fundamental change. . . . Change began to take place because people began to act as if they were free to act. . . . That had an amazingly contagious effect. . . . We sort of revolted along, which was perhaps one of our biggest mistakes."*

In contrast to the reasoning articulated by fellow oppositionists like Frank Eigenfeld or Rainer Eppelmann, by religious reformers like Klaus Kaden, or party reformers like Werner Bramke, Sebastian Pflugbeil explains in the following pages why opposition activists like himself believed that a very realistic alternative to the annexation of East Germany by West Germany did, in fact, exist. His explanation as to why such political alternatives were never pursued in earnest merits close attention, I be-lieve, for it is not only indicative of the problems currently haunting the citizens of every East-Central European country, but the alternatives he

37. For background information on Pflugbeil, see Part I, chapter 3, pp. 160–65.

discusses also clearly transcend the kinds of narrow political debates currently being fought out within the recovered "political normalcy" of the new united Germany.

■ *Can you summarize broadly how and why you think the many disparate grass-roots groups you have been telling me about coalesced into what appeared to be a large-scale civic movement in the Fall of 1989?*

Well, the big problems of the previous few years had been quite obvious to everyone. Every normal human being saw those problems. And people who met in their kitchens, in the church, at their workplace, or wherever, and started to talk about those problems, at some point came to the conclusion that they had the same enemy. Of course, that produced a large and rather pleasant unanimity among all the oppositional groups, a unanimity, however, that merely derived from a clearly identifiable opponent.

Exactly how and why this broad dissatisfaction began to surge ahead in the Fall of 1989 we do not know. It is clear, however, that a number of factors contributed to the decision by many people that it was "time to act," that we could no longer simply stand on the sidelines and observe the whole process, but, instead, that we had to get actively involved.

There were a lot of catalysts for people to come to this conclusion: we had no reform-minded party politician like Gorbachev in the GDR; there was this whole election fraud in May of 1989; there were the political changes in Hungary that led to the opening of its border with Austria; there was a clear decline in economic performance; there was an obvious inability to act or respond to all these problems within the government— the leadership was, among other things, just too old; it was way past the time in which the leadership should have been replaced; then there was the spectacle of Politburo member [and later general secretary] Egon Krenz congratulating the Chinese for the Tiananmen Square repression; and then, of course, the huge wave of people fleeing the country through Hungary and Czechoslovakia. All these combined factors resulted in people saying "enough is enough." Somehow things started to happen; no one knew exactly how. And the population understood that there was a real chance to move things. People understood that very quickly after it began.

In fact, it happened much faster than the organized opposition had expected. We had thought that it would take many years to fight for fundamental change. The speed of subsequent events was much too fast for us. It was simply overwhelming. Developments far exceeded our abilities to cope.

*When you are saying "we," you are referring to the few nationwide opposi-
tional groups that were founded in the Fall?*

Yes. All these groups were founded almost at the same time. It was pure
coincidence that New Forum was the first one—the others followed soon
thereafter.

*Could you describe from your perspective how you came to be a member of New
Forum, and not one of the other groups?*

That was also more or less coincidental. Bärbel Bohley and a few
friends of hers had, for a number of months, tried to figure out exactly who
would be available for and helpful to a possible project founding a national
group that would approach the fundamental question of "where to go
from here." So they had drawn up a list of people whom they invited to
Katja Havemann's house. I was asked to participate as the expert on
questions concerning energy in general, and nuclear energy in particular. . . .

Most of the participants had not previously known each other. On the
very same weekend, we drafted a paper about where we thought we stood
and what we thought should happen next. That was the paper which
was subsequently made public and which got such a stunning reception
among the population.[38]

People began to inquire about who we were and what we wanted to do.
They began to copy our founding statement at home, in the factory, or
wherever else they could, and began to disseminate it on their own. We
had not at all anticipated such an overwhelmingly positive response. This
in turn pushed things ahead quite a bit. People everywhere began to
meet—all over the GDR. Virtually everyone began to think about further
steps that one could possibly take. A lot of people tried to join us and
participate in whatever needed to be done.

*If you had to describe what ideas this initial group of founding members of New
Forum had in terms of what should be done, what would you say?*

The central thought was that we should, first of all, try to push for the
full practical realization of all the rights every citizen already enjoyed
according to our constitution. It is important to understand that theoretically we enjoyed all basic rights, but on the other hand we had a politicized criminal law which in reality had annulled all such rights. The
situation was so absurd that no citizen who got up in the morning could be
sure that he or she would not overstep the narrow boundaries of some of
these political criminal laws during the course of the following day. To the

38. Parts of this document are reproduced in the epilogue, p. 383–84.

government, every citizen was—in case there was any doubt—"guilty by suspicion," and thus not able to move around freely at all. So that is what we wanted to change first of all. We had hoped that if we succeeded in that, we could perhaps at some point achieve the right of free expression and free assembly, so that we could finally speak out freely, meet with one another, publish things, so that we would no longer have to be scared all the time about speaking up. We also thought that this, in and of itself, would suffice to destroy the multitude of political taboos that existed at the time.

What we tried to do, basically, was to act as if these rights already existed, and thus we went ahead publicly saying what we thought and what we wanted. To our utter surprise, that had an amazingly contagious effect. A lot of people very quickly began to do the same thing. In effect, what happened was exactly what we had hoped for, except that it happened much more quickly than we had anticipated, or even imagined, in our wildest dreams.

Change began to take place because people began to act as if they were free to act. At first, there was an immense buildup of tension toward the government, but then everything became very exciting.

Could you give me some examples for concrete actions which directly resulted from the founding of New Forum and the initial phase following its founding?

Very simple. The very fact that the first huge demonstrations took place, for instance. Or the fact that so many people began to get organized in one way or another. Within a few days, New Forum began to appear as a group in virtually every city in the GDR. Throughout the country, people began to set up these New Forum contact addresses. People began to meet there even though this was still a time in which the Interior Minister of the GDR had declared New Forum as "hostile to state and constitution." You have to keep in mind what this meant: everyone who either participated or associated with such an organization faced twelve to fifteen years in prison. And yet hundreds of thousands of people contacted us and signed up, despite such dangers. The churches were fuller than they had been since the times of the Reformation. Everywhere, even in small towns, an incredible number of people came to the churches in order to hear representatives of New Forum speak.

We really had stunning experiences with the population—like when one of the thousands of people who regularly attended such meetings suddenly stood up and gave a fiery speech, covering all of the relevant political points of this time. I am talking about people who understood precisely what the problems were, and who were very sophisticated in talking about them. We had simply not expected anything like that. We were extremely surprised to discover this potential within the population. In fact, we probably got a little intoxicated by these dynamics. I am afraid we began to perceive the situation in much more favorable terms than was realistic.

Could you be a little more specific when you say people understood exactly what the problems were and what should be done next? What exactly were the problems, and what was it that should have been done?

Well, one issue, for example, was to secure basic human rights, to abolish the ties between party and state, and to destroy the Stasi. People raised questions that ran the gamut from basic economic issues to the organization of the educational system. They mostly articulated these problems in a very sophisticated fashion, very much to the point. They did it without any preparation. Even their rhetoric was good most of the time. We were not just very surprised by that; we were also euphoric about it.

But this phase only lasted for a short time, a very exciting time during which we went through some very critical conflicts. Today, we know that we barely escaped being thrown into internment camps. We learned that from the documents we obtained later from the Stasi, after it was disbanded. They had set up internment camps for people like us, and they had very detailed plans as how to arrest us, how to get us into those camps, and so forth. They had very elaborate lists of all of us—who we were, what we did, or in what specific ways we had been active in the opposition. They even had these extremely detailed fascist plans concerning what we would be allowed to take along after we had been arrested, such as a book, a pair of underwear, one toothbrush, and so on. You can imagine the very cold feet we got when we learned about all these plans. At the time, we did not know about such plans, but we had clearly noticed that the tensions between state and opposition had reached the breaking point.

During all these church meetings, for example, the surrounding territory was always covered with Stasi plainclothesmen. The Stasi followed me around for 24 hours a day during these weeks. This was not only very unpleasant, it was downright eerie. Many of us were also arrested and interrogated for a few days, and so on. They never arrested me, though. But I now know that they had bugged my apartment for many months.

So despite this general situation of fear and intimidation, New Forum found widespread support across all sections of the population, from plain workers all the way to the intelligentsia. A lot of Protestant pastors also got involved, if for no other reason than that the only places where we could meet continued to be the churches. So they got involved automatically.

They were also the ones who were best-trained in speaking publicly, and thus they were, in many cases, quickly elected as the spokespersons of such groups. Yes, it was a very interesting time, indeed.

Before we go past this point, let me ask you to try to draw a comparison with what happened in other Eastern European countries. Two things I noticed: first, whether one looks in Hungary, Poland, or Czechoslovakia, one finds that party reformers and nonparty dissidents always had some degree of contact with one another. I have not found much evidence of any such contacts in the GDR. Secondly, the big difference between the opposition in the GDR and a movement such as Solidarność was that very little seemed to have come out of the factories here . . .

. . . Yes, that was beyond a doubt true, even though I am not sure why that was. What was unique about the GDR, perhaps, was that we had not experienced any open debate of political questions after 1933. In other words, even the generation of our parents, and sometimes even the generation of our grandparents, had grown up and had lived with the tremendous fear of speaking up. They had simply been scared all their lives. In effect, we had been molded into an oppressive state of existence for a much longer period of time than the Poles, for example.

Two other major differences between here and Poland were, first, that the Catholic church played a significant role in the formation of an opposition in Poland, and, secondly, the Poles managed to build an independent union. I have difficulties explaining why no such efforts were ever made in the GDR.

But I think the reason why very little dissent ever found any articulation within the party itself might have something to do with our Nazi past, with this particular kind of German perfectionism with which "our socialism" was built. Based on the Stasi and their entire apparatus, the party literally succeeded in penetrating every corner of this society. Nowhere else, not even in the Soviet Union, was this done as thoroughly, was this done with the kind of perfection that was carried through in the GDR.

All of this, of course, had tremendous ramifications in terms of how much someone could politically articulate one's self, like at one's job, for example.

I don't quite understand yet. If we just take the example of the party. It seems to me that there were quite a few members who were, at least potentially, open to hearing criticism and who were themselves in favor of change or reform. But somehow no one ever tried to establish connections with those people . . .

. . . It wasn't quite that simple. In my opinion, the barriers were set up by the party and its members, and not by us. We were absolutely willing to negotiate or talk, but it was always the party which blocked any such attempts. The kinds of people who were in the party and who at least had vaguely similar ideas about what the problems were, and what should be done about them, and who still remained in the party—I could count those people on the fingers of one hand. The overwhelming majority of people who joined the party, on the other hand, did so in order to gain some personal advantage. Any attempt to get into the party with the goal of changing it would have had absolutely no chance. It was never an option for any of us.

But even those few people inside the party who might actually have been interested in change really couldn't have done much. Until the very end the party discipline was so harsh, and the possible repercussions for anyone not conforming so severe, that being a dissenter within the party must have been outstandingly difficult. I know this from party colleagues at work, people whom one could talk to, people who were relatively independent. But even they never had the courage to do anything against the "party line." They might have complained about the same things we were complaining about, but they never would have dared to raise such issues at their party meetings. Exceptions to that virtually never comprised more than a handful of people.

And you think this kind of party discipline was considerably more severe in the GDR than in Poland or Hungary?

Oh yes, it was both much more dogmatic and more rigid. You have to understand that we were the frontline state toward the West. And we did not have any oppositional past . . .

. . . You had the large-scale worker's uprising of 17 June 1953?

That was too long ago and, above all, something very different from the Prague Spring or Solidarność. It did not even come close to an organized movement. . . .

I interrupted you in your chronological description. You had told me about the beginnings of New Forum. Could you tell me how things developed in October, which, as I understand it, was a very decisive month for the opposition, the month in which the change from repression to publicly permissible opposition took place?

It is important to note that no one was directing the course of events. Also, things happened much faster and on a scale much larger than anyone had expected. Why exactly the Stasi and the police folded the way they did is not quite clear to this very day. . . . No one was prepared for this. We possessed neither a theoretical nor a practical substitute for the old system.

The old system—which had already been rather shaky, as we now know—was simply pushed a little at the right place and the right time, and then collapsed like a house of cards. Since this came very unexpectedly, there was no one who could have immediately put a workable alternative in its place.

Throughout October we basically tried to pursue what we had already started. To some extent we were pushed forward by all those people who suddenly assembled in the churches and streets. We were also suddenly forced into some kind of leadership position by that. Few of our activities were very goal-oriented. We sort of revolted along, which was perhaps one of our biggest mistakes. The reason behind this was simply not to lose the momentum of the movement.

Of course, "step one" of most successful revolutions in the past has been to destroy the old state apparatus. We, on the other hand, had a peaceful revolution in which we abstained from destroying anything, for good reasons. But the price we had to pay for that was that the old apparatus, the old mafia, could continue doing its thing for several more months, and without much interference. We allowed them, if you will, a very orderly retreat.

The result is that today the majority of those primarily responsible for some of the most abominable actions, the very people who were largely responsible for the terrible conditions we currently find ourselves in, got off scot-free. As we speak [in the summer of 1990, shortly before unification] we are already a long way from any possibility that some of these people will ever be held accountable.

Some of the very same people under whom we have suffered a great deal, for a very long time, are now holding positions in the Treuhand-gesellschaft [a trust committee controlling the distribution of capital for the economic recovery of East Germany] or on the board of directors of some big corporations. The same people are back on the top again. Perhaps even worse, many ex-Stasi agents are once again working for the interior ministry, the only difference being that they now work for a different boss. We were the ones who succeeded in dissolving the Stasi, but today the old Stasi archivists are again handling, without interference, the material gathered about us, while the citizens' committees are standing outside and cannot get in.

I just wanted to give you a few examples which clearly indicate to us that we should have pursued this revolution much more decisively, with much more force.

Let's see if we can be a bit more concrete. You came together with Berlin district party secretary Günter Schabowski on 26 October for a public panel discussion organized by the opposition. What was the purpose behind this panel discussion? Could it be interpreted as your acceptance of the one-party state, except that you wanted to make clear that they would have to deal with some kind of organized opposition from now on?

We had demanded fundamental reforms for a long time. But we had always tried to phrase such demands in a way that would make it clear that we stood behind the principles of the existing constitution. We thought it was necessary to create some kind of mutual basis for conversations and controversial debates. And we felt that the constitution could very well be used for such an endeavor.

Basic democratic rights were all guaranteed by the constitution, something we thought was important and useful to point out. Our initial goal had *not* been to bring down this state. In fact, at first that had not been our intention at all. In the beginning, we were very hesitant to launch a full attack against the party.

But, of course, the "leading role of the party" was just as much part of the constitution. We had deliberated for a long time whether right from the start we should call into question the basic pillar of the party's power, the "leading role." Many of us—and I was among them—had argued that we should first fight for a full guarantee of basic human and democratic rights, because that would eventually lead to an inevitable self-dissolution of the phrase "leading role of the party." The reason I had initially shied away from touching this issue had to do with my fear of a very likely irrational reaction on the part of the party.

One could say in general that we had always been very careful. Perhaps we followed existing laws too much for too long. We did not want to break any laws, but, on the contrary, wanted those laws abolished which were in clear conflict with our constitution. That was our main and most decisive demand. In other words, we attempted to take off slowly.

But then it became clear very quickly that we could take the whole struggle to a much higher plateau, that the population was willing to go much farther. In fact, it turned out that it was simply not possible to take such small steps, one at a time. As a result, events simply overtook us on numerous occasions, because things were moving ahead much faster than we had anticipated.

What do you mean by that? The fall of Honecker, the opening of the Wall?

Yes, for example. You see, of course we had been strongly opposed to the Wall for all these years. Yet neither the Wall nor the question of unification were part of our agenda, or part of our debates, at the time. What was important to us was to get out from under the total political domination of the party. We wanted finally to get the chance to participate in directing the future course of the GDR. We basically wanted to have independent political rights. We wanted to become citizens who would fully share political responsibilities. We certainly did not want Western conditions here. Unification had not been an issue at all among any of the opposition activists, whatever else their differences may have been.

What we really wanted is to become independent, as a country of free citizens. The opening of the Wall and the subsequent whining for the West German Mark thus came as a severe blow to our first careful deliberations as to how to build a sensible society.

Again, with "we" you are referring to the leading people within New Forum, Democracy Now, Democratic Awakening, and so on?

Yes, that's correct.

Many people considered some kind of "third way" as completely unrealistic . . . ?

. . . Whether this would have been workable or not is impossible to say. It is true that it was made impossible by the situation following the opening of the Wall, but that does not mean that it was not possible in general.

One argument was that the economic situation turned out to be much worse than what anyone had expected, and that therefore any political effort without the help of West Germany was doomed to fail.

Yes, but this line of reasoning is much too simplistic. You see, the current conditions represent something no one had expected as well, certainly not among those currently in power in the Federal Republic. We had already predicted in November of 1989 many of the problems we are currently facing. We are not at all happy about what is now taking place in the GDR. For very good reasons we are greatly worried that the GDR is going to see a very stormy winter.

Above all, and I think one can particularly argue this from hindsight, it was absolutely possible for new people in leadership positions in the GDR to be much tougher bargaining partners with the Federal Republic. There was no question that we would run into severe problems surviving without any help from the outside. But what is taking place now represents the most profitable bargain the Federal Republic has ever entered, while the current government of the GDR acts as if we are nothing but the biggest beggars history has ever seen.

I am, in short, absolutely certain that we were in a good position to negotiate about conditions, and to think about who to strike a deal with. We could have avoided many of the negative aspects of the Federal Republic, if only we had shown the necessary political will.

Could you give me an example of such "negative aspects"?

Well, one very obvious example is individual transportation, the expansion of the infrastructure for automobiles at the expense of public transportation. There is no question whatsoever that we had the option to solve this problem differently. But we did not choose to do that. Now our cities are beginning to get more polluted than ever, and the death toll on our streets has already risen by 80 percent. We are basically replicating all the errors made in the West over the last three decades.

Or if you look at what is now happening to our department stores, or what is happening in terms of a national energy policy. One can find examples in virtually every sphere of life. We had made sensible and realistic proposals concerning the reorganization of a very wide range of issues. But no one listened to us any longer. We even had people in the Federal Republic who were quite interested in investing their money in new, alternative forms and structures of organization, whether concerning environmentally safe ways of providing energy, alternative products, public transportation, or what have you. In fact, in many areas we could have become a model, simply because we were pretty much starting at zero again. We had the best chances to begin something completely new.

You see, even though many West Germans realize that there are very realistic opportunities for developments far in advance of what they currently have, in the Federal Republic these developments have never taken place because of the need to maintain existing structures, such as the existing strong monopolies. In the GDR, however, all of these structures were completely demolished, thus we could really have started anew at a very high level. That's precisely the chance we missed, a chance we might never get again.

A common argument in the West has been that these ideas are the kinds of typical visions of a few intellectual dreamers, and that they in no way represented the wishes of the people. This argument continues that people were in fact fed up with bad working conditions, a bad infrastructure, bad cars, bad roads, and so forth, and that they saw no alternative to the West in order to improve these conditions.

Well, yes, except that no one knows what that means. Above all, the "West" does not equal the West. The West also means, for instance, that there will now be millions of unemployed, something we did not have before. The West also means that our next national energy policy will be dictated by a few big Western energy concerns. But all of this is not "Western" per se, because in the West there are also many people who see these problems, and there are also other structures available. In other words, one could have selectively learned and adopted a lot of different things from the West, without necessarily swallowing up everything in such a wholesale fashion. All we actually ended up doing was to opt for the largest bags of money.

What I am saying is that we would have succeeded as well in finding investors and supporters if we had created a different system. In fact, with smaller investors we probably would have achieved a much better bargain. But that's not what we did. Just look, for instance, how the very same people in the energy sector who are responsible for the pollution and devastation in the GDR are now negotiating with West German energy concerns about future cooperation—thereby securing their own personal interests. Things like that generate a lot of anger. We are, in effect, experiencing a more or less smooth transition with a lot of the same people. We have never been able to get these people.

I understand, and this is very helpful. But the question I had asked was actually going in a slightly different direction. Wasn't there a rather huge gap of alienation between the opposition intellectuals and the vast majority of the population? Exactly what the vast majority of people really wanted is still unclear, because no one ever made a sustained effort to find out. All that has been done up to now has been to interpret symbolic politics, such as what people voted for, or whether they wave German flags. Could it not be that the main problem was that the majority of people simply did not see a realistic alternative?

Yes, I guess that's possible.

On the one hand, they were constantly being told how terrible things actually looked in the GDR, and, on the other hand, West Germany seemed all too willing to come in and take over things. Thus, their impression might have been that the GDR is not much more than a completely bankrupt enterprise, and that the best thing that could happen, whether one liked it or not, was to be taken over by the wealthy brother in the West?

Well, yes, that is a rather accurate description. What was, above all, fatal in this situation was that things happened so quickly, that we never had sufficient time to think about all these questions. . . . No one had any convincing concept in their pocket as to what to do next. And, of course, no one could generate such a concept in a matter of a few weeks.

The other fatal factor was that, as the election campaign took off, the big West German parties forced themselves into this political no-man's-land. With their huge political machines, they effectively killed all attempts in the GDR to articulate independent political ideas and to build independent political structures. Of course, they tried to convey the message that the West, or Kohl, offered the only possible solution. It did not require all that many political skills to sell such a message to a people who had absolutely no experience with this kind of political campaign. Yet it was all empty phraseology. We considered this to be an extremely unfair and self-interested move on their part.

I think this largely accounts for why people in the GDR subsequently appeared to be screaming so loudly for bananas. There is no question that we could have had a much more differentiated campaign had the West German Christian Democrats and Social Democrats not decided to fight out *their* struggles in *our* election campaign. They committed a severe sin by doing this, one that is largely responsible for the mess we are now facing. . . .

Let me ask you a question about your particular attempts to influence political decision-making as a member of the Central Round Table and as minister without portfolio in the Modrow government. Perhaps you could describe a little how this round table worked and address the question as to why the round table never tried to take power away from the SED by attempting to take over the government?

The round tables were an extremely interesting experiment, one that had never been tried in this form, and one that will probably never take place again. Each round table, whether on a local, state, or national level, represented the attempt to bring the civic movement—as the new political force—together with the old forces around one table in order to talk with one another on an equal basis. That wasn't bad at all. We achieved a lot through these discussions at the round table, there is no question about that. Our biggest success was the dissolution of the secret police apparatus. On the other hand, our negotiations with the party were concentrated too much on disbanding the secret police. We never managed to cut through the ties between the secret police and the party itself, nor did we manage to get the party apparatus itself dissolved. But at the time we were confronted with such a huge array of problems, and they were all supposed to be solved at the same time by the same group of people—much of that was simply not possible. After all, our days still had only twenty-four hours in them. In some ways this continues to be a problem: we do not have enough people to occupy all the positions that *need* to be occupied. . . .

It is important to note that these round tables existed on all levels, all the way down to small towns. Together they made possible a number of things that had never been achieved before. . . .

Most instructively, however, the debates at the round tables were conducted in an amazingly constructive fashion—there was very little of this empty rhetoric one usually associates with conventional forms of the political process. Everyone, including the SED/PDS representative, tried really hard to bring the problems we discussed to a meaningful solution. It was very different from the way democratically elected parliaments function, where everyone is mostly interested in how most effectively to score some political points off one's opponent, while the actual issues and problems have only secondary importance—if that. You see, people were *actually talking to one another*, across all party or organizational lines. We had established what one might call a "real cooperation," even with the SED/PDS or with the Christian Democrats.

A lot of the usual aggression was effectively kept down, perhaps due to the fact that the churches were moderating the whole process. We had all agreed that some major problems needed to be tackled, and this common understanding created a strong bond between us, despite all the difficulties.

Why do you think this experiment failed as quickly as it did? Or did it fail? Why, in any case, did it not continue after the 18 March elections?

Yes, it did fail in the long run, and there is no doubt that the Social Democrats were mainly responsible for that. They were very certain that they would win the absolute majority at the elections, and so they wanted to run the show by themselves. First, they tried really hard to keep us out of the election process altogether; they did not want the civic movement to run for election. And then they attempted, in an extremely arrogant fashion, to push for a very early election date [and succeeded in moving it forward from 6 May to 18 March]. All this created big problems between us and the representatives of the SPD, some of whom we knew from many years of common struggle. These were people with whom we used to stand on the same side of the barricades. To this very day I do not understand what they thought they were doing during this time.

You see, we had created a common election alliance of all opposition groups which was supposed to run against the communist party and their satellite parties. And then the SPD people in East Germany single-handedly left this alliance in order to run by themselves. That was clearly a big mistake. It is really hard to fathom how these people began to have such different views just by being members of the SPD—which was, in the case of most of them, pure coincidence. They just as easily could have ended up in one of the other oppositional groups. The fact that they joined the SPD somehow fundamentally changed their attitudes concerning what was previously a common political understanding within the opposition.

You are saying that the Social Democrats ceased to act in a democratic manner?

Yes.

That is interesting. Let me ask you one more question concerning the round table. Ulrike Poppe [co-founder of Women for Peace, leading member of and representative at the Round Table for Democracy Now] told me that the opposition, in her view, had, or has, a very conflicted attitude toward power, and that that is why it did not even make an attempt to take power. In retrospect, she thinks that this was a big mistake because she believes that a serious attempt at taking power in October or November could not only have been successful, but would also have changed all of the political dynamics, particularly the ones relating to West Germany.

Yes, one could put it that way. On the other hand, the situation exceeded all of our abilities—in terms of energy, in terms of particular qualifications, in terms of time. Therefore, I believe that this is a rather theoretical consideration, constructed after the fact. But it is true, there was at least one point at which we could have come very close to taking power. In January of 1990 Prime Minister Hans Modrow offered to the opposition all ministries except the ministry of economics. All we had to do was to say "yes." If we had accepted this offer, our position would have been very different.

But, again, this was also sabotaged by the SPD. They did not want to be implicated in what they called this old kind of "party-dominated" government before the elections. The compromise that came out of our dispute with the SPD members, as you know, was that the remaining opposition groups did not take over the existing ministries, but instead became ministers without portfolio. Of course, that was a very bad compromise, because as ministers without portfolio there was very little we could do against those huge existing state and party apparatuses.

You were such a minister without portfolio. How did you perceive your own tasks or responsibilities?

Well, everyone could do whatever they wanted. I tried to tackle the issue of a national energy policy. More than anything else I tried to get access to the existing documents concerning power plants such as Greifswald [a Chernobyl-type nuclear plant that had long been considered extremely unsafe].

How, specifically, did you do that? Did you go to the Ministry of Energy and demand to see the files on Greifswald as a representative of the government?

The Council of Ministers had a lot of those files, and I received access to those. Or I went to the Department for Nuclear Safety, or I went to Lublin where the nuclear plant was located and talked to the people running it. And those people, of course, had to talk to minister Pflugbeil, even though a few weeks earlier they would not have even let me past the security guards. It was actually sort of funny since now they had to unroll the red carpet for me.

But, of course, there were severe limits to what I could do, or to the extent to which I could get access to all these apparatuses. It was mostly restricted to getting access to files that had previously been top secret.

In other words, the party apparatus made no attempts to cooperate with you?

No, no, not at all.

Did they openly try to sabotage your work?

Yes, pretty much wherever they could.

I guess you, in turn, went back to the round table with such experiences . . .

. . . Yes. Above all I tried to bring up the whole problem surrounding nuclear energy, since I was now able to document my deep concerns. That whole endeavor was very frustrating, however.

But to get back to your initial question. Yes, that was definitely a missed chance. When Modrow offered us all those positions, we should have taken them. Of course, we would have run into big problems taking over the old and deeply entrenched party apparatuses, particularly since we did not even come close to having enough competent people to replace all those party bureaucrats. But on the other hand, the people who now are doing it face the same problems. They somehow seem to manage rather well. So we definitely should have made use of that opportunity.

All the opposition groups were in favor of going ahead with that except for the SPD?

Yes, that's correct.

That is quite revealing. Now, let me ask you this: most of the opposition activists who were disappointed about the course of the revolutionary transformation, people who were particularly disappointed because to them it seemed that most fellow citizens primarily wanted "better cars, more consumption, and the West German Mark," still say that the situation is now better than what it was before. Most think, it seems to me, that a lot has been achieved, even though things have not gone in the direction they wanted. On the other hand, it appears as if the civic movement is currently in a state of disintegration. Most oppositionists have either joined some of the already existing parties, particularly the Social Democrats and the Greens, or they are returning to their private lives. How do you see this development?

It is very possible that you are right about this development. Most of the previously existing grass-roots groups have now disappeared or have joined one or the other of the national civic movement organizations or the newly founded parties. The hard core of these groups are, in fact, all deeply involved in local politics in one way or another, as members of the city council, or the local parliament, or something else like that. One of the problems connected with such local involvement, however, is that oppositionists find themselves awash in local politics, and therefore unable to focus on the broader issues concerning a national oppositional network. I consider this to be a big danger, particularly since we are now running into the very same problems we did a year ago, namely the growing and tension-filled gap between normal citizens and the governing elite. That tension today has almost reached the same degree as it reached during the days of one-party rule.

You mean that the citizens are again effectively divorced from political decision-making processes?

Yes. Absolutely. The degree of powerlessness toward what is being done "up there" is now very comparable to what it was before. We successfully managed to bring down the secret police, for instance. But when you look at how the current minister of the interior, Diestel, is treating the whole problem of domestic security and of state secrecy, you find virtually no difference from how the Stasi treated those problems before the revolution. That really makes one wonder how that happened and why. . . .

But I would be cautious with any predictions, because, after all, everything that has happened over the last year was simply not foreseeable. All predictions that were made during this time quickly turned out to be quite wrong. It has been an exciting, strange, and sobering experience.

■ INGRID KÖPPE, independent activist, recruited to the opposition movement. New Forum representative at the Central Round Table, delegate to the Berlin city parliament, Köppe was subsequently elected to the national parliament of the new united Germany on 2 December 1990 and became domestic policy spokesperson of The Greens/Alliance 90/Civic Movement.[39] ■ *"There was a definite sense in the air that this whole thing could escalate, that buildings might be stormed, that a civil war might break out. . . . We had developed a lot of self-confidence, and we were not about to cave in to someone else."*

Inge Köppe became deeply involved in attempts to build a coherent opposition immediately after her first meeting with the original New

39. For background information on Köppe, see Part I, chapter 3, pp. 181–93.

Forum contact person in her district—in September 1989. As previous interviews have illustrated, the tasks facing East German activists between October and December of 1989 often seemed simply overwhelming. Literally within a few days, oppositionists had moved from being in a marginal and illegal position to a position in which their decisions appeared decisive for the future course of the entire country. As Sebastian Pflugbeil, Ludwig Mehlhorn, and others have pointed out, the breathtaking pace of this development was not only entirely unexpected; it also inevitably caught the opposition ill-prepared. What was suddenly needed, and had to be built pretty much from scratch, was an elaborate communicational network between various opposition groups as well as organizational structures that could "get things done." But even beyond such complications, the new situation required concrete proposals as to how to deal with a wide range of specific problems, and one needed hundreds of people with all kinds of expert credentials. It was, in short, a situation which, most fundamentally, required time and space—both of which did not exist in East Germany at the time.

In often dramatic ways Inge Köppe here recaptures some of the major issues with which the opposition was struggling during the decisive weeks of the East German Revolution. In the end, she comes to the same conclusion as Sebastian Pflugbeil: whether or not it might have succeeded, the opposition should have seized various political openings (between October 1989 and January 1990) by attempting to take over the government and assume state power.

■ *You were one of the 200,000 or so East Germans who very quickly responded to the first public declaration by New Forum. And you immediately became a "contact person" yourself, setting up the first such office of New Forum in Köpenick. And hundreds of people showed up to offer support and to add their names to the founding document. Did this mean that you pretty much decided for Köpenick what people could do, what the next organizational steps should be?*

Yes. But for the most part you just talked to these people. It was amazing, because all these people came with all their frustrations, wanted to have an outlet for all their complaints. They just swamped us with their stories. They all said "something has to happen now." Young people, retirees, a very well-off couple who told me that they had built a house and that they wanted the best for their children—literally people from all walks of life, in other words.

When I try to imagine this situation, it would seem that there must have been a lot of concern about all sorts of people coming together who only shared one thing in common, namely, their opposition to the existing state or party, but perhaps had very little in common concerning the question as to what should be done next?

That's true. There was very little that people had in common other than their opposition to the party. That's why we tried to build a sort of replica of the entire society within New Forum, to set up groups dealing with literally every aspect of the organization of a society. The intention was to generate a new model of society, to see what could be done differently. Of course, nobody took into consideration that we might not have any time for all of this.

A few demands were shared by everyone, however, such as the freedom to travel, or a drastic restructuring of the legal system. Everyone who joined had a great desire to experiment with all these problems on their own. When we organized our first large-scale meetings in Köpenick at the end of September, it was just an incredible experience. These meetings lasted for hours; people could not get enough of talking to one another. They did not want to go home. We had this powerful sense of togetherness. . . .

How did the various contact persons from the different districts in turn communicate or organize among themselves?

We had regular meetings of the contact persons. Of course, we knew that we were infiltrated by the Stasi.

How often did you meet?

Every other week. A really important meeting took place just prior to 7 October [the fortieth anniversary of the GDR]. We were told at the meeting that it was known that orders to shoot at demonstrators were given [by the party] for the demonstration that was planned for the 7th. It was suggested that we should perhaps not ask people to come to the demonstration.

Who exactly was suggesting that?

People at the meeting.

Was there a consensus that you should not go because orders to shoot were given by the party?

No. Eventually, we decided to go with the demand for "no violence," for having a nonviolent demonstration, and to just demand this over and over again. Because, even among the people who came to see me [in her position as district contact person], it became clear that the willingness to use violent means was tangibly growing—not just within the party leadership, but even among large portions of the population. You could really notice that. There was a definite sense in the air that this whole thing could escalate, that buildings might be stormed, that a civil war might break out. . . .

In the end, quite a few large demonstrations took place on the 7th. Did New Forum support those?

Yes, of course. But, you see, at that time we were already in a situation in which nobody had to organize this anymore. To anyone who wanted to know, it was absolutely clear that something would take place on 7 October. You see, on top of everything else, the fortieth anniversary happened on the 7th, that is, on the very date that we had used for our monthly demonstrations ever since the May 7th elections. So there was no doubt that something would happen on that day.

I got arrested by the Stasi without ever getting a chance to participate in the demonstrations. By that time the police had become much more brutal than we had ever experienced before. I had to stand in a cold, dark garage all night long, guarded by policemen with dogs. I was scared that I might not ever make it out of there again. . . .

What about the demonstrations two days later, on the 9th. Is it correct, in retrospect, to say that this marked the day after which everything began to turn?

Yes, absolutely.

Was that your understanding at the time as well? I would imagine that it was a very liberating feeling to have those mass demonstrations without the state making any attempts to suppress them?

Yes, that's true. What was even more important to me at the time, however, was 4 November, even though we now know that the old system had already collapsed at that point. But this demonstration was simply overwhelming [about 1 million people demonstrated in East Berlin]. The communication among us was just incredible.

Would it be precise to say, and please correct me if I am wrong, that the main thrust of the political demands voiced on 4 November in East Berlin, among the participants and the banners they were carrying as well as among the speakers, was still addressing the need for reforms in the GDR and still very much had what you called "democratic socialism" on the agenda? From what people have told me so far, "Germany" or a "united Germany" played absolutely no role in this demonstration.

Oh yes, that's certainly true.

How would you interpret this from today's perspective? Was that out of fear, out of opportunism, or because those attending really did not want to hear anything about a "united Germany?" I am asking because it still seems very much undetermined whether the demonstrators after 9 November [the opening of the Wall], who increasingly began to demand unification, were the same or perhaps entirely different people?

Well, I think some were the same, but most of them were not. I really think that most people at the demonstration on 4 November were clearly in favor of something entirely new, of something that became known as the "third way." I think they also believed that something new was indeed possible.

You know, it is extremely interesting to think back to those days: there were even some first signs of arrogance vis-à-vis the West. This became clear to me, for example, at an event we had at the Erlöserkirche [Redeemer Church]. Previously, we had always felt a kind of exotic awe toward people from the West, but all of a sudden it was the other way around. Wherever we appeared, the "Wessies" [East German nickname for West Germans] turned around and looked at us, as if we were something really special, whereas we no longer paid any attention to them. We had developed a lot of self-confidence, and we were not about to cave in to someone else.

But it seems it did not take long for this to change again?

Yes, that's true, the whole dynamic changed dramatically after 9 November.

There were quite a few people who rejoiced over 9 November, and others who perceived it as a tragedy, as something that came much too early and therefore destroyed everything independent that was just beginning to grow. How did you experience 9 November?

Well, what was much more important to me at the time was that New Forum received an official recognition by the government on 8 November. I did not really consciously experience 9 November. [she laughs] You see, we were supposed to have a republic-wide meeting of all New Forum contact persons the following weekend, and on the evening of the 9th we had an organizing meeting for that. Our meeting was scheduled for 7 P.M., and when I got there someone said "did you hear, the borders are open," and I thought "that can't be right, this is not possible." We immediately turned on the news, and, yes, in fact the Wall had been opened. But, somehow, incredible as it now must sound, I subsequently forgot about it again. We had many important issues to discuss and future steps to organize, and only after the meeting, after I had returned home did it dawn on me what had happened that evening. But somehow it did not touch me, did not interest me all that much. I was also not one of those who immediately predicted the consequences of this, who were pretty clear about what this meant for the future of the GDR. . . .

Let me ask you a few questions about this period between 9 November and 18 March, that is, between the opening of the Wall and the first free elections in East Germany. Could you tell me about efforts by the opposition to gain control of this fundamental restructuring process after 9 November?

This is a very difficult question. As you know, I was a member of the

Central Round Table right from the start. At first, we thought the whole idea was just meant to be some kind of "token." But then we quickly realized that we could achieve quite a few things at the round table—such as when we demanded that Modrow should come to the round table and negotiate with us directly. All of this was very exciting. It felt like we were part of the government. The government was, in effect, no longer able to make decisions without first consulting the Central Round Table.

All in all, I think the round table was a very significant experiment. Just going through the experience of finding out that you were actually capable of doing work like that, you know. Of course, none of us had ever been in a comparable position before. It certainly was a lot of hard work, because we had certain pretty clear ideas as to what results we wanted to achieve. And, above everything else—in clear distinction to what is now happening in parliament—we had genuine debates concerning issues of political substance. Our debates actually stayed with and centered on the specific topic that was on the agenda, something I now miss a great deal. Every decision we arrived at was exciting, partly because no one would have been able to predict the outcome beforehand.

It was my understanding, however, that your relations with the government were extremely difficult . . .

. . . Yes, that's correct. In the beginning, the government did not take the round table seriously at all. Later on they *had* to start taking us seriously, but we still had the impression that too many things were still going on behind our backs.

In other words, you did not have any control over the government or the administrative apparatus?

No, for us to be able to exert such control, we would have needed access to all the relevant documents and papers. It had been one of our central demands right from the start that the government should no longer make any decisions without first informing us, but that's not what actually happened. Of course, we were well aware of this; we experienced it over and over again on certain issues.

Why do you think this could not be achieved?

Simply because the government would not let anyone control its work unless it was forced to. Particularly during this period of time the government wanted to manufacture "hard facts," which they did, for example, by quickly selling numerous houses to former party functionaries, or actively preventing a thorough dissolution of the Stasi by attempting to portray it as a legitimate and necessary "intelligence agency," or by undercutting attempts by the opposition to gain access to crucial files.

So how would you evaluate or interpret the position of the round table at the time? Was it more or less a gift to the opposition by the party and the Modrow government, an attempt to create some sort of a playground for oppositionists in order to quiet them down?

Yes, but on the other hand we did achieve more than they would have liked us to. Our work definitely went beyond the limits which the government had set for us.

But didn't Modrow, at some point, make a sincere effort to share responsibility with the round table, as when he offered positions in his government to the round table?

Yes. Afterward, we realized that we made one decisive mistake, namely, we should have attempted to take over the government somewhere between October and December. I realized that in January. When I asked myself why we had not tried that, I could not come up with a good reason. Our attitude had in many ways been that the ones who got us into this mess should also now be responsible for getting us out of it. Our part in this was supposed to be one of making sure that they would, in fact, do that. . . .

In any case, I am very confident that we could have taken over the government before December. I think our crucial mistake was that we did not make that attempt.

Well, and when we received this offer from Modrow, the members of the different opposition groups came together and talked about it. We initially wanted to enter the government by taking over certain ministerial positions. But, on the other hand, we realized that this meant that we would have to give up our basic principle, that is, "grass-roots democracy." Reinhart Schult and I sat down together at one point and drafted a program, a platform for the government.

It's incredible when I think about that now. Actually, it was a very detailed program in terms of what the next steps should look like. Our idea had been that the opposition people would join the government, but only on the condition that they could operate within governmental positions along the lines of their own program. But this was precisely the point at which we failed, because the Social Democrats refused to participate in this endeavor.

We had long and intense debates among the opposition groups about that, and the Social Democrats quite openly said that they wanted to become the governing party after May [the initial date for the first free elections] and that they did not want to be seen as being associated with the Modrow government. So their goal was to establish a traditional party with all the hierarchies and apparatuses that inherently go along with this process. This was also the time when they first said that they "did not want to share governmental responsibility with chaotic people like us." On this issue the initial break between the SPD and us substantially solidified. At the same time, the Social Democrats also left the alliance of all oppositional groups and parties that we had previously formed for the upcoming elections. I think that was a terrible mistake on their part. . . .

How do you explain, in this context, the fact that there were so many different oppositional groups in the first place?

That's a good question, a question many people, even inside the opposition, have asked ever since the Fall of 1989. I think the main reason was that people were responding to this monolithic one-track kind of politics we had previously experienced with one-party rule. Most people thought it would be extremely important to experiment with various different kinds of strategies, particularly since all the different groups were in constant contact. So the idea was that there should be as many groups as people had a desire for.

I had the impression that there were very few differences, if any, between the ideas and goals of these different groups. Is that a fair characterization in your opinion?

Yes. One of the problems later on was that each of these opposition groups had a seat at the round table. I remember that Konrad Weiss [leading spokesperson of Democracy Now] told me in January that they were thinking about joining New Forum, simply because they themselves did not have much of an active membership. But they also said that they could not do that immediately because otherwise they would lose their seats at the round table. So they said they would do it in March.

But when the elections came around, they suddenly said they wanted to run independently because they thought the name "Democracy Now" should not be lost. To this very day we have not managed to bring all these groups together, which is, in my opinion, another fatal failure on the part of the opposition. But the main failure was not to try to take power between late October and early December. . . .

So, if I may summarize, you think that two developments were most decisive for the collapse of any viable alternative to unification with West Germany: (1) the breaking apart of a unified oppositional front because of the SPD, and (2), the fact that the old communist regime resisted change for too long, as indicated by their decision to choose Krenz rather than Modrow. Perhaps if Modrow had risen to power right after Honecker, things could have proceeded very differently?

Yes. For me the main mistake was that we pretty much restricted ourselves to observing what *they* were doing, instead of doing more ourselves.

Ulrike Poppe called this "our torn relationship toward power" [gebrochenes Verhältnis zur Macht], that is, the opposition never wanted to take power, in fact, never even wanted to have anything to do with power, but later on realized that they should have tried to take power anyway, because the alternative of either the party keeping power or Western elites taking it was far worse.

Yes, I think that captures it rather nicely.

PART III
TAKING STOCK: THE SEARCH
FOR A HISTORICAL
PERSPECTIVE

Ludwig Mehlhorn (in an interview with the author, June 1990): One important reason as to why we call this a "revolution" has to do with the fact that a large portion of the population came out from hiding and began to think, and act, differently. For most people this moment lasted only for a rather short period, but it happened nonetheless. It was a rare moment of democratic experimentation. What was, ironically, also typical for a revolution was that the result looked very different from what the revolutionaries had been striving for. I know of no revolution that has generated the kinds of results the revolutionaries had initially been struggling for—including the Russian and the American Revolutions.

East German bishop (in a letter to former West German Chancellor Helmut Schmidt[1]): We are expected merely to listen all the time. It is constantly suggested that we are not capable of anything, and that everything we have done was wrong. We are the only ones who have to learn something, because, it is said, all of our experiences belong on the trashpile of history. Apparently it is not worth listening when we are saying anything. But we can no longer take this permanent know-all manner and our degrading treatment as disenfranchised failures.

Klaus Kaden (in an interview with the author, July 1990): I just hope that we will not once again fall victim to some kind of ideology that promises to have all the answers. The worst irony is that because people were socialized so materialistically, they now easily fall victim to the economic miracle, to the West German Mark. They almost can't help it. They will see very quickly that corporate capital makes a big profit at their expense—and they will be disappointed. They necessarily will have to be disappointed.

1. Quoted in Helmut Schmidt, "Uns Deutsche kann der Teufel holen," *Die Zeit*, no. 21 (17 May 1991), 3. My translation.

A worker in Magdeburg, East Germany (in an interview with the author, August 1990): In their opinion pretty much everything we've done, everything we've had here was somehow wrong, or at least deficient. In their eyes we are basically all failures, whether it was our fault or not. I don't think that's correct, and I certainly don't think it's fair. I am not going to let them steal my whole past, and I don't want to be a second-class citizen for the rest of my life.

■ As I drove through the cities and towns of the GDR during the summer of 1990, I wished time and again that I could find a citizen who had kept a day-to-day diary of the drastic changes the East German society had undergone over the preceding year. Within a few months, a whole people had lost the previous normality of everyday life. First there was the hopeful moment of momentous political change, of mass demonstrations, meetings, and the frantic rear-guard lurches of the once all-powerful party as it lost control over the machinery of the state and the citizenry as a whole. Then came the time, soon after the opening of the Wall, in which Western party organizers arrived with flashy handouts and Western politicians began to campaign for "freedom and wealth after unification." Used-car salesmen brought automobiles they could no longer sell in the West, real-estate agents searched for cheap bargains and businessmen for quick "deals." All took place within a struggling economy that was in no position to survive immediate and direct competition with the West. Amid this unfamiliar commercial swirl, escalating numbers of West Germans arrived on the scene to reclaim property they considered to have been illegally confiscated from them in the aftermath of World War II.

Meanwhile, East Germans paid less attention either to the old rules and regulations or to the layers of state functionaries who had once successfully enforced them. As the black market not only appeared, but soon intruded into the daily life of virtually everyone, many observers—defenders of communist order and capitalist order alike—detected "anarchy in the air." In short order, received habits of authority and deference visibly disintegrated throughout the GDR. People no longer worried about the perils of speeding on highways, or of expressing to party bureaucrats what they had always wanted to say but had not dared to tell them. Citizens even exchanged money illegally for black market rates right in front of police officers.

All of which is to say that long-established relationships everywhere simply broke apart. People who had been friends or colleagues yesterday suddenly left for the West or became political opponents. In many cases, people learned that some of their closest friends had turned out to be Stasi informants.

This process of fundamental social disintegration was by no means over during the summer of 1990: less than one year after the first signals of far-reaching revolutionary change had surfaced, East Germans found themselves about to be "unified" into an entirely different social, political, economic, legal, and cultural system. On July 1, 1990, the social and currency union between West and East Germany went into effect, and the East German Mark ceased to be a valid currency. Only up to 4,000 East Marks could be exchanged 1 : 1 with West Marks, the rest had to be exchanged 1 : 2, despite the fact that the average income in East Germany was less than one third of what it was in West Germany. From one day to the next East German enterprises lost half of their already meager assets at the same moment that they lost their former trading partners in the East. The latter had, with equal abruptness, found that they no longer were able to honor contracts if they had to pay in hard Western currency.

The cumulative result of all these developments was nothing short of staggering: thousands of jobs disappeared daily as an increasing number of enterprises were forced to close down. As social workers and psychologists attested in alarm, families broke apart on an unprecedented scale, the rate of suicides quadrupled, and thousands sought relief in alcohol. A growing majority of East Germans began to wonder whether there was any chance at all for genuine recovery. And yet, in the end, it seemed only of secondary importance whether one perceived this entire process with hope or resignation, whether one had supported this kind of change or whether one had struggled against it. In all instances, the observable result was most fundamentally dislocating. For the great majority of East Germans, the security of knowing what to expect, of knowing how to behave, and oftentimes of just knowing how to get by, had simply vanished.

In ways that proved extremely difficult for outsiders to grasp, this array of tribulations simply flattened the normal cause-and-effect contours of public life, public opinion, and, in the end, of what is normally considered politics itself. In terms of understanding the East German revolution, the very speed of the cataclysm has had the effect of washing aside historical causation, of leveling experiences and choices of East Germans in such a way as to make the political result, "German unification," appear much more orderly, and far more logical, than was actually the case.

To the casual observer, unification appeared to be a simple expression of understandable consumer hunger. The evidence seemed plain: East Germans rose as one to join hands with "a society that works."

As the East German voices in this book make abundantly evident, it did not happen that way. To continue to think so only insures that the drives that produced East Germany's revolutionary autumn will continue to elude us.

The issue here, it seems to me, is not just one of understanding recent history. Viewed as frozen pieces of evidence, little of what happened during the revolutionary months in East Germany can be of much enduring significance. A simplistic reading which portrays the events of 1989–90 as "inevitable" in its outcome because that outcome was solely determined by the desire for a higher standard of living completely misses what is historically significant: a vital democratic moment in European and world history. Fully considered, it is a moment rich in instruction for those many millions of people, inside and beyond the borders of Germany, who aspire to overcome conditions which have produced massive resignation, and often deep cynicism, concerning a political process largely divorced from their own concerns or, for that matter, from their own input. East German events, in short, provide an instructive example not only of people attempting to think and act democratically, but also of their achievements and failures in experimenting with ways to achieve a fuller democratic participation in the workings of their own society. In order for the East German revolution to be of any relevance to outsiders, it needs to be understood as such a process, and thus as inherently open-ended and experimental. It was not a frozen series of mere "events" that somehow pointed in a predetermined direction. Instead, East Germans continuously learned and changed as they were going through this process of self-generated change.

The sources and meaning of the initial insurgency have remained unclear because the process was not allowed to run its course. The domestic revolution was dramatically interrupted and thus became invisible to everyone except to those who participated in it. First hundreds, then thousands and finally hundreds of thousands had engaged in a great variety of courageous and often creative acts. Yet no one had anticipated that "change" could happen so quickly, and that, once underway, a mounting revolution could be altered so irrevocably by outside factors.

The deepest irony lay in the simple but awesome fact that very few East Germans had fought for the specific kinds of change actually taking place in 1990 and beyond. Simply stated, under the wreckage of the old regime lay most of the certainties of life that people had long taken for granted. These included a number of structural and cultural achievements that, upon closer consideration, they would have preferred to keep when suddenly confronted with the Western alternative.

In an extensive poll conducted by the newsweekly *Der Spiegel* in July 1991, 83 percent of former East Germans expressed their opinion that the former GDR had provided "more social security" for them than West Germany, 63 percent said that "West Germany has conquered the GDR like a colonial empire," 92 percent thought that the former GDR was considered to be little more than a "new market" for the West, and 84 percent believed that they would remain "second-class citizens" in the new united Germany for a long time to come. While all of these things happened on broad institutional, social, and also cultural levels, their impact was dramatically personal: individual patterns of perception and behavior became radically transformed within a breathtakingly short period of time. To journalist and writer Andreas Lehmann, "they are asking us for a complete renunciation of the old and a cheerful subordination to the culture of the West, which above all does not translate into the surrender of some 'ideals' (political or otherwise), but, worse, into a total loss of one's own biography."[2]

From hindsight it seems clear that the East German transformation passed through four distinct phases. The first began somewhere around May of 1989, when the growing opposition in the GDR conclusively documented pervasive election fraud on the part of the CP, when Hungary began to tear down its border fences to Austria, and when the first free election in the Eastern Bloc took place in Poland. This first phase lasted through August and September, with the founding of New Forum, Democracy Now, and Democratic Awakening, the halting emergence of small-scale popular protests in widely disparate parts of the country, and the departure of tens of thousands of citizens fleeing their country for good. Its culminating point was the demonstration of 9 October in Leipzig, when over 70,000 citizens from all walks of life defied the publicly announced warning by the party leadership that it would crush any further show of popular opposition. That Monday in Leipzig saw a showdown between peaceful demonstrators and a hardline leadership in Berlin during which the latter effectively lost its ultimate power—the ability to repress dissent with force.

The second phase lasted four weeks. These four weeks constituted the heart of the "revolutionary moment" in East Germany, when thousands and then hundreds of thousands of citizens demonstrated, held organizing meetings and public discussions, and when, in the face of it all, the party began to crumble. It was revolutionary because few people continued to acquiesce to traditional authority or showed any willingness

2. Andreas Lehmann, letter to the author, June 1991.

to accept old formulas as viable political solutions for the future. Instead, increasing numbers of East Germans organized, debated, experimented, and collectively sought new solutions. It was a time that most East Germans enthusiastically described in terms of "coming alive" or some alternate descriptions of excitement, drama, and unexpected promise. Meanwhile, New Forum exploded in membership, and even the party's rank-and-file became threateningly assertive toward its own leadership. On 4 November one million demonstrators gathered in East Berlin and issued demands ranging from the resignation of the party and a thorough reform of socialism to free elections and the recognition of New Forum as the main representative of the civic movement. This second phase, which began in the aftermath of the 9 October demonstration in Leipzig, ended on 9 November when the Berlin Wall came down.

It was only several weeks later that the organized opposition began to realize that this period had constituted little more than the initial, embryonic stage of the citizens' movement. As was soon to become clear, oppositionists were still far from prepared for the profound alteration of political dynamics that accompanied the opening of the Wall. No one had anticipated the enormous implications flowing from unrestricted travel of people, ideas, political concepts, capital, and goods between the two Germanies.

The third phase—roughly 9 November, 1989, to mid-January 1990—can perhaps best be characterized by the emergence of West Germany as the dominant political force in the GDR, and by the concomitant, Western orchestrated resurfacing of German nationalism. It was a period during which the size of the organized opposition peaked, but also a time of first calls for a "united fatherland" during demonstrations in Leipzig and Dresden. On 7 December the first Central Round Table negotiations took place between the CP and its satellite parties on the one side, and representatives from all opposition groups on the other. In the following weeks, the opposition at the Central Round Table not only succeeded in dissolving the hated Stasi and setting a date for the first free elections, but also, and more importantly, it mounted increasingly forceful pressure on the Modrow government to meet the demands of the civic movement. Even the party's rank-and-file demonstrated in front of the CP headquarters in early December and chanted, "We are the party."

But in early January of 1990 the Social Democrats at the Central Round Table defected from the "election alliance" of the previously united opposition, and refused either to participate in a "government of national responsibility" or to attempt with the other oppositional groups to take over the government. Instead, they bet on winning a majority of the vote at the parliamentary elections set for May 6, 1990. With these moves the SPD-East decisively contributed to the fundamental change of political dynamics in East Germany: first, their decision to affiliate with their bigger sister party in the West initially opened the gates through which Western political influence immediately began to flood into the GDR; secondly, and perhaps even more importantly, it effectively broke apart the clear distinction in the GDR between groups and parties associated with the opposition and parties closely connected with the CP. This blurring of political clarity made possible the sudden reemergence of the old CP satellite party CDU in a new guise—not that of sister party to a ruling communist party, but as a sister party of the conservative West German governing party of Chancellor Helmut Kohl, the CDU. Almost all of the East-CDU leaders were the same ones who had historically cooperated closely with the CP, and who had explicitly supported socialism and the "leading role of the party." Just a few weeks earlier, they had also entered the Round Table discussions on the side of the CP—that is, explicitly in a manner divorced from and unassociated with the civic movement mounted by the democratic opposition!

This wondrous turnabout built on two events. First, the decision of the East-SPD to regroup under the leadership of the West-SPD, to defect from the unified opposition and to run for election as a Western-type party effectively precluded both the last chance of the opposition to assume state power and the possibility of a stronger East German voice in the ensuing negotiations with the West German government. It represented the Wende of the revolution, the end of any independent East German political course. Second, the decision of Kohl's West-CDU to coalesce with the East-CDU effectively destroyed what little coherence the East German electorate might still find in public politics. It no longer mattered what the East German opposition believed—as a political force, it had been structurally marginalized. With part of the opposition deserting to the West German Social Democrats, and with the puppet party of the communists quickly refashioning itself as a puppet party of Kohl's West German CDU, the recently achieved space for political clarity became suddenly and radically reduced.

The fourth and last phase encompassed the remaining weeks of electoral politics—mid-January to election day of 18 March, 1990. Ever since the beginning of February the Modrow government, now including opposition representatives as ministers without portfolio, had served little more than a caretaker function, and the Central Round Table had steadily declined in significance. Its last—failed—attempt was to prevent Western money and Western parties from interfering in the East German campaign for national parliament. Moreover, after the unified opposition had broken apart due to the defection of the SPD, political forces ranging from the governing West German Christian Democrats to the East German communists successfully portrayed unification as the only viable option. Under such circumstances, there was no longer a place in the political landscape of the GDR for yesterday's revolutionaries, for they continued to debate the pros and cons of unification and, at the very least, wanted East Germans to have the power to negotiate the terms through which this process might take place. As it turned out, the groups which had been central in the first two phases of the revolution, above all New Forum, Democracy Now, and the Initiative for Peace and Human Rights, were not only successfully outmaneuvered and outspent during the campaign by the vast professional political machineries of West Germany's major parties, they had effectively lost their underlying political context as a civic movement experimenting in new democratic forms. The ignominious end to all the efforts of the democratic opposition was codified in a disarming statistic: thanks largely to the political machinations of West German parties and their Eastern subsidiaries, the truncated remnants of the civic movement, running under the hurriedly constructed labels of "Alliance 90" and "Greens/UFV," received a meager 4.9 percent of the vote.

March 18, 1990, instead saw the unexpected victory of the conservative "Alliance for Germany." And unexpected it was: even the latest polls conducted in East Germany had predicted a landslide victory of over 50 percent for the Social Democrats and a scanty 10 to 20 percent for the Christian Democrats, who, it was widely believed, would still be remembered by the East German electorate for their past as little more than stepping stones for the continuation of Communist Party control. The actual results, however, looked remarkably different: 21.8 percent for the SPD and a stunning 40.9 percent for the CDU, which made it by far the largest party in the new political landscape of the dying East Germany.[3]

This is the bizarre outcome that is now commonly described as "inevitable." Before accepting this explanation, it is perhaps well to keep in

---

3. See, for example, the polling results cited in Darnton, *Berlin Journal,* 248. While election results are inherently difficult to analyze, and this is particularly true for times of momentous political changes, it seems safe to suggest that a majority of East Germans voted for those parties who were in the best position to speed up a process that was, by then, already considered eminent—that is, annexation by West Germany.

mind some of the wholly unforeseeable events which attended this result. All of the three major players with whom West German chancellor Helmut Kohl formed the Alliance for Germany, namely the General Secretary of the CDU, Martin Kirchner, the chairman of the CDU and later Prime Minister, Lothar de Maizière, and the chairman of Democratic Awakening, Wolfgang Schnur, had for many years served as Stasi informants. And, it is now clear, the West German government and Kohl himself possessed conclusive evidence of this fact at the time.[4] Not surprisingly, all three of East Germany's leading politicians publicly denied any involvement with the Security Police, and they were joined by their West German sponsors in a cloak of silence. Wolfgang Schnur of DA was the only one not as lucky as the others: just days before the election, revelations unearthed by journalists and members of the civic movement irrefutably implicated him in having been a dutiful informant of the old regime's security police. Understandably, East German voters were outraged. Schnur's party received a total of 0.9 percent of the vote.

Even more significantly, of course, had the same revelations also emerged into public view concerning the Stasi connections of de Maizière and Kirchner, the CDU would have suffered a similar fate. Indeed, a nice bipartisan symmetry reinforced the Stasi revelations about East Germany's Christian Democrats. Also emerging after the elections was the discovery that Ibrahim Böhme, chairman of East Germany's Social Democrats, and an architect of that group's defection from the civic movement and its re-alignment with the West German SPD, had also been a Stasi informant. Had the role played by Stasi-connected politicians in both the CDU and the SPD been known by the East German public, their voting patterns would have borne no resemblance to the actual election result of 18 March, 1990. So much for the "inevitability" of the electoral destruction of the democratic opposition in East Germany.

In any event, with the advent of the coalition government under Prime Minister de Maizière, which was formed shortly after the elections and which consisted entirely of Eastern subsidiaries of large, well established West German parties, East Germany ceased, for all intents and purposes, to be a separate country.

By the time of my visit in the summer of 1990, almost everyone in East Germany had begun to speak of a "deep crisis." A child care teacher in East Berlin vividly captured this sense of anxiety and loss: "I am somehow no longer able to find my way through day-to-day life. I will probably lose

4. See, for example, *Der Spiegel*, no. 14, 1992.

my job, many of my friends are gone, and I don't even know whether some new owner—probably from the West—will not throw me out of my apartment." Karin Witte[5] had never been a member of the party, nor had she participated in any of the early oppositional grass-roots groups. But she had gone to the frequent large-scale demonstrations in Berlin since early October. "Of course I went. I felt we had to go, because otherwise nothing ever would have changed." When the Wall came down she could scarcely contain her emotions: "Finally, *finally,*" she emphasized with a great sense of relief, "to be able just to walk right through." Nevertheless, as Karin Witte paid extended visits to the other half of the city, "discovering how people on the other side live," she had her first "mixed reactions." Many West Germans seemed to "look down on us, even though they were very friendly at first—that changed quite a bit later on, however." Also, "everything and everybody seemed to move a lot quicker. People never seem to take the time to talk to one another over there."

When I talked to Karin in July of 1990, she had not visited "over there" for more than eight weeks, despite the fact that the Wall had been largely torn down. "I wouldn't know why to go anymore," she said. While she was not sure whether there could have been a viable alternative to the looming Western takeover, she was "very angry about how all the West German parties came in here, with all their money and their glossy handouts," and how "they took over everything we had just made possible." Her conclusion: "Maybe we should have paid much more attention much earlier to what was happening in our own country—you know, get involved, do it ourselves. Perhaps it wouldn't have worked either, but we should have tried harder anyway."

At the time, of course, few of these intricate relationships were apparent—not for most East Germans themselves, and certainly not for outside observers. With the benefit of hindsight it becomes evident that unity in purpose within the East German opposition—and, arguably, within the East German population at large—disappeared the moment the common enemy, the one-party state, was gone. For obvious reasons, no one had endeavored to design a clear-cut plan for this unlikely event, much less had anyone succeeded in bringing to life a popularly constructed organization capable of providing support for any such plan. Nothing containing such futuristic sweep had been remotely possible on such short notice. Viewed from a distance, little that transpired within such circumstances seemed to make sense. It appeared, rather, as chaotic

5. Personal interview, 16 August 1990. Name changed.

and contradictory. What Bärbel Bohley has called the opposition's "desperate" attempts "to create a space in which people could help change the country" turned out to be an extremely complicated process that was quickly cut short by the emergence of West German predominance over the future fate of the GDR.

The prominent dissident Ulrike Poppe, Democracy Now founding member and representative at the Central Round Table, explained a few months after the revolution that East Germans had collectively gone through "an emancipatory process, a general sense that something new could be created," adding that this sense was not restricted "to Berlin or Leipzig, but also existed in smaller towns" throughout the GDR. While she did not object in principle to the idea of an eventual unification with West Germany, pointing out that she had moved away from "many fundamentalist positions" which had not previously been tested "against political realities," Ulrike Poppe above all lamented that "suddenly there was only one big picture left that crushed everything else—the West."[6] For the East German civic movement, the moment of self-generated democratic possibility seemed irrevocably lost.

Despite this unwanted and unforeseen result, East Germans collectively had created a moment in time that had the effect of fatally undermining the old power apparatus. Somehow they had managed to overcome the silent acquiescence that had characterized their lives for two generations. By the tens of thousands they came out of their private "niches" and began to occupy public spaces, thereby transforming their own environment and generating experiences that would, in turn, transform them. No one remained unaffected by these drastic changes. For an undetermined time, the future shape of their society had been wide open. Depending on one's own viewpoint, East Germans had, in different ways, "threatened" or "liberated" some deeply internalized convictions about what was possible and what was not. It is precisely this achievement which, I believe, offers numerous lessons for people engaged in the ongoing struggle of creating more authentic democratic forms in every society in the world.

And yet, none of these popular achievements provided concrete answers as to "where to go from here." The main task surfaced as an immense organizing challenge—one more complex and demanding than oppositionists themselves had realized at the time. Within constantly changing conditions, the opposition needed to create well-functioning

6. Ulrike Poppe, *Der Spiegel*, no. 14, 1990.

lines of communication among its members; establish democratic decision-making procedures; and, above all, recruit many more citizens for
the seemingly endless tasks that suddenly demanded attention. Only after
the fact did it occur to opposition activists that large sectors of the East
German population had not found a way to participate in this hard-won
moment of transformative opportunity. But little of this was clear at the
time, much less was it obvious how these prerequisites to democratic
activity could be quickly or effectively put into place. As Ludwig Mehlhorn pointed out, "We were not at all prepared for that."[7]

In order to grasp the magnitude of the organizing challenge that confronted all those seeking to transform the East German social context, it
might be helpful, for a moment, to imagine a comparable situation in the
United States. Expanding a bit on already existing conditions, let us just
speculate that years of governmental neglect and corporate complacency
have led to a further deindustrialization of the country and have thrown it
into an insurmountable debt crisis. The S&L and bank bailouts have far
exceeded the projected $10 billion originally announced, and a $500
billion figure later substituted, a sequence that has effectively revealed the
dependence of elected representatives on corporate interests.

The social results (in this imaginary scenario) are also terrifying: home-
lessness has reached unprecedented proportions, and unemployment is
approaching Great Depression levels; the cities continue to deteriorate,
while violence begins to reach into the previously safe citadels of middle-
class suburbs; health care and education allocations are ravished by the
austerity deemed necessary for economic "recovery" plans; and environmental destruction becomes depressingly visible throughout the country.
At the same time, military allocations continue to drain away vital resources needed for social and economic reconstruction. In such a setting,
church, community, and campus-based groups begin to organize against
what was increasingly perceived as some sort of structural flaw in the
system itself, until—some years down the road—millions of people demonstrate in Washington, New York, Chicago, and Los Angeles; the Re-
publican and Democratic parties, along with the banking community,
effectively retreat from the seats of power; and more than 5,000 disparate
grass-roots groups across the country emerge to demand drastic political
change. While the situation seems to transform and retransform itself on a
week-to-week and even day-to-day basis, hundreds of thousands of people suddenly begin packing up and leaving for Canada and Western
Europe. All of this transpires amid increasingly devastating revelations

7. See Part II, chapter 4, p. 214.

about the state of the economy and the extent of private corruption among previously sanctioned elite groups.

Clearly, even among those who might agree that serious structural changes were now necessary, it would be far from obvious precisely what should be done—either long term or, even, at the moment. Among other things, reliable information about actual conditions in the country has just begun to become available. What would quickly become apparent is the fact that no one had remotely considered the possibility of such a development, much less drawn up detailed plans for it. On the contrary, even the few earlier demands and projections of the most "radical" opposition groups would now seem timidly inappropriate. As activists in East Germany told me over and over, "You have to understand that this happened very unexpectedly for us. No one had thought that the state would collapse so quickly like a house of cards." Instead, they had thought that "many years of struggle for step by step reforms" would be necessary.

Whether in our imaginary American context or in the actual East German context, the shock that is present turns on one controlling social fact: many generations of political experience have proven that people were not conditioned to think in terms of the possibility of structural change—that is, no one was quite prepared (psychologically or intellectually) to think in such broad, organic terms. Structural change had been so effectively relegated to the margins for such a long time that it was almost impossible to possess the conceptual range to think beyond narrow social limits.

Indeed, in most modern societies it is settled folk wisdom that change—if it is perceived as necessary at all—can only take place in small steps within what is intuitively understood as "the existing system." Political questions of a broader nature are either not debated at all or have been consigned to the outer fringes of obscure academic discourse. But even beyond these conceptual realities, East Germans faced crushing practical constraints. Few among the oppositionists, for example, had any experience in holding public office or, for that matter, in running a factory. But the ultimate challenge existed at an even deeper level: in the United States as well as in East Germany, only a small fraction of the population had previously participated in anything that could authentically be described as self-generated democratic activities. Most "activist" groups that had managed such participation were relatively small, had not been around for a very long time, were not very well organized, and, in many cases, were not as internally democratic as participants liked to think they were. In short, no one was experientially prepared for the opportunity at hand.

To be sure, such a comparison between East Germany and the United

States is transparently overdrawn. Above all, the American scenario, complex as it already seems, lacks a final complexity that haunted the East Germans: the "big brother in the West" ready to come in and take over. What both the imaginary U.S. and the real East German situation have in common, however—though to clearly differentiated degrees—are the political realities that attend a structural breakdown of the economy and a social breakdown of the legitimacy of certain existing state institutions and their nominally sanctioned representatives. As these dynamics worked themselves out in East Germany (and both outside observers and East German participants have equally acknowledged this point), "power was lying on the streets during October and November" in the GDR. A political space, a political opportunity, had been opened up. But now the most pressing and immediate question to be answered was who would fill it—and how.

All things considered, it is therefore not merely idle speculation to ask whether events could have taken a different turn in East Germany's Revolutionary Autumn. What we call history is, after all, not an objectively guaranteed march toward some premeditated goal. It is a process mediated by given social realities, but one set in motion by the transforming activities of human beings. In fact, events in East Germany during the Fall of 1989 offer a truly rare example of people acting upon the future by unexpectedly articulating and subsequently enacting long-repressed aspirations.

Quite naturally, many outside factors had an influence on events: Gorbachev's willingness to allow and occasionally even support radical structural changes in East-Central Europe, the free elections in Poland that produced the first noncommunist government within the Eastern Bloc, Hungary's decision to open its borders to Austria, and the existence of the "big brother in the West." All testify to the range of outside influence defining the realm in which the East German revolution took place. Yet none of these factors predetermined the specific political trajectory of the events that unfolded in the country. Nor did economic grievances, Stasi infiltration and repression, or party corruption explain, in themselves, the shape of subsequent events. All of these factors represented certain necessary or helpful preconditions (and need, therefore, to be specifically considered) but they do not help illuminate how different people in different situations either acted or reacted to the cataclysm. Above all, they do not help us understand changing forms of human action and human consciousness over time. They do not help us understand the emergence of democratic forms.

To focus on East German events in this way is to bring into view the most fundamental issues of historical possibilities and constraints, human agency and structural determinants, human self-actualization and the confining consequences of existing power relations. But it is also necessary to stress that these relationships cannot be addressed within a presumed set of static, unchanging preconditions; rather, these preconditions inherently exist within a dynamic flux of constantly changing social relations. Only by keeping this premise in mind can we begin to approach the central historical question of what was possible in East Germany, and what was not. Only then can we equip ourselves to assess in coherent ways the course that eventually emerged as predominant—and why.

All of which is to suggest that the most confining conceptual problem in studying the East German revolution—or any other social movement, for that matter—grows out of the prevailing habit of result-oriented interpretation. The *outcome* of a historical process is routinely used to explain certain decisions and the availability of options actually existing at the *outset* of the process. Something that may be seen as utterly foolish after it has failed might well have been considered courageous, farsighted, and intelligent had it succeeded. Yet the distance between success and failure is often a deceptively thin line. Today, most observers of the East German revolutionary transformation, for instance, would dismiss the idea of the opposition taking power in November or December of 1989 as "chimerical." Yet, had the attempt been made, perhaps even successfully, obviously our line of interpretation would show no resemblance to the explanations now prevailing. The point, of course, is that this thin line, defined by divergent "senses of possibility," is decisive not only for the observer after the fact, but for the potential participant before the fact as well.

It is precisely in this way, in my view, that the East German revolution lies in danger of being fundamentally misread. Shining through interview after interview is a rich complexity of aspirations, a tremendously expanded "sense of possibility" that cannot in any way be seen as the sole province of imaginative intellectuals, or be dismissed as the fancies of a few hundred "social dreamers." Beyond this, citizens from all sectors of society—sometimes actively, sometimes passively—supported the expansive social visions that informed the struggles of the growing East German civic movement. While the Western media saw "freedom and democracy" (as defined by the West) triumphing in the GDR, Harald Ebert, a 60-year-old worker from Leipzig with no prior party affiliations, commented in a much more complex manner during an interview that had a remarkably similar thrust to many others that the author conducted during the summer of 1990. "Yes," he said, "we need a real democracy, but we should combine it with the many good things we have achieved for common people in this country, instead of giving it all up." By this he meant things ranging from "full employment," "more equality," and "less competitiveness" to "a greater sense of solidarity among us." The dilemma was that by the time of this interview it had already become clear that those "many good things" could have no place in the future united Germany. The dreams of all the Harald Eberts of East Germany had been forfeited as a necessary price of "freedom and democracy." Shaking his head, Mr. Ebert acknowledged this unwanted tradeoff by saying, "I can't grasp why anyone would try to convince us that we've worked for nothing over the last forty years."[8]

People throughout East Germany shared the doubts and worries of citizens like Harald Ebert. Much was at stake. While the Western takeover seemed to confirm some deeply internalized apprehensions (the "victory of capitalism"), surrounding events also put into question the feasibility of a lifelong dream, one for which generations of people had risked, and sometimes lost, their lives: the dream of an egalitarian society without oppression and without poverty (the idea of "socialism"). Both abstractions, "capitalism" and "socialism," in turn took on a new meaning.

Observers across the world had invested a great deal of hope in the "democratic quality" of popularly generated changes occurring throughout East-Central Europe—first in Poland, then in East Germany and Czechoslovakia. Yet it was undeniable, as 1990 progressed, that the movements which had brought about these changes were increasingly pushed into the background. Politics was returning to "normal," away from the churches, cafés, factories, and streets back to the paneled board rooms of traditional political decision-making. To all appearances, tangible beginnings of democratic popular politics were once again replaced by conventional elite politics. Evidence of this was abundant. The East German leadership caved in to the annexation of the GDR by West Germany even as the opposition became marginalized, and the Polish government negotiated with the IFM while the elaborate popular network of Solidarność languished in isolation on the sidelines. As a result, ongoing broad-scale debate about options and alternatives suddenly vanished. The days of the Gdansk shipyard strike in Poland were now quite remote—"ancient history"—as, indeed, were the earnest and impassioned colloquies conducted in the churches of Leipzig and the universities of

8. Personal interview with the author, Leipzig, 12 July 1990. Name changed.

Budapest, or the peaceful and courageous mass demonstrations in Prague and East Berlin. Things had "returned to normal" with a vengeance.

The irony is that East European citizens themselves were increasingly persuaded (sometimes against their deepest beliefs) to accept this state of affairs as "inevitable"—even though many early on detected striking similarities between certain features of "the old" they had just collectively overcome, and certain features of "the new" that had descended upon them with the promise of "changing everything." And yet no other explanation seemed to carry weight; after all, it was said, the new governments were brought into office by what were generally considered "democratic elections." Didn't 46 percent of East German voters, for instance, opt for the West German-controlled conservative Alliance for Germany on 18 March 1990? Didn't the whole election process, furthermore, represent a clear mandate for unification?

In due course, as the date for unification drew closer and the moment of revolutionary transformation in the Fall of 1989 turned into little more than a quaint historical footnote, thousands of more or less sophisticated justifications as to why things had happened as they did were cited by observers from all over the ideological spectrum. In this context it should be emphasized once again that the idea of an immediate unification, controlled by West Germany, initially generated widespread opposition among Germans (East and West) and also among non-Germans. Whether West Germans were worried about the eventual tax burden that unification would be likely to generate; whether East Germans were concerned about losing their jobs, their homes, their child care places, or about becoming second-class citizens in the new Germany; or whether European neighbors were troubled by the potential economic and political predominance of a united Germany in Europe, the objections were both multiple and vocal. Yet as soon as a West German-controlled unification process had been successfully portrayed as the only viable option, thereby making it apparent that both the activists and the ideas of the East German opposition movement would have little if any role to play within the new unified structures of political decision-making, an almost obsessive debate was launched by commentators in East and West as to how to evaluate this outcome of the revolution. The argument essentially centered on the rather narrowly conceptualized question of whether a Western-controlled unification process was good and necessary or wrong and avoidable, or perhaps even lamentable but nevertheless inevitable.

Among the vast majority of commentators, the result quickly came to be taken for granted; concomitantly, everyone's attitude toward it was now read as a litmus test for one's political realism and reliability. Alternative routes toward unification—or even alternatives to unification as such—were no longer taken into consideration. It was not that the idea of the debate itself was counterproductive, but rather that any retrospective appraisal necessarily would have (and still has) to turn on what actually happened in East Germany, not only during the few months following the revolution, but throughout the 1970s and '80s. Only then can we come to a historically informed conclusion as to which options were realistically available and which ones were not. Thus, if we are not careful, the meaning of 1989—grounded as it is in what happened within opposition circles in the years and months *before* the Fall of 1989—stands in danger of being artificially frozen into a much too narrow and hence essentially irrelevant context.

As the interviews in this book make clear, for instance, the political agenda of East German opposition activists never centered on the issue of unification, but rather on the question of what kind of society they wanted to build, and how they envisioned life within new democratically-constructed social and political structures. The merger with the larger and well-established "big brother" thoroughly displaced such questions.

The role of result-oriented assumptions in all this is self-evident. It did not matter whether commentators thought that the specific shape of the final outcome was disappointing or promising, or the extent to which it could be taken to reflect "the wishes of the people." A kind of abstract historical determinism seemed to settle across the ideological landscape.

Above all else, as soon as politics had returned to "normal," virtually all observers immediately shifted their cameras to focus upon elite forms of politics again. This occurred whether the observer was a journalist reporting on governmental decision-making, or a professor engaging in broad academic reflections. The result was the same in either case. The most important questions were passed over—questions as to why and how the entire process of popular politics had happened, and, what it all meant in real historical terms as part of the ongoing legacy of human striving. It was almost as if "the people" had done their duty, that is, "they" had brought the party to its knees, and now "they" could safely be forgotten again. East German citizens were once again—bitter irony of history—handled so abstractly as "masses" that they disappeared from view. Across a wide range of occupations and ideological backgrounds, self-perceived experts, including some leading East German opposition intellectuals, effortlessly joined the chorus of re-established elite politics.

The results were often grotesque. Stefan Heym, probably the best-known "critical intellectual" in the GDR, voiced his personal despair just a few weeks after the opening of the Wall: "The people who had just recently been striving, with a noble vision, for a promising future, turned into a horde of brutes . . . who stormed . . . Hertie and Bilka [West German department stores] with cannibalistic lust."[9] Having thus reduced a wide range of apparently "alien" men and women to a faceless collection of "brutes," remote observers such as Heym launched with great ease into all sorts of descriptively vivid interpretations of what "the people" wanted and what was good for "them." In this rhetorical manner, the unfamiliar and unsettling time of "street politics" had passed, and everybody had been put back into their proper place. Further inquiry appeared to be no longer necessary; all the big questions had been asked, and the proper answers duly recorded. The energizing dynamics of the East German revolution—the democratic polity itself—had once again been exiled from thought.

Beyond this form of widespread condescension, however, there was also anger and frustration—even a sense of betrayal—particularly on the part of East German opposition activists who had often risked their physical safety by speaking out. A highly prominent figure in the East German opposition movement, a very kind and thoughtful man, told me in June of 1990, after I had turned off my taperecorder: "You know, people are now worried about losing their jobs and such. I have to say it serves them right if they *do*, in fact, lose their jobs. Where did they hide during all this time when we fought for them against the party, and what did they do after we had succeeded?"

It may be seen that, by the time of this conversation, the period of collective democratic struggle for a better society, one in which everyone would have a voice, was over. In retrospect, it is instructive to note that this had not been a revolution that had "devoured its children." Rather, it was a revolution that quickly ran out of time and space. Before viable alternatives could be articulated—or even effective steps taken toward their implementation—forces largely beyond the control of East German citizens effectively eclipsed the process of self-determined transformation. The society at large became a casualty of time—of time not granted.

Not surprisingly, as East Germans lost the fragile control they had won over the possible shape of their own future, and lost it to unseen "forces" originating on the Western side of the Wall, many of the revolution's

---

9. Stefan Heym, "Aschermittwoch in der DDR," in Michael Naumann (ed.), *"Die Geschichte ist offen"* (Reinbek bei Hamburg, 1990), 71–72.

children began to turn against each other, against those, in Sebastian Pflugbeil's words, "who used to stand on the same side of the barricades." Yet Pflugbeil remained confident that the struggles and collective experiences of the East German civic movement—what he called a "rare moment of democratic experimentation"—had not been in vain, despite the fact "that the result of the revolution looked very different from what the revolutionaries had been striving for." His conclusion is worth pondering for all those who perceived the goals of the organized opposition as "illusory" and impractical when put to the test of realpolitik. "I have considerable hope that the experiences of the last half year will carry our society along for quite some time to come. We have created experiences that really are fundamentally different from the ones that the opposition in the Federal Republic, for instance, has ever generated. We are not quite certain yet what will grow on this fertile soil—that is hard to calculate. But you should keep in mind that we . . . have accomplished much more on our own than the West German opposition has ever achieved."[10]

The central point, one that ultimately comes to define the range of democratic possibility in every modern society, it seems to me, is this: as politics returned to "normal," most internalized prejudices and condescending attitudes resurfaced in an old form. The less one had been actively involved in the process of democratic transformation, the more this appeared to be true. Evidentially unsupported (and unsupportable) perceptions once again were substituted for the subtle knowledge that comes out of active participation in the political processes of one's own environment. What East Germans described as the "unique opportunity to create something new," something beyond the narrow and misleading alternatives of "market and democracy" or "state planning and socialism," a time during which people from all walks of life "began to talk and listen to each other" in their communal efforts to create "a better society on our own," had all too quickly slipped away.[11]

As East German society was getting ready for the complete adoption of an already well-established political, economic, and legal system, most of

10. See Part III, chapter 8, pp. 351–53.

11. In this context, I believe, it is difficult not to agree with one of the most perceptive chroniclers of the East German events, Peter Marcuse, when he concluded that "'state' vs. 'market' as a formulation of the alternatives that were facing the DDR is badly misleading. Not only does it suggest a factually incorrect separation of the two; not only does it conceal the substantive forces operating through the two forms; not only does it blend into one term very different concepts; it also, and here lies its practical danger, excludes alternative approaches from consideration." Peter Marcuse, *Missing Marx* (New York, 1991), 86.

the popularly organized Citizens' Committees and Round Tables quickly disappeared. The citizens' voices seemed no longer relevant. Self-organization, East Germans were instructed by Westerners, could not work. As the well-informed observer Peter Marcuse aptly noted, "the West continues what has just recently been rejected" in that it treats East Germans "as stupid children" and is "infantalizing in its every tone and gesture." The time in which "almost everyone with integrity is questioning, probing, looking for solutions, unwilling to take things for granted or accept answers just because they are authoritatively given" had passed.[12] Perhaps in no other way had the return of political "normality" produced more debilitating consequences. By the summer of 1990, in fact, many East German opposition activists considered the new situation as strikingly similar to the one that confined the democratic opposition "just one year ago"—that is, the comparison was to a time when no one had even considered possible the collapse of the one-party state.

In short, the return to conventional modes of politics not only overpowered (and thereby disempowered) the East German civic movement, but it also led, above all, to a reemergence of widespread popular passivity in the GDR. Someone else had effectively "taken over." Most crucial issues concerning the future would again be decided in chambers to which most East Germans were not privy. The most common rationalizations among East Germans for this unsuspected development were both ironic and sobering, although, perhaps, entirely predictable. The source for deeply felt grievances and frustrated dreams was increasingly sought among some undefined "other" within the GDR, such as "all those intellectuals in the opposition," or, quite frequently, "those associated with the party," and sometimes even simply and sweepingly "the people of East Germany" in general. What such remote abstractions suggested, in effect, was the need among citizens to find a villain for disappointing developments, developments over which East Germans felt they had again lost all control.

In this sense, the East German experience also came to foreshadow both the possibilities and dangers of political changes occurring in the rest of East-Central Europe and in the Soviet Union itself. In all cases the search toward a self-articulated and independent democratic future necessarily occurs within the context of long-repressed public debates about political choices and as a result of dilapidated economies which have denigrated human beings into a "production force" and nature into a

12. Marcuse, *Missing Marx,* 97.

"production tool." In each country this democratizing process also happens in the face of strong Western interests, ready to "export" their particular tradition of democracy and, above all, eager to step in with their ideas of "how to do business." Only if one is content with low standards of evaluation, however, can this "solution" be perceived as an unalloyed step forward. As the former dissident activist and current president of Czechoslovakia, Václav Havel, has eloquently pointed out:

the traditional parliamentary democracies can offer no fundamental opposition to the automatism of technological civilization and the industrial-consumer society, for they, too, are being dragged helplessly along by it. People are manipulated in ways that are infinitely more subtle and refined than the brutal methods used in the posttotalitarian societies. But this static complex of rigid, conceptually sloppy and politically pragmatic mass political parties run by professional apparatuses and releasing the citizen from all forms of concrete and personal responsibility; and those complex foci of capital accumulation engaged in secret manipulations and expansion; the omnipresent dictatorship of consumption, production, advertising, commerce, consumer culture, and all that flood of information: all of it . . . can only with great difficulty be imagined as the source of humanity's rediscovery of itself.[13]

The summary statements in the following pages chronicle the vivid internal argument among East Germans on what happened and what it all meant. It is *their* understanding of their own revolution. The reader will probably find much with which to agree and disagree and much simply to ponder. Beyond this, the conclusions that follow represent an individual and collective meditation on the process of democratic social change in the modern world. As we all know, such a meditation has significance far beyond the borders of the now extinct German Democratic Republic.

13. Václav Havel, "New Year's Day Speech, 1990," in Gale Stokes (ed.), *From Stalinism to Pluralism* (New York, 1991), 261; Václav Havel, et al., *The Power of the Powerless* (Armonk, N.Y., 1990), 91.

8 BETWEEN OPPORTUNITY
AND FAILURE

■ SEBASTIAN PFLUGBEIL, physicist, leading environmentalist, and nationally prominent opposition spokesman.[14] ■ *"The whole society was turned upside down. . . . It certainly did not collapse by itself."*

■ *How would you describe the outcome of the revolution for the civic movement, from the perspective of East German opposition activists?*

We are in the opposition again, just as we had been before. In fact, we are in about the same situation as we were just one year ago. But we can live with that, just as we can live with the fact that we did not get to nominate the new federal president, because we had never intended to play that game in the first place.

Perhaps it represented one of the weaknesses of this civic movement that we never seriously attempted to take over the government. Almost everyone in the opposition apparently belonged to that breed of humanity that was not very interested in exercising power. We sort of like that about ourselves, but of course such an attitude makes it very difficult to gain positions of power.

I have considerable hope that the experiences of the last half year will carry our society along for quite some time to come. We have created experiences that really are fundamentally different from the ones that the opposition in the Federal Republic has ever generated. We are not quite certain yet what will grow on this fertile soil—that is hard to calculate. But you should keep in mind that we have experienced a much tougher past

---

14. For background information on Pflugbeil, see Part I, chapter 3, pp. 160–65, and Part II, chapter 7, pp. 303–19.

than the opposition in the Federal Republic, and we have accomplished much more on our own than the West German opposition has ever achieved.

If you just look at the example of the West German secret police [or, as it is called in West Germany, the Agency for the Protection of the Constitution], nothing has been done about that in the West. After we had managed to dissolve *our* secret police, we had hoped that the West German left would also try to make some efforts in this direction, but none of that ever happened. I think it is very possible that some of the things that had been quietly accepted for a long time in the Federal Republic will now come out into the open again. Perhaps after unification, political issues will be thought about in more fundamental terms again.

But whatever the long-term developments will look like, it will be extremely difficult for us to accept unification of the two Germanies with the existing "Verfassungschutz" [Agency for the Protection of the Constitution]. The same is true for the NATO membership of the Federal Republic, just to give you two obvious examples. I think we will see a lot of very serious debates about many such issues. And, of course, a considerable number of people will be very critical of the kind of capitalism that is currently being forced down our throats. You see, things have already begun to develop in ways that are very different from what people in East Germany had originally expected.

A particular form of "left ideology" in the broadest sense continues to have wide support among the people of the GDR. But keep in mind that what we consider "left" had little to do with what people in the West associate with "left." Since we possess a much better, experientially grounded knowledge of what certain forms of left-wing ideology can lead to, we also possess much better preconditions to reach a sober, more rational program than people who are extremely well-off and who are mostly left-wing because they are bored, like most people who perceive themselves to be "left-wing" in the West.

At an earlier point in our conversation you called what has happened in the GDR a "revolution" . . . ?

Yes, that's what we call it. Perhaps it was only a tiny revolution. It was a revolution in the sense that very much happened very quickly, things that could no longer be reversed, and the citizens of the GDR made it happen. Again, no one had expected that all these things would be possible within just a half a year. The whole society was turned upside down.

Some commentators have argued that it was little more than simply the sudden collapse of a moribund system . . .

. . . It certainly did not collapse by itself.

But perhaps it would also have collapsed without the opposition, as a response to the wave of emigration, to Gorbachev, to the opening of the border between Hungary and Austria, and to the deteriorating economic conditions?

I am very skeptical of such a line of argument. I find it very hard to imagine what would have happened without the opposition. One thing seems certain, however: it would not have been as peaceful. . . .

One important reason as to why we call this a "revolution" has to do with the fact that a large portion of the population came out from hiding and began to think, and act, differently. For most people, this moment lasted only for a rather short period, but it happened nonetheless. It was a rare moment of democratic experimentation. . . .

What was, ironically, also typical for a revolution was that the result looked very different from what the revolutionaries had been striving for. I know of no revolution that has generated the kinds of results the revolutionaries had initially been struggling for—including the Russian and the American revolutions.

■ KLAUS KADEN, Protestant pastor, and a central facilitator within the church for the opposition in Leipzig.[15] ▮ *"The breaking of silence in the face of injustice . . . was our biggest achievement."*

▮ I would just like to say it in a completely unguarded way. Ever since the early eighties I had this terrible sense that something had broken inside people, even among many of my colleagues in the church. They were not as engaged anymore, they had simply begun to "suffer through" by, in effect, gritting their teeth.

But worst of all, as a part of this, something else is beginning to happen; people now begin to glorify this terrible past. Now they allude to "the teachings of Christ" and so on, claiming that under the new conditions "even this will be taken away from us." In other words, the past, though almost totally regimented, is suddenly portrayed as better than the present. This is very crippling, because it means that people are thinking about the present in a wholly resigned way, instead of thinking about the future in terms of completely new opportunities, new possibilities for talking

15. For background information on Kaden, see Part I, chapter 3, pp. 140–60, and Part II, chapter 4, pp. 217–24.

about the teachings of Christ. Why can't we think about conveying the message in new and creative ways if we are convinced that it is the best message?

And when I bring this up, I always realize how empty people are. Some mourn the loss of the "old ideals," saying how terrible it is that those are now being buried. So many churchmen act as if they are the only ones who care about social matters. It will be interesting to see whether those people are not all going to drive around in big Western cars in three years, or even earlier than that, or whether we will be able to generate a sort of awakening in our church. We need an awakening concerning the real issues in our church. We need to go back to the roots of Christianity, to those questions that also brought about the Wende, such as nonviolence, or the breaking of silence in the face of injustice, which was our biggest achievement, and which made the revolution possible in the first place. . . .

At bottom, we have to realize, however, that there were about ten to twelve pastors in Leipzig—out of about eighty—who became actively involved in the oppositional efforts. Throughout the country I don't think there were more than about 100 pastors worth mentioning. . . .

You have stated earlier that you did not think that there was any alternative to unification, that in fact the GDR would have had no other chance than to be annexed by the Federal Republic. You also said "we are a clear-cut failure." There is something I still don't quite understand about this: I can see your reasoning concerning the obvious economic imbalance between the two Germanies. But in a political sense, particularly since you were the ones who brought about the downfall of the old communist one-party state, I don't see why you could not have been an equal political partner with the other Germany?

In using the word "we," I did not refer to the 1.5 percent who brought about the Wende, but rather to "the people" as a whole. We as a people have simply failed. We have simply put up with this system far too long. The people in the factories and in the various institutions knew all along which direction this country was heading. Why didn't they stand up? Why didn't they resign from their posts, thereby signaling to the rest of the population that they would no longer be willing to take responsibility for all this? Why did they build themselves dachas out of the national wealth? Just so that they could bear the whole mess?

If you look at all these factors, you just have to come to the conclusion that the people have failed. They even perceive it that way themselves, even though, of course, they will not admit it. Who likes to admit something like that?

People now want to get rid of the aura of being failures. They can now hide behind the "new Germany," behind "being somebody again," by being able to go to the other Eastern European countries playing the wealthy uncle with the West German Mark. Sure, this is very dangerous, because this is the soil on which chauvinism can blossom.

So, in effect, you think that any kind of different development would not have been possible because of the existence of the Federal Republic of Germany?

Well, I am not sure. But I think, for example, that the civic initiatives [the opposition movement] simply ran a very bad election campaign. They were on such bad terms with one another. They held such differing views, and they had not even made up their minds as to whether they wanted a parliamentary democracy in the first place. . . .

Parties like the SPD, even though they were not very successful either, at least told people what they wanted and what they did not want, and they could refer to an outstanding tradition with which many people still associated themselves—the tradition of the organized German working class.

The fact that the Christian Democrats ultimately came out first primarily had to do, beyond doubt, with the fact that chancellor Helmut Kohl represented the "big power" in the West and all the money that comes along with that. He was thus in the position to promise that he would help. The others could make promises as well—and they all did it—but they controlled neither power nor capital. . . .

A campaign manager for the Social Democrats from North Rhine-Westphalia [West Germany] taught me once that about 80 percent of the people vote for short slogans, and not for ideas, concepts, or ideologies. So ultimately it is a question of power, and those who can best capture in five words or less what the people want to hear get elected.

This is a pretty cynical view of people, isn't it?

Yes, very cynical. Back then I also protested against it by saying to my West German friend that "it is outrageous how you judge people." He only responded by saying, "Well, you just go ahead, you will find out soon enough." Party platforms and political concepts are something for intellectuals, a small elite of less than 20 percent, but not for the people. This is a very sobering insight, but that's how people are. Anybody who successfully promises a lot will be elected; that's just the way it is. . . .

As a GDR citizen, I would also once again like to point out that those who come from the outside, particularly journalists, have contributed a great deal to making this transformation possible in the first place. What I find particularly impressive, though, is that you make such extensive efforts to understand the GDR citizens before you arrive at any kind of judgment or conclusion. This is very important to me since my experience with my West German friends has always been that somehow no one from the West could quite grasp what had happened here over the last forty years; what this system had done to its people; what our educational system had been like; how this overpowering state apparatus had regimented every aspect of life; how we had to fit in with this system—everybody who had not managed to get out by 1961 was, after all, imprisoned; how people had repressed their feelings, their anger; how people freed themselves by yelling out for the first time "we are the people." I had to cry the first time I could scream "we are the people," I had not dared to say something like that earlier. For the first time in our lives, we had the feeling "we are somebody, they can do whatever they want to now, this we will not let them take away from us again."

I think this newly gained self-confidence will stay with the GDR citizenry. The party big shots are badly mistaken if they think they can lull us with the West German Mark or anything. The economy is one thing. Somehow we have to find a way to start our lives all over again. We have to have an entirely new tax system, we have to have a new banking system, we need work. Too many people are already unemployed.

If we can get all these things consolidated after about two or three years, then we have to try to come to terms with what we have experienced during all these years, with what they have done to us. We will most certainly never forget that.

I just hope that we will not once again fall victim to some kind of ideology that promises to have all the answers. The worst irony is that because people were socialized so materialistically they now easily fall victim to the economic miracle, to the West German Mark. They almost can't help it. They will see very quickly that corporate capital makes a big profit at their expense—and they will be disappointed. They necessarily will have to be disappointed.

So people from the West should not judge East Germans too quickly, after they themselves have lived so well for more than 20 years by now. If you have been extremely well off for so long, it is much easier to criticize your own system. But you simply cannot expect that kind of criticism from the citizens of the GDR who have not had any of this, who have not been exposed to your system.

■ FRANK EIGENFELD, biologist and founding member of New Forum, and HARALD WAGNER, mathematician, pastor, and founding member of Democratic Awakening, now a leading member of Democracy Now.[16] ▮ *"You have to rebuild what lies in ruins. . . . The transition toward the new united Germany should take place as fast as possible."*—Frank Eigenfeld ▮ *"Ten years of mindless euphoria about unification may have devastating effects."*—Harald Wagner

■ *Taking the reality of unification into consideration, do you think there was anything that could have been done differently in order either to avoid unification, or at least slow it down, so that the future course of the GDR could have been influenced a bit more by the opposition movement, or by East German citizens at large?*

Wagner: That's of course very difficult to say. . . . There is no question that we should have tried to deprive the communist party of its power much earlier, if only to prevent it from taking this devastating step of opening the border on 9 November. But after 9 November, I could not have imagined a development anymore that would have looked substantially different from the one we got. We did try, however. There were initiatives that looked rather promising, like the Alliance 90 proposal to transfer all state ownership into a democratically run public holding. It had become clear that individual firms were simply no longer able to manage their own property. Yet the old enterprise directors continued to act as if they were some kind of masters. . . .

Our real chance lay in October 1989. At that point we should have pushed much more decisively and quickly for the implementation of the Central Round Table. . . . Only then would we have had a chance to proceed in a somewhat thoughtful and democratic manner with the drastic transformation taking place throughout this society. Very many mistakes have been made, as it turns out. And yet you also have to see how much we *did* do, day and night. A relatively small number of people accomplished a great deal. There were just certain limits to what we could possibly do—in terms of time, available people, and in terms of energy.

Eigenfeld: I have to say, on the other hand, that it became very obvious that the division of Germany, which was a result of World War II, constituted an extremely abnormal state of affairs. . . . I think most people felt that. There was a definite wish to overcome this division. That we were going to face grave problems in the process of overcoming this division, however, was an issue very few had really thought about. . . .

16. For background information on Eigenfeld and Wagner, see Part I, chapter 1, pp. 35–44, and Part II, chapter 4, pp. 224–35.

The will to overcome this division was so great that it now articulates itself at the speed with which unification takes place. I don't think there is anyone able to offer a catch-all solution, either within the various sectors of the civic movement or among the established parties. This is what I meant when I talked earlier about "times of fundamental change": once they occur and a certain route has been taken, those problems have to be dealt with as quickly as possible. I am not a proponent of either slowing down or even stopping this process. The shorter this period of fundamental change, the better. This transition toward the new united Germany should take place as fast as possible—now—since it is decided upon anyway . . .

But wasn't it rather a question of control over a process than a question of speed? The party-state collapsed like a house of cards and there was apparently no one to take its place from within the GDR . . .

Eigenfeld: What remained was no more than a ruin.

But in the last instance the ruin was taken over by West Germany as a bankrupt enterprise . . .

Eigenfeld: No. You have to rebuild what lies in ruins. We are now facing the results of 40 years of the existence of the GDR, an existence we were all part of upholding. The longer this existence lasted, the greater the damage. The reconstruction of normal conditions requires time.

Wagner: How did Walter Benjamin say it?—referring not to the East but rather to Western capitalism: the biggest catastrophe is if everything remains normal. If we consider what is happening in the Federal Republic as normal . . .

Eigenfeld: But this is not where the story ends . . .

Wagner: Of course, it does not end there. But there is little doubt that we got caught in a very unfavorable situation. The space for broad political and social alternatives had not been expanded during the unification process—as it could have been—but rather it has considerably narrowed . . .

Eigenfeld: But this is only a temporary phenomenon.

Wagner: What do you mean by "temporary"? If you just look at the environmental disaster, 10 years are now a very long time, maybe too long a time. I don't want to come across as overly pessimistic, but if you look at this development from a global perspective, 10 years of mindless euphoria about unification may have devastating effects.

My ideal would have been if the two Germanies had never grown together again but rather would have become parts of a confederated Europe in which Saxony, Thuringia, and Germany in general would have been a cultural unit but not a social, political, and military one any longer. This may sound fanciful now, but for global processes, for global justice, it would have been the only solution. . . . But currently all of this has been pushed from view.

Eigenfeld: Well, for the moment, but not forever. We can only solve such problems—ecological problems, problems concerning the Third World—*after* we have finished this unification process.

Wagner: No, I think the exact opposite is true. If we had set out on a process toward European confederation, we would have been in a much better situation to solve these problems.

Eigenfeld: But that will be one result of unification. A united Europe would never have come about if we had sustained an independent East Germany for a long time to come.

Wagner: But that is not what I said. Basically, you are also falling into the trap of arguing as a German centrist by saying that European unity will be advanced by German unification. But that is very hard to believe. The Germans are going to "help" everyone now, that is for sure. But the important bottom line is that it is an extremely profitable business for them. The strength they are now going to be able to acquire, they could not have gotten even with a war.

Eigenfeld: But that exactly relates to the question as to what kinds of politics will be implemented in the new Germany, which is an open question. What is not an open question is the fact that Germany will be a leading economic and political force in Europe.

If I may interrupt one more time. We seem to be caught in a false contradiction, aren't we? The question was not "unification or not," but rather under what conditions unification should occur. Please correct me if I am wrong, but did not, or does not, the question of unification turn primarily on how much input East Germany or the East German civic movement has in this process—rather than a debate about what might be possible at some later point after unification? My sense is that the decisive issues have been decided without your input, and there are those who would argue that this was not necessarily inevitable. Power was passed on from Honecker to Krenz to Modrow to de Maizière, while the opposition was left out. It seems to me that the very people who had generated the revolution have now completely lost control over the outcome.

Eigenfeld: Even if we had been in charge, things would not have developed very differently. As I mentioned earlier, unification has always been a latent issue in the history of East Germany. We should now go ahead with it as soon and as fast as possible, regardless of who is going to be in charge of it.

But aren't those two different issues? I do not quite see the connection. Unification is based on the historical fact that this separation between East and West Germany was an artificial political construct. But exactly how the process of unification takes place, the fact that it is not being done in a spirit of partnership but rather looks more like a takeover of a bankrupt enterprise, that, it seems to me, cannot merely be explained by saying that unification had to occur.

Eigenfeld: Well yes, I agree. But who of us East Germans could possibly influence any of this in the current situation? I am really convinced that regardless of who is at the top, whether it is Hans Modrow, Jens Reich [spokesperson of New Forum], Wolfgang Ullmann [spokesperson of Democracy Now], or Gregor Gysi [chairman of PDS], things would have run their course. There was and is nothing we can do to counter it, because we are simply dependent on the economic aid of the West. We simply have to go through the process of unification and equalization first, and then we can think about these other issues under new preconditions.

Wagner: I don't understand how you can say this. I still think you are turning events on their head—there was nothing inevitable about this whole process, nor are the conditions very favorable for us today. But you are right about the fact that it is probably too late by now to think about fundamental alternatives. We allowed that train to leave without us.

■ BÄRBEL BOHLEY, artist, founder of New Forum.[17] ■ *"Conflict was always repressed, we never had any space to deal openly with problems and conflicts."*

■ *Earlier in our conversation you said something that I found extremely interesting, namely, that one cannot present people with abstract political ideas that do not correspond at all with their own experiences or needs. But it seemed to me that what you said later on about "the Third World" or about "capitalism" made sense only in similarly abstract terms—that is, terms that were also unclear. Isn't it extremely difficult to begin the process of mutual communication with the population in such remote language, particularly if one is in desperate need of opening genuinely serious lines of communication—if one, in short, is trying to build a democratic movement?*

Yes, I suppose so. The election exemplified really well what was going on. Nobody talked in specific terms about how unification could be

17. For background information on Bohley, see Part I, chapter 2, pp. 131–39, and Part II, chapter 7, pp. 292–303.

brought about. Instead, they all claimed to know exactly how to do it, and said that it would not cost anything, everything would be wonderful from now on, and so on. I guess the people just wanted to be told "that it would all be wonderful." If someone had told them that we are most certainly going to have more than 1 million unemployed at the end of 1990 if we take the road proposed by Western politicians . . .

. . . But a lot of people said just that . . .

. . . No, who?

. . . Everyone who was part of Alliance 90, and even some Social Democrats . . .

. . . Yes, but Mr. Kohl did not, and he was the one with all the money. Mr. Kohl had the money and said, "This will not cost anything; it will all be wonderful."

And you think the majority of people believed it like that?

Yes. It was quite obvious to everyone that we did not possess sufficient means for the development of a new GDR ourselves. We were only citizens of the GDR.

But wasn't the economic situation of the GDR portrayed in terms that sounded worse than what the conditions actually were or are?

Oh yes, much worse. But, you see, this is very complicated; there are not these simple connections. One might have hoped that people would realize if we just told them, but they didn't. There was always this old habit of believing what those "up there" were saying, except that we had now replaced an "up there" that people had come to reject [the old party and its entire apparatus] with an "up there" that one could allegedly trust [the West German government]. So people thought if Helmut Kohl says so, it's probably going to be all right.

I believe many people just wanted to have some kind of "better" power, but they were not really opposed to power itself. There was very little consciousness about oneself, very little confidence in oneself, and there still is very little of that. I guess people can only gain some self-confidence as competent citizens if a society had organized *itself*, that is, in resistance to existing state power. To give you an example. If you were the parent of a handicapped child, only if you forced the state to provide you with a school for handicapped children would you gain some self-confidence in your relationship to the state. But you cannot gain this self-confidence if things are just handed down to you, if you play no role in the entire process. This is just one example, but the dynamic holds true within every realm of society. It was the kind of experiential knowledge that did not exist anywhere in East Germany.

But what about the people who took to the streets and who made many more or less creative demands and who said "we are the people"—that is, prior to 9 November. Have those really been the same people who later on carried banners saying "Germany, united Fatherland" or "Helmut, you are our chancellor too" or who were waving German flags?

By and large, I think they were the same people.

So you think what they said earlier was quite opportunistic, or was it perhaps simply because of their fear about going even further?

I do not think it was opportunistic. You see, I think what happened in the GDR was, in the sense Camus has written about it, a revolt, people standing up and saying, "I don't want this anymore." And everything else was steps that came later. There was no system behind their actions, but neither was it opportunistic. People just did not want to go along anymore, yet it did not go beyond that either. "We are the people," is what they said, but that did not yet say anything about what "the people" wanted. What they did was to stand up and to say, "Forty years is enough; we can and will no longer take this."

But that still does not mean the same as saying, "We want things to be like they are in the West."

No, no, at first it did not mean anything, except that people really did not want the old anymore. But what came afterward gets very complicated; you have all sorts of layers to this. There are a whole variety of people and groups which wanted different things. And in this sense it is not necessarily a contradiction that the same people who had just stated "we are the people" ran around waving West German flags eight weeks later, because they thought "this is it." You have to understand that this is not dishonest. Both statements were honest at the time they were made.

I have to say time and again that when it comes right down to it, you can only blame the system for this, because the system was not capable of dealing with the problems people had. Conflict was always repressed; we never had any space to deal openly with problems and conflicts. . . .

■ HANS MODROW, last communist prime minister in East Germany, parliamentary spokesperson for the PDS.[18] ■ *"The opposition did not have sufficient strength for that."*

18. For background information on Modrow, see Part I, chapter 1, pp. 89–96, and Part II, chapter 5, pp. 254–62.

■ *I have been told by many leading members of the opposition that they consider it their biggest mistake not to have been attempting to take power between October and December 1989—that the only possible path toward the continuation of an independent East Germany and some kind of socialism would have been without the party, based on the civic movement alone. As the last leader of the party-state, how do you react to that interpretation?*

I think this is a justified claim. Yet they would have had to understand that this would only have been possible if they had come together with a certain core of people from within the party. That is, with people like Gregor Gysi—and I do not want to say Modrow—but with that group of people who were interested in the same project.

So you are saying that without certain party people, this effort could never have succeeded?

Absolutely. The opposition did not have sufficient strength for that . . .

You mean because they did not have enough competent people, not enough experience?

Exactly right. They did not have the strength or the influence. But otherwise this would have been a viable path. In fact, it could have been attempted as early as October, if only the reformers in the party and the opposition had come together differently. I was already on the streets with those forces in Dresden prior to 18 October [the fall of Honecker], something for which I was subsequently accused and criticized. I was openly communicating with those forces even then. So that's where we should have come together; then it would have been possible.

■ **WERNER BRAMKE,** long-time party member, chairman of the history department of the Karl Marx University, Leipzig.[19] ■ *"The vast majority of the population was fed up with actually existing socialism."*

■ *As a leading academic spokesman of the party, how did you perceive the turn or transition between the collapse of the party-state and the subsequent political opening on the one hand, and the annexation of the GDR by West Germany on the other?*

The "annexation" of the GDR by the West—and unfortunately I think you were correct in using that term—could not be avoided, at least not as

19. For background information on Bramke, see Part I, chapter 2, pp. 97–111, and Part II, chapter 5, pp. 262–70.

late as 1989. The vast majority of the population was fed up with "actually existing socialism."

What exactly do you mean by that?

Well, I don't think they were fed up for ideological or ethical reasons, because those were rather convincingly transmitted by the official ideology. No, I think they were fed up because of the pent-up anger that resulted from the permanent lack of consumption. The GDR was a society of shortages, particularly in comparison with the Federal Republic. And then there was the problem with limited travel opportunities, in the eighties more than ever.

Does that mean I accuse the citizens of the GDR of being too materialistically minded? No, this was not only an expression of very understandable wishes, but behind those wishes loomed the fundamental desire to rid oneself finally of those all-pervasive, all-regulating limitations.

In the Fall of 1989 the population of the GDR would no longer have given a dime for the democratic renewal of the socialist structure. I think they simply had had to wait for too long.

Do you think there were any viable alternatives to the ensuing development toward unification?

I don't think there were many possibilities left for changing the course of events that followed. There may have been some space prior to October of '89—not much, but some.

The civic movement counted some thousands of participants, which is not very many in order to influence solidified state structures, much less to break them open. Yet it was sufficient to force a rotten system to collapse during a time of acute crisis. . . .

The mass of the population had long said good-bye to this system, and it was pretty certain, particularly after what Gorbachev had said on 7 October 1989, that the Soviet Union would not intervene in support of the SED. Yet the only issue the civic movement and the majority of the population agreed upon was to bring to an end the reign of the party. That's why the organized opposition, relatively small as it was, came to be strong enough to initiate the activities that led to the subsequent transformation. But their intentions to fight for a renewal of socialism, or an entirely different type of democracy, were shared, I think, by only a small minority of the population.

So why, in the end, do you think that the historical opening of the Fall of 1989 in the GDR led to such a rapid process of annexation?

If there had still been any chance in the Fall of '89 for creating a democracy in the GDR that would—in confederation with, but also in clear distinction from the FRG—have a clear grass-roots democratic profile and property relations that would be characterized by the strong influence of society at large, then this chance was already missed by October, if not before. That had nothing to do with the civic movement— which, in my opinion, did not commit any real errors—but rather with what I would call the "critical potential" in the SED.

Could you explain what you mean by "critical potential"? You mean people like yourself who were interested in a reformed kind of socialism?

Yes. The party had a membership of over 2 million, and there was, in that number, no longer a majority for actually existing socialism. There were a lot of confusing currents in the party, but among them were members—I would estimate their strength in the tens of thousands—who wanted a kind of "democratic socialism" which differed little from what the civic movement wanted. And those people should have joined the civic movement even before October, but certainly no later than that. I have to say this as a substantial correction of my own earlier position as a member of that group. I should have done the same thing.

Within the existing system of the GDR, the proponents of the civic movement . . . were certainly not in any positions of authority. On the other hand, the party's critical reformers, who had long severed their ties to their own party leadership, were also not in key positions of power, but they at least held many midlevel administrative and managerial positions. In other words, these two groups together, the civic movement and the critical reformers of the SED, may have had a chance. During times of general disaffection, insecurity, and eagerness for something new, such a determined minority could have done much more than just bring the old system to a point of collapse.

Let me ask you a quick last question about this. How would you evaluate the experience of the round tables in this respect?

Well, again, I think they were to a large extent determined by a tenuous cooperation between the civic movement and the party, a cooperation which can be characterized by both trust and suspicion.

The round tables were a kind of historical successor to the revolutionary councils of 1918–19. Similar to those, they exerted real power during a time of severe crisis. Had this understandable suspicion between the civic movement and the PDS not existed, they would have had a genuine chance to develop elements of a real grass-roots democracy. As such, it might have turned into a long-term institution which could have functioned as a democratic corrective to the parliaments and the state apparatus.

I think the round tables would have needed about one year to become accepted as an institution among the majority of the population. However, the unfavorable conditions in the spring of 1990 did not allow them more than four months.

■ ANDRÉ BRIE, vice chairman in 1990 of the PDS.[20] ■ *"Socialism as an abstraction is no longer an attractive political goal. . . . But I also do not think that the current forms of Western-style societies have a chance of survival in the long run."*

■ *May I ask you to expand upon your earlier statement that "one can no longer work with the term 'socialism.'" Do you mean to advise people that they cannot work in politics with those terms, even if they understand themselves to be socialists or Marxists or whatever, as I presume you do? What brings this question to mind is the fact that the West German left has been saying for quite some years that any kind of socialism in the Federal Republic was made impossible by the existence of the GDR, simply because there was an unbridgeable chasm between the terms used by the party in the GDR and the political substance articulated by West German socialists. Yet the newly formed PDS is holding on to this same terminology, running the risk—it is, in fact, a certainty more than a risk, in my opinion—that they will largely be discredited because they will be identified by the German population with the former Socialist Unity Party. So why do you hold on to that terminology anyway, particularly in light of your own statements on the subject?*

Well, that is an extra problem. In many ways the identification with the old party is, of course, justified. It would be ridiculous if the PDS thought of itself merely as a "new" party. The PDS developed out of the Socialist Unity Party, and it thus has to carry the responsibility that goes along with that fact. We are in urgent need of beginning a critical process of coming to terms with this history, without ever closing the books on it. The reason why the PDS explicitly associates itself with the term "socialism," on the other hand, is not only because of a willingness to take responsibility for this history, or to take the risk of being discredited, but is also because of the fact that its membership would immediately fall apart if we did not stick to the term "socialism."

20. For background information on Brie, see Part I, chapter 3, pp. 171–81, and Part II, chapter 5, pp. 270–79.

As a social scientist I can begin to use the term "modern society" instead of "socialism," for example, but within the party I cannot do that, because the members would not support it. I think three things are necessary in this respect. First, we have to cleanse this term, which will require many years, particularly in the public consciousness. We need to point out the deep chasm between actually existing socialism and the original ideas behind socialism. Secondly, we have to arrive at a fundamentally different concept of socialism, a modern concept. And to such a modern concept of socialism necessarily belongs, thirdly, the concrete specificity of socialist politics. We have to move away from a claim of absoluteness, saying that we want "*the* socialist society." Instead, we have to engage in concrete socialist politics, which encompasses many steps that we had better begin valuing as such—things like a radical equalization of the position of men and women, or breaking the predominance of corporate business. Those would represent decisive steps in and of themselves.

Let's not give up on such fundamental issues simply because we have failed so far. Societies function very differently from those of Marx's and Lenin's times, and thus we have to find fundamentally different ways to address the challenges posed by such societies. There are numerous areas in which we could try to break the dominance of big business, step-by-step. But if we do that, many of those will mourn who want to hear that "we are going to create the socialist revolution, we are going to create the socialist society." This whole process will take a very different route from what we have thought in the past—not because everything we did in the past was wrong, but because we live in societies that operate very differently because of the technical-scientific revolutions they have since undergone and because of the globalization of the conditions of their existence. . . .

Socialism as an abstraction is no longer an attractive political goal. An example of a very attractive and concrete political goal, on the other hand, would be a radical economic democracy, just to name an example. . . .

I think we have a tremendous chance today—of course, starting at a very low level—to create something new out of this terrible defeat of actually existing socialism, out of this failure, or out of this apparent "triumph of capitalism," whichever you prefer. Of course, we are not only talking about a chance; we are also talking about an absolute necessity. But I also do not think that the current Western-style societies have a chance of survival in the long run. In fact, this is not a question that merely concerns the distant future, but rather a question of pressing immediacy.

Many irreversible issues concerning our entire survival are on the agenda already. If we want to survive, we simply have to create something new quickly. I am not without hope in this respect. We are, for example, already experiencing an increasing individualization of the vast majority of the population, including workers. I know that this process is currently corporate-dominated, that it leads in many cases to loneliness or egotism. But, on the other hand, these dynamics also provide a basis from which we can again think about the correct statement by Marx that "the free development of every individual is a precondition for the free development of all." . . . There is no question that education, culture, and the development of a public democracy play a far more significant role in the lives of much larger portions of the population in modern societies than they did a mere 50 years ago. . . .

■ LUDWIG MEHLHORN, prominent oppositionist, East European expert, founding member of Democracy Now.[21] ■ *"We had lost all influence on future developments the week after the opening of the Wall."*

■ *If you look back on the revolutionary transformation of 1989 from today's perspective—and you have self-critically stated that the organized opposition did not have sufficient structures and communicational networks to find an adequate response to the appearance of a mass movement of people in the streets—what would you do differently if you could start all over again?*

I think prior to the Fall of 1989 there was not much we could have done differently. But during the Fall we made two decisive mistakes, or rather failed at two crucial junctures.

The first thing was that we allowed all these different, disparate, and unconnected organizational beginnings to take place, and I mean by that the founding of New Forum, of Democracy Now, of Democratic Awakening, or the Social Democratic Party. We definitely should have insisted on organizational unity, despite all programmatic diversity. . . .

I mistakenly argued *for* this diversity at the time, which irritated a great many people. Everyone seemed to offer his or her organization as the gathering ground for the opposition. Even at the time, many people asked why one collective organization would not suffice, when in fact most

21. For background information on Mehlhorn, see Part I, chapter 1, pp. 76–89, and Part II, chapter 4, pp. 209–16.

oppositionists would clearly have preferred that. I defended this diversity with the argument that we needed, after so many years of party monopoly, the largest possible plurality. But, of course, we could also have continued this plurality, could have continued our work as Democracy Now within the organizational framework of New Forum. . . .

If I take our own group, Democracy Now, as an example, it becomes absolutely clear that we should have decided after September or October to join New Forum. We could have accepted New Forum as a sort of organizational roof and could have worked pretty independently as a group within New Forum. As such, we would have concentrated on programmatic questions, for example. That way we could have been much more successful in building a nationwide organizational structure and a nationwide communicational network. These things require immense amounts of energy—many people, previous connections, and much more. All of which we could have accomplished better within New Forum. Instead, all those different groups tried it on their own, wasted a lot of energy that was lost for other equally or more important things. This is definitely a question each individual group has to ask itself now. . . .

The other thing in which we failed was perhaps inevitable at the time and has to do with the week following 9 November. As everyone knows, no one had anticipated that the Wall would come down that quickly. It was a last stunt by the party to relieve some of the boiling pressure that had built up throughout the country. What we had sort of expected was that they would substantially ease some of the travel restrictions, and perhaps that they would even allow everyone at least one free visit to the West, beginning sometime the following year. So that would have been a scenario we could, perhaps, have dealt with. But we had not at all realized the inner dynamic undergirding this international question, the pressure building up from the outside as well. In other words, we completely failed to take into proper consideration at one and the same time the question of Germany East and West as a nation and the problem of internal democratization in the GDR. . . .

Our biggest failure was probably that we were completely unable to analyze the mood and the sentiments among the population, and we thus did not at all succeed in becoming the authentic voice of these sentiments.

Immediately after 9 November we should have come out with a plan for a possible confederation with West Germany, perhaps even together with the newly formed Social Democratic Party. Then we could possibly have prevented, or at least made it much more difficult, for the West German Christian Democrats to make such effective use of the previous satellite parties in order to push through their specific concepts. Of course, these are all thoughts that none of us had at the time. So the question becomes, "Why didn't we think about this?" But whatever the answer may be, to me this represents a definite failure on the part of the civic movement. We did not thematize the national question in an open and democratic fashion— at no point, I must say.

In the context of people running away by the millions, breathing freely for the first time, and then coming back to talk about their experiences, we did not have any answer to the national question. And, despite this situation, we still did not expect the GDR to collapse so quickly and helplessly as it did.

Did this perhaps partly have to do with the fact that no one knew how bad the conditions in the country actually were?

Yes. We had simply miscalculated the entire situation. One way to define our mistake, or failure, is to point out that the organized opposition did not do anything against the growing gap between the oppositional elite and the people in the streets, a gap that quickly widened after 9 November. To allow such a gap to develop is always very dangerous, because you lose all control of events. . . .

How did this election date, first 6 May 1990, and later brought forward to 18 March 1990, come about?

Well, this was essentially a proposal of the Social Democrats, obviously under advice from and in agreement with the West SPD. They pushed this through against our will.

What created both this election date in the first place and what subsequently even brought it forward to 18 March were a number of factors: as the selling out of the GDR picked up in full force, as the East Mark was exchanged at horrendous rates against the West Mark, as the people stopped going to work, as one corruption after another in the party was revealed, it became clear very quickly that the very statehood of the GDR was under imminent threat. The very "idea" of the GDR was imperiled. There was also the question of whether a tough winter might not produce serious problems in providing sufficient goods and services to people, and thus lead to another massive wave of emigration to the West. So this immense pressure resulted in an even earlier election date.

Of course, the SPD had also calculated that it would achieve a landslide victory, which turned out to be a gross miscalculation of their own strength. From the way things had developed as of January or February in 1990, there were probably, in fact, a number of objectively good reasons to have the elections as soon as possible. But again, let's not forget that no one, absolutely no one, had anticipated that things would develop that quickly, no one had a political concept for such an event. . . .

What I am about to say, of course, is merely hypothetical, but I do believe that we could have substantially influenced these dynamics in a different direction if we had never given the Modrow government a chance to proceed relatively unchecked. We should have—pretty much the way it happened in Prague—done everything possible to establish a transition government formed by the civic movement itself. . . .

It is true that we would have had to include part of the old apparatus, but the decisive positions would have been under the opposition's control. Only if we had taken over the power structures in a determined and self-confident fashion, only if we had picked up part of the power which was literally lying in the streets, could things have turned out differently.

But at the end of December this opportunity had already passed. At that time, the West SPD proclaimed its support for unification at the party congress in Berlin. Willy Brandt gave his pathos-ridden speech in favor of unification. And in January the SPD announced its plans for an economic and currency union. People tend to forget that this was initiated by the SPD, and not by the conservatives. . . .

There are, as you well know, those voices who claim that the organized opposition, or the "elite," as you called them at one point, in no way expressed the needs of the larger population . . .

That's exactly right . . .

. . . Nor did they know about these needs, problems, grievances, or whatever one may call them, that existed within the population as a whole. And, this line of argument continues, as soon as the common enemy had collapsed, everyone promptly headed off in different directions . . .

Yes, I would largely agree with that. The opposition in this country was—perhaps with the partial exception of our group—mostly inspired by this abstract political model called "democratic socialism." And within this model we did not succeed in giving voice to the needs of the largest circles of the population. To put it succinctly: we had lost all influence on future developments the week after the opening of the Wall.

If we had possessed a consensus among the opposition in mid-November concerning a possible confederation with West Germany, for instance, a plan, in other words, that would have come out of our own ranks, and if we could have held people in the streets for such a plan, then we would have effectively prevented something like the Modrow government from acquiring so much space to maneuver. In such a case the civic movement—instead of Kohl or Modrow—would have been the spokespersons for the interests and needs of the population. And then it would also have been very possible, very realistic, for us to take power during this period—in other words, to follow the Czechoslovakian example.

But perhaps the Czechoslovakian example is not quite analogous owing to the fact that there was no West Czechoslovakia, no big brother to the West ready to jump in?

Well, yes, that's why it was so much harder in the GDR. But still, the GDR opposition at the time should have, and could have, formulated a real alternative to both the strategy of continuing East German statehood under the program of some kind of "third way," as postulated by the party reformers around Luft and Modrow, and to the classical reunification or annexation concepts as put forward by all the conservatives. We should have developed a genuine trajectory of confederation, buttressed by further pressure from the streets against the then existing political executive. If we had not left open the change of slogans from "we are *the* people" to "we are *one* people" to spontaneous and predictable interpretations, but instead had captured this sentiment and had placed it into a political concept of our own, then we could have effectively taken the wind out of the sails of Kohl and those who were marching in here in their economic-nationalist manner.

But wouldn't that also have meant that you would have had to actively recruit parts of this population, attempt to incorporate them in the movement, and not just change the organizational leadership and their goals?

Yes, you are absolutely right. If we had only managed to install a government in the GDR before Christmas that had consisted of the very people who later constituted one-half of the Central Round Table [the oppositional half], . . . then we could have forced West Germany to invest enough into the GDR to stop this mass emigration and create some time and space for a democratic renewal. Then we could have also taken bold steps on our own concerning the question of a transformation toward a market economy, without letting pace and content of policies be entirely determined by the West. Maybe not all of this would have worked, but at least it would have prevented the kind of total marginalization we subsequently experienced during the elections in March of 1990.

The main problem, it seems to me, was our inability to find a democratic answer to the national question. It has always been a big problem for Germans to think simultaneously of democracy and nation in Germany, or to bring them together politically. I have also consistently rejected this characterization of the transformation in the GDR as a "peaceful revolution." It was certainly not a revolution in the sense that it achieved its own goals, and what happened to it quickly thereafter is not very peaceful either.

But what were "its" goals . . . ?

For me, or for us, the goal was, beyond doubt, democracy, or rather a fundamental democratization of society. And none of us had any illusions about the fact that this meant a lot more than merely free formal elections or the creation of certain state institutions, such as the classical division of powers and such. We knew that it was essential for a democratic society to have a democratic infrastructure, structures of a civil society that we could not build from one day to the next after 40 years of communist dictatorship and another 12 years of Nazi dictatorship.

For almost 60 years any independent initiatives from within society had been brutally suppressed. So the whole process—psychologically, politically, socially—would have had to take a long time, particularly if it were to grow or develop from below—as we wanted it—rather than be implemented in such an orderly way from above or from outside. This was also the main reason why we in Democracy Now held on to the concept of independent statehood for such a long time. We thought that we needed an independent GDR in order to work on such goals in a democratic fashion, and in order to reach this goal, rather than stop dead halfway through. But this is precisely what we did not achieve. We successfully toppled a dictatorship, but that does not, as we now see, automatically encompass anything new. . . .

How, do you think, could one explain the many differences between the various routes of transformation from communist one-party rule to something else that took place in Poland, in Czechoslovakia, in Hungary, or in the GDR?

In Poland, it seems to me, you had a massive, self-generated working-class movement; in Czechoslovakia, the popular unrest was also not very well-organized, but there was a small, well-organized, and consistent group of dissident intellectuals who could staff a new government, at least at the very top; in Hungary, change mostly emanated from within the party itself, with some pressure from the streets; and the East German case is once again different from all the others. How would you explain that as an Eastern European expert?

Well, I don't think that one can explain such differences with the different postwar developments of communism in each of these countries. I think the main difference of the East German route has more to do with the fact that the GDR perceived the other German state as a constant threat to its very existence. There was just no question that the two Germanies had common roots in a common national history, with its values and myths, its successful and failed struggles. The entity called

"GDR" alone did not have such roots, a history that could provide a ground for identification. The only thing that was unique to the GDR, namely its ideology of Marxism-Leninism, thus played a much more significant role as the glue that holds together the system than in any other Eastern European country. This is the ultimate reason why the party and state leadership held on to and continued to push forward this ideology until the very end. They knew that if they lost this basis, they would probably lose everything, which is, of course, exactly what happened. . . .

Even to most Eastern European oppositionists, like those in Poland or Czechoslovakia, we merely represented "the other German state." Whenever dissidents from those countries thought about a possible future political constellation of Europe, they assumed that the separation of the two Germanies would not—in fact, could not—be maintained. . . . They thought about this much earlier and much more clearly than we did. . . . And when unification actually took place, they even welcomed it, despite the fact that it created further problems for them.

In other words, other Eastern European oppositionists were already thinking about German unification at a time when the East German opposition was still holding on to the concept of independent statehood for the GDR?

Oh, yes, absolutely . . .

You yourself have written earlier that you considered an independent path of the GDR toward something new as the most feasible option. . . .

I had simply assumed that it would take at least another generation before the question of unification would come up as a realistic option. And, you know, to some extent that is still true. That which is currently going on at the level of the state [that is, unification] will take a lot longer within society. It will be a long time before we have gotten rid of Stalinism in our heads, before the consequences of our socialization have been replaced by a different kind of education. It is certainly not as if the huge differences between the GDR and the Federal Republic will suddenly wither away just because we unified the two states.

But to return to this question of the Eastern European opposition once again. Charter 77 had already proclaimed in one of its "Prague Appeals," I think it was in 1983, . . . that they could not imagine the continued division of Germany within a new European framework. Or if you read some of the earlier statements of Solidarność theorists, some of whom are now part of the government, like Jan Josef Lipski, you will always find the argument that German unification is not only necessary because even Germans have a right to national self-determination, but it would also be preferable for the Eastern European neighbors to have a democratic state on its western border rather than an old Stalinist bastion like the GDR. . . .

On the other hand, I think that the Polish opposition, for example, vastly underestimated the role of the GDR in such a process. They were simply not very concerned about the East German opposition or how this unification would actually take place. Instead, they seemed mostly concerned about what the future relation to this Western neighbor would look like. And in this regard they always stated: "If we want to talk to the Germans, we might as well only talk to the West Germans. At least with the West Germans we can be sure that they say what they mean." The East German opposition was just not representative enough for them.

You see, the Poles had undergone an experience with East Germany; they understood that most East Germans, all the way into the oppositional grass-roots groups, had not shown much sympathy for their struggles in the early to mid-eighties. Most of the East German opposition had taken a position that may best be called the "social-democratic stance," which argued that we should work for détente between the two military and political blocs, but that we should not yet strive to overcome these blocs. In this sense, a movement such as Solidarność, one that effectively began to undermine these blocs from below, was looked upon as rather more destabilizing and distracting than helpful.

The Poles, of course, perceived such a stance as mere ignorance toward their conditions and their struggles, which in turn had a tremendous effect on how they viewed our oppositional movement. And in this context the few personal contacts that existed between members of the respective opposition movements, contacts that could never be made public, did not do much to influence or enlighten the impression people had of one another. . . .

You said at some earlier point that it was simply "hopeless" to try to use Solidarność as an example of what could be done in the GDR. Could you explain that?

The situation for workers was just very different in the GDR. They did not at all feel the same kind of economic hardship and social pressure as the Poles. Therefore, workers in the GDR would never have been willing to risk everything like their Polish counterparts had. The general sentiment against strikes was very stable in the GDR. And the GDR workers were acutely aware of the fact that they might be worse off than West German workers, but that they were extremely well-off compared to most of their Polish or Czechoslovakian counterparts.

There is a problem with this kind of reasoning, though. Generally speaking, if you look at the historical record, hardships do not, in themselves, produce social movements. And, more specifically, if you look at who was most active within Solidarność, you find two particular groups. One, those who were least skilled and worst-off, like the ones who worked in the hulls on the shipyard. But the second group were those who were highly skilled and relatively well-off, that is, workers who potentially had a lot to lose. It was the latter group that provided the experienced core of activist leadership.

Well, but that's always true . . .

. . . What is?

That the weakest members of a given society do not have the strength anymore to fight for their own rights, which is probably the main reason why the strike movement of 1980 in Poland was mainly generated by those who were the relatively highest salary earners, that is, the shipyard workers on the coast and the miners of Silesia.

I was just wondering because you said that a Solidarność-type movement could not have happened in the GDR because workers here were relatively well-off, and what you are saying now about the relatively well-paid shipyard workers seems to contradict that. Moreover, it seems to me that workers in the GDR had a number of justified grievances, severe grievances, in terms of working conditions, in terms of safety, and so on. So therefore it seems quite questionable that it suffices merely to look at the assumed social conditions of workers in order to explain why they did, or did not, perform certain acts.

[long pause] I guess you are right; it certainly does not suffice. Perhaps it is not even the most decisive factor. [again, long pause] But on the other hand, how can I put it, the extent of mismanagement, of waste of resources and labor power, of time and energy, was much more obvious in Poland. So it was more than just a problem of material living standards; it was a problem that had to do with the dignity of the individual workers. So much of what the worker was capable of doing was simply wasted, and thus the worker was also continuously devalued as a person. Somehow they managed to raise this to a level of collective consciousness within the Solidarność movement.

I completely agree. But that makes me wonder, again, as to why that could not have been possible in the GDR as well, particularly because the GDR worker was, in addition, always faced with the comparison to the situation in West Germany, where working conditions were generally better despite the fact that it was a capitalist society?

[pause] Well, again, I do not think anyone was willing to take that risk. It was just simply impossible to make any inroads with these issues among the workers of the GDR. The vast majority of the population had simply made their peace with the existing system. I think there were a lot of illusions about that during the Fall of 1989, when hundreds of thousands of previously quiescent citizens took to the streets. That was just a peculiar

moment in time. Furthermore, everything that happened afterward was clearly intended to destroy this moment.

This society had never come to terms with itself. There were only traces of something like an independent identity. People did not even show any solidarity with the opposition in their own country, like with the ones who had been arrested, or deported, or with people who had lost their jobs because of oppositional activity. There was the solidarity of your friends, but beyond that there was very little. No one among the workers would have ever considered going on strike for the release of a political prisoner, or something like that, something that was an almost daily feature in Poland during 1980/81.

Let me ask you this then. I see considerable frustration, all the way to bitter cynicism, on the part of opposition activists in the GDR about what they perceive the population at large to be like. On the other hand, it is pretty clear to me that most of these grand and abstract generalizations about "the people in the GDR" contain precious few specifics—they cannot convey much of an understanding of what we are really talking about. In short, these abstractions conceal more than they clarify. Examples for this are statements to the effect that "people were mostly passive" or "all people were interested in was the West German Mark." Obviously, this is too simplistic and can in no way do justice to the vast number of people under consideration . . .

I agree with that . . .

. . . Yet one can hear such assessments over and over again when oppositionists try to explain why things happened the way they did, or why contact with other sectors of the population—like workers—were so hard to establish, or why they did not try to establish them. On the other hand, the question of whether or not communication between various sectors of society is successfully established represents the decisive issue for any social movement; and it ultimately determines whether a movement actually evolves or whether organized opposition remains confined to small elite circles . . .

Right, and that is exactly what happened here, because we did not have the time and space to create a process of sustained and functioning communication about the real aspirations, about the hopes and desires of people. More or less out of necessity, the organized opposition found itself in utter isolation. We were confined to back rooms or spaces within the church, but we could never occupy any public spaces.

This, by the way, also explains why so many opposition activists in the Fall came out of the realm of the church. The study of theology was the only thing you could engage in that was free of party ideology. Many people merely entered the realm of the church because they wanted to have nothing to do with the state and the party. Most critical thinking was imprisoned within the walls of the church. Whether we talk about philosophy, sociology, or history, it was probably much easier to pursue these fields in Hungary, Czechoslovakia, or Poland than in the GDR. Just look at the opposition intellectuals in Poland. There you find literary critics, philosophers, historians, and so on. And who are these people here? Either they are Protestant ministers, or they are natural scientists. In other words, they came out of those sectors in which ideology was not as important, where you did not have to be a member of the party. This is true almost across the board. Look at the people who played a decisive role in the opposition here: Gerd Poppe, Sebastian Pflugbeil, and Hans-Jürgen Fischbek are all physicists; Jens Reich is a biologist, just to name a few obvious examples. . . .

How would you respond to the argument that the opposition movement basically failed because of an internal contradiction, that is, between their theoretical goals and their practical implementation of these goals. The intention had been to go beyond a mere formal democracy, that is, to help build a broad-scale democracy with active popular participation, and on the other hand the organized opposition groups did not practically reflect this intention within their own structures. It was exclusive rather than inclusive, elite rather than democratic, was it not?

Well, there is a lot of truth to that. This certainly represents one possible way of putting it. On the other hand, this goal or aspiration of building a democratic infrastructure within society still exists, and we now have somewhat better conditions in which to reach such a goal. We now have certain basic rights that are guaranteed. We can now organize a public meeting anytime we want to, or we can now organize political education. All of these things still need to be created, but the conditions needed to create them are better now than they were prior to the Fall of 1989.

I guess we just initially had this illusion that this whole process could take place within the framework of the GDR itself, that we could, in fact, do this on our own in order to allow people to go through the experiences of self-generated political activity and change. People should have seen themselves becoming active and making change happen, so that we could have proved to ourselves that we could not only get rid of a dictatorship on our own, but that we were also capable of building something new from the bottom up.

As it turned out, we only succeeded in the first step, but for the second step of independent democratic renewal we did not have the energy. . . .

The result is that we will be annexed and will simply have to take over the existing Western model. So in some way we are unfortunately continuing an old German tragedy of conforming to something that is already in place, instead of creating something new on our own.

In this respect, I was a bit surprised to hear that you think conditions are better now than they had been prior to the Fall of 1989? Is there an element here I do not understand?

Well, you are right. Concerning this very aspect it has actually become much harder. What I meant was that it is easier in terms of the state apparatus we are facing. The state apparatus is at least formally speaking under the rule of law now. Students are now freely demonstrating in front of the People's Assembly.

True, West Germany, like the United States, represents a formally democratic political system, but many critics would argue that both are far from what you called a "civil society," much less an economic democracy. Are you worried, like many of your friends in New Forum, that East Germany is now going to turn into the low-wage labor source for West Germany, into a kind of Mexico for West Germany?

Yes, of course. We had warned people that this would happen, which may have been one of the reasons why we did not get any votes, because this is not what people wanted to hear. They wanted to believe the outrageous promises of Helmut Kohl. But again, this had to do with the fact that we did not succeed in conveying our ideas and programs to a large section of the population.

Do you think these topics will come back as issues of broad-scale debates in the GDR (or, rather, by then the "former GDR")? What will happen if people begin experiencing extremely high unemployment rates here, when they start facing forms of poverty that they have never experienced before . . .?

Of course, we are going to have these conflicts. People are utterly unprepared for the social and economic reality that is currently invading us.

I have heard some lone East German voices who speculated about a second phase to this revolution. What do you think?

No, I don't think that we will see a second phase of the revolution, but rather simply a lot of social conflict over the question of who gets what and why. But this will never lead into a second revolutionary phase, at least I cannot imagine that. There is no way that the goals of last fall will be realized through conflicts concerning economic and social distribution.

I just raised this question because of what you said earlier. You had explained to me that the national question had been high on the agenda of the East German

*population, and you said that the opposition found no substantive way to respond
to that. Might it not be possible that because of the social and economic hardships
which the East German population will now experience (much more severely than
their West German "cousins"), that this may create a dynamic of new identification with the old GDR amongst most former East Germans?*

No, I don't think so. The national question was, after all, not resolved
by the opposition, but rather by the former satellite parties. We thus lost
much of our influence. There will be no identification with the GDR, or
any other kind of independent consciousness vis-à-vis West Germans.
More likely, people will begin identifying with their own social group or
class. So you have students who demonstrate for scholarships, the unemployed for jobs and benefits, or the house builders for whatever. Everyone
will organize around their own interests. You will see many special interest
lobbies emerging, and that's what will provide a possible ground for a new
identity. But it will not lead to anything comprehensive, not to anything
that will bring these different groups together, certainly not to a social
movement.

■ WOLFGANG K., newly elected trade union secretary at the second-
largest heavy machinery plant (Magdeburg) in the GDR.[22] ■ *"I think we
need to look out for ourselves."*

■ I don't have any hope that we can save this factory. I think total
bankruptcy is now inevitable. More than 20,000 people are going to lose
their jobs, and for many colleagues those will have been the last decent
jobs they will have ever had. . . . You see, we are completely export-
oriented. We would only have had a chance if they had not converted our
currency. Now, with the West German Mark, our Eastern Bloc trading
partners, especially the Soviet Union, cannot afford to do business with us
any longer. And even if they could, we would now get about 2 West Mark
30 for every ruble, and we used to get about 4 East Mark 60 for every
ruble. There is no way we can stay alive like that. . . .

And cooperation with some West German firm? Well, not very likely.
First of all, they do not need us, and secondly, nothing of what we are
producing fits with their stuff—our parts don't fit, our norms and standards are different, and so on. And on top of that, we don't have any

22. For background information on Wolfgang K., see Part II, chapter 6, pp. 287–91.

capital, and therefore cannot make the necessary investments in order to become an "attractive" business partner of some sort. I just don't see any hope. . . .

Probably most of us will have to learn everything all over again, that is, if we are lucky enough to at least get *that* chance. Because some of us will simply be thrown on the trash heap of history.

You know, we were never really asked whether we wanted all this, and I guess we never had the guts to stand up and fight for our own rights. Anyway, I am not at all sure things will really get better for us now. On the contrary, I think for many of us things will get a lot worse. But we will see. . . .

We should never have given up as much as we did. Despite all the failures and shortcomings, you know, we had achieved quite a bit. . . . What? A basic security, much more equality—we used to help each other out. I don't know, we were just all in the same boat together, not all fighting against each other all the time—which is, as far as I can tell, exactly what we are going to get now. . . .

Look, now the boss of the West German unions is going to come visit us [Ernst Maier, chairman of the Alliance of German Trade Unions (DGB)]. It's the very first time he has ever made it over here; he doesn't know much about our situation. They don't even know how to talk to us. Yes, they feel sorry for us, and somehow I guess they really want to help. But do they take us seriously? I don't think so. And when push comes to shove, I am not sure they will look out for our interests very well. Maybe that's a little unfair as it concerns the West German unions, but it's certainly true concerning everything else "West German." . . .

I think we need to look out for ourselves. In fact, we should have done that all along. You see, in the opinion of West Germans pretty much everything we've done, everything we've had here, was somehow wrong, or at least deficient. In their eyes we are basically all failures, whether it was our fault or not. I don't think that's correct, and I certainly don't think it's fair. I am not going to let them steal my whole past, and I don't want to be a second-class citizen for the rest of my life.

EPILOGUE

■ East Germany's revolutionary autumn: the reflections contained in this book may be seen as representing, above all else, a *lament* about a loss, a *reproach* to those who were unable to see, and an *appeal* to all those who have not yet given up on the idea of a more genuine democratic polity— the objective which East Germans sometimes refer to as a "civil society," a space outside the state that is occupied by an actively engaged democratic citizenry.

It is a *lament* in that the struggles, the goals, and, perhaps most importantly, the very life experiences of East Germans have been lost in the fast pace of a Western-controlled unification process. Most East Germans never have found—and probably will not find in the foreseeable future— a comfortable place in this process.

Despite a wide range of viewpoints, the interviews also constitute a *reproach* to political pundits whose condescension, or alienation, has never allowed them to pay sustained attention to the (necessarily complex) experiences, aspirations, and beliefs of those GDR citizens who are routinely labeled "ordinary people"—that is, all those who do not happen to inhabit elite circles of society. One wonders why it is not self-evident by now that people are more than simply workers or intellectuals, women or men, bureaucrats or dissidents, whose actions and thoughts can be summarily characterized by one or two presumed "interests," and that whatever they are and think changes over time—sometimes quite drastically, as in moments of self-propelled radical transformation. Yet much of the prevailing debate about the ostensible "meaning" of the East German revolution or, for that matter, of the revolutionary transformations across East-Central Europe suggests the opposite. Those who have, for a moment, populated public spaces—streets, churches, and round tables—and thereby forced, in the end, the one-party state to collapse, have not only again disappeared from view, but the lenses of most commentators have never even been focused enough to "see" them in the first place. The very idea of popular democratic striving, of active involvement rather than passive acquiescence, of probing rather than accepting, of active questioning rather than passive submission, seemed too alien ever to reach the level of "official discourse."

In this sense, the East German voices I have encountered unmistakably constitute an *appeal,* an appeal to listen and to take seriously those citizens who strive for a much more active democratic voice in their society—in East Germany as, indeed, all over the world. They are precisely the ones who are unable to recognize themselves—or their efforts—within misleading, remote, and often unhistorical abstractions that largely constitute traditional forms of political description. The attempt to categorize East Germany's revolutionary autumn in lofty political terms—many of which have their origins in the nineteenth century—suggests a rather profound inability to recognize the presence of a broadly politicized popular constituency.

One of the most instructive documents of the East German revolution remains the New Forum Founding Appeal of 12 September 1989. I would here like to call attention to certain particularly relevant sections:

Communication between state and society in our country has clearly broken down. The all-pervasive sullenness finds a variety of expressions, from withdrawals into private life to massive emigration. . . .

The political and economic interests of groups and strata are poorly balanced, and communication is obstructed. In private, people casually offer their diagnoses and remedies without regard for either their mutual compatibility or their practicality. . . . We want room for economic initiative without degeneration into ruthless competition. We wish to retain our achievements and yet create space for renewal, that we might live more simply and in greater harmony with nature. We want order without being patronized. We want individuals to be free and self-confident, yet socially conscious. We want protection from violence without being saddled with informers and police spies. Idlers and braggarts should be turned out of office without disadvantaging the socially weak and defenseless. We want an efficient health system for all, but no one should play sick at the expense of others. We want to participate in international trade and commerce, but do not wish to become either the debtors and servants of the leading industrial states or the exploiters and creditors of weaker nations.

For these contradictions to be recognized, for opinions and arguments to be aired and evaluated, and to distinguish particular from general interests, a democratic dialogue about the tasks of a constitutional state and about the economy and culture is necessary. The broadest public participation must be sought; we need to reflect and discuss with one another, openly and throughout the entire country. Our readiness and desire to do so will determine whether we will find a way out of the current crisis in the foreseeable future.

Social development now depends on whether a greater number of people will participate in the social reform process, and whether the various individual and group activities can find a common ground.

We are therefore uniting to form a political platform for the whole GDR, enabling people from every walk of life, from every party or group, to participate in discussing the vital issues facing our society. . . .

We call upon all GDR citizens who wish to take part in restructuring our society to join New Forum. The time has come to act.[1]

Though people could still lose their jobs or go to jail for what was broadly defined as "activities directed against the state," this appeal was signed, within weeks, by more than 200,000 East German citizens. Yet both the New Forum Founding Appeal and the rich variety of views contained in this book are intrinsically part of a moment in history which is now over. While it was a truly rare moment in the annals of democratic human striving, its long-term meaning is not yet clear—not for East Germans themselves, nor for anyone else interested in advancing democratic social forms. There is still much to be learned both from the legacy of 40 years of "actually existing socialism" and from East Germans' popular attempt to find a more democratic and humane alternative.

For most of the issues that their revolutionary effort began to address are haunting the West as much as the East.

1. New Forum Founding Appeal, in Charles Schüddekopf (ed.), *"Wir sind das Volk!"* (Reinbek bei Hamburg, 1990), 29.

CHRONOLOGY OF
EAST GERMAN HISTORY,
1945–1990

BASIC FACTS AND FIGURES

Official name	Deutsche Demokratische Republik (German Democratic Republic)
Land area	108,333 square kilometers (about the size of Ohio)
Capital	East Berlin (1.2 million inhabitants)
Population	16.4 million (1989)
Urban population	75 percent (1985)
Governing party	Socialist Unity Party of Germany (SED). The opening words of the East German constitution stated: "The German Democratic Republic is a socialist state of workers and farmers. It is the political organization of the working people in town and country under the leadership of the working class and its Marxist-Leninist party."
Religious affiliation	7.2 percent Roman Catholic
	46.2 percent Protestant (1985)
Total work force	8.6 million
Percentage of women	49.6 percent (percentage of female students in universities and colleges of higher education: 49.3 percent [1982])
Party membership	2.3 million—18 percent of the adult population (1986)

CHRONOLOGY OF EVENTS

1945

8 May	Capitulation of Nazi Germany; the four wartime Allies take over administration of their respective occupied zones.
21–22 April	In the Soviet zone the Communist Party (KPD) and the Social Democratic Party (SPD) are merged to form the Socialist Unity Party of Germany (SED), which assumes an increasingly dominant role through the support of the Soviet occupational administration.

1949	
23 May	American, British, and French zones of occupation become the Federal Republic of Germany (FRG, or "West Germany").
7 October	Soviet zone of occupation becomes the German Democratic Republic (GDR, or "East Germany").
1953	
5 March	Death of the Soviet dictator, Joseph Stalin.
17 June	Popular upheaval spreads to 270 localities throughout the GDR. Some 350,000 East Germans, mostly workers, participate. This massive self-assertion is crushed with the help of Soviet tanks. Twenty-one demonstrators are killed, many more injured. Some 1,000 demonstrators are sent to prison, seven of them sentenced to death.
1956	
18 January	Creation of the National People's Army (NVA).
24 February	Soviet General Secretary Nikita Khrushchev delivers speech in front of Soviet Central Committee denouncing his predecessor, Stalin, and many of the policies associated with the Stalin era.
June	Workers' strikes and violent mass demonstrations in Poznan, Poland.
18 October	Soviet tanks move toward Warsaw.
23 October	First mass demonstration of the Hungarian Revolution.
1957	
27 July	The GDR government proposes a confederation between the two Germanies.
1958	
16 July	Fifth Party Congress of the SED; the party declares that the GDR's standard of living will surpass West Germany's by 1961.
1961	
13 August	Erection of Berlin Wall, labeled the "Anti-Fascist Protection Bulwark" by the SED. More than 3 million GDR citizens have fled the country to West Berlin or West Germany since October 1949.
1962	
24 January	Conscription introduced in the GDR (without provisions for conscientious objection).
1964	
7 September	Provisions for conscientious objection introduced in the GDR ("construction soldier decree").
1968	
20–21 August	Participation of the East German army in the occupation of Czechoslovakia and the crushing of the Prague Spring by Warsaw Pact troops.

1969
10 June

Protestant churches in GDR break formal ties with West German churches to form the Federation of Protestant Churches in the GDR.

1970
19 March

First meeting of the two German heads of government, Willy Brandt and Willy Stoph, in Erfurt, East Germany.

1971
31 January

After 19 years of complete interruption, a few telephone lines are reconnected between the two Berlins.

21 June

Erich Honecker replaces Walter Ulbricht as first secretary of the SED.

1972
May

Twenty-five former construction soldiers organize first unofficial peace seminar in Königswalde. They subsequently meet every year.

8 November

The way is cleared for West German journalists to open offices in East Berlin.

21 December

Basic Treaty signed (fundamental cornerstone of Willy Brandt's Ostpolitik) as a first step toward "normalizing" relations between GDR and FRG and facilitating contacts between the citizens of the two states.

1973
21 February

A new regulation against foreign journalists "slandering the GDR, its institutions, and leading figures."

1974
7 October

Law on the revision of the constitution comes into effect. Concept of one German nation is dropped, and closer ties with the Soviet Union are stressed.

1975
1 August

Helsinki Final Act signed. The GDR commits itself to the guarantee of human rights.

1976
16 November

The songwriter/author Wolf Biermann is deprived of GDR citizenship after a concert tour to West Germany. Numerous writers and artists of the GDR send Honecker a petition of protest the following day; some are subsequently arrested. In the end, more than 100 prominent GDR intellectuals sign the petition.

26 November

Robert Havemann, prominent dissident, is placed under house arrest. One month later, the GDR Foreign Ministry requests foreign journalists to refrain from contacting him.

1977

23 August — Party member Rudolf Bahro arrested after extracts from his book *Die Alternative,* sharply criticizing "actually existing socialism," appear in the West German magazine *Der Spiegel.*

7 October — Clashes between police and young people on the Alexanderplatz in East Berlin after a rock concert. Reports of some deaths.

30 December — *Der Spiegel* publishes the first part of the "Manifesto," allegedly written by SED functionaries, clandestinely organized as the League of Democratic Communists of Germany. The league, following the ideas developed by Rudolf Bahro, calls for fundamental reforms such as the abolition of "one-party dictatorship" or any other dictatorship, "party pluralism," an "independent parliament and judiciary," and a government "free of party control." After publication of the second part, *Der Spiegel's* office in East Berlin is closed down by GDR authorities.

1978

31 January — Before the UN Human Rights Committee in Geneva, the GDR argues that its law allows restrictions on civil rights such as freedom of movement and retention of GDR citizenship.

6 March — In meeting between Protestant church leadership (Bishop Schönherr) and state and party leaders, Honecker acknowledges the church as an independent organization with social relevance even in a socialist society.

30 June — Rudolf Bahro sentenced to eight years' imprisonment.

1 September — Pre-military training introduced as a new subject in schools for 15 and 16 year olds.

1979

14 April — A new regulation requires Western journalists to obtain permission to conduct interviews of any kind.

9 May — House arrest for Robert Havemann ends, but proceedings are started against him for alleged currency offenses.

May–June — Havemann and Stefan Heym [well-known critical communist writer] are fined heavily for publishing work in the West without permission. Heym is expelled from the Writers' Union together with eight others who protested against these moves.

28 June — Reform of the penal code, increasing maximum penalties for "agitation against the state," "establishing illegal contacts," and "public vilification." Law on taking up illegal contacts extended to apply to GDR writers who publish critical work in the West.

Autumn — USSR begins withdrawal of 20,000 troops and 1,000 tanks from GDR.

6 October — Nico Hübner (East Berliner conscientious objector who refused to do any service for the military because of the "demilitarized status" of Berlin) and Bahro are released from prison as part of an amnesty to celebrate the thirtieth anniversary of the GDR. They both go to the West.

December	Central Committee-sponsored review of communist party members results in 3,944 expulsions.
12 December	NATO decides to deploy Cruise missiles and Pershing IIs in Western Europe, mainly in West Germany.

1980

23 August	First negotiations between striking workers and the communist government in Gdansk, Poland.
30 October	GDR government introduces strict travel restrictions between the GDR and Poland.
9–19 November	First all-German church "Peace Week."

1981

Spring	Supported by Protestant pastor Wonneberger, an initiative of construction soldiers demands the implementation of a "Social Peace Service" (SoFd) as a legitimate alternative to military service.
June	The East Berliner Protestant pastor, Rainer Eppelmann, writes open letter to Honecker suggesting a 17-point plan to help overcome militarization and conflict.
20 September	Communist dissident Havemann writes open letter to Leonid Brezhnev calling for peace and unilateral disarmament. The letter carries more than 200 signatures. Among the signers is Eppelmann, who is once again placed under house arrest.
13–14 December	Peace meeting of writers and scientists in East Berlin. Criticism from writers of the authorities' actions against activists in the unofficial peace movement.
13 December	The Polish government declares martial law, ending 15 months of the legal existence of the independent trade union, Solidarność.

1982

9 February	Eppelmann is arrested after publishing the Berlin Appeal, "Make Peace Without Weapons" (25 January; more than 200 signatures). He is released two days later.
13 February	Peace forum on the occasion of the thirty-seventh anniversary of the bombardment of Dresden in the Kreuzkirche attended by more than 5,000 East Germans.
March	New military service law makes it possible for women to be called up in case of need.
9 April	Robert Havemann dies. Some 600 friends and sympathizers attend his funeral.
July	First "Peace Workshop" with nationwide participation takes place in Berlin; 5,000 peace activists participate.
24–28 September	Synod of the Protestant Church in Halle takes peace as its theme. The symbol bearing the slogan "Swords into Ploughshares," worn by members of the unofficial peace movement, is dropped "for the sake of peace" within East German society.
October	Women for Peace write open letter to Honecker protesting against the March 1982 conscription law.

24 December	Some 200 to 300 peace activists attempt to hold a silent vigil in the city center of Jena; many are temporarily taken into custody.

1983

Spring	Founding meeting of Peace Concrete [Frieden Konkret] in Berlin, the first nationwide network with representatives from all unofficial grass-roots peace groups in the GDR.
14 February	About 100,000 East Germans demonstrate for peace in Dresden.
May	Petra Kelly, Gert Bastian, Antje Vollmer, and other West German Greens demonstrate for peace and disarmament on the Alexanderplatz. They are taken away by the police.
8 June	Peace activist Roland Jahn of Jena is expelled from the GDR.
23 July	Around 200 East Germans hold a silent demonstration in Jena as part of their campaign to leave the GDR.
1 September	Initiated by Women for Peace, some 70 people attempt to form a human chain between the American and Soviet embassies in East Berlin to "remind both nuclear powers of their responsibility for world peace." Security police break up the demonstration.
17 September	Five hundred women attend meeting in the Berlin-Lichtenberg Auferstehungs Church and discuss the link between the arms race and male domination.
10 October	The GDR decides to deploy middle-range nuclear missiles of the Warsaw Pact following a corresponding decision by West Germany.
16 October	Bärbel Bohley, Ulrike Poppe, and 30 other women, dressed in black, demonstrate at Alexanderplatz against any military service of women. They barely escape arrest.
12 December	Bohley and Poppe are arrested after involvement in peace initiatives and setting up autonomous nursery. As a result of international pressure, they are released on 24 January 1984.

1984

24 January	Twelve East Germans enter the West German Permanent Mission in East Berlin and are allowed to leave for West Germany.
March	Protestant church synod at Görlitz calls upon the government to create social conditions in East Germany which will encourage its citizens to stay.
6 April	Thirty-five East Germans leave the West German Embassy in Prague after five weeks and return to the GDR when they receive an assurance that they will be permitted to move to the Federal Republic.
15 May	*Neues Deutschland* reports that in response to the stationing of American missiles in Western European countries, long-range missiles have now been stationed in the GDR.
27 June	The West German Permanent Mission in East Berlin is closed after 55 East Germans enter in an effort to move to the West. They leave the mission three days later.
17–21 July	END (European Nuclear Disarmament) conference in Perugia attended by East German peace activists. They criticize repression

in the GDR, excessive church influence on the unofficial peace movement, and point out that the number of peace activists in the GDR has fallen dramatically as a result of people being allowed to leave the country for the West more easily.

9 November   The West German authorities announce that 36,123 GDR citizens moved to the Federal Republic in the first nine months of 1984.

1985
11 March   Mikhail Gorbachev is elected new general secretary of the Soviet Communist Party.

1986
In Berlin alone, about 20 different grass-roots political groups are founded in 1986.

24 January   Rainer Eppelmann, Peter Grimm, Ralf Hirsch, and Wolfgang Templin write an appeal to Honecker in which they demand the guarantee of full human rights.

Spring   After being rejected by the church, human rights activists found the Initiative for Peace and Human Rights (IFM).

2 April   IFM writes a petition to the Central Committee of the SED at the occasion of the Eleventh Party Congress.

September   Founding of the unofficial Environmental Library under the roof of the Zions-Parish in Berlin; publication of the oppositional (and illegal) "Umweltblätter." The IFM begins to publish the "Grenzfall" (also illegally).

1987
8 June   After a rock concert in West Berlin that could be heard on the Eastern side as well, East Germans protest against the Wall and clash with police.

24–28 June   Environmental, peace, women's, and Third World groups organize an alternative "Church Day from Below" on the occasion of the Protestant Church Day in East Berlin, "because the church has already lost part of its basis—workers—and it is about to lose the rest."

17 July   Abolition of the death penalty.

September   Founding of first organized group of would-be émigrés, called Working Group Citizen's Rights. The League of Protestant Churches in the GDR questions the politics of nuclear deterrence and the value of military service.

7 September   Honecker pays official visit to West Germany. He is the first East German head of state to do so.

18 November   The Environmental Library in Berlin is searched by the secret police. Printing equipment, documents, and books are confiscated or destroyed. More than 30 people who came in order to show solidarity with the library are arrested. Library personnel are also arrested. Vigils for their release are subsequently organized all over the country.

1988

15 January	The party sponsors traditional demonstration commemorating the 1919 murder of Rosa Luxemburg and Karl Liebknecht in East Berlin. Numerous members of GDR human rights groups are arrested. Unofficial demonstrators portray the absurdity of the official demonstrations by carrying signs with the famous Luxemburg quotation, "freedom is always the freedom of the one who thinks differently." Many of the most prominent spokespersons of the GDR opposition are subsequently expelled to the West, among them Bärbel Bohley, Freya Klier, Stephan Krawczyk, Werner Fischer, Wolfgang Templin, and Lotte Templin.
19 November	The Soviet magazine *Sputnik,* which has become a leading exponent of glasnost and perestroika, is banned in the GDR. Five new wave Soviet films are also banned.

1989

11 January	Twenty East German citizens leave the West German Permanent Mission in East Berlin, where they had stayed for almost two weeks, after assurances that they will not be prosecuted. The Hungarian parliament in Budapest votes to allow a multiparty system and to call 1956 uprising a "popular rebellion."
6 February	First negotiations in Poland between government and opposition at the Round Table. Meanwhile, GDR border guards shoot and kill a 20-year-old East German mechanic while he attempted to cross the Wall in Berlin.
12 March	Demonstration of would-be émigrés at Spring Industrial Fair in Leipzig. After confrontation between police and demonstrators, numerous protestors are arrested.
26 March	Elections in the USSR for the First Congress of People's Deputies, which in the future will be the highest institution of the Soviet state.
10 April	First Peace Prayer at the Nikolai Church in Leipzig under the auspices of grass-roots groups since June 1988; 900 participants.
2 May	Hungary begins to tear down its barbed-wire border fences to Austria.
7 May	Local elections throughout the GDR. The opposition attempts to oversee the election process; major cases of election fraud are detected. The party denies any wrongdoing.
4 June	Poland holds the first free election with opposition candidates in a Warsaw Pact country. The opposition movement Solidarność gains 99 of the 100 possible seats in the Senate, and all the seats (161) open for contest in the 460-member lower house, the Sejm. In China, on the same day, brutal crackdown of a mass demonstration at Tiananmen Square in Beijing occurs (estimated 3,000 to 20,000 demonstrators killed).
5 June	The official GDR party newspaper, *Neues Deutschland,* comments on the bloodbath at Tiananmen Square by stating that "it was a

	necessary answer to the counterrevolutionary upheaval of a minority."
12 June	Gorbachev pays a four-day visit to West Germany. People greet him enthusiastically.
28 June	Honecker and Gorbachev meet in Moscow.
7–9 July	Alternative Church Day takes place simultaneously to the official Church Day in Leipzig.
9 July	U.S. President George Bush visits Poland.
August	Hundreds of GDR citizens escape into the West German embassies in East Berlin, Budapest, and Prague. The would-be émigrés are estimated to be more than 1 million.
8 August	The West German Permanent Mission in East Berlin is closed because of crowding; 131 East Germans have sought refuge in the mission.
14 August	The West German Embassy in Budapest also closes for the same reason (more than 100 GDR citizens).
20 August	About 660 GDR citizens use a border checkpoint festivity between Hungary and Austria for their escape. Authorities in Bonn, Budapest, and Vienna are informed of the planned escape and offer back-door support. Hungarian border guards aid the escape.
22 August	Lithuanian parliament declares Moscow's annexation of the republic in 1940 as invalid.
23 August	The West German Embassy in Prague also closes because of overcrowding (more than 100 GDR citizens sought refuge).
24 August	Tadeusz Mazowiecki, a Solidarność official, is elected first non-communist prime minister within Warsaw Pact countries.
28 August	In the East Berlin Golgatha Parish four Protestant pastors and one member of the IFM sign a declaration of intent to found a Social Democratic Party in the GDR.
4 September	Popular activities are proliferating across the GDR. The majority of about 1,200 participants of the traditional "Monday demonstration" at the Nikolai Church in Leipzig demand exit visas, while some 300 debate with Protestant pastor Schorlemmer on the possibility of renewing socialism. Representatives of the socialist opposition in the GDR meet in Böhlen and decide to work for "a united left in the GDR."
7 September	GDR police forces brutally prevent a demonstration protesting the election fraud of 7 May. Some 40 people are arrested.
10 September	Hungary decides to let thousands of East Germans with valid documentation leave for the West.
11 September	Thirty oppositionists from across the country found the opposition group New Forum and sign an appeal entitled "Departure '89." The Hungarian government permits 6,500 East German citizens to go free after it abandoned part of a bilateral travel agreement with the GDR. Meanwhile, the East German government authorizes mass arrests following the traditional Monday prayer at the Nikolai Church in Leipzig.

12 September	New Forum publicizes its first manifesto. A second civic movement, Democracy Now, agrees on a founding statement entitled "Getting Involved," which calls for a "fundamental democratic restructuring" of the GDR.
19 September	GDR oppositionists attempt to register New Forum in districts throughout the country. The synod of the Alliance of Protestant Churches in the GDR issues a statement calling for "necessary reforms." The West German embassy in Warsaw is closed because of overcrowding by GDR refugees.
21 September	The GDR Ministry of the Interior declares New Forum as "hostile to the state" and rejects official recognition.
24 September	Representatives of New Forum, Democracy Now, Democratic Awakening, and the United Left escape secret police surveillance and meet at a clandestine location in Leipzig.
25 September	The largest demonstration in the GDR since 1953 takes place in Leipzig after the traditional Monday Peace Prayer. About 8,000 people demand reforms and the recognition of New Forum.
30 September	A total of 6,299 East German refugees, some of whom have spent weeks in West German embassies in Prague and Warsaw, receive permission to leave for the West. Their train passes through the GDR, causing major clashes between police and people trying to get aboard the train.
2 October	Some 20,000 demonstrators participate in the traditional Monday Peace Prayer in Leipzig.
3 October	GDR government suspends visa-free travel to Czechoslovakia.
4 October	More than 7,600 GDR refugees are taken by special trains from Prague to West Germany—across the GDR. Violent clashes between police and demonstrators occur alongside the tracks in the GDR.
6 October	Some 2,500 oppositionists agree in the East Berlin Erlöserkirche on a "common declaration" of all oppositional groups. Mikhail Gorbachev visits the GDR for its fortieth anniversary.
7 October	Near Potsdam, 43 persons illegally found the Social Democratic Party of the GDR.
	State and party celebrations of the GDR's fortieth anniversary. At the official ceremony in the Palace of the Republic, Honecker again invokes the "successes of socialism" and states that "there is no need for changes." Gorbachev issues a statement that "dangers await only those who do not react to life."
7–8 October	Tens of thousands of people demonstrate for political change and more freedom in East Berlin, Dresden, Leipzig, Plauen, Jena, and Potsdam. GDR police forces respond to the "hooligans" with great brutality. Thousands of demonstrators are arrested and beaten.
	The Hungarian Communist Party dissolves itself; some decide to found a new party under the principles of democratic socialism.
8–9 October	Thousands of East Germans again demonstrate throughout the country. The largest demonstration to date takes place in Leipzig with 75,000 participants despite threats by the party to "suppress

any and all demonstration, if necessary with all due force." The police, it turned out, had received orders to shoot. Everything remains peaceful on this Monday evening.

11 October   The Politburo of the SED announces proposals for a more "attractive socialism." They state that the mass exodus of citizens does not "leave us indifferent" and "socialism needs everyone."

14 October   New Forum, by now grown to about 25,000 members, attempts to fashion a nationwide organizational structure at a coordinating meeting in East Berlin. Democracy Now, about 1,000 members strong, also calls upon its sympathizers to organize regional structures. With the beginning of autumn vacations, the number of refugees to West Germany picks up again.

17 October   Workers at the Berliner firm Wilhelm Pieck withdraw from the party union FDGB, found an independent factory union called "Reform," and ask others to join them in founding an independent union. About 4,000 students discuss reforms at East Berlin's Humboldt University; the FDJ attempts to lead the reform movement within the universities, but its hegemony, previously unquestioned, is now challenged.

18 October   Erich Honecker resigns after being "first man" (erster Mann) for more than 18 years. Egon Krenz, Politburo member and Central Committee secretary for security issues, is unanimously elected as the new first general secretary of the SED. Krenz admits certain mistakes by the party, announces reform—without any specifics—and reiterates the "leading role of the party."

19 October   East Germans across the country show their dissatisfaction with Krenz's election. Wherever the new leader goes, he is subjected to severe criticism.

21 October   Tens of thousands of East Germans again take to the streets. The church in Saxony publicizes a study documenting more than 100 cases of severe police brutality against demonstrators during the fortieth anniversary celebration.

23 October   About 300,000 people in Leipzig demonstrate for reforms after the traditional Monday Peace Prayer, the largest demonstration ever in the GDR (2 October: 20,000; 9 October: 75,000; 16 October: 150,000).
Hungary declares itself an independent republic.

24 October   The GDR People's Chamber elects Krenz as chairman of the State Council and as chairman of the National Defense Council. Some 12,000 East Berliners demonstrate against Krenz and the party. The GDR State Council admits to, and apologizes for, police brutalities on the fortieth anniversary. First official panel discussion between representatives of the government and the opposition takes place in East Berlin, with Markus Wolf (ex-chief of the Military Intelligence Service), Christoph Hein (dissident author), Stefan Heym (communist critic, author), and the prominent dissident Bärbel Bohley.

26 October   Public debate between East Berlin first party district leader Günter

Schabowski and two representatives of New Forum, Jens Reich and Sebastian Pflugbeil. Public "dialogue" in Dresden between 100,000 demonstrators and city party functionaries. Though East Berlin's chief of police warns against any further protests, 25,000 demonstrate in Rostock, 15,000 in Erfurt, and 5,000 in Gera.

28 October　　In Prague the arrest of prominent dissident and playwright Václav Havel provokes a protest rally attended by some 10,000. The police use force to break it up.

29 October　　Open debate between party functionaries and tens of thousands of demonstrators in East Berlin, Leipzig, and Karl Marx Stadt. Prominent artists and scientists invited to an organizing and action meeting. More than 3,000 participants follow their call entitled "Against the Sleep of Reason" and cram into the Erlöser Church in East Berlin.

30 October　　More than 400,000 people demonstrate in various cities for reforms, free elections, and free travel. Hundreds of thousands surround Leipzig's inner city.

31 October　　Krenz visits Gorbachev in Moscow; he publicly rejects any ideas concerning a plural party system or German unification.

During October more than 24,000 GDR citizens have fled across the Hungarian/Austrian border into West Germany.

2 November　　Under mounting public pressure, Free German Trade Union Alliance boss Harry Tisch and the minister of education, Margot Honecker, both resign. New, elected chairperson of the official East German trade union is for the first time a woman: Annelis Kimmel.

3 November　　GDR government allows visa-free travel to Czechoslovakia again, which means that GDR citizens can now freely leave the country via Czechoslovakia. In two days more than 15,000 citizens make use of this option. Krenz announces a reform package that includes the creation of a supreme court and a dismantling of party privileges. The package does not, however, alter the "leading role of the party." Most remaining members of the old party elite are forced to resign.

5 November　　Almost 1 million demonstrators gather at the Alexanderplatz in East Berlin. It is the largest public demonstration in German history.

6 November　　GDR government announces new travel law according to which all citizens can, from now on, freely travel for a total of 30 days a year. The opposition rejects the law as an insufficient token.

7 November　　Despite the new travel law, the mass exodus continues. The GDR Council of Ministers under Prime Minister Willi Stoph collectively resigns.

8 November　　The SED Politburo resigns collectively. New Forum receives official recognition as a political organization.

9 November　　East Berlin First Party Secretary Schabowski announces immediate free travel rights for every citizen. The Wall no longer is a wall. Until midnight, hundreds of thousands crowd through the few

border crossings into West Berlin. Over the next two weeks more than 8 million East Germans visit West Germany and West Berlin. In its 28 years of existence the Wall has been the site of the deaths of 188 East Germans who attempted to cross it.

12 November   Krenz announces an extraordinary party convention for 15–17 December. As in previous days, the borders to West Germany are jammed with East Germans flooding west.

13 November   Former first district party secretary of Dresden, Hans Modrow, is elected as new prime minister. The former satellite parties announce their determination to scratch the constitutional article concerning "the leading role of the party." More than 200,000 people participate in another peaceful Monday demonstration in Leipzig.

14 November   Czechoslovakian Prime Minister Ladislav Adamec announces in Prague the suspension of all travel limitations for the country's citizens as of 1 January 1990.

16 November   West German Chancellor Helmut Kohl agrees to substantial economic aid to the GDR under the condition that "a fundamental change of the economic and political system in the GDR" will take place.

17 November   Police in Prague brutally suppress a peaceful demonstration of some 30,000 participants.

18 November   Oppositionists in Czechoslovakia found a Civic Forum.

19 November   More than 100,000 demonstrate in Prague for democratic reforms.

20 November   Some 250,000 attend the traditional Monday demonstrations in Leipzig, along with 40,000 demonstrators in Karl Marx Stadt and tens of thousands in Dresden, Cottbus, East Berlin, and other places across the country. For the first time the slogan "We are *one* people" appears.

West German minister of the chancellory, Rudolf Seiters, meets with Modrow and Krenz and unequivocally sets conditions for any possible economic aid, among them: free elections, plural party system, elimination of "the leading role of the party," and introduction of elements of a market economy.

22 November   SED Politburo offers satellite parties and opposition negotiations at the round table. Both a new election law and the possible elimination of paragraph I—the leading role of the party—to be discussed. Prague is the site of the largest Czechoslovakian demonstration since 1968.

24 November   Krenz announces the elimination of the "leading role of the party." In Prague the party leadership resigns; prominent 1968 party reformer Alexander Dubček speaks to a huge rally.

26 November   The East German communist party begins to disintegrate; according to new statistics, more than 200,000 GDR citizens have apparently left the party over the last two months, 70 percent of them workers.

27 November   Kohl presents a ten-point program for cooperation and eventual

unification. At a Monday demonstration in Leipzig more than 200,000 are in the streets again. More and more demands are for unification. A group of prominent oppositionists, intellectuals, party reformers, and clergymen issues a call against "selling out" to the West and for creating a "socialist alternative" to the FRG.

30 November   The Modrow government apologizes to the Czechoslovakian people for GDR participation in the 1968 invasion of Czechoslovakia. Gorbachev warns an increasingly demanding Kohl: "We cannot allow clumsy conduct and provocative declarations to cause harm to the epochal changes currently taking place."

1 December   After only 15 minutes of debate, the East German parliament scratches the "leading role of the party" from the constitution. The West German parliament supports Kohl's ten-point program for cooperation and eventual unification between the two Germanies, with Social Democratic Party abstention and Green Party opposition.

3 December   Both the Central Committee and the Politburo collectively resign. Krenz is also forced out as first secretary.

7 December   First negotiations at the Central Round Table. Long debates as to who should be included. Decision made for 6 May 1990 as the date for first free elections. It is agreed that the secret police apparatus will be dissolved.

8 December   An extraordinary party congress of the SED begins in East Berlin. At the same time, part of the old party elite is arrested. In a surprise vote, 95 percent of the 2,700 delegates elect Gregor Gysi as their new chairman. The idea to dissolve the party and found a new one is unanimously rejected.

11 December   Pro- and anti-unification demonstrators try to shout each other down in Leipzig and East Berlin.

15–17 December   The GDR Christian Democrats call for unity of the German nation at the opening of their extraordinary party congress. Intense debates at the party founding congress of Democratic Awakening over social-ecological vs. market economy alternatives, GDR autonomy vs. unification. Wolfgang Schnur elected chairman, while a left minority faction elects the spokesperson. The SED changes its name to SED-PDS (Party for Democratic Socialism). The old/new party adopts a tentative program to be valid until its next ordinary party congress.

18 December   Party congress of the West German Social Democrats in West Berlin also opts for unification. In East Germany, additional new members are added for the second round-table meeting—Peasants' Party, Green League, Women's Alliance, and FDJ. Discussions develop about "the legitimacy" of the government. The Modrow government accepts the decision to dissolve secret police, but also wants to create two new organs: an intelligence service and a "department for the protection of the constitution." Final Monday demonstration in Leipzig commemorates the victims of Stalinism.

19 December	Kohl visits Dresden and is enthusiastically welcomed. First anti-Kohl demonstration in East Berlin. Kohl and Modrow sign two treaties concerning future economic cooperation. New Forum decides not to become a party but will nominate candidates for the upcoming national elections.
24 December	The symbolic Brandenburg Gate is reopened; for the first time free access is allowed for West German citizens to the GDR. As of 1 January 1990, the exchange rate of West German Mark to East German Mark is set at 1:3.

1990	
3 January	The SED organizes an old-style mass demonstration against the desecration of the Soviet memorial in Treptow. About 100,000 people participate. Rumor had it that not neo-Nazis, as claimed by the party, but the Stasi itself has spray-painted the anti-Soviet slogans. The eight opposition groups at the round table protest in a common declaration against the formation of a Nachrichtendienst and a Amt für Verfassungsschutz [foreign and domestic security service].
4 January	The left-wing of Democratic Awakening leaves the party as a result of its defeat at the party congress in December. Pastor Friedrich Schorlemmer and others now want to join the Social Democrats.
5 January	The national delegates' conference of New Forum in Leipzig decides not to found a party. A quota system is also rejected.
8 January	The opposition at the round table passes a vote of no-confidence for the government's representative, Peter Koch. Also passed is an ultimatum to Prime Minister Hans Modrow to appear at the round table by 4 P.M. that same day. Opposition members ask the government to confirm the authenticity of a fax of the Gera section of the Stasi that could be interpreted as a call for a putsch; it turns out the fax is authentic. Meanwhile, more than 50,000 workers demonstrate in Karl Marx Stadt for free unions and a right to strike.
9 January	The West German Confederation of Unions (DGB) announces it seeks a broad cooperative agreement with the FDGB in order to avoid the possibility that the GDR will become "the new low-wage country of Europe."
11 January	The People's Assembly sets the date for the first free elections in East Germany for 6 May 1990.
12 January	After intense debate, Modrow agrees to wait until after the elections to form a new security service.
13 January	The East German Social Democrats (SDP), rename themselves after their Western counterpart (SPD—tellingly, the "D" which stood for "Democratic" now stands for "Deutschland" [Germany]) and leave the joint election alliance with the other opposition groups in order to run independently. Last chance for a united opposition to take state power in the GDR is thus effectively eradicated.

20 January	Egon Krenz, Kurt Hager, and ten former members of the Politburo are thrown out of the party by the new leadership.
21 January	The prominent party leader, reformer, and mayor of Dresden, Wolfgang Berghofer, and 39 others leave the SED-PDS.
22 January	In Leipzig and other cities, close to 200,000 demonstrate for unification. Modrow offers substantial government participation to the opposition; the SPD rejects the offer.
26 January	Cochairmen Edelbert Richter and Harald Wagner leave Democratic Awakening after the party has moved considerably to the right.
27 January	The left wing and founding generation of New Forum is defeated on crucial programmatic issues at the conference of delegates in Berlin. A quota for women gets rejected, as does a plan to give factory councils a veto power over major decisions of their plants; no majority is evident for a clear vote toward East German independence.
28 January	Prime Minister Hans Modrow and representatives of the opposition agree to form a "government of national responsibility." The 27-member cabinet will be enlarged by eight ministers without portfolio, to be filled from among the groups at the round table. Government and SPD decide, behind the backs of the opposition, to bring forward the date of the election from 6 May to 18 March.
30 January	Modrow visits Gorbachev in Moscow. Gorbachev now considers the "unification of Germans" as inevitable, but he says that this process has to be embedded in the European unification process. SED-PDS chairman Gregor Gysi also thinks that unification cannot be avoided anymore. Says he: "it is no longer a question of 'if,' but 'how.'"
1 February	Modrow comes out in favor of unification: "Germany shall be the united fatherland of all Germans again." The prime minister proposes a four-step plan for "the creation of a unified German state." Kohl meets with Wolfgang Schnur and Lothar de Maizière for the purpose of creating a conservative election alliance.
3–4 February	In a desperate last-ditch effort to break with its now publicly discredited SED past, the SED-PDS drops half of its abbreviation and reappears as PDS. According to state secretary for work and salaries, Roland Schneider, the GDR currently counts 51,000 unemployed, most of them former security police agents.
5 February	Eight members of the opposition enter Modrow's government as "ministers without portfolio." A conservative election alliance is formally established under Kohl's guidance. Christian Democrats from East and West, Democratic Awakening, and the German Social Union form the so-called "Alliance for Germany." The round table unsuccessfully attempts to prohibit West German politicians from participating in the East German election campaign; its authority is generally dwindling.
7 February	To already existing conditions for currency union with the GDR,

	the West German government adds that the GDR's economic and judicial system has to become fully compatible with the West.
10 February	Kohl visits Gorbachev, who agrees to respect German self-determination and eventual unification.
13 February	Modrow and Kohl agree on setting up a "commission of experts" to prepare for currency union; Kohl, however, rejects all other proposals and demands by the Modrow government, particularly for necessary immediate financial aid.
14 February	The four foreign ministers of the allied powers, and the two German foreign ministers, agree on "two-plus-four" negotiations about the future status of Germany.
18 February	Since 1 January some 89,000 GDR citizens have left the country for West Germany.
19 February	Wolfgang Ullmann from Democracy Now calls for a new constitution in case of German unification.
22 February	New Forum, PDS, and various other groups call for a demonstration against "capitalist unification." Though several thousands participate, the tide is clearly running in the opposite direction.
12 March	A by now effectively marginalized round table meets for the last time and agrees on proposals to give all state property to the people and to hold a referendum on a new constitution. Both issues are not even considered by West German parties.
14 March	Wolfgang Schnur, chairman of Democratic Awakening, admits his work for the security police and resigns from all positions.
18 March	First free elections in the GDR

First free elections in the GDR
(93 percent participation): (in percentages)

Christian Democratic Union (CDU)	40.9
Social Democratic Party (SPD)	21.8
Party for Democratic Socialism (PDS)	16.3
German Social Union (DSU)	6.3
Alliance of Free Democrats	5.3
Alliance 90 (New Forum, Democracy Now, Initiative for Peace and Human Rights)	2.9
Greens	2.0
Democratic Awakening (DA)	0.9
Other	3.6

| 12 April | Christian Democrat Lothar de Maizière becomes first (and last) freely elected prime minister of the GDR. He forms a coalition government of CDU, SPD, DSU, DA, and liberals. |
| 3 October | Formal unification between the Federal Republic of Germany (West Germany) and the German Democratic Republic (East Germany). Name of the new united Germany: Federal Republic of Germany. |

SELECTED BIBLIOGRAPHY

PERIODICALS/JOURNALS/NEWSPAPERS

Across Frontiers
Archiv für Sozialgeschichte
Deutschland Archiv
East European Quarterly
Eastern European Politics and Society
German Politics and Society
Jahrbücher für Geschichte Osteuropas
Labour Focus on Eastern Europe

Neues Deutschland (East Berlin)
Oral History
Problems of Communism
Socialism and Democracy
Der Spiegel (Hamburg)
Studies in Comparative Communism
Die Tageszeitung (West Berlin)
Die Zeit (Hamburg)

BOOKS

Abel, Elie, *The Shattered Bloc: Behind the Upheaval in Eastern Europe.* Boston: Houghton Mifflin, 1990.

Adam, Jan, *Economic Reforms in the Soviet Union and Eastern Europe Since the 1960s.* New York: St. Martin's Press, 1989.

Allen, Bruce, *Germany East: Dissent and Opposition.* Montreal: Black Rose Books, 1989.

Andert, Reinhold, and Wolfgang Herzberg, *Der Sturz: Erich Honecker im Kreuzverhör.* Berlin: Aufbau Verlag, 1990.

Arato, Andrew, "Civil Society Against the State." *Telos* 47 (1981), pp. 23–47.

——, *Crisis and Reform in Eastern Europe.* New Brunswick, N.J.: Transaction, 1991.

——, and Mihaly Vajda, "The Limits of Leninist Opposition." *New German Critique* 7, no. 19 (1980), pp. 167–75.

Ardagh, John, *Germany and the Germans: An Anatomy of Society Today.* London: Hamish Hamilton, 1987.

Ash, Timothy Garton, *"Und du willst nicht mein Bruder sein": Die DDR heute.* Reinbek: Rowohlt, 1981.

——, *The Magic Lantern.* New York: Random House, 1990.

——, *The Uses of Adversity: Essays on the Fate of Central Europe.* New York: Random House, 1990.

Bahro, Rudolf, *The Alternative in Eastern Europe.* London: Verso, 1981.

Baring, Arnulf, *Uprising in East Germany: June 17, 1953.* Ithaca, N.Y.: Cornell University Press, 1972.

Berger Gluck, Sherna, and Daphne Patai (eds.), *Women's Words: The Feminist Practice of Oral History.* New York/London: Routledge, 1991.

Berghahn, V. R., *Modern Germany: Society, Economy and Politics in the Twentieth Century.* Cambridge: Cambridge University Press, 1990.

Beyme, Klaus v., and H. Zimmermann, *Policymaking in the German Democratic Republic.* New York: St. Martin's Press, 1984.

Biermann, Wolf, *The Wire Harp: Ballads, Poems, Songs.* New York: Harcourt Brace & World, 1968.

——, *Demokratisierung in der DDR?* Hattingen: Scandia, 1982.

Blackburn, Robin (ed.), *After the Fall: The Failure of Communism and the Future of Socialism.* London/New York: Verso, 1991.

Blanke, Thomas, and Rainer Erd, *DDR—Ein Staat Vergeht.* Frankfurt am Main: Fischer Taschenbuch, 1990.

Böhme, Irene, *Die da drüben: Sieben Kapitel DDR.* West Berlin: Rotbuch Verlag, 1983.

Bohley, Bärbel, et al., *40 Jahre DDR . . . und die Bürger melden sich zu Wort.* Frankfurt am Main: Büchergilde Gutenberg, 1989.

Borneman, John, *After the Wall: East Meets West in the New Berlin.* New York: Basic Books, 1991.

Bowers, Stephen R., "The East European Revolution." *East European Quarterly* 25, no. 2 (June 1991), pp. 129–43.

Brandt, Willy, *Reden zu Deutschland—". . . was zusammengehört."* Bonn: Dietz Taschenbuch, 1990.

Brendl, Cajo, *The Working Class Uprising in East Germany.* Paris: Échanges et Mouvement, 1982.

Brown, J. F., *Eastern Europe and Communist Rule.* Durham, N.C.: Duke University Press, 1988.

——, *Surge to Freedom: The End of Communist Rule in Eastern Europe.* Durham, N.C.: Duke University Press, 1991.

Bruns, Wilhelm, *Von der Deutschlandpolitik zur DDR-Politik?* Opladen: Leske & Budrich.

Brus, Wlodzimierz, *From Marx to Market: Socialism in Search of an Economic System.* New York: Oxford University Press, 1989.

Büscher, Wolfgang, *Friedensbewegung in der DDR: Texte 1978–1982.* Hattingen: Scandia, 1982.

——, and Peter Wensierski, *Null Bock auf DDR: Aussteigerjugend im anderen Deutschland.* Reinbek: Rowohlt, 1984.

Bugajski, Janusz, and Maxine Pollack, *East European Fault Lines: Dissent, Opposition, and Social Activism.* Boulder, Colo.: Westview Press, 1989.

Bundesministerium für innerdeutsche Beziehungen, *DDR Handbuch.* Cologne: Verlag Wissenschaft und Politik, 1979.

Burens, Peter Claus, *Die DDR und der Prager Frühling.* Berlin: Duncker & Humblot, 1981.

Bussiek, Hendrik, *Notizen aus der DDR.* Frankfurt am Main: Fischer Taschenbuch, 1979.

Bust-Bartels, A., *Herrschaft und Widerstand in den DDR-Betrieben.* Frankfurt am Main; New York: Campus Verlag, 1980.

Childs, David, ed., *Honecker's Germany.* London: Allen & Unwin, 1985.

——, *The GDR: Moscow's German Ally.* London: Allen & Unwin, 1988.

——, ed., *East Germany in Comparative Perspective.* London/New York: Routledge, 1989.

Comisso, Ellen, "Property Rights, Liberalism, and the Transition from 'Actually Existing' Socialism." *East European Politics and Society* 5, no. 1 (Winter 1991), pp. 162–88.

Connor, Walter D., *Socialism's Dilemma: State and Society in the Soviet Bloc.* New York: Columbia University Press, 1988.

Curry, J. L. (ed.), *Dissent in Eastern Europe.* New York: Praeger, 1983.

Dahrendorf, Ralf, *Reflections on the Revolution in Europe.* New York: Times Books, 1990.

Darnton, Robert, *Berlin Journal, 1989–1990.* New York: W. W. Norton, 1991.

Decker, Peter, *DDR kaputt, Deutschland ganz.* Munich: Resultate Verlag, 1989/90.

Dennis, Mike, *German Democratic Republic: Politics, Economics, and Society.* London: Pinter Publishers, 1988.

Deppe, Rainer, Helmut Dubiel, Ulrich Rödel (eds.), *Demokratischer Umbruch in Osteuropa.* Frankfurt am Main: Suhrkamp Verlag, 1991.

Dubiel, Helmut, and G. Frankenberg, and Ulrich Rödel, *Die Demokratische Frage.* Frankfurt am Main: Suhrkamp Verlag, 1989.

East European Solidarity Committee (ed.), *Peace in the East.* Edmonton: East European Solidarity Committee, 1983.

Edwards, G. E., *GDR Society and Social Institutions: Facts and Figures.* New York: St. Martin's Press, 1985.

Ehring, Klaus, and Martin Dallwitz, *Schwerter zu Pflugscharen: Friedensbewegung in der DDR.* Reinbek: Rowohlt, 1982.

END, *Ecology in Eastern Europe: An END Briefing Sheet.* London: END, 1986.

Evans, Richard J., *In Hitler's Shadow: West German Historians and the Attempt to Escape from the Nazi Past.* New York: Pantheon Books, 1989.

Feher, Ferenc, *Eastern Left, Western Left: Totalitarianism, Freedom, and Democracy.* Atlantic Highlands, N.J.: Humanities Press, 1987.

Fessen, Bertolt, "The People and the Power in East Germany 1989." *Labour Focus on Eastern Europe* (May 1991), pp. 8–13.

Fischer, Alexander, *Die Deutsche Demokratische Republik.* Freiburg: Ploetz, 1988.

Fischer Welt Almanach, *Sonderband DDR.* Frankfurt am Main: Fischer, 1990.

Foley, John M., *The Theory of Oral Composition: History and Methodology.* Bloomington: Indiana University Press, 1988.

Frey, Eric G., *Division and Détente: The Germanies and Their Alliances.* New York: Praeger, 1987.

Fricke, Karl Wilhelm, *17. Juni 1953: Arbeiteraufstand in der DDR.* Cologne: Edition Deutschland Archiv, 1982.

——, *Die DDR-Staatssicherheit: Entwicklung, Strukturen, Aktionsfelder.* 2nd rev. ed. Cologne: Verlag Wissenschaft und Politik, 1984.

——, *Opposition und Widerstand in der DDR.* Cologne: Verlag Wissenschaft und Politik, 1984.

Fulbrook, Mary, *The Divided Nation: History of Germany, 1945–90.* London: Fontana Press, 1991.

Gelb, Norman, *The Berlin Wall.* London: Michael Joseph, 1986.

Glenny, Misha, *The Rebirth of History: Eastern Europe in the Age of Democracy.* London/New York: Penguin Books, 1990.

Gleye, Paul, *Behind the Wall: An American in East Germany, 1988–89.* Carbondale: Southern Illinois University Press, 1991.

Goeckel, Robert F., *The Lutheran Church and the East German State: Political Conflict and Change Under Ulbricht and Honecker.* Ithaca, N.Y.: Cornell University Press, 1990.

Goodwyn, Lawrence C., *Breaking the Barrier: The Rise of Solidarność in Poland.* New York: Oxford University Press, 1991.

Grabner, Wolf-Jürgen, Christiane Heinze, et al. (eds.), *Leipzig im Oktober: Kirchen und alternative Gruppen im Umbruch der DDR.* Berlin: Wichern Verlag, 1990.

Griffith, William E. (ed.), *Central and Eastern Europe: The Opening Curtain?* Boulder, Colo.: Westview Press, 1989.

Habermas, Jürgen, "Der DM-Nationalismus." *Die Zeit,* no. 14 (March 1990), pp. 62–63.

——, *Die nachholende Revolution.* Frankfurt am Main: Suhrkamp, 1990.

Hahn, Annegret, et al. (eds.), *Protestdemonstration Berlin DDR—4/11/89.* Berlin: Henschelverlag, 1990.

Harman, Chris, *Bureaucracy and Revolution in Eastern Europe.* London: Pluto Press, 1974.

——, *Class Struggles in Eastern Europe.* London: Pluto Press, 1983.

——, *The Fire Last Time: 1968 and After.* London/Chicago: Bookmarks, 1988.

Hartung, Klaus, *Neuzehnhundertneunundachtzig.* Frankfurt am Main: Luchterhand, 1990.

Havel, Václav, et al., *The Power of the Powerless.* Armonk, N.Y.: M. E. Sharpe, 1990.

Havemann, Katja, and Irena Kukutz, *Geschützte Quellen: Gespräche mit Monika H. alias Karin Lenz.* Berlin: BasisDruck Verlag, 1991.

Havemann, Robert, *Questions, Answers, Questions: From the Biography of a German Marxist.* Garden City, N.Y.: Doubleday, 1972.

——, *Ein deutscher Kommunist.* Reinbek: Rowohlt, 1978.

——, *Ein Marxist in der DDR,* ed. H. Jickel. Munich and Zurich: R. Piper, 1980.

Henrich, Rolf, *Der vormundschaftliche Staat: Vom Versagen des real existierenden Sozialismus.* Reinbek bei Hamburg: Rowohlt, 1989.

Herles, Helmut, and Ewald Rose, *Vom Runden Tisch zum Parlament.* Bonn: Bouvier Verlag, 1990.

Honecker, Erich, *From My Life.* Oxford/New York: Pergamon Press, 1981.

"Hundreds of Women Make Pacifist Protest, 1982–83." *Labour Focus on Eastern Europe* 5, nos. 5–6, pp. 39–40.

Kimmel, Michael S., *Revolution.* Philadelphia: Temple University Press, 1990.

Klier, Freya, *Abreisskalender: Ein deutsch-deutsches Tagebuch.* Munich: Droemersche Verlagsanstalt Th. Knaur Nachf., 1989.

Köhler, Anne, and Volker Ronge, " 'Einmal BRD-einfach': die DDR-Ausreisewelle im Frühjahr 1984." *Deutschland Archiv* 17, no. 12 (1984), pp. 1280–86.

Königsdorf, Helga, *Adieu DDR—Protokolle eines Abschieds.* Reinbek: Rowohlt, 1990.

Krisch, Henry, *The German Democratic Republic: The Search for Identity.* Boulder, Colo.: Westview Press, 1985.

——, *Politics and Culture in the German Democratic Republic.* Ann Arbor: Center for Political Studies, Institute for Social Research, University of Michigan, 1988.

Kroh, Ferdinand (ed.), *"Freiheit ist immer Freiheit . . .": Die Andersdenkenden in der DDR.* Frankfurt am Main/Berlin: Ullstein, 1988.

Kuczynski, Jürgen, *Schwierige Jahre—mit einem besseren Ende?* Berlin: Tacheles Verlag, 1990.

Kuppe, Johannes, " 'Neues politisches Denken' auch in der DDR?" *DDR Report* 19, no. 12 (1986), pp. 56–61.

Lane, Christel, "Women in Socialist Society with Special Reference to the German Democratic Republic" *Sociology* 17, no. 4 (1983), pp. 489–505.

Lane, David, *The End of Social Inequality? Class, Status, and Power Under State Socialism.* London: Allen & Unwin, 1982.

Lange, Horst, and Uwe Matthes, "Ein Jahr Danach: Auf der Suche nach Fragen und Antworten zur Wende in der DDR." *Deutschland Archiv* 11, no. 22 (November 1990), pp. 1744–49.

Lau, Karin, *Deutschland auf dem Weg zur Einheit: Dokumente einer Revolution.* Braunschweig: Westermann, 1990.

Lemke, Christiane, *The Quality of Life in the GDR.* Armonk, N.Y.: M. E. Sharpe, 1989.

——, *Die Ursachen des Umbruchs 1989: Politische Sozialisation in der ehemaligen DDR.* Opladen: Westdeutscher Verlag, 1991.

——, and Gary Marks (eds.), *The Crisis of Socialism in Europe.* Durham, N.C.: Duke University Press, 1992.

Leonhard, Wolfgang, *Child of the Revolution.* Chicago: Henry Regnery, 1958.

Lewis, Paul G. (ed.), *Eastern Europe: Political Crisis and Legitimation.* London: Croom Helm, 1984.

Links, Christoph, and Hannes Bahrmann, *Wir sind das Volk: Die DDR im Aufbruch.* Berlin/Wuppertal: Aufbau Verlag/Peter Hammer Verlag, 1990.

Lochner, Axel (ed.), *Linke Politik in Deutschland.* Hamburg: Galgenberg, 1990.

Ludz, Peter Christian, *The German Democratic Republic from the Sixties to the Seventies.* Cambridge, Mass.: Center for International Affairs, 1970.

McAdams, A. James, *East Germany and Détente: Building Authority After the Wall.* Cambridge: Cambridge University Press, 1985.

McCauley, Martin, *Marxism-Leninism in the German Democratic Republic: The Socialist Unity Party (SED).* New York: Barnes & Noble, 1979.

——, *East Germany: The Dilemmas of Division.* London: Institute for the Study of Conflict, 1980.

——, *East-West German Relations: A Turning Point?* London: Institute for the Study of Conflict, 1983.

——, *The German Democratic Republic Since 1945.* New York: St. Martin's Press, 1983.

——, *The Origins of the Cold War.* New York: Longman, 1983.

Mallinckrodt, Anita, "Environmental Dialogue in the GDR: The Literary Challenge to the Sanctity of 'Progress.'" *GDR Monitor,* no. 16 (1986/87), pp. 1–26.

Marcuse, Peter, *Missing Marx: A Personal and Political Journal of a Year in East Germany, 1989–1990.* New York: Monthly Review Press, 1991.

Menge, Marlies, *"Ohne uns geht nichts mehr": Die Revolution in der DDR.* Stuttgart: Deutsche Verlags Anstalt, 1990.

Minnerup, Günter, "German Reunification and the Legacy of German Communism." *Labour Focus on Eastern Europe* (June 1991), pp. 4–7.

Mitter, Armin, and Stefan Wolle (eds.), *"Ich liebe euch doch alle": Befehle und Lageberichte des MfS.* Berlin: Basis Druck, 1990.

Moore, Barrington, Jr., *Social Origins of Dictatorship and Democracy.* Boston: Beacon Press, 1966.

——, *Authority and Inequality Under Capitalism and Socialism.* Oxford: Oxford University Press, 1987.

Moreton, N. Edwina, *East Germany and the Warsaw Alliance: The Politics of Détente.* Boulder, Colo.: Westview Press, 1978.

——, *Germany Between East and West.* New York: Cambridge University Press, 1987.

Mühler, Kurt, and Steffen H. Wilsdorf, "Die Leipziger Montagsdemonstration Aufstieg und Wandel einer basisdemokratischen Institution des friedlichen Umbruchs im Spiegel empirischer Meinungsforschung." *Berliner Journal für Soziologie.* Berlin: Sonderheft, 1991.

Müller-Enbergs, Helmut, Marianne Schulz, and Jan Wielgohs (eds.), *Von der Illegalität ins Parlament: Werdegang und Konzept der neuen Bürgerbewegungen.* Berlin: LinksDruck Verlag, 1991.

Naumann, Michael, ed., *Die Geschichte ist offen, DDR 1990: Hoffnung auf eine neue Republik: Schriftsteller aus der DDR über die Zukunftschancen ihres Landes.* Reinbek: Rowohlt, 1990.

Neues Forum Leipzig, *Jetzt oder Nie—Demokratie! Leipziger Herbst, 1989.* Leipzig: Forum Verlag, 1989.

Niethammer, Lutz, *"Lebenserfahrung und kollektives Gedächtnis"—Die Praxis der Oral History.* Frankfurt am Main: Suhrkamp, 1980.

———, *Die volkseigene Erfahrung: Eine Archäologie des Lebens in der Industrieprovinz der DDR.* Berlin: Rowohlt, 1991.

Offe, Claus, "Prosperity, Nation, Republic: Aspects of the Unique German Journey from Socialism to Capitalism." *German Politics and Society,* no. 22 (Spring 1991), p. 18.

Oktober 1989—Wider den Schlaf der Vernunft. Berlin: Neues Leben/Elefanten Press, 1989.

Pelikan, Jiri, *Socialist Opposition in Eastern Europe.* New York: St. Martin's Press, 1976.

Peltzer, Michael, *Sozialistische Herrschaft und Materielle Interessen.* Opladen: Westdeutscher Verlag, 1987.

Plock, Ernest D., *The Basic Treaty and the Evolution of East-West German Relations.* Boulder, Colo.: Westview Press, 1986.

Prolingheuer, Hans, *"Kirchenwende oder Wendekirche?" Die EKD nach dem 9. November 1989 und ihre Vergangenheit.* Bonn: Pahl-Rugenstein Verlag Nachfolger, 1991.

Ramet, Pedro, "Disaffection and Dissent in East Germany." *World Politics* (1985).

Reich, Jens, *Rückkehr nach Europa: Zur Lage der deutschen Nation.* Munich: Carl Hanser Verlag, 1991.

Rein, Gerhard (ed.), *Die Opposition in der DDR—Entwürfe für einen anderen Sozialismus.* Berlin: Wichern Verlag, 1989.

———, *Die protestantische Revolution, 1987–90: Ein deutsches Lesebuch.* Berlin: Wichern Verlag, 1990.

Röder, Hans-Jürgen, "Weil es eben typisch ist die Klappe zu halten!" *Kirche im Sozialismus* 12, no. 34 (1986), p. 106.

Roehricht, Karl Hermann, *Lebensverläufe: Innenansichten aus der DDR.* Berlin: Morgenbuch Verlag, 1991.

Rothschild, Joseph, *Return to Diversity: A Political History of East Central Europe Since World War II.* New York: Oxford University Press, 1990.

Sanford, John, *The Sword and the Ploughshare: Autonomous Peace Initiatives in East Germany.* London: Merlin Press/END, 1983.

———, "The Church, the State, and the Peace Movement in the GDR." *GDR Monitor* no. 16 (1986/87), pp. 27–54.

Scharf, C. Bradley, *Politics and Change in East Germany: An Evaluation of Socialist Democracy.* Boulder, Colo.: Westview Press, 1984.

Schmid, Thomas, *Staatsbegräbnis von ziviler Gesellschaft.* Berlin: Rotbuch Verlag, 1990.

Schmidt, Helmut, "Uns Deutsche kann der Teufel holen." *Die Zeit* no. 21 (May 1991), p. 3.

Schneider, Eberhard, *The G.D.R.: The History, Politics, Economy, and Society of East Germany*. New York: St. Martin's Press, 1978.

Schneider, Gernot, *Wirtschaftwunder DDR—Anspruch und Realität*. Cologne: Bund Verlag, 1990.

Schorlemmer, Friedrich, interview in "Mit Vordenkern und Akteuren der Wende im Gespräch." *Deutschland Archiv*, no. 23 (December 1990), pp. 1935–37.

Schüddekopf, Charles (ed.), *"Wir sind das Volk!" Flugschriften, Aufrufe und Texte einer deutschen Revolution*. Reinbek bei Hamburg: Rowohlt, 1990.

Sievers, Hans-Jürgen, *Stundenbuch einer deutschen Revolution: Die Leiziger Kirchen im Oktober 1989*. Göttingen: Vandenhoeck & Ruprecht, 1990.

Simmons, Michael, *The Unloved Country: A Portrait of East Germany Today*. London: Sphere Books, 1989.

Spittmann, Ilse, and Karl Wilhelm Fricke (eds.), *17. Juni 1953: Arbeiteraufstand in der DDR*. Cologne: Edition Deutschland Verlag, 1962.

Staritz, Dieter, *Geschichte der DDR 1949–1985*. Frankfurt am Main: Edition Suhrkamp, 1985.

Steele, Jonathan, *Socialism with a German Face: The State that Came in from the Cold*. New York: Urizen Books, 1977.

Süss, Walter, "Mit Unwillen zur Macht." *Deutschland Archiv*, no. 24 (May 1991), pp. 470–78.

——, "Bilanz einer Gratwanderung—Die kurze Amtszeit des Hans Modrow." *Deutschland Archiv*, no. 24 (July 1991), pp. 596–608.

Thaysen, Uwe, *Der Runde Tisch. Oder: Wo blieb das Volk? Der Weg der DDR in die Demokratie*. Wiesbaden: Westdeutscher Verlag, 1990.

Thompson, Paul, *Our Common History: The Transformation of Europe*. Atlantic Highlands, N.J.: Humanities Press, 1982.

——, *The Voice of the Past: Oral History*. Oxford/New York: Oxford University Press, 1988.

Tökés, Rudolf (ed.), *Opposition in Eastern Europe*. London: Macmillan, 1979.

Tucker, Robert C., *The Marx-Engels Reader*. 2nd Ed. New York: W. W. Norton, 1978.

Turner, Jr., Henry Ashby, *The Two Germanies Since 1945*. Binghamton, N.Y.: Vail Ballou Press, 1987.

Ullmann, Wolfgang, *Demokratie—Jetzt oder nie! Perspektiven der Gerechtigkeit*. Munich: Kyrill & Method Verlag, 1991.

Wallace, Ian (ed.), *The GDR Under Honecker, 1971–1981*. GDR Monitor Special Series, No. 1. Dundee: University of Dundee, 1981.

——, *East Germany: The German Democratic Republic*. Oxford/Santa Barbara, Calif.: Clio, 1987.

Weber, Hermann, *Geschichte der DDR*. Munich: Deutscher Taschenbuch Verlag, 1986.

——, *Die DDR, 1945–1986*. Munich: R. Oldenbourg, 1988.

Wensierski, Peter, "Friedensbewegung in der DDR." *Aus Politik und Zeitgeschichte* no. 17 (1983), pp. 3–15.

Wettig, Gerhard, *Community and Conflict in the Socialist Camp: The Soviet Union, East Germany, and the German Problem, 1965–1972*. New York: St. Martin's Press, 1975.

Whetten, Lawrence L., *Germany East and West: Conflicts, Collaboration, and Confrontation*. New York: New York University Press, 1980.

——, *Interaction of Political and Economic Reforms Within the East Bloc*. New York: Crane Russak, 1989.

Wilkening, Christina, *Staat im Staate: Auskünfte ehemaliger Stasi-Mitarbeiter.* Berlin: Aufbau Verlag, 1990.

Woods, Roger, *Opposition in the DDR Under Honecker, 1971–85.* London: Macmillan, 1986.

Zagorin, Perez, *Rebels and Rulers.* Cambridge: Cambridge University Press, 1982.

Zeman, Z. A. B., *Pursued by a Bear: The Making of Eastern Europe.* London: Chatto & Windus, 1989.

INDEX

A specialist in comparative history and social movements, Dirk
Philipsen teaches in the History Department at Duke University

Library of Congress Cataloging-in-Publication Data
Philipsen, Dirk, 1959–
We were the people : the voices of East Germany's revolutionary
autumn of 1989 / Dirk Philipsen.
Includes bibliographical references and index.
ISBN 0-8223-1282-4 (alk. paper). — ISBN 0-8223-1294-8 (pbk. :
alk. paper)
1. Germany (East)—Politics and government—1989–1990.
2. Revolutions—Germany (East)—History.   3. Germany—
History—Unification, 1990.   I. Title.
DD289.P48   1992
943.1087′8—dc20   92-12762 CIP